AWAKE, BRIDE
We are in the Great Tribulation

By Eve Clarity

Awake, Bride: We are in the Great Tribulation
Copyright ©2009 Eve Clarity   July 19, 2009

All rights reserved. No part of this publication may be reproduced except for brief quotations in printed reviews without the prior permission of the author.

All Scripture quotations are from the American King James Version of the Holy Bible which is in the public domain. It is available for free at www.crosswire.org. Scripture has been *italicized*. **Bold lettering** and underlining has been added to some of the text for emphasis.

ISBN 978-1-931203-17-3
Published by Inspired Idea
in the United States of America
www.InspiredIdea.com

Share the News

To share this message with friends who don't have the time or money for the whole book, I wrote an extended version of the chapter, "7 Seals, 7 Trumpets and 7 Vials" as a 36 page booklet with the Great Tribulation Time-Line as an evangelistic tool titled *Seals, Trumpets and Vials* available at for $5.50 currently at http://stores.lulu.com/awakebride.

For bulk purchase of 25-99, the price drops to $3.22 each; for 100 it's $2.97 per book.

View Slide Presentations

Slide shows of the material are available at http://www.kneelingmedia.org/AwakeBride and in Second Life on KMTV or the Kneeling Media building on Eternal Creations island.

Contact Author

My e-mail address is also at the above website. Please be courteous. I did not force you to read my book; I will not force myself to read or respond to e-mails which are rude. I will do my best to answer honest questions in a timely manner.

Dedicated to Our Groom, King Jesus

Contents

	Page #
Foreword	vii

CHAPTER TITLE	
1. Jewish Calendar	9
2. Spring Feasts	25
3. Fall Feasts	41
4. Ten Toes & Ten Horns (Daniel 2 and 7)	55
5. Resurrections & Rapture	69
6. 70 X 7 (Daniel 9)	85
7. Prophetic Devolution of the Greek Empire (Daniel 11)	99
8. Biblical Astronomy (Rev. 12 and 20)	113
9. Israel (Daniel 7 & 8)	127
10. Abominations (Daniel)	145
11. Little Horn with the Blasphemous Mouth (Daniel 7 & 8)	161
12. Gog (Ezekiel 38-39)	179
13. End-Times Overview (Matthew 13-25)	197
14. Judgments and Rewards (Rev. 2-3)	215
15. Great Tribulation Angels	229
16. The Beasts and Whore of Babylon (Rev. 13-18)	245
17. 7 Seals, 7 Trumpets and 7 Vials (Rev. 6-11; 16)	261
18. Day of the LORD	285
19. Millennium (Rev. 19-22)	303
20. Conclusions	323
Sources and Resources	343
Appendix	345

Foreword

Jesus wants His Bride to be ready for His coming. His Bride is composed of all who believe in Jesus as their Lord and Savior. The Bride continues to love God and others while patiently waiting for Jesus' return (2 Thessalonians 3:5). Jesus wants His Bride to understand the prophecies regarding His return. He gave us His Words in the Holy Bible and His Holy Spirit to reveal His future plans to us.

However, when he, the Spirit of truth, is come, he will guide you into all truth: for he shall not speak of himself; but whatever he shall hear, that shall he speak: and **he will show you things to come**. *(John 16:13)*

The entrance of your words gives light; it gives understanding to the simple. (Psalm 119:130)

The simple can understand prophecy even though prophecy is a complex subject. Just as Jews had difficulty separating prophecies regarding Jesus' first and second comings as Redeemer then King, so we have difficulty compartmentalizing prophecies into those pertaining to Hebrews (Judah and Israel), those pertaining to pagan Gentiles, and those pertaining to the "one new man" composed of both. We have disagreements on which prophecies have been fully or partially fulfilled, and in which order they will be fulfilled, and how they relate to current events. One passage of scripture can contain several prophecies pertaining to different circumstances. So we need to keep our focus on Jesus, and worship Him; *"for the testimony of Jesus is the spirit of prophecy"* (Revelation 19:10).

The Spirit of the Lord GOD is on me; because the LORD has anointed me to preach good tidings to the meek; he has sent me to bind up the brokenhearted, to proclaim liberty to the captives, and the opening of the prison to them that are bound; To proclaim the acceptable year of the LORD, and the day of vengeance of our God; to comfort all that mourn; (Isaiah 61:1-2)

When Jesus announced who He was in a synagogue, this is how He read the passage:

The Spirit of the Lord is on me, because he has anointed me to preach the gospel to the poor; he has sent me to heal the brokenhearted, to preach deliverance to the captives, <u>and recovering of sight to the blind,</u> to set at liberty them that are bruised, To preach the acceptable year of the Lord. (Luke 4:18-19)

Jesus then stated, *"This day is this scripture fulfilled in your ears."* From a parallel passage, Jesus inserted Isaiah 42:7 (the underlined portion). Jesus combined two passages into one scripture which He fulfilled. Jesus also stopped mid-sentence prior to *"and the day of vengeance of our God,"* which was not yet time to be fulfilled. Jesus set precedent of combining similar prophetic passages into a single prophecy, and being able to differentiate between prophecies in the same sentence. This necessitates our reliance on God's Holy Spirit to guide us into all truth.

I approached this end-time prophecy study asking God to show me what the Holy Bible really taught about the subject. I was shocked when my long-held beliefs about end-times dissolved under the light of scripture and history. Human interpretation of Scripture is faulty, but God's Word remains true. Jesus told of great tribulation prior to His coming.

> *For then shall be great tribulation, such as was not since the beginning of the world to this time, no, nor ever shall be. And except those days should be shortened, there should no flesh be saved: but for the elect's sake those days shall be shortened. Then if any man shall say to you, See, here is Christ, or there; believe it not. For there shall arise false Christs, and false prophets, and shall show great signs and wonders; so that, if it were possible, they shall deceive the very elect. Behold, I have told you before. Why if they shall say to you, Behold, he is in the desert; go not forth: behold, he is in the secret chambers; believe it not. For as the lightning comes out of the east, and shines even to the west; so shall also the coming of the Son of man be. (Matthew 24:21-27)*

Jesus will return from heaven with the clouds in the same manner in which He ascended (Acts 1:9-11), and there will be much lightning and signs in the sky (black sun, red moon, fallen stars) making His return obvious to the whole world. DON'T BELIEVE ANYONE ON EARTH CLAIMING TO BE JESUS CHRIST, THE MESSIAH, regardless of what amazing and miraculous signs he might perform.

Many more Christians will be martyred for their faith. A religious economical system will be imposed upon the world, preventing people from buying or selling unless they receive the mark of allegiance to that religious system. DON'T TAKE THE MARK OF THE BEAST! It would be better to starve to death or be beheaded than to endure the plagues of those who worship the Beast and be thrown into lake of fire with them.

> *There shall come in the last days scoffers, walking after their own lusts, And saying, Where is the promise of his coming? (2 Peter 5:3b-4b)*

DO KEEP BELIEVING IN JESUS' PROMISE TO RETURN.

I wanted to share my discoveries to better prepare Christians for their amazing future. To understand prophecy regarding the Son of God who was crucified for being the "King of the Jews" you will need background on the Hebrew people (ch. 1-3). In order to recognize prophecies which have already been fulfilled, you'll also need some world history (ch. 4, 6-12). Be patient; it will all come together wondrously, and the book of Revelation will make sense (ch. 13-19).

Hebrew Calendar

And God said, Let there be light: and there was light.
And God saw the light, that it was good:
and God divided the light from the darkness.
And God called the light Day, and the darkness he called Night.
And the evening and the morning were the first day.
(Genesis 1:3-5)

Jesus was born a Jew, lived as a Jew (and learned Hebrew and Aramaic), and will return as the "*Lion of the tribe of Judah*". Those who wrote the Bible were Hebrews, descendants of Eber, whose great-grandfather was Shem (Genesis 10:11-14, 21), and so they are also called S(h)emites; and Hebrew is called a Semitic language. The Bible is about Hebrew history, and most of it was written in the Hebrew language using Hebrew idioms and calendars. The more Hebrew understanding Gentiles (non-Hebrews) gain, the clearer the Bible will become. Gentile believers have been grafted into the marvelous Hebrew stock through the blood of Jesus Christ. All believers in the Lord Jesus Christ are members of the Bride of Christ. Brides want to understand the culture of their groom, especially to know what is pleasing and acceptable in that culture. As such, we seek to understand Hebrew culture and to understand the last days we are living in so as to prepare for our Groom's return.

The Hebrew Day

On the first of the six days God terra-formed the earth, He called light into existence and separated it from the darkness. God called the light 'day', but He also called an entire rotation of the earth 'day'. This Hebrew word for day is '*yom*'. It can refer to the lighted time of day, or more often to the evening and morning returning to dusk constituting a day. The first day began with darkness; and Hebrews, taking their cue from creation, begin their days at dusk when the sun is no longer visible. A Hebrew day is from dusk to dusk, sundown to sundown. Gentile days have often been from dawn to dawn, sunup to sunup; or now, from midnight to midnight. Though they both contain twenty-four hours, Gentile days are not in sync with Hebrew days. When a Gentile day is cited, like September 11th, it is considered to be from midnight to midnight. When a Hebrew day is cited, like Tishri 1, it is considered to be from sundown to sundown.

The Hebrew Week

God did His work in six days and rested on the seventh to give us a pattern to follow. None of the Hebrew days of the week were named except for the special seventh day, which was called 'sabbath'. The Hebrew days were simply numbered throughout the month. This concept of six days of work followed by a day of rest was reiterated in the ten commandments.

> *Remember the sabbath day, to keep it holy. <u>Six days shall you labor, and do all your work: But the seventh day is the sabbath of the LORD your God: in it you shall not do any work</u>, you, nor your son, nor your daughter, your manservant, nor your maidservant, nor your cattle, nor your stranger that is within your gates: <u>For in six days the LORD made heaven and earth, the sea, and all that in them is, and rested the seventh day</u>: why the LORD blessed the sabbath day, and hallowed it. (Exodus 20:8-11)*

Again the Hebrew word for day here is '*yom*'. '*Sabbath*' means 'intermission' from a root word with meanings to repose and desist from exertion; cease, celebrate, rest, and be still. It was Father God's date-night with His wife, the Hebrews. This contract we call the Ten Commandments, was the wedding contract the Hebrews agreed to with God fifty days after He redeemed them from bondage in Egypt.

Many believers still set aside the sabbath to commune with their Lord. Since Jesus rose from the dead on the first day of the week, some believers began to especially meet for teaching and fellowship on that day. In Colossians 2:16, Paul urged no one to judge another regarding which days they held special. Jesus infuriated legalistic Jews by healing people and doing good on the sabbath.

> *And he said to them, The sabbath was made for man, and not man for the sabbath: Therefore the Son of man is Lord also of the sabbath. (Mark 2:27-28)*

Clearly the Hebrew week has seven days, with the seventh being "set apart", sanctified and made holy.

The Ancient Hebrew Month

In Antediluvian (pre-flood) times, all months had thirty days, as is calculated from Genesis 7 and 8 regarding the waters abating from the earth after 150 days in five months.

> *In the six hundredth year of Noah's life, in<u> the second month, the seventeenth day of the month,</u> the same day were all the fountains of the great deep broken up, and the windows of heaven were opened. (Genesis 7:11)*

> *And the waters returned from off the earth continually: and **after the end of the hundred and fifty days** the waters were abated. And the ark rested <u>in the seventh month, on the seventeenth day of the month,</u> on the mountains of Ararat. (Genesis 8:3-4)*

The ancient months and days did not have names associated with them, but were simply numbered. After Noah's flood, the people populated the land of Shinar (Sumer). The Sumerians, Noah's descendants, had a calendar that divided the year into 30-day months, divided the day into 12 periods from dusk to dusk, and had a sexagesimal (base 60) numbering system. They had no official names for their months, but referred to them according to agricultural or local events. After they built the tower of Babel and God confused their languages, the Babylonian empire eventually ruled Mesopotamia. The Babylonian month names were in the following order beginning with spring: Nisanu, Ayaru, Simanu, Du'uzu, Abu, Ululu, Tashritu, Arakhsamna, Kislimu, Tebetu, Shabatu, and Adaru. The end of the Babylonian empire was called the Chaldean Era, into which Abram was born, six generations from Eber (Genesis 11:17-28). Abram married Sarai and traveled to Canaan and miraculously gave birth to Isaac, who was the father of Jacob (renamed Israel by God), who had twelve sons from whence we get the twelve tribes of Israel. Because of famine, Jacob's family emigrated to Egypt, where his son Joseph was governor. One hundred and thirty years later the Hebrews were slaves in Egypt, and Moses was born to deliver them. The Egyptians used three calendars, one of which was close to the Babylonian calendar, but called Nisan the seventh month. When God brought the Hebrews out of Egypt, He corrected their calendar, clarifying Nisan as the first month (Exodus 12:2). The Hebrew month names were in the following order beginning with spring: Nisan (also called Abib in Exodus 13:4), Iyar, Sivan, Tammuz, Av, Elul, Tishri, Cheshvan, Kislev, Tevet, Shevat, Adar I, and Adar II (for 'pregnant' years to realign their lunar calendar with the solar year). The similarity with the Babylonian names is to be expected, since that's what Abraham used and passed onto his family.

New Moons

It takes the moon about 29.5 days to go through its phases as we observe from the earth. When the moon is between our line of sight on the earth to the sun, it looks like a black disc, and is called a 'new moon'. When just the tiniest sliver of the waxing (growing) moon appears, it is also still called a 'new moon,' and was considered so by the Jews who would establish the declaration of a 'new moon' after two eye-witnesses concurred.

Though God clearly told Moses the date to start their calendar, further direct information on how to keep it accurate is absent from Scripture. When God created the sun, moon, and stars, He stated their purpose *"for signs, and for seasons, and for days, and years"* (Genesis 1:14). Astronomical calculations were expected, but God specifically instructed the Hebrews against worshiping the heavenly bodies (Deuteronomy 4:12-35). Instead they were to celebrate the beginning of their months when the tiniest sliver of the moon was observed.

> *And the sons of Aaron, the priests, shall blow with the trumpets; and they shall be to you for an ordinance for ever throughout your generations. Also in the day of your gladness, and in your solemn days, and <u>in the beginnings of your months, you</u>*

shall blow with the trumpets over your burnt offerings, and over the sacrifices of your peace offerings; that they may be to you for a memorial before your God: I am the LORD your God. (Numbers 10:8, 10)

The Hebrew Year

A strict, twelve lunar month calendar will fall eleven days short of a solar year, as does the Islamic calendar of 354 days. A solar calendar of 365 days has to add an extra day every four years because the earth's orbit around the sun takes 365.24 days. The Hebrews had a combined lunar-solar calendar which included a 13th month every six years until reaching the 36th year when an extra month was added to the 40th year. Every forty years this ancient Hebrew 360-day calendar was in sync with the modern 365.25-day calendar.

Just as we recognize different years within our twelve month calendar: school year, fiscal year, campaign year, and so on; so did the Hebrews. They had their religious year which was from Nisan to Nisan, and the king's regnal year which was from Tishri to Tishri. Biblical scholars also note their use of a 360-day prophetic year used in the books of Daniel and Revelation. Dean of 360calendar.com suggests this 360-day prophetic calendar was also their normal use calendar, since it includes the patterns of the week, the sabbath, and the forty-year generation. [see Appendix]

A Hebrew Generation

After Noah's flood, a generation was established as forty years (Job 42:16); time for a man to mature and have children.

And the LORD's anger was kindled against Israel, and he made them wander in the wilderness forty years, until all the generation, that had done evil in the sight of the LORD, was consumed. (Numbers 32:13)

The Hebrew Sabbath Year

Every seventh year the Hebrews were commanded to let their land rest. God would provide them with bumper crops in the sixth year with plenty to store for food through the seventh year, much like He allowed them to gather double the manna on the sixth day because He did not provide manna on the seventh day when they were in the wilderness (Exodus 16:12-27).

And the LORD spoke to Moses in mount Sinai, saying, Speak to the children of Israel, and say to them, When you come into the land which I give you, then shall the land keep a sabbath to the LORD. Six years you shall sow your field, and six years you shall prune your vineyard, and gather in the fruit thereof; But in the seventh year shall be a sabbath of rest to the land, a sabbath for the LORD: you shall neither sow your field, nor prune your vineyard. (Leviticus 25:1-4)

The Hebrew Jubilee Year (Sabbath of Sabbaths)

Then after the seventh sabbath year, the Hebrews were commanded to celebrate another special sabbath year called the year of jubilee. Any lands that had been sold were returned to the original owner or the ownership of their tribesmen. Those who had sold themselves into slavery were freed. All debts were canceled. All farmers took another 'sabbatical' from working the fields.

And you shall number seven sabbaths of years to you, seven times seven years; and the space of the seven sabbaths of years shall be to you forty and nine years. <u>Then shall you cause the trumpet of the jubilee to sound on the tenth day of the seventh month, in the day of atonement shall you make the trumpet sound throughout all your land.</u> And you shall hallow the fiftieth year, and proclaim liberty throughout all the land to all the inhabitants thereof: it shall be a jubilee to you; and you shall return every man to his possession, and you shall return every man to his family. A jubilee shall that fiftieth year be to you: you shall not sow, neither reap that which grows of itself in it, nor gather the grapes in it of your vine undressed. (Leviticus 25:8-11)

The tenth day of the seventh month is the holy day of Yom Kippur, one of seven feasts commanded by God for the Hebrews to celebrate.

The Seven Feasts

Seven is a very important number in the Bible which is emphasized by the sabbaths, and reinforced by seven feasts. There are three spring feasts held in the first month of Nisan, one early summer feast, and three fall feasts held in the seventh month of Tishri. These feasts were memorials of what God had done for the Hebrews which were to be celebrated annually as a means to teach their importance to the following generations. We will look at the Hebrew history of each.

Passover: Nisan 14

Speak you to all the congregation of Israel, saying, In the tenth day of this month they shall take to them every man a lamb, according to the house of their fathers, a lamb for an house: And if the household be too little for the lamb, let him and his neighbor next to his house take it according to the number of the souls; every man according to his eating shall make your count for the lamb. Your lamb shall be without blemish, a male of the first year: you shall take it out from the sheep, or from the goats: And you shall keep it up until <u>the fourteenth day of the same month: and the whole assembly of the congregation of Israel shall kill it in the evening. And they shall take of the blood, and strike it on the two side posts and on the upper door post of the houses, wherein they shall eat it. And they shall eat the flesh in that night, roast with fire, and unleavened bread; and with bitter herbs they shall eat it.</u>

Eat not of it raw, nor sodden at all with water, but roast with fire; his head with his legs, and with the entrails thereof. And you shall let nothing of it remain until the morning; and that which remains of it until the morning you shall burn with fire. <u>And thus shall you eat it; with your loins girded, your shoes on your feet, and your staff in your hand; and you shall eat it in haste: it is the LORD's passover. For I will pass through the land of Egypt this night, and will smite all the firstborn in the land of Egypt, both man and beast; and against all the gods of Egypt I will execute judgment: I am the LORD.</u> And the blood shall be to you for a token on the houses where you are: and <u>when I see the blood, I will pass over you</u>, and the plague shall not be on you to destroy you, when I smite the land of Egypt. And this day shall be to you for a memorial; and you shall keep it a feast to the LORD throughout your generations; you shall keep it a feast by an ordinance for ever." (Exodus 12:3-14)

The feast of Passover required preparation. On the 10th of Nisan a family would select an unblemished, undamaged lamb and take it home and care for it for four days. God wanted to create an attachment to this sacrifice unlike any other. At twilight at the beginning of the fourteenth day all of these lambs were to be slain and their blood applied with hyssop to the doorpost's sides and top (and as the blood dripped from the top to the ground, the four points of a cross are made). The lambs were to be roasted whole, likely on a spit, which would take between three to four hours. If twilight was about 7:00 pm, then the family would have been eating their meal between 10:00 pm and midnight. Unleavened bread and bitter herbs accompanied the meal which they were to eat quickly in their traveling clothes. The lamb's bones were not to be broken (Ex. 12:46), and any uneaten lamb was to be burned.

*And it came to pass, that <u>at midnight the LORD smote all the firstborn in the land of Egypt</u>, from the firstborn of Pharaoh that sat on his throne to the firstborn of the captive that was in the dungeon; and all the firstborn of cattle. And Pharaoh rose up in the night, he, and all his servants, and all the Egyptians; and there was a great cry in Egypt; for there was not a house where there was not one dead. And he called for Moses and Aaron by night, and said, Rise up, and get you forth from among my people, both you and the children of Israel; and go, serve the LORD, as you have said. Also take your flocks and your herds, as you have said, and be gone; and bless me also. And the Egyptians were urgent on the people, that they might send them out of the land in haste; for they said, We be all dead men. <u>And the people took their dough before it was leavened, their kneading troughs being bound up in their clothes on their shoulders.</u> And the children of Israel did according to the word of Moses; <u>and they **borrowed** of the Egyptians jewels of silver, and jewels of gold, and raiment: And the LORD gave the people **favor** in the sight of the Egyptians, so that they lent to them such things as they required. And they **spoiled** the Egyptians.</u> And the children of Israel journeyed from Rameses to Succoth, about six hundred thousand on foot that were men, beside children. And a mixed multitude* *went up also with them; and flocks, and herds, even very much cattle. <u>And they baked unleavened cakes</u> of the dough which they brought forth out of Egypt, for it was not leavened; because they were thrust out of Egypt, and could not tarry, neither had they prepared for themselves any victual. Now the sojourning of the children of Israel, who dwelled in Egypt, was four hundred and thirty years. <u>And it came to pass at the end of the four hundred and thirty years, even the selfsame day it came to pass, that all the hosts of the LORD went out from the land of Egypt.</u> It is a night to be much observed to the LORD for bringing them out from the land of Egypt: this is that night of the LORD to be observed of all the children of Israel in their generations. (Exodus 12:29-42)*

Not long after midnight the Hebrews were given word to go to the houses of the Egyptians who were grieving the losses of their first born to ask them for gold, silver, polished brass mirrors, clothing, tents, cookware, swords and armor ("harnessed" is armed for battle in Exodus 13:18), and whatever else they desired to put into their carts and wagons as they left; now that's a miracle! The Egyptian people didn't kill them, spit in their faces, or send them away empty handed, but "lent" them whatever they wanted because God gave His people favor in their sight. Wow.

They traveled that night for a few miles and camped at Rameses. The 430 years refers to when Abram first entered Egypt because of a famine after God had promised him his seed would inherit the land of Canaan (Genesis 12:6-10 and Galatians 3:16-17). The day of Passover was also to remind the Hebrews of God's covenant with Abraham to give his descendants the land of Canaan; a very special celebration indeed as Passover is the catalyst to the fulfillment of that promise.

The Feast of Unleavened Bread: Nisan 14-21

The feast of unleavened bread coincides with and is an extension of Passover. Leaven is yeast which enables bread to rise. Unleavened bread is flat, and can be baked soft like a tortilla or hard like a cracker. The Hebrews had been commanded before they left Egypt not to take any leaven with them.

*Seven days shall you eat unleavened bread; even the first day you shall put away leaven out of your houses: for whoever eats leavened bread from the first day until the seventh day, that soul shall be cut off from Israel. And in the first day there shall be an holy convocation, and in the seventh day there shall be an holy convocation to you; no manner of work shall be done in them, save that which every man must eat, that only may be done of you. And you shall observe <u>the feast of unleavened bread</u>; for in this selfsame day have I brought your **armies** out of the land of Egypt: therefore shall you observe this day in your generations by an ordinance for ever. In the first month, on the fourteenth day of the month at even, you shall eat unleavened bread, until the one and twentieth day of the month at even. <u>Seven days shall there be no leaven found in your houses: for whoever eats that which is</u>*

leavened, even that soul shall be cut off from the congregation of Israel, whether he be a stranger, or born in the land. You shall eat nothing leavened; in all your habitations shall you eat unleavened bread. (Exodus 12:15-20)

If they did not put the blood on the doorposts, a physical death would ensue; but if they ate any leaven during this seven day feast, they would be excommunicated from Israel and suffer a spiritual and relational death. So after selecting the lamb on the 10th of Nisan, women would have been cleaning their homes of any leaven crumbs, so that their children would not mistakingly eat leaven from the 14th to the 21st of Nisan and be parted from them. This seven day feast was to remind them of God bringing their "armies" out of Egypt; it was a seven day journey from Goshen to the crossing of the Red Sea. By the end of the feast they would retrieve weapons of the defeated Egyptian army (Exodus 14:30). The word used for "armies" can also mean a host prepared to worship, which would also be fulfilled after they crossed the Red Sea (Exodus 15:1-21).

In the fourteenth day of the first month at even is the LORD's passover. And on the fifteenth day of the same month is the feast of unleavened bread to the LORD: seven days you must eat unleavened bread. (Leviticus 23:5-6)

A distinction is made in the seven day feast: the fourteenth is the LORD's Passover, and the fifteenth and five following days are the feast of unleavened bread, because it was on the fifteenth that the Hebrews actually left Egypt with unleavened bread dough in their kneeding bowls (Numbers 33:3). Yet their is another holy day in connection with the feast of unleavened bread with a special name and purpose which can occur after the fifteenth, depending upon when the Sabbath comes after Passover.

The Feast of First Fruits: Nisan Sunday after Passover

The Hebrews did not celebrate the feast of first fruits until after they entered the land of Canaan and harvested barley. Moses described it in conjunction with Passover and the feast of unleavened bread.

And the LORD spoke to Moses, saying, Speak to the children of Israel, and say to them, When you be come into the land which I give to you, and shall reap the harvest thereof, then you shall bring a sheaf of the first fruits of your harvest to the priest: And he shall wave the sheaf before the LORD, to be accepted for you: on the morrow after the sabbath the priest shall wave it. And you shall offer that day when you wave the sheaf an he lamb without blemish of the first year for a burnt offering to the LORD. And the meat offering thereof shall be two tenth deals of fine flour mingled with oil, an offering made by fire to the LORD for a sweet smell: and the drink offering thereof shall be of wine, the fourth part of an hin. And you shall eat neither bread, nor parched corn, nor green ears, until the selfsame day that you have brought an offering to your God: it shall be a statute for ever throughout your generations in all your dwellings. (Leviticus 23:9-14)

Since the feast of unleavened bread occurs over a period of seven days, a sabbath must occur sometime during it. Sabbath is from sundown Friday to sundown Saturday on our calendars, so the "morrow after the sabbath" would be from sundown Saturday to sundown Sunday. It is not specified as an evening offering, and gives an injunction not to eat until bringing this offering "the selfsame day," which makes it Sunday before sundown. Regardless of which day of the week Passover begins, the feast of first fruits would always be during the light of day on Sunday. The Hebrews celebrated the first Passover on a Sabbath, making the dawn after safely crossing the Red Sea during the night the "*morrow after the sabbath*" or First Fruits.

The Feast of Weeks (Seven Sabbaths): Sivan 6

[Some Jews count fifty days from Nisan 15, the "morrow after the sabbath" of Passover, so that Feast of Weeks is always on Sivan 6.] From the Sunday of the feast of First Fruits, the Hebrews were to count seven sabbaths, and celebrate the "morrow after the seventh sabbath", the fiftieth day, which would be another Sunday. The Feast of Weeks is similar to the jubilee celebration of the fiftieth year after seven sabbaths of years.

And you shall count to you from the morrow after the sabbath, from the day that you brought the sheaf of the wave offering; seven sabbaths shall be complete: Even to the morrow after the seventh sabbath shall you number fifty days; and you shall offer a new meat offering to the LORD. You shall bring out of your habitations two wave loaves of two tenth deals; they shall be of fine flour; they shall be baked with leaven; they are the first fruits to the LORD. And you shall offer with the bread seven lambs without blemish of the first year, and one young bullock, and two rams: they shall be for a burnt offering to the LORD, with their meat offering, and their drink offerings, even an offering made by fire, of sweet smell to the LORD. Then you shall sacrifice one kid of the goats for a sin offering, and two lambs of the first year for a sacrifice of peace offerings. And the priest shall wave them with the bread of the first fruits for a wave offering before the LORD, with the two lambs: they shall be holy to the LORD for the priest. And you shall proclaim on the selfsame day, that it may be an holy convocation to you: you shall do no servile work therein: it shall be a statute for ever in all your dwellings throughout your generations. (Leviticus 23:15-21)

The feast of First Fruits is during the feast of Unleavened Bread and offers the other two ingredients found in bread: barley flour and oil. The offering of the Feast of Weeks combines wheat flour, oil, and leaven into two loaves of bread. Feast of First Fruits harvested barley; feast of weeks harvested wheat. On the Feast of Weeks, the Hebrews heard God proclaim His ten commandments to them as His people from Mount Sinai (Exodus 20).

Awake, Bride

The Feast of Trumpets (*Rosh Hashanah*): Tishri 1

And the LORD spoke to Moses, saying, Speak to the children of Israel, saying, In the seventh month, in the first day of the month, shall you have a sabbath, a memorial of blowing of trumpets, an holy convocation. You shall do no servile work therein: but you shall offer an offering made by fire to the LORD. (Leviticus 23:23-25)

This is the only feast on the first of a month; the new moon. The first of Tishri was a memorial of blowing trumpets. The passage does not specify what is being memorialized. Traditionally, Jews suspect it commemorates the day Abraham prepared to sacrifice Isaac on Mount Moriah, but God provided a two-horned ram instead. A ram's horn is a *shofar* or trumpet. Others surmise it commemorates the giving of the ten commandments, since a trumpet is involved (Exodus 19:13,16,19), but that has its own celebration: Feast of Weeks. There was another important day in the history of the Hebrews which scripture associates with blowing trumpets, and that is the day of Joseph's inauguration.

And it came to pass <u>at the end of two full years</u>, that Pharaoh dreamed: . . .Then Pharaoh sent and called Joseph, and they brought him hastily out of the dungeon: and he shaved himself, and changed his raiment, and came in to Pharaoh. And Pharaoh said to Joseph, I have dreamed a dream, and there is none that can interpret it: and I have heard say of you, that you can understand a dream to interpret it. And Joseph answered Pharaoh, saying, It is not in me: God shall give Pharaoh an answer of peace. . . . <u>And Pharaoh said to Joseph, For as much as God has showed you all this, there is none so discreet and wise as you are: You shall be over my house, and according to your word shall all my people be ruled: only in the throne will I be greater than you.</u> And Pharaoh said to Joseph, See, I have set you over all the land of Egypt. And Pharaoh took off his ring from his hand, and put it on Joseph's hand, and arrayed him in clothing of fine linen, and put a gold chain about his neck; And he made him to ride in the second chariot which he had; and they cried before him, Bow the knee: and <u>he made him ruler over all the land of Egypt</u>. And Pharaoh said to Joseph, I am Pharaoh, and without you shall no man lift up his hand or foot in all the land of Egypt. And Pharaoh called Joseph's name Zaphnathpaaneah; <u>and he gave him to wife Asenath the daughter of Potipherah priest of On</u>. **And Joseph went out over all the land of Egypt**. *And <u>Joseph was thirty years old</u> when he stood before Pharaoh king of Egypt. And Joseph went out from the presence of Pharaoh, and went throughout all the land of Egypt. (Genesis 41:1a, 15-16, 39-46)*

Joseph is a type of Christ. He was thirty years old, the same as when Jesus began His ministry. Joseph was wrongly imprisoned; yet saved the world much as sinless Jesus died to save the world. After two full years Joseph was made ruler over all the land; after two thousand years, King Jesus will rule over all the earth and marry His Bride. Jesus is "*the bread of life*" (John 6:48). One translation of *Zaphnathpaaneah* is 'living bread man' since he was to store the grain to provide bread that would sustain life in Egypt. In one day God took him from the prison to the palace, gave him a wife, and gave him an empire to rule. Though the scripture here does not mention trumpets being blown as Joseph was paraded through the streets; it is clear in Psalms.

> <u>*Blow up the trumpet in the new moon, in the time appointed, on our solemn feast day*</u>*. For this was a statute for Israel, and a law of the God of Jacob.* <u>*This he ordained in **Joseph** for a **testimony**, when he **went out through the land of Egypt**:*</u> *where I heard a language that I understood not. I removed his shoulder from the burden: his hands were delivered from the pots. (Psalm 81:3-6)*

This is a clear reference to the holy day on the 1st of Tishri. The Hebrew word for 'testimony', *ayduth,* can also mean witness, and its root means 'prince'. The Jews call this holiday *Rosh Hashanah,* which literally means 'head of the year' or new year. The blowing of the *shofar* was also associate with the inaugurations of king Solomon (1 Kings 1:34) and king Jehu (2 Kings 9:13).

The Fast Day of Atonement (*Yom Kippur*): Tishri 10

> *And the LORD spoke to Moses, saying, Also on the tenth day of this seventh month there shall be a day of atonement: it shall be an holy convocation to you; and you shall afflict your souls, and offer an offering made by fire to the LORD. And you shall do no work in that same day: for it is a day of atonement, to make an atonement for you before the LORD your God. For whatever soul it be that shall not be afflicted in that same day, he shall be cut off from among his people. And whatever soul it be that does any work in that same day, the same soul will I destroy from among his people. You shall do no manner of work: it shall be a statute for ever throughout your generations in all your dwellings. It shall be to you a sabbath of rest, and you shall afflict your souls: in the ninth day of the month at even, from even to even, shall you celebrate your sabbath. (Leviticus 23:26-32)*

This is the only day of fasting amidst the seven festivals. Though it is officially celebrated on Tishri 10, it is reiterated that means beginning with the evening of Tishri 9. Day of atonement in Hebrew is *Yom Kippur*. After the tabernacle is erected and the priesthood established, this becomes a very busy day for the high priest. Only the high priest was allowed in the Holy of Holies, and only on this day could the Name of God *YHWH* be pronounced audibly by him. During a jubilee year, the trumpet was to be blown on this day (Leviticus 25:9).

Feast of Ingathering and Booths/Tabernacles (*Succoth*): Tishri 15-23

And the LORD spoke to Moses, saying, Speak to the children of Israel, saying, The fifteenth day of this seventh month shall be the feast of tabernacles for seven days to the LORD. On the first day shall be an holy convocation: you shall do no servile work therein. <u>Seven days you shall offer an offering made by fire to the LORD: on the eighth day shall be an holy convocation to you</u>; and you shall offer an offering made by fire to the LORD: it is a solemn assembly; and you shall do no servile work therein. . . . Also in the fifteenth day of the seventh month, when you have gathered in the fruit of the land, you shall keep a feast to the LORD seven days: on the first day shall be a sabbath, and on the eighth day shall be a sabbath. And <u>you shall take you on the first day the boughs of goodly trees, branches of palm trees, and the boughs of thick trees, and willows of the brook; and you shall rejoice before the LORD your God seven days.</u> And you shall keep it a feast to the LORD seven days in the year. It shall be a statute for ever in your generations: you shall celebrate it in the seventh month. <u>You shall dwell in booths seven days; all that are Israelites born shall dwell in booths: That your generations may know that I made the children of Israel to dwell in booths, when I brought them out of the land of Egypt</u>: I am the LORD your God. And Moses declared to the children of Israel the feasts of the LORD. (Leviticus 23:33-36, 39-44)

The feast of ingathering is that of grapes, figs and olives in the fall. After the harvest they were to make booths and celebrate for a week; a community camp-out to remember God's faithfulness to them when He delivered them from Egypt, again emphasizing it took seven days to get the Hebrews from Goshen to the Red Sea. That first Passover began on a Sabbath, with the "*morrow after the sabbath*" (First Fruits), eight days later on the morning of Nisan 22. So the eighth day was one of great victory. They were not to work on the first and eighth days, but could work and party during the rest of the week.

Males Required to Appear before God for Three Feasts

Three times you shall keep a feast to me in the year. You shall keep the <u>feast of unleavened bread:</u> (you shall eat unleavened bread seven days, as I commanded you, in the time appointed of the month Abib; for in it you came out from Egypt: and none shall appear before me empty:) And the <u>feast of harvest, the first fruits</u> of your labors, which you have sown in the field: and the <u>feast of ingathering</u>, which is in the end of the year, when you have gathered in your labors out of the field. Three items in the year all your males shall appear before the LORD God. (Exodus 23:14-17)

The <u>feast of unleavened bread</u> shall you keep. Seven days you shall eat unleavened bread, as I commanded you, in the time of the month Abib: for in the month Abib *you came out from Egypt. And you shall observe the <u>feast of weeks, of the first fruits of **wheat** harvest</u>, and the <u>feast of ingathering</u> at the year's end. Thrice in the year shall all your male children appear before the LORD God, the God of Israel. (Exodus 34:18, 22-23)*

The "first fruits" is an agricultural term related to those fruits and grains which mature first, and is not to be confused with the feast of First Fruits (of barley) which occurs after Passover. The middle feast (of wheat) is Weeks or Pentecost. When this command was given, there was no permanent place for God's tabernacle, so they would go wherever it was located. After the building of Solomon's temple, then Jerusalem became the place where God set His Name. The three feasts in which the Hebrew males are required to go to Jerusalem are the feast of Unleavened Bread (14th-21st of Nisan), the feast of Weeks (around 6th of Sivan), and the feast of Booths (15th-23rd of Tishri).

These feasts and their prophetic meanings will be explored in the next two chapters.

Why Don't Most Contemporary Christians Celebrate God's Feasts?

When Paul began preaching to the Gentiles, the Jews placed no prerequisites on them besides not eating blood or fornicating (Acts 15:28-29). Gentiles were not required to become Jewish and obey the Law in order to receive salvation through faith in Christ Jesus. Monotheistic Jews and Christians were severely persecuted by polytheistic Romans, until 313 AD when Constantine declared toleration of Christianity. But Constantine was anti-semitic. Constantine wrote laws restricting Jewish religious services and access to Jerusalem.

In 325 AD Constantine convened over 500 bishops in Nicea to come to a consensus on Christian practices. They concluded "Let us, then, have nothing in common with the Jews, who are our adversaries." They purposefully set resurrection Sunday on a date other than feast of First Fruits, and chose to appease the pagans by renaming it Easter after their fertility goddess Ishtar. They also picked December 25th, the birthday of the war god Mithras, to celebrate Christ's mass. In 387 AD John Chrysostom, bishop of Antioch, wrote sermons "Against the Jews" which further distanced Gentile believers in Jesus from Jews who had accepted Him as Messiah. These new celebrations became a major part of our cultures which most Christians blindly accept. More churches are teaching the importance of God's feasts, but few actually celebrate them.

Why not use the Contemporary Jewish Calendar?

The Jews sensed the need to prepare a calendar for another wave of persecution in which they would not be able to establish the new moons from Jerusalem. In 360 AD Rabbi Hillel created an astrologically calculated calendar and had the Sanhedrin bless all the new moons until the Jewish year 6000 (2240 AD). Years are either 12 or 13 months, corresponding to the 12.4 month solar cycle. Thus giving their 12 month year 354 days, and their 13 month year 384. The 13th month is added in the 3rd, 6th, 8th, 11th, 14th, 17th and

19th years of the cycle started in the fourth century. 2008 was the 11th year in this metatonic cycle. Though this calendar began correctly, it occasionally drifts a month out of sync with the spring equinox. Rabbis know this but are unwilling to change it because they believe only a modern Sanhedrin or the Messiah has the authority to do so.

A modern Jewish calendar will place the holiday name on the day and sometimes note it begins the prior evening. According to the contemporary Hebrew calendar, Rosh Hashanah will occur on September 17, 2012; so it actually begins at dusk on September 16th. The new moon will be visible earlier, around 2:00 am on September 16th, so that pious Jews could declare Tishri 1 begins at dusk on September 16th. This date is key to the rest of the book.

Two Additional Historical Feasts

The seven feasts are God's appointed times. The next two feasts were added by the Hebrews to commemorate God's victories on their behalf.

Purim: Adar 13-14

After Nebuchadnezzar conquered Israel and Judah, he transported many Hebrews throughout his Babylonian empire to keep them from becoming a national threat again. Eventually the Persians conquered his empire. The Persian capital was in Susa, and so were many Hebrews because of the earlier dispersion. King Xerxes (sometimes called Ahasuerus) held a great banquet for his nobles for 180 days and summoned his queen to appear. When she refused, his nobles suggested he look for a new queen. Eventually he chose Esther. Queen Esther was made aware of a plot to exterminate the Jews on Adar 13. Because of her bravery, the king allowed the Jews to defend themselves against their enemies on Adar 13 and 14 which then became the Jewish holiday called Purim.

Hanukkah (Feast of Dedication): Kislev 24 - Tevet 2

Then spoke Jesus again to them, saying, I am the light of the world: he that follows me shall not walk in darkness, but shall have the light of life. (John 8:12) And it was at Jerusalem the <u>feast of the dedication</u>, and it was winter. And Jesus walked in the temple in Solomon's porch. (John 10:22-23)

Hanukkah was mentioned in John as the "*feast of dedication*" of the Temple. This referred to when the Maccabees fought off the armies of Antiochus Epiphanes who had sacrificed a pig on the altar. They cleansed the temple from his "abomination of desolation", but there was only enough holy oil for one day. Miraculously the oil lasted eight days. This festival starts on the evening of Kislev 24 and lasts eight days.

Hannukah was also referred to as the "festival of lights". Four young priests would climb 50 cubit poles to light several gallons of olive oil using wicks of worn priestly robes, thus illuminating all Jerusalem. There was dancing and singing well into the night. It is possible that Jesus was conceived during this feast to be born nine months later at Rosh

Hashanah. It's clear Jesus used this feast to declare Himself to be "*the light of the world*" (John 9:5).

Summary

The Biblical Hebrew day goes from sundown to sundown because the first day in the creation in Genesis begins in darkness. God established a pattern of six days of work followed by a day of rest as one week. Hebrew months at the time of Noah's flood had thirty days each. Hebrew years typically contained twelve months of thirty days each which equaled 360 days. The Hebrews had a combined lunar-solar calendar which included a 13th month every six years until reaching the 36th year when an extra month was added to the 40th year as well. Every forty years this ancient Hebrew 360-day calendar was in sync with the modern 365.25-day calendar. Forty years is equivalent to a Hebrew generation. Every seventh year the land was given rest from farming, and the fiftieth year was a year of Jubilee when all debts were canceled and slaves were freed, and it was celebrated on Yom Kippur.

When God delivered the Hebrews from bondage in Egypt, He reoriented their religious calendar to begin in spring with the first of seven feasts they were to hold throughout the year. The spring feasts are Unleavened Bread, Passover, and First Fruits. The early summer feast is Feast of Weeks, later known as Pentecost in Greek due to its counting of 'fifty' days. The fall feasts are Feast of Trumpets, Day of Atonement, and Feast of Booths. Two additional Jewish holidays which celebrate victories over their enemies are Purim and Hanukkah.

Spring Feasts

O Judah, keep your solemn feasts, perform your vows:
(Nahum 1:15b)

Taking and Renewing Betrothal Vows

The Spring feasts not only commemorate the historical deliverance of the Hebrew people, they also portray the betrothal of God to His people. During the Spring feasts, God's people renew their vows as His Bride to love and obey Him. God gave them gifts, promising a Groom. In America, Spring brides and June weddings continue to persist.

Hebrew Marriage Traditions	Fulfillment in Scripture
Betrothal covenant was a witnessed and sealed contract called a *shitre erusin*	Ten Commandments and Law sealed in blood. (Exodus 20-24)
If the woman drank the wine offered, that **sealed the covenant**; they were 'betrothed'.	The 70 elders ate and drank with God. Exodus 24:3-11; 1 Corinthians 10:3-4
Groom's covenant (*ketubah*) would pay a **"bride price"** to the father of the bride.	Spotless lambs for first born sons Exodus 12-13
Bride accepts a **gift** from groom; *kiddushin*, which means sanctification.	Salvation, deliverance, and freedom Redeemed (Exodus 15:13)
Bride had a ritual immersion [**baptism**] transferring her obedience to her husband.	Baptism through the Red Sea 1 Corinthians 10:1-2
Groom returned to his father's house to build an addition, the **bridal chamber**.	The Promised Land: a prepared place Exodus 23:20-23
After father deemed bridal chamber finished, he allowed son to leave at sunset to get bride.	God sent His Angel with His Name Exodus 23:20-23
Groom to bride's house with **shofars, shouting**, "*Behold, the bridegroom comes.*"	Joshua took Jericho with trumpets and shouting. (Joshua 6)
Wedding ceremony took place under a *chupah*, a white canopy.	God appeared as a thick **cloud**. Exodus 19:9,16; 24:15-17
Vows consummated that night; celebrate the wedding feast for seven days.	Exodus 24:3-12 Exodus 24:16

Brides want to understand the culture of their groom, especially to know what is pleasing and acceptable in that culture. I am indebted to Edward Chumney who wrote of the Hebrew marriage traditions and their Biblical fulfillments in "*The Seven Festivals of the Messiah*" which was published by Treasure House in 1994.

The father chooses a bride for his son and approaches with an offer of betrothal. The bride's responsibilities were in the betrothal covenant, *shitre erusin*, (Law on Mt. Sinai); the groom's responsibilities were in the wedding covenant, *ketubah*, ("new covenant" Jeremiah 31:31-37 fulfilled at Pentecost).

The Exodus Betrothal

God flexed His muscles and got the Hebrew people's attention with the ten plagues. God demonstrated His choice of the Hebrews by the fourth plague, clearly separating them to Himself. The tenth plague revealed to God which of the Hebrews would not accept His offer of betrothal by their refusal to place blood on their door posts. Throughout their generations, He would continue to see those who would refuse to sacrifice for the first born (Ex. 13:2). Father God's betrothal offer to the Hebrews began with the **bride price** on Passover, followed by the **gift** of freedom from bondage and **baptism** in the Red Sea on First Fruits, and formalized with the **betrothal contract** spoken with fire from Mount Sinai on Sukkot.

On the full moon of the fourteenth of Nisan, the angel of the LORD 'passed over' the homes which had lamb's blood on them, but killed the first born son of the homes which did not. The Hebrews hastily ate their Passover meals in their traveling apparel, burned the leftover lamb, packed the rest of the flat bread and the unleavened bread dough in their kneading bowls, and gathered together after midnight at Rameses on the edge of the land of Goshen to sleep for a few hours before making preparations for a larger trek the next day with the rest of their people and animals. The land of Goshen occupied much of the Nile delta, and they needed a day for everyone to gather in Rameses and plan their departure. They would march and camp according to tribe. While the Egyptians buried their dead, they retrieved the bones of Joseph from his tomb in order to rebury them in Canaan. After a good night's sleep, they left Egypt triumphantly for Succoth less than 20 miles away, but outside the eastern border of Egypt. *Succoth* means booths or tents, and it may just have been a plain large enough for over a million people to camp. (The Feast of *Sukkot*/Booths also celebrates the seven days it took the Hebrews to escape Egypt, crossing the Red Sea on the eighth day, the highlight of the festival.)

Exodus Journey to the Red Sea

There was one day's travel from Rameses to Succoth. From Succoth, ancient Tharu, to Etham on the edge of the wilderness was about 80 miles. It could be traversed by a million people with animals in four days traveling day and night (Ex. 13:21) with God's help who "bore them on eagle's wings" (Ex. 19:4). From Etham they could have gone around the northern tip of the Gulf of Aqaba easily, but then so could the Egyptians for whom God set

Spring Feasts

a trap. Instead, God sent them south to Nuweiba beach at Pihahiroth, which was about a 50 mile trip and likely took them two days; totaling seven days to reach the Red Sea.

> *Seven days you shall eat unleavened bread, and in the seventh day shall be a feast to the LORD. . . . And you shall show your son in that day, saying, This is done because of that which the LORD did to me when I came forth out of Egypt. And it shall be for a sign to you on your hand, and for a memorial between your eyes, that the LORD's law may be in your mouth: for with a strong hand has the LORD brought you out of Egypt. (Exodus 13:6, 8).*

The Hebrews were to eat unleavened bread for seven days to commemorate the seven days it took them to flee Egypt, 'eating on the run'. ["In 1967, Moshe Dyan marched his troops from Nuweiba (the crossing site) to Suez City (near ancient Tharu/Succoth) in six days. And they camped at night." www.wyattmuseum.com]

At Nuweiba beach there is an engraved column, and ten miles away on the opposite shore there is a matching engraved column. According to John Wyatt, these two columns are memorials placed there by King Solomon to commemorate the miraculous crossing of the Red Sea. There is a 7 to 10 mile wide land bridge in shallow water connecting the two shores. All night of Nisan 21, God's column of fire kept the Egyptians at bey, and God's wind blew the sea floor so the people could walk across on dry ground at dawn and be safely across by dusk. In "*the morning watch*" on Nisan 22, three hours before dawn, the Egyptians pursued them; but God removed their chariot wheels and closed the Red Sea over them so that not one of them was left alive (Ex. 14:24-31). So, that first Passover began on a Sabbath, with the "*morrow after the sabbath*" (First Fruits), eight days later on the morning of Nisan 22. The dead pharaoh was most likely Amen-hotep III.

Exodus Journey to Mount Sinai

Exodus 13-19 and Numbers 33 describe the exodus of the Hebrews and the places they camped. They journeyed three days without water (Ex. 15:22). Then at Marah, God turned the bitter waters to sweet using a tree (Ex. 15:23-26). Then they camped at Elim which had 12 wells and 70 palms (Ex. 15:27). They left Elim and camped at the Red Sea (Num. 33:10). Then they camped by the Desert of Sin (Num. 33:11). Thirty days after their departure, on the 15th of Iyar, the Hebrews murmured for meat in wilderness (Ex. 16:1). God gave them quail at twilight and manna in the morning (Ex. 16:12), but no manna on the Sabbath (Ex. 16:25-26). At Rephidim there was no water, and God told Moses to strike the rock for water to come out; and Moses renamed the place Massah and Meribah (Ex. 17:1-7). God gave the Hebrews their first military victory over Amelek (Ex.17:8-16). Since they traveled in the land of Midian, Moses met with Jethro, his father-in-law, who gave him sound advice (Ex. 18:7-26).

The Hebrews arrived and made camp at Mount Sinai on the third new moon of the year, the month of Sivan. God talked to Moses (day one), Moses talked to the elders (day two) and the people said they would obey God (Ex. 19:8), and then Moses gave God's command to the people to abstain from sex for three days (days three, four, five) and to wash their clothes to prepare themselves to hear the audible voice of God. The traditional date for the feast of weeks is the 6th of Sivan, fifty days after the Hebrews left Egypt on Nisan 15.

> *And it came to pass on the third day in the morning, that there were <u>thunders and lightning, and a thick **cloud** on the mount, and the voice of the trumpet exceeding loud</u>; so that all the people that was in the camp trembled. And Moses brought forth the people out of the camp to meet with God; and they stood at the nether part of the mount. And mount Sinai was altogether on a smoke, because the LORD descended on it in **fire**: and the smoke thereof ascended as the smoke of a furnace, and the whole mount quaked greatly. And when the voice of the trumpet sounded long, and waxed louder and louder, Moses spoke, and God answered him by a voice. And the LORD came down on mount Sinai, on the top of the mount: and the LORD called Moses up to the top of the mount; and Moses went up. (Ex. 19:16-19)*

The underlined are also characteristics of God's throne in heaven as portrayed in Revelation. Mere mortals met with God Almighty as Mount Sinai quaked and smoked. A mountain in ancient Midian, now Saudi Arabia, is called Jebel el Lawz. It is roughly forty miles away from the Red Sea crossing point, and twenty miles from Jethro's home (now Al Bad). The top of it is burnt. At its base are the remains of twelve pillars and an altar.

The Betrothal Vows

A Hebrew wedding is very formal. The choosing and betrothal (*kiddushin*, meaning holy and set apart) is binding. The betrothal contract (*shitre erusin*) spells out the bride's responsibilities, and is proffered with a gift. Then the marriage covenant (*ketubah*) spells out the groom's responsibilities and his bride price (*mohar*), and the bride's rights.

The Hebrews heard God proclaim His ten commandments to them with His Own voice (Exodus 20). The Talmud for Shabbat 88b on Psalm 68:11 teaches that "Every single word going out from the Omnipotent was split up into seventy languages." Jewish tradition holds that a "tongue as fire" had presented itself to each person at Sinai, to ask if he or she would accept the Covenant. Those present were from all seventy nations, a "mixed multitude." Each was presented with the bride's responsibilities, and they accepted (Ex. 24:3). And they pleaded with Moses to go talk to God for them, lest they continue to hear Him and die. So Moses heard the rest of God's commands (Exodus 21-23) and relayed them to the people. Then Moses wrote them down. This was God's marriage contract with them; a **blood covenant**. They would be His people, and He would be their God. <u>They sent 70 representatives to **seal** the covenant with a meal in God's presence.</u> Their description of God is akin to that in Revelation 4.

> *<u>And Moses came and told the people all the words of the LORD, and all the judgments: and all the people answered with one voice, and said, All the words which the LORD has said will **we do**.</u> And Moses wrote all the words of the LORD, and rose up early in the morning, and built an altar under the hill, and twelve pillars, according to the twelve tribes of Israel. And he sent young men of the children of Israel, which offered burnt offerings, and sacrificed peace offerings of*

*oxen to the LORD. And Moses took half of the **blood**, and put it in basins; and **half of the blood he sprinkled on the altar**. <u>And he took the book of the covenant, and read in the audience of the people: and they said, All that the LORD has said will we do, and be obedient.</u> And **Moses took the blood, and sprinkled it on the people, and said, Behold the blood of the covenant, which the LORD has made with you concerning all these words**. Then went up <u>Moses, and Aaron, Nadab, and Abihu, and seventy of the elders of Israel: And they saw the God of Israel</u>: and there was under his feet as it were a paved work of a sapphire stone, and as it were the body of heaven in his clearness. And on the nobles of the children of Israel he laid not his hand: also they saw God, <u>and did eat and drink</u>. (Exodus 24:3-11)*

. . . Return, you backsliding Israel, said the LORD; and I will not cause my anger to fall on you: for I am merciful . . . Only acknowledge your iniquity, that you have transgressed against the LORD your God, . . . you have not obeyed my voice, said the LORD. Turn, O backsliding children, said the LORD; <u>for I am married to you</u>: . . . (Jeremiah 3:12-14 edited)

*Moreover, brothers, I would not that you should be ignorant, how that <u>all our fathers were under the **cloud**</u>, and <u>all passed through the sea</u>; And <u>were all **baptized** to Moses in the cloud and in the sea</u>; And <u>did all eat the same spiritual meat; And did all drink the same spiritual drink: for they drank of that spiritual Rock that followed them</u>: and that Rock was Christ. But with many of them God was not well pleased: for they were overthrown in the wilderness. Now these things were our examples, to the intent we should not lust after evil things, as they also lusted. (1 Corinthians 10:1-6)*

During a betrothal a couple is considered to be married and are called husband and wife even though the marriage won't be consummated until the wedding.

Forty Days of Fasting and the Tabernacle

God's glory **cloud** rested on the mountains for six days, and on the seventh day He called Moses into the cloud where he remained forty days and nights (Exodus 24:16-18) receiving instructions for the tabernacle and two stone tablets of the testimony engraved by God (Exodus 25-31). On the fortieth day, Moses came down the mountain and saw the naked people worshiping the calf Aaron had made, and threw and broke the tablets at the base of the mountain; and asked those who were on the Lord's side to kill the worshipers. The Levites killed about 3,000 men that day, and received a blessing from God (Exodus 32:27-28). Mountain climbing after forty days without food is not recommended. To regain his strength, Moses had a tent of meeting built at the base of the mountain away from the camp in which to talk with God (Exodus 33). After a month, Moses spent another 40 days and nights fasting on the mountain (Exodus 34:28). According to Jewish tradition, Moses went up on the 1st of Elul and returned on the 10th of Tishri, which is Yom Kippur. When Moses came down, the people started working on the tabernacle. After several months it was completed and erected on the 1st of Nisan (Exodus 40:1), completing the first year of the Hebrews under their new calendar with Yahweh.

The Promised Land: A Prepared Place

*Behold, I send an Angel before you, to keep you in the way, and to bring you into the **place which I have prepared**. Beware of him, and obey his voice, provoke him not; for he will not pardon your transgressions: for my name is in him. But if you shall indeed obey his voice, and do all that I speak; then I will be an enemy to your enemies, and an adversary to your adversaries. For my Angel shall go before you, and bring you in to the Amorites, and the Hittites, and the Perizzites, and the Canaanites, the Hivites, and the Jebusites: and I will cut them off. (Ex. 23:20-23)*

And he said to Abram, Know of a surety that your seed shall be a stranger in a land that is not their's, and shall serve them; and they shall afflict them four hundred years; And also that nation, whom they shall serve, will I judge: and afterward shall they come out with great substance. And you shall go to your fathers in peace; you shall be buried in a good old age. But <u>in the fourth generation they shall come here again</u>: for the iniquity of the Amorites is not yet full. (Genesis 15:13-16)

The Promised Land was promised to Abram and his seed (Genesis 13:14-17). The land of Canaan took 400 years for God to "prepare" for Abraham's descendants, waiting for the iniquity of the Amorites to come to the point He was ready to destroy them. The Hebrews only spent 215 years in Egypt. If you count the generation that died in the wilderness as one of the "four generations," then they spent roughly 120 years of their time in slavery in Egypt. The Hebrews plundered the Egyptians as they left. Disobedience kept the Hebrews from entering Canaan for forty years. Moses died and God raised up Joshua to lead them. Joshua obeyed God's instructions, and they took Jericho.

*So the people shouted when the priests blew with the trumpets: and it came to pass, when the people heard the sound of the **trumpet**, and the people shouted with a great **shout**, that the wall fell down flat, so that the people went up into the city, every man straight before him, and they took the city. (Joshua 6:20)*

The Feasts of the LORD Fulfilled in the LORD Jesus Christ

The LORD spoke to Moses, saying, Speak to the children of Israel, and say to them, Concerning the feasts of the LORD, which you shall proclaim to be holy convocations, even these are my feasts. (Leviticus 23:2-3)

These feasts were not devised by Moses nor any man, they are the *moed*, the 'appointed times' of the Lord. They are holy and set apart for the Lord's purposes as convocations, *miqra*, public meetings or 'rehearsals'. They rehearse Israel's past, but they are also shadows of future events which find their complete fulfillment in the Lord Jesus Christ.

Let no man therefore judge you in meat, or in drink, or in respect of an holy day, or of the new moon, or of the sabbath days: Which are a shadow of things to come; but the body is of Christ. (Colossians 2:16-17)

The Lord Jesus Christ fulfilled the spring feasts and the early summer feast in His death, resurrection, and sending His Holy Spirit at His first coming.

Passover: the Bride Price (*mohar*)

When we take communion, we reaffirm our belief that Jesus' physical death on the cross imparts life to us through His body, represented by the bread, and His blood, represented by the wine. Jesus made this requirement clear, and many of His followers left Him because they thought they would have to drink real blood which was forbidden in the Law (Genesis 9:4 and Leviticus 17:14).

And the <u>passover</u>, a feast of the Jews, was near. When Jesus then lifted up his eyes, and saw a great company come to him, he said to Philip, From where shall we buy bread, that these may eat? . . . There is a lad here, which has five barley loaves, and two small fishes: but what are they among so many? . . . And Jesus took the loaves; and when he had given thanks, he distributed to the disciples, and the disciples to them that were set down; and likewise of the fishes as much as they would. . . . When Jesus therefore perceived that they would come and take him by force, to make him a king, he departed again into a mountain himself alone. . . . Jesus answered them and said, Truly, truly, I say to you, You seek me, not because you saw the miracles, but because you did eat of the loaves, and were filled. . . . Then Jesus said to them, Truly, truly, I say to you, <u>Moses gave you not that bread from heaven; but my Father gives you the true bread from heaven. For the bread of God is he which comes down from heaven, and gives life to the world.</u> Then said they to him, Lord, ever more give us this bread. And Jesus said to them, <u>I am the bread of life</u>: he that comes to me shall never hunger; and he that believes on me shall never thirst. . . . Truly, truly, I say to you, <u>He that believes on me has everlasting life. I am that bread of life.</u> Your fathers did eat manna in the wilderness, and are dead. This is the bread which comes down from heaven, that a man may eat thereof, and not die. I am the living bread which came down from heaven: if any man eat of this bread, he shall live for ever: and <u>the bread that I will give is my flesh, which I will give for the life of the world.</u> The Jews therefore strove among themselves, saying, How can this man give us his flesh to eat? Then Jesus said to them, Truly, truly, I say to you, Except you eat the flesh of the Son of man, and drink his blood, you have no life in you. <u>Whoever eats my flesh, and drinks my blood, has eternal life; and I will raise him up at the last day. For my flesh is meat indeed, and my blood is drink indeed. He that eats my flesh, and drinks my blood, dwells in me, and I in him.</u> As the living Father has sent me, and I live by the Father: so he that eats me, even he shall live by me. This is that bread which came down from heaven: not as your fathers did eat manna, and are dead: he that eats of this bread shall live for ever. . . . Many *therefore of his disciples, when they had heard this, said, This is an hard saying; who can hear it? . . . From that time many of his disciples went back, and walked no more with him. (John 6:4-66 edited)*

The next day John sees Jesus coming to him, and said, Behold the <u>Lamb of God</u>, which takes away the sin of the world. (John 1:29)

For even <u>Christ our passover</u> is sacrificed for us (1 Corinthians 5:7b)

Scripture is clear that Jesus is our Passover Lamb. We apply His blood to the door posts of our life in faith that when the angel of death comes our way, we will not die spiritually but passover into eternity with Jesus. We commemorate this by taking the Lord's Supper, or communion, which is actually a part of the Passover service.

The Passover Seder

Seder means 'order'. The instructions to the Hebrews in Egypt regarding the passover meal were the starting point to a much fuller feast both in foods and drink consumed and in their analogies to Jesus. Luke warm water is added to the wine, representing the water and blood which flowed from Christ's side. The unleavened bread, or *matzoh*, which is eaten has very unique characteristics: it is pierced so that it won't rise (Ps. 22:16; Zech. 12:10), and it appears striped and bruised (Isaiah 53:5). At the beginning of the seder, three matzah are placed into a white cloth bag called a *matzah tosh*. After the first cup of wine, the *kiddush* for sanctification, the middle matzoh is removed and broken in half. One half is wrapped in a white cloth and 'hidden' in the home as the *afikomen*, which means 'that which comes after' or dessert. The second cup of affliction in remembrance of the plagues of Egypt is consumed prior to washing the hands and eating the meal. After the meal is eaten, the children look for the *afikomen*, and the child who finds it is given a piece of silver or a gift. The *afikomen*/dessert is eaten with the third cup of wine which is for redemption; this is the part of the passover we celebrate as communion.

*And he said to them, With desire <u>I have desired to eat this passover with you before I suffer</u>: For I say to you, I will not any more eat thereof, until it be fulfilled in the kingdom of God. And he took the cup, and gave thanks, and said, Take this, and divide it among yourselves: For I say to you,| I will not drink of the fruit of the vine, until the kingdom of God shall come.| And he took bread, and gave thanks, and broke it, and gave to them, saying, <u>This is my body which is given for you: this do in remembrance of me. Likewise also the cup **after supper,** saying, This cup is the new testament in my blood, which is shed for you.</u> (Luke 22:15-20)*

The fourth cup, which Jesus declined to drink with His disciples until the kingdom of God, is one of praise (*hallel*) which is also known as the cup of His coming to complete/establish His kingdom. Psalm 136 is sung recounting God's deliverance of the Hebrews. The fifth cup for Elijah remains untouched as they open the door for him. The evening ends with everyone proclaiming, "Next year in Jerusalem."

Spring Feasts

The Hebrew traditions which flowed from God's heart are full of meaning to His Bride, and do not counter God's written Word but affirm It. There were other traditions which conflicted with God's Word which Jesus condemned (Mark 7:7-14). The Jews later added a hard-boiled egg to their passover meal. In 197 AD, the Christian Council at Edessa had lost connection with its Jewish roots and the facts of Christ dying on Passover and rising on First Fruits, and the correct day to celebrate Christ's resurrection began to be debated. By the Council of Nicea in 325 AD, laws and attitudes against celebrating Jewish feasts rose as did the number of pagans in the church, and so the 500 bishops mixed Christ's resurrection with the pagan celebration to Ishtar, the fertility goddess; hence the reproductive symbols of rabbits and eggs. Christians do not celebrate Ishtar/Easter, but the resurrection of their Passover Lamb, Jesus.

Now let's see how the Passover Seder dovetails with the traditions of a Hebrew wedding.

Hebrew Marriage Traditions	Traditional Passover Seder
Bride price is established and witnessed; *kiddushin*, which means sanctification.	The first cup of sanctification, *kiddush*.
Bride had a ritual immersion [baptism] transferring her obedience to her husband.	Washing of hands
Bride may wait a year or more	The second cup of affliction
If the woman drank the wine offered, that <u>sealed the covenant</u>; they were 'betrothed'.	The third cup of redemption; known as the "cup of the covenant" (Jer. 31:31-33)
The groom would pay "bride price" to the father of the bride.	The middle matzah, *afikomen*, is eaten.
Groom returned to build bridal chamber, and retrieved bride when it was finished.	The fourth cup of *hallel* (praise)
Wedding ceremony took place under a *chupah*, a white canopy.	After meal, go out and look at sky; opening the door for Elijah to come.
Marriage is consummated.	The fifth cup of Elijah, who was raptured. "Next year in (New) Jerusalem"

Jesus Last Days on Earth as Our Passover Lamb

Nisan 10, Saturday night to Palm Sunday: Jesus rides into Jerusalem to cries of *"Hosanna, Blessed is he that comes in the name of the Lord"* (Mark 11:9). The people have selected their sinless, spotless Lamb and lambs.

Nisan 11, Sunday night to Monday: Jesus cursed the fig tree and cleansed the Temple from the leaven of the money changers (Mark 11:11-19).

Nisan 12, Monday night to Tuesday: The fig tree was withered from its roots. Jesus said, *"You know that after two days is the feast of the passover, and the Son of man is betrayed to be crucified"* (Matthew 26:2).

Nisan 13, Tuesday night to Wednesday: Jesus tells Kingdom parables and prophesies future events (Matthew 24-25), including *"Behold, your house is left to you desolate. For I say to you, You shall not see me from now on, till you shall say, Blessed is he that comes in the name of the Lord"* (Matthew 23:38-39). Jesus sent the disciples to prepare the passover meal, because His 'appointed time' was near. *"Now the first day of the feast of unleavened bread the disciples came to Jesus, saying to him, Where will you that we prepare for you to eat the passover? And he said, Go into the city to such a man, and say to him, The Master said, My time is at hand; I will keep the passover at your house with my disciples. And the disciples did as Jesus had appointed them; and they made ready the passover"* (Matthew 26:17-19).

Nisan 14, Wednesday night to Thursday: *"Now when the even was come, he sat down with the twelve"* and ate the Passover meal (Matthew 26 20). Then they went to the Mount of Olives to pray, and were betrayed by Judas and the temple guards. Peter denied Christ before the cock crowed.

"When the morning was come, all the chief priests and elders of the people took counsel against Jesus to put him to death: And when they had bound him, they led him away, and delivered him to Pontius Pilate the governor" (Matthew 27:1-2) The soldiers scourged Him and then crucified Him at noon. *"And it was about the sixth hour, and there was a darkness over all the earth until the ninth hour. And the sun was darkened, and the veil of the temple was rent in the middle. And when Jesus had cried with a loud voice, he said, Father, into your hands I commend my spirit: and having said thus, he gave up the ghost"* (Luke 23:44-46). This darkness was not an eclipse, but akin to the darkness when Egypt's first-born were slain. Jesus died at three o'clock. The soldier had no need to break His legs to hasten His death (Ex. 12:46). Joseph, a rich man like governor Joseph of Egypt, arranged for Christ's burial a new tomb; and he and Nicodemus inter Jesus' body before sunset. *"And that day was the preparation, and the sabbath drew on. And the women also, which came with him from Galilee, followed after, and beheld the sepulcher, and how his body was laid."* (Luke 23:54-55)

Nisan 15, Thursday night to Friday: Recall that the fifteenth is specifically the feast of unleavened bread celebrating the day the Hebrews departed from Egypt. The Pharisees, the majority of the Sanhedrin in Jesus' time, considered the fifteenth a holy convocation in which no work was to be done; a sabbath, for which a Jew would be excommunicated if he or she violated it.

Nisan 16, Sabbath, Friday night to Saturday: *"And they returned, and prepared spices and ointments; and rested the sabbath day according to the commandment"* (Luke 23:56).

Nisan 17, Saturday night to Sunday: *"Now on the first day of the week, very early in the morning, they came to the sepulcher, bringing the spices which they had prepared, and certain others with them. And they found the stone rolled away from the sepulcher. And they entered in, and found not the body of the Lord Jesus. And it came to pass, as they were much perplexed thereabout, behold, two men stood by them in shining garments: And as they were afraid, and bowed down their faces to the earth, they said to them, Why seek you the living among the dead? He is not here, but is risen: remember how he spoke to you when he was yet in Galilee, Saying, The Son of man must be delivered into the hands of sinful men, and be crucified, and the third day rise again. And they remembered his words,"* (Luke 24:1-8) While Christ's disciples were verifying the fact of Jesus' resurrection, other Jews were taking their first sheafs of barley to the priests for his blessing on the harvest in accordance with the feast of First Fruits. Jesus appeared to Mary and later to Peter.

Nisan 18, Sunday night to Monday: Jesus revealed himself to Cleopas and another man in a village on the road to Emmaus. They ran back to Jerusalem to tell the eleven disciples, and while they were speaking, Jesus stood among them and ate some fish. *"And he said to them, These are the words which I spoke to you, while I was yet with you, that all things must be fulfilled, which were written in the law of Moses, and in the prophets, and in the psalms, concerning me. Then opened he their understanding, that they might understand the scriptures"* (Luke 24:44-45). This was the second day of appearances Jesus made in a total of forty days (Acts 1:3). Using the 30-day month, 360-day calendar, the next seven sabbaths are Nisan 23 and 30; Iyar 7, 14, 21, and 28; and Sivan 5. So Sivan 6 would be the Feast of Weeks (*shavuot*).

Iyar 29, Saturday night to (Ascension) Sunday: Jesus gives final instructions to His disciples to stay in Jerusalem until they receive the promise of the Father, saying, *"For John truly baptized with water; but you shall be baptized with the Holy Ghost not many days hence"* (Acts 1:5). Then Jesus ascends into heaven. The 120 men, women, and children faithfully remained in prayer in the upper room for the next seven days.

Sivan 6, Saturday night to Sunday, Feast of Weeks, also called Pentecost (3+40+7=50): Father-God sent His promised Holy Spirit as a mighty wind Who appeared as tongues of fire resting upon each disciple on Sunday morning. The disciples began proclaiming the wonders of God in foreign languages, and left the upper room and went to Solomon's porch at the Temple in which foreign visitors understood them (Acts 2).

The Feast of Unleavened Bread (*Hag HaMatzah*)

Kosher foods are those which are in accordance to Jewish dietary laws. The Hebrew word *kasher* means 'fit', as in fit for consumption. Leaven causes fermentation which causes bread to rise. Unleavened bread is *matzah* in Hebrew. The rules for making kosher *matzah* of just flour and water is to mix it, roll it, poke it with a fork or a similar tool to keep the finished product from puffing up like pita bread, and to cook it at a high heat until it develops dark spots. It is also customary to create matzah with rows. Thus matzah appears bruised, striped, and pierced.

> *But he was wounded for our transgressions, he was <u>bruised</u> for our iniquities: the chastisement of our peace was on him; and with his <u>stripes</u> we are healed. (Is. 52:5)*

For dogs have compassed me: the assembly of the wicked have enclosed me: they <u>pierced</u> my hands and my feet. (Psalm 22:16)

And I will pour on the house of David, and on the inhabitants of Jerusalem, the spirit of grace and of supplications: and they shall look on me whom they have <u>pierced</u>, and they shall mourn for him, as one mourns for his only son, and shall be in bitterness for him, as one that is in bitterness for his firstborn. (Zechariah 12:10)

God prepared the Hebrews at each Passover to be looking for Him as a suffering savior who would be striped (whipped), bruised, and pierced. Traditionally at the beginning of the Passover meal, three matzah are placed in a cloth, representing the Father, Son, and Holy Spirit. The middle one is removed, covered in another cloth and hidden. Toward the end of the meal it is 'found', broken, and the pieces are considered as the desert (*afikomen*) to be eaten with the third cup of wine, known as the 'cup of redemption'; these are the elements of communion.

Know you not that a little leaven leavens the whole lump? Purge out therefore the old leaven, that you may be a new lump, as <u>you are unleavened</u>. For even Christ our passover is sacrificed for us: Therefore let us keep the feast, not with old leaven, neither with the leaven of malice and wickedness; but with <u>the unleavened bread of sincerity and truth</u>. (1 Corinthians 5:6b-8)

The first believers in Jesus were Hebrew and continued to celebrate the feasts, but even the Gentiles in the cosmopolitan church of Corinth were celebrating the feast of Unleavened Bread. What former idolater wouldn't want to party for a week, but they had to learn to party with purity.

The Feast of First Fruits: Freedom from Sin and Death

In winter the ground is cold and hard and bleak; it is in a type of death. But in spring new life appears. The farmer would go out to his field and tie a string around the first shoot from the ground, and later present that sheaf to the priest who would wave it before the Lord on the feast of First Fruits.

Jesus is called Abraham's Seed. *"Now to Abraham and his seed were the promises made. He said not, And to seeds, as of many; but as of one, And to your seed, which is Christ"* (Galatians 3:16). The covenant God made with Abraham was based upon his faith, not works of the law which was given 430 years later. Christ, the Seed, was buried in the ground, and rose up in a glorified body. *"But some man will say, How are the dead raised up? and with what body do they come? You fool, that which you sow is not quickened, except it die: And that which you sow, you sow not that body that shall be, but bore grain, it may chance of wheat, or of some other grain"* (1 Corinthians 15:35-37)

*But now is Christ risen from the dead, and become the **first fruits** of them that slept. For since by man came death, by man came also the **resurrection** of the dead. For as in Adam all die, even so in Christ shall all be made alive. But every man in his own order: Christ the first fruits; afterward they that are Christ's at his coming.*

Then comes the end, when he shall have delivered up the kingdom to God, even the Father; when he shall have put down all rule and all authority and power. For he must reign, till he has put all enemies under his feet. The last enemy that shall be destroyed is death. (1 Corinthians 15:20-25)

The order of resurrection of the dead is as follows: 1) Christ, who is the first fruits, 2) those who belong to Christ at His coming; and, after His millennial reign on earth, 3) the unbelieving dead who will be judged at the great white throne and cast into the lake of fire with death and Hell (Rev. 20).

The Feast of Weeks (Pentecost): Gift of the Holy Spirit

Two hundred and fifteen years transpired from the time Joseph brought the rest of his family to live with him in Goshen to the time the Hebrews left Egypt. That's plenty of time for families to learn new languages and begin to forget their native tongue; especially if it was banned when they were slaves. Think about all the different languages spoken in America. The English of the King James Bible was not what we spoke in the nineteenth century. Fifty days after the Hebrews left Egypt, they heard Almighty God command them to obey Him. We assume God spoke in Hebrew. In the Hebrew oral teachings, it is said that "tongues of fire" came down the mountain in front of each person and that person heard the ten commands in his own language.

For you are not come to the mount that might be touched, and that burned with fire, nor to blackness, and darkness, and tempest, And the sound of a trumpet, and the <u>voice of words</u>; which voice they that heard entreated that the word should not be spoken to them any more: And so **terrible** *was the sight, that Moses said, I exceedingly fear and quake:) . . . For our God is a consuming fire. (Hebrews 12:18-21, 29)*

Why would a fire way up on the top of a mountain be scary? But if a million parts of that fire came streaming down as a "voice of words" to the hearers in their native languages, that would truly be frightening (*phoberos* = terrible). The Talmud for Shabbat 88b on Psalm 68:11 teaches that "Every single word going out from the Omnipotent was split up into seventy languages." Jewish tradition holds that individual "tongues as fire" spoke the commandments to each person at Sinai. God's voice shook the earth (Hebrews 12:26) like an amplified bass, and the people didn't want to hear it again. So the next time God decided to speak to His people directly, He toned it way down. God still represented Himself with "tongues of fire" and spoke in the native languages of His hearers, but He used human vessels who were much less frightening; and instead of commandments, He just told people His awesome qualities and all the wonderful things He'd done.

At Mount Sinai, after waiting around for over a month for Moses to come back with the rest of the commands, the people created their own god and ways of 'worship', and 3,000 men were killed. This time God's Son had compacted the 613 laws down to the two most important: *"Jesus said to him, You shall love the Lord your God with all your heart, and with all your soul, and with all your mind. This is the first and great commandment. And the second is like to it, You shall love your neighbor as yourself. On these two commandments hang all the law and the prophets"* (Matthew 22:37-40). After Peter explained the gospel, 3,000 men got saved. The Old Covenant of the Flesh that was performed at Mt. Sinai was the Bride's vows to God. The New Covenant of the Spirit was the Groom's vows to His Bride, about which Jeremiah prophesied.

> *Behold, the days come, said the LORD, that I will make a <u>new covenant</u> with the house of Israel, and with the house of Judah: <u>Not according to the covenant that I made with their fathers in the day that I took them by the hand to bring them out of the land of Egypt; which my covenant they broke, although I was an **husband** to them, said the LORD</u>: But this shall be the covenant that I will make with the house of Israel; After those days, said the LORD, <u>I will put my law in their inward parts, and write it in their hearts; and will be their God, and they shall be my people</u>. And they shall teach no more every man his neighbor, and every man his brother, saying, Know the LORD: <u>for they shall all know me</u>, from the least of them to the greatest of them, said the LORD: for I will forgive their iniquity, and I will remember their sin no more. (Jeremiah 31:31-34; and see Hebrews 8:7-13)*

> *There is therefore now no condemnation to them which are in Christ Jesus, who walk not after the flesh, but after the Spirit. For the [new covenant] law of the Spirit of life in Christ Jesus has made me free from the [old covenant] law of sin and death. (Romans 8:1-2; text added)*

The Hebrew wedding covenant was a written agreement, or contract, which set the "bride price" the groom would pay the father of the bride. [God is our Father, and Jesus paid with His life-blood.] Then the prospective groom would pour a glass of wine. If the intended bride drank it, that sealed the covenant, and they were considered 'betrothed'. [The disciples, representing the Bride, received from Jesus *"the cup after supper, saying, This cup is the new testament in my blood, which is shed for you"* (Luke 22:20), and the Bride became engaged to Jesus.] The bride would undergo a ritual immersion [baptism]. After the Hebrew wedding contract was accepted, the groom returned to his father's house to begin building an addition called the bridal chamber. Only when the father deemed the bridal chamber finished would he allow his son to leave at sunset to go get his bride.

> *In my Father's house are many mansions: if it were not so, I would have told you. I go to prepare a place for you. And if I go and <u>prepare a place</u> for you, I will come again, and receive you to myself; that where I am, there you may be also. (John 14:2-3)*

> *Abraham had two sons, the one by a female slave, the other by a free woman. But he who was of the female slave was born after the flesh; but he of the free woman was by promise. Which things are an allegory: for these are <u>the two covenants; the one from the mount Sinai, which engenders to bondage</u>, which is Agar. . . . <u>But Jerusalem which is above is free</u>, which is the mother of us all. (Galatians 4:22-26)*

The place which Jesus is preparing for us is the new Jerusalem which comes out of heaven (Rev. 21:2).

History and Fulfillment of Spring Feasts and Pentecost

Nisan 10: Hebrews select an unblemished lamb to take into their homes for four days.
Jesus, the sinless Lamb of God rides into Jerusalem.

Nisan 14: Hebrews apply lamb's blood to doors so that death will "pass over" them.
Jesus eats Passover then becomes Passover Lamb on the cross, and is buried.

Nisan 15: Hebrews to Joseph's tomb to retrieve his bones; leave Egypt without leaven.
The sinless body of Jesus is in the tomb.

Nisan 16: Hebrews leave Succoth for Ethan.
Jesus' body is in the tomb.

Nisan 17: Jesus arose from the dead as the First Fruits who would be resurrected.

Nisan 22: Hebrews are on the Arabian side of Red Sea by morning of First Fruits.
[Since First Fruits is on the "*morrow after the sabbath*" after Passover, the number of days between Passover and First Fruits varies.]

Iyar 27: Moses appoints leaders to judge the smaller matters (Ex. 18:21-26).

Iyar 29: Jesus gives final instructions to His disciples and He ascends into heaven.

Sivan 6: God, as a fire, speaks Ten Commandments to the Hebrews. Feast of Weeks
God's Spirit of fire on disciples telling God's wonders in tongues. Pentecost

And out of the throne proceeded lightning and thunder and voices: and there were seven lamps of fire burning before the throne, which are the seven Spirits of God" (Revelation 4:5)

Feast of Weeks (Pentecost) is when humans on earth experience a bit of heaven. And we should not be surprised at how God has orchestrated His feasts to be fulfilled in His Son according to His appointed times. Since God so dramatically fulfilled the Spring feasts through the first coming of Jesus Christ, we should expect nothing less dramatic in Jesus' fulfillment of the Fall feasts through His second coming.

Purim's History interlaced with Jesus' Last Days.

Purim is not one of God's appointed times, but was added by the Hebrews to commemorate God's victory on their behalf. Yet there are stunning correlations between it and Christ's last days.

Nisan 13 was the day Haman and his buddies cast lots (*purim*) to find the best day to annihilate the Jews; it fell to Adar 13. Haman requested king Xerxes to have all the Jews in his kingdom killed and their properties confiscated. Letters were written in all the languages and sent out so that on the 13th of the twelfth month of Adar all the Jews would be exterminated. (Esther 3:12-14)

[Jesus was anointed for His burial.]

Mordecai relayed the plot to Esther who requested three days of fasting before she approached the king unbidden to appeal for her people and possibly be slain right then. (Esther 4:14-17)

Nisan 14 was the first day of the fast.

[Jesus was tried, beaten, crucified, and placed in a tomb on the Feast of Passover.]

Nisan 15 was the second day of the fast.

Nisan 16 was the third day of the fast, and Esther approached the king uninvited, but was accepted by the king who was ready to grant her any request, but she arranged a banquet with Haman. (Esther 5:1-4) This allowed time for Haman's pride to escalate to his own ruin.

On Nisan 17, Esther held a second banquet with Haman and the king in which Haman's evil plans for Mordecai and the Jews are both turned around for their good and Haman's destruction. (Esther 7-9)   [Jesus rose from the dead on the Feast of First Fruits.]

The original letters could not be revoked, so King Xerxes sent a second dispatch which encouraged the Jews throughout his Persian empire to defend themselves against their enemies on Adar 13. In Susa they were allowed to continue on Adar 14 as well. The Jews defeated their enemies and they held great festivities on Adar 13 and 14 and called it the feast of Purim.

Summary: Parallel Portions of Wedding Covenant

When Father God sought betrothal of the Hebrew nation for His Son, His 'bride price' would be giving His "*firstborn*" Son as the "*passover*" lamb (Exodus 11:5-11). In the light of the full moon they left Egypt, and a week later (7 days of Unleavened Bread) God parted the Red Sea while they crossed to Arabia safely, and then He closed the sea upon their enemies, giving the Hebrews the gift of freedom from bondage. Six weeks later, fiery Father God declared the Bride's contract, the Ten Commandments, and the people responded with a fearful 'I do' (Exodus 19:1, 19). The pattern is the **bride price is given on Passover**, **freedom from bondage** is given on First Fruits, and the **wedding contract is spoken with fire** on the Feast of Weeks.

When Jesus proclaimed the bride price of the "new covenant" to His Bride, many were offended at the thought of eating His body and drinking His blood (John 6), except for His disciples (Mark 14:22-24). After eating the Passover meal that night, Jesus became the Passover Lamb that day, then three days later arose victorious over sin and death and appeared to hundreds of witnesses for forty days. The disciples prayed for a week and then were baptized with the Holy Spirit on Pentecost. Jesus, the first born Son of God, gave His blood as the **'bride price'** of the ***"new covenant"*** on Passover, He rose redeeming all who trust in Him **from sin and death** on First Fruits, and Jesus sent the **gift of His Comforter with tongues of fire** on Pentecost.

Fall Feasts

It shall be a statute for ever in your generations: you shall celebrate it in the seventh month. (Leviticus 23:41b)

Jesus' Betrothal and Wedding to His Bride

Hebrew Marriage Traditions	Fulfillment in Scripture
The father chose the bride for his son.	God chose us. (Eph. 1:4; 2 Thess. 2:13)
Bride's betrothal covenant (*shitre erusin*) Groom's wedding covenant (*ketubah*)	Ten Commandments (Exodus 20) New covenant is "*Love one another*"
If the woman drank the wine offered, that sealed the covenant; they were 'betrothed'.	The disciples (Bride) drank the "new testament" in Christ's blood. (Luke 22:20)
The groom would pay "bride price" to the father of the bride.	Jesus paid Father God with His life-blood, so ketubah is also a will.
Bride accepts a gift from groom; *kiddushin*, which means sanctification.	Jesus gave us His Holy Spirit, sanctifying and sealing us to Himself (Eph. 1:13; 4:30)
Bride had a ritual immersion [baptism] transferring her obedience to her husband.	Baptism and obedience Romans 6-8
Groom returned to his father's house to build an addition, the bridal chamber.	"*Prepare a place*": New Jerusalem John 14:2-3 and Rev. 21:9-27
After father deemed bridal chamber finished, he allowed son to leave at sunset to get bride.	"*Only the Father knows*" Mark 13:32-37
Groom to bride's house with shofars, shouting, "*Behold, the bridegroom comes*".	Trumpets are *shofars* (1 Thess. 4:16-17). Matthew 25:6
Wedding ceremony took place under a *chupah*, a white canopy.	Bride meets Groom in clouds. Acts 1:9-11; 1 Thess. 4:14-18
The cantor greeted groom like a king, "*Blessed is he who comes*".	When Jews chant same, Jesus will come. Matthew 23:39
Celebrate wedding feast for seven days.	Honeymoon during Tishri 2-9, 2012

Jesus, the first born Son of God, gave His blood as the **'bride price'** of the **"new covenant"** on Passover, He rose redeeming all who trust in Him **from sin and death** on First Fruits, and Jesus sent the **gift of His Comforter with tongues of fire** on Pentecost.

Jesus left to "*prepare a place*" for us called New Jerusalem, and promised, "*I will come again, and receive you to myself*" (John 14:2-3). Jesus will return when Jews receive Him as Messiah and say, "*Blessed is he who comes in the Name of the Lord*" (Matthew 23:39). Jesus will come with the clouds and trumpet and a shout like a "*thief in the night*" for His Bride (1 Thess. 4:14-18; 5:2). Then He will take us to the heavenly New Jerusalem for the wedding feast for seven days (Rev. 21:9-27).

The feasts were instituted by God; they are the *moed*, the 'appointed times' of the Lord. They are holy and set apart for the Lord's purposes as convocations and 'rehearsals', wedding rehearsals. They rehearse Israel's past, but they are also shadows of future events which will find their complete fulfillment in the Lord Jesus Christ (Colossians 2:16-17). The Lord Jesus Christ completely fulfilled the spring feasts and the early summer feast in His first coming. Jesus partially fulfilled the fall feasts during His first coming, and will completely fulfill the fall feasts in His second coming when He judges the wicked.

> *Yes, the stork in the heaven knows her appointed times [moed]; and the turtle and the crane and the swallow observe the time of their coming; but my people know not the judgment of the LORD. (Jeremiah 8:7 with addition)*

Trumpet Call to Fasting and Repentance

The year of the exodus, Moses fasted for forty days on two occasions. The second time was from Elul 1 to Tishri 10, the traditional Hebrew period of repentance (*teshuvah*) in which the **shofar** is blown. Moses prophesied, "*The LORD your God will raise up to you a Prophet from the middle of you, of your brothers, like to me; to him you shall listen*" (Deuteronomy 18:15). At the beginning of Christ's ministry, He was baptized and immediately taken into the desert where He fasted forty days and night, likely from Elul 1 to Tishri 10.

> *Blow you the **trumpet** in Zion, and sound an alarm in my holy mountain: let all the inhabitants of the land tremble: for the day of the LORD comes, for it is near at hand . . . Therefore also now, said the LORD, turn you even to me with all your heart, and with <u>fasting</u>, and with weeping, and with mourning: And <u>rend your heart</u>, and not your garments, and turn to the LORD your God: for he is gracious and merciful, slow to anger, and of great kindness, and repents him of the evil. . . . Blow the **trumpet** in Zion, sanctify a <u>fast</u>, call a solemn assembly: Gather the people, sanctify the congregation, assemble the elders, gather the children, and those that suck the breasts: <u>let the bridegroom go forth of his chamber, and the bride out of her closet</u>. . . . Then will the LORD be jealous for his land, and pity his*

people. Fear not, O land; be glad and rejoice: for the LORD will do great things. . . . And you shall know that I am in the middle of Israel, and that I am the LORD your God, and none else: and my people shall never be ashamed. And it shall come to pass afterward, that I will pour out my spirit on all flesh; and your sons and your daughters shall prophesy, your old men shall dream dreams, your young men shall see visions: And also on the servants and on the handmaids <u>in those days will I pour out my spirit. And I will show wonders in the heavens and in the earth, blood, and fire, and pillars of smoke. The sun shall be turned into darkness, and the moon into blood, before the great and terrible day of the LORD</u> come. And it shall come to pass, that whoever shall call on the name of the LORD shall be delivered: for in mount Zion and in Jerusalem shall be deliverance, as the LORD has said, and in the remnant whom the LORD shall call. (Joel 2:1, 12-13, 15-16, 18, 21, 27-32)

Beginning on Elul 1 the people would have heard broken staccato blasts each day to help remind the people to break with evil by repenting. During the month of Elul the shofar was blown to prepare people to meet Messiah, except for the last day of Elul when it remains silent. So there was a day of **silence** prior to Rosh Hashanah, in which a special midnight service called *Selichos* (repentant prayers) was held to prepare people.

*And when he had opened the seventh seal, there was **silence** in heaven about the space of half an hour. And I saw the seven angels which stood before God; and to them were given seven **trumpets**." (Revelation 8:1-2)*

The Feast of Trumpets (*Rosh Hashanah*)

In the Bible this feast is not actually given a name, but is known for the blowing of the trumpet (*shofar*), which sounds 100 notes. The Hebrews called it by many prophetic names. *Rosh HaShannah* means Head of the Year or New Year. *Yom Teruah* means Day of the Awakening Blast. *Yom HaDin* means Day of Judgment. *HaMelech* means The King or Coronation of the Messiah. *Yom Hazikkaron* means Day of Remembrance. It is also known as the Hidden Day, the Wedding Day, the Day of the Open Gates and Open Books, and the day to end "Jacob's trouble" (Jeremiah 30:5-10) which is synonymous with the Great Tribulation. Also associated with this day are the resurrection of the dead and the rapture (*natzal*).

Rosh Hashanah (New Year)

According to Hebrew tradition, the following events occurred on *Rosh Hashanah:* Adam and Eve were created, Enoch was taken by God (Genesis 5:24), the flood waters stopped (Genesis 8:1-4), Joseph was delivered from prison and made governor of Egypt (Genesis 41), and the exiles who returned to Jerusalem with Ezra offered sacrifices on the new altar (Ezra 3:1-6).

Yom Teruah (Day of the Awakening Blast)

*Why he said, **Awake** you that sleep, and arise from the dead, and Christ shall give you light. See then that you walk circumspectly, not as fools, but as wise, Redeeming the time, because the days are evil. Why be you not unwise, but understanding what the will of the Lord is. (Ephesians 5:14-16)*

'Awake' (e*igiro*) means both 'wake up' and 'rise up' from a root to collect one's faculties. Those who have died in Christ will 'arise' (*anestemi*) and 'stand up' with Christ at His return, and then those who are alive in Christ will be caught up together with them at the "*trump of God*". The resurrection precedes the rapture, and both occur at Christ's coming with the blowing of a trumpet.

*For if we believe that Jesus died and rose again, even so them also which sleep in Jesus will God bring with him. For this we say to you by the word of the Lord, that we which are alive and remain to the coming of the Lord shall not prevent them which are asleep. For the Lord himself shall descend from heaven with a shout, with the voice of the archangel, and with the **trump** of God: and <u>the dead in Christ shall rise first: Then we which are alive and remain shall be caught up together with them in the clouds, to meet the Lord in the air</u>: and so shall we ever be with the Lord. Why comfort one another with these words. (1 Thessalonians 4:14-18)*

*And then shall appear the sign of the Son of man in heaven: and then shall all the tribes of the earth mourn, and they shall see the Son of man coming in the clouds of heaven with power and great glory. And he shall send his angels with a great sound of a **trumpet**, and <u>they shall gather together his elect from the four winds</u>, from one end of heaven to the other. (Matthew 24:30-31)*

*And the LORD shall be seen over them, and his arrow shall go forth as the lightning: and the LORD God shall blow the **trumpet**. (Zechariah 9:14)*

The Long, Hidden Day

Like as a woman with child, that draws near the time of her delivery, is in pain, and cries out in her pangs; so have we been in your sight, O LORD. We have been with child, we have been in pain, we have as it were brought forth wind; we have not worked any deliverance in the earth; neither have the inhabitants of the world fallen. Your dead men shall live, together with my dead body shall they arise. Awake and sing, you that dwell in dust: for your dew is as the dew of herbs, and the earth shall cast out the dead. Come, my people, enter you into your chambers, and shut your doors about you: <u>hide</u> yourselves as it were <u>for a little moment, until the indignation be over.</u> For, behold, the LORD comes out of his place to punish the *inhabitants of the earth for their iniquity: the earth also shall disclose her blood, and shall no more cover her slain. (Isaiah 26:17-21)*

Before Jesus returns He will hide a remnant of His people during the "*indignation*". His Bride will go through the Great Tribulation as He punishes the wicked. *"For in the time of trouble he shall hide me in his pavilion: in the secret of his tabernacle shall he hide me; he shall set me up on a rock"* (Psalm 27:5) The day of Tishri 1 itself is also hidden. Since they had to wait for the signal fires to begin the celebration, they did not know the day or hour; so it was determined to celebrate for two days which were considered one long day. To not know *"the day nor the hour"* was a tip to Hebrews who celebrate Rosh Hashanah, because it's the only feast on a new moon.

The Wedding Day

The Hebrew wedding covenant was a written agreement, or contract, which set the "bride price" the groom would pay the father of the bride. Then the prospective groom would pour a glass of wine. If the intended bride drank it, that sealed the covenant, and they were considered 'betrothed'. After the Hebrew wedding contract was accepted, the groom returned to his father's house to begin building an addition called the bridal chamber. Only when the father deemed the bridal chamber finished would he allow his son to leave to go get his bride. Between the contract and the ceremony if someone asked the groom when the wedding would be, he would reply, "*No one knows the day nor the hour, only my father knows*" (See Matthew 24:36). Our Groom has had to build a chamber with many rooms. (*Mone* is translated 'mansions' here and 'abode' in John 14:23.)

In my Father's house are many <u>mansions</u>: if it were not so, I would have told you. I go to prepare a place for you. And if I go and prepare a place for you, I will come again, and receive you to myself; that where I am, there you may be also. (John 14:2-3)

The bride would go through a ritual immersion signifying leaving her old life to get ready for her new life. The bride was in a state of constant preparedness after the signing of the wedding contract. Her focus would be on preparing items for her home: dishes, utensils, linens, coverings, and such. Each evening she would wait with a lit lamp until she fell asleep. The groom's party would arrive with trumpets and a great noise, waking up the whole neighborhood to let them know the wedding was about to take place. The groom would escort his bride in grand procession back to his father's house where the wedding canopy and feast were ready for the ceremony. The new couple would consummate their marriage in the bridal chamber that night, emerging to celebrate with wedding guests throughout the seven days (Genesis 29:26-28).

And I heard as it were the voice of a great multitude, and as the voice of many waters, and as the voice of mighty thunder, saying, Alleluia: for the Lord God omnipotent reigns. Let us be glad and rejoice, and give honor to him: for <u>the</u>

marriage of the Lamb is come, and his wife has made herself ready. And to her was granted that she should be arrayed in fine linen, clean and white: for the fine linen is the righteousness of saints. And he said to me, Write, Blessed are they which are called to the marriage supper of the Lamb. And he said to me, These are the true sayings of God. (Revelation 19:6-9)

HaMelech (Coronation of the Messiah)

HaMelech literally means 'the king'. Hebrew kings were inaugurated on this date and/or had their reigns calculated from this date. Edwin Thiele, in *The Mysterious Numbers of the Hebrew Kings*, states the following: "a Tishri-to-Tishri year was used in the reckoning of Solomon's reign" (p. 51), and "that Judah almost at the close of its history was still counting its regnal years from Tishri-to-Tishri is indicated by 2 Kings 22:3 and 23:23" (p. 52).

*And let Zadok the priest and Nathan the prophet <u>anoint him there king</u> over Israel: and blow you with the **trumpet**, and say, God save king Solomon. (1 Kings 1:34)*

And the seventh angel sounded [the last trumpet] *and there were great voices in heaven, saying, The kingdoms of this world are become the kingdoms of our Lord, and of his Christ; and he <u>shall reign</u> for ever and ever. (Revelation 11:15 [clarification added])*

Satan offered Jesus all the kingdoms of the world in exchange for His submission (Matthew 4:8-11). People who ate His miraculous bread tried to force Jesus to be a king (John 6:14-15). Jesus told His disciples, *"You are they which have continued with me in my temptations. And I appoint to you a kingdom, as my Father has appointed to me"* (Luke 22:28-29). The 'crime' for which Jesus was persecuted was that He was the King of the Jews, but Jesus fully understood His kingdom and the timing of its fulfillment.

<u>Jesus answered, My kingdom is not of this world</u>: if my kingdom were of this world, then would my servants fight, that I should not be delivered to the Jews: but now is my kingdom not from hence. Pilate therefore said to him, Are you a king then? Jesus answered, <u>You say that I am a king. To this end was I born</u>, and for this cause came I into the world, that I should bear witness to the truth. Every one that is of the truth hears my voice. (John 18:36-37)

And Pilate wrote a title, and put it on the cross. And the writing was JESUS OF NAZARETH THE KING OF THE JEWS. This title then read many of the Jews: for the place where Jesus was crucified was near to the city: and it was written in Hebrew, and Greek, and Latin. Then said the chief priests of the Jews to Pilate, Write not, The King of the Jews; but that he said, I am King of the Jews. Pilate answered, What I have written I have written. (John 19:19-22)

When King Jesus returns and He gathers His Bride unto Himself, we will defeat the armies of the Antichrist at Armageddon, and then we will rule and reign with Him a thousand years (2 Tim. 2:11-12 and Rev. 20:6).

His eyes were as a flame of fire, and <u>on his head were many crowns</u>; and he had a name written, that no man knew, but he himself. And he was clothed with a clothing dipped in blood: and his name is called The Word of God. And <u>the armies which were in heaven followed him</u> on white horses, clothed in fine linen, white and clean. And out of his mouth goes a sharp sword, that with it he should smite the nations: and <u>he shall rule them with a rod of iron</u>: and he treads the wine press of the fierceness and wrath of Almighty God. And he has on his clothing and on his thigh a name written, <u>KING OF KINGS</u>, AND LORD OF LORDS. (Revelation 19:12-16)

Yom HaDin (Day of Judgment) and *Yom Hazikkaron* (Day of Remembrance)

Before Jesus died as King of the Jews, He cleansed His Father's house. When Jesus comes to rule as King of kings, He will cleanse the world of wickedness, and only the righteous will enter His Kingdom. The Hebrews believe that the gates of heaven are opened to the righteous on Tishri 1.

Open you the gates, that the righteous nation which keeps the truth may enter in. (Isaiah 26:2)

Open to me the <u>gates of righteousness</u>: I will go into them, and I will praise the LORD: This gate of the LORD, into which the righteous shall enter. (Ps 118:19-20)

Blessed are they <u>that do his commandments</u>, that they may have right to the tree of life, and may <u>enter in through the gates</u> into the city. For without are dogs, and sorcerers, and fornicators, and murderers, and idolaters, and whoever loves and makes a lie. (Revelation 22:14-15)

*For the LORD most high is terrible; he is a great King over all the earth. <u>He shall subdue the people under us</u>, and the nations under our feet. He shall choose our inheritance for us, the excellency of Jacob whom he loved. Selah. God is gone up with a **shout**, the LORD with the sound of a **trumpet**. (Psalm 47:2-5)*

*With **trumpets** and sound of cornet make a joyful noise before the LORD, the King. Let the sea roar, and the fullness thereof; the world, and they that dwell therein. Let the floods clap their hands: let the hills be joyful together <u>Before the LORD; for he comes to judge the earth: with righteousness shall he judge the world, and the people with equity</u>. (Psalm 98:6-9)*

The Hebrew *Tanach* refers to the books as the book of the righteous (Book of Life), book of the wicked, and the book of remembrance (Exodus 17:14; Psalm 112:6). The Jews have the ten days of awe to make sure they're in the book of the righteous before the books and gates are closed on Yom Kippur. The common greeting on Rosh Hashanah is "May you be inscribed in the Book of Life."

He that overcomes, the same shall be clothed in white raiment; and I will not blot out his name out of the <u>book of life</u>, but I will confess his name before my Father, and before his angels. (Revelation 3:5)

Then they that feared the LORD spoke often one to another: and the LORD listened, and heard it, and a <u>book of remembrance</u> was written before him for them that feared the LORD, and that thought on his name. And they shall be mine, said the LORD of hosts, in that day when I make up my jewels; and I will spare them, as a man spares his own son that serves him. Then shall you return, and discern between the righteous and the wicked, between him that serves God and him that serves him not. (Malachi 3:16-17)

I beheld till the thrones were cast down, and the Ancient of days did sit, whose garment was white as snow, and the hair of his head like the pure wool: his throne was like the fiery flame, and his wheels as burning fire. A fiery stream issued and came forth from before him: thousand thousands ministered to him, and ten thousand times ten thousand stood before him: the judgment was set, and the <u>books</u> were opened. . . .I saw in the night visions, and, behold, one like the Son of man came with the clouds of heaven, and came to the Ancient of days, and they brought him near before him. And there was given him dominion, and glory, and a kingdom, that all people, nations, and languages, should serve him: his dominion is an everlasting dominion, which shall not pass away, and his kingdom that which shall not be destroyed. (Daniel 7:10-14 edited)

The sun shall be turned into darkness, and the moon into blood, before the great and terrible day of the LORD come. And it shall come to pass, that <u>whoever shall call on the name of the LORD shall be delivered</u>: for in mount Zion and in Jerusalem shall be deliverance, as the LORD has said, and in the remnant whom the LORD shall call. (Joel 2:31-32)

The day of Christ's coming will be a great day for the righteous and a terrible day for the wicked. But at the end of the 1,000 year reign of Christ, Satan will be loosed to deceive and foment one last rebellion stemming from Gog and Magog which Jesus will destroy with fire. Then Jesus will sit on His great white throne and open the books and judge those who are not written in the Book of Life and cast them into the lake of fire along with Satan (Revelation 20:6-15).

The Fast Day of Atonement (Yom Kippur)

Yom HaKippurim means the 'day of covering'; canceling, pardon, and reconciling. It is a day of fasting, confession of sins, repentance and humble prayer. The synagogues are draped in white and the people wear white to symbolize purity. The Hebrews believe the closing of the gates to God's Kingdom is signaled by the sound of the Great Shofar. The Hebrews refer to three main shofars during the year: the First Trumpet at Pentecost, the Last Trumpet at New Year, and the Great Trumpet on the Day of Atonement.

> *Cry aloud, spare not, lift up your voice like a **trumpet**, and show my people their transgression, and the house of Jacob their sins. Yet they seek me daily, and delight to know my ways, as a nation that did righteousness, and forsook not the ordinance of their God: they ask of me the ordinances of justice; they take delight in approaching to God. Why have we fasted, say they, and you see not? why have we afflicted our soul, and you take no knowledge? Behold, in the day of your fast you find pleasure . . . Is not this the <u>fast</u> that I have chosen? to loose the bands of wickedness, to undo the heavy burdens, and to let the oppressed go free, and that you break every yoke? Is it not to deal your bread to the hungry, and that you bring the poor that are cast out to your house? when you see the naked, that you cover him; and that you hide not yourself from your own flesh? Then shall your light break forth as the morning, and your health shall spring forth speedily: and your righteousness shall go before you; the glory of the LORD shall be your rear guard. (Isaiah 58:1-3, 6-8)*

Jesus is our High Priest

Only on this day would the high priest go beyond the thick veil into the Holy of Holies and sprinkle blood on the mercy seat of the ark of the covenant. The high priest would *"make reconciliation for the sins of the people"* (Hebrews 2:17). Jesus Christ became the *"Apostle and High Priest of our profession"* of faith (Hebrews 3:1). When the testator of a will dies, that will is finalized. Jesus, the Son of God, died and finalized the old covenant (nailing the Law to the cross, Colossians 2:14), and instituted a new covenant (the royal law of Love, James 2:8) to which He alone is the Mediator (Hebrews 12:24). A mediator helps to resolve disputes between parties in legal matters. God was legally obligated to punish sin with death, but now Jesus has fulfilled our legal obligations to the Law, and now stands as our Advocate (1 John 2:1-2) before the Father when Satan accuses us (Rev. 12:10).

> *Then said I, See, I come (in the volume of the book it is written of me,) to do your will, O God. Above when he said, Sacrifice and offering and burnt offerings and offering for sin you would not, neither had pleasure therein; which are offered by the law; Then said he, See, I come to do your will, O God. <u>He takes away the first, that he may establish the second. By the which will we are sanctified through the offering of the body of Jesus Christ once for all.</u> (Hebrews 10:7-10)*

> *Seeing then that <u>we have a great high priest, that is passed into the heavens, Jesus the Son of God,</u> let us hold fast our profession. For we have not an high priest which cannot be touched with the feeling of our infirmities; but was in all points tempted like as we are, yet without sin. Let us therefore come boldly to the throne of grace, that we may obtain mercy, and find grace to help in time of need. (Hebrews 4:14-16)*

Jesus is our Atonement

Having therefore, brothers, boldness to enter into the holiest by the blood of Jesus, By a new and living way, which he has consecrated for us, through the veil, that is to say, his flesh; And having an high priest over the house of God; Let us draw near with a true heart in full assurance of faith, having our hearts sprinkled from an evil conscience, and our bodies washed with <u>pure</u> water. Let us hold fast the profession of our faith without wavering; (for he is faithful that promised;) And let us consider one another to provoke to love and to good works: Not forsaking the assembling of ourselves together, as the manner of some is; but exhorting one another: and so much the more, as you see the day [of His return] *approaching. (Hebrews 10:19-24* clarification added*)*

But God commends his love toward us, in that, while we were yet sinners, Christ died for us. Much more then, being now justified by his blood, we shall be saved from wrath through him. For if, when we were enemies, we were reconciled to God by the death of his Son, much more, being reconciled, we shall be saved by his life. And not only so, but we also joy in God through our Lord Jesus Christ, by whom we have now received the <u>atonement</u>. (Romans 5:8-11)

'Atonement' is *katallage* which means an exchange, reconciliation, and restoration to favor. Jesus' blood redeemed us from the consequences of our sins. He exchanged His perfect life for our sinful ones. Jesus reconciled us (2 Corinthians 5:17-21) to Father God and restored us to His favor. Jesus fulfilled the Feast of Atonement for our spirits, but the earth and the bodies of all believers are still awaiting the physical redemption (Romans 8:18-32).

The Feast of Ingathering and Booths/Tabernacles (*Sukkot*)

Five days after Yom Kippur is the Feast of Ingathering, which is also called the Feast of Booths (*Succoth*) or Tabernacles, the Season of our Joy, the Feast of the Nations, and the Celebration of Water. The Hebrew word *Sukkot* (a modern variation of the spelling) can also be translated 'stable'. Many theologians believe Jesus was born during Tabernacles; *"The Word of God was made flesh and 'tabernacled' among us" (John 1:14a).* Biblical astronomy provides evidence that Jesus was born on Tishri 1, 3 AD as befits the King of kings.

At the end of Genesis, 70 nations are listed in the world; 70 bullocks are sacrificed during Tabernacles. Seventy people of Jacob's family met Joseph in Egypt, and millions came out 215 years later. Moses descended Mount Sinai on *Yom Kippur* after his 2nd fast of 40 days for the second set of stone commands, which represented God's forgiveness of the people's idolatry. This brought relief and great joy. The next day Moses gave them instructions to build the tabernacle for God's Presence. The Feast of Tabernacles is 5 days after the Day of Atonement. Solomon dedicated the first temple during *Sukkot*.

Also in the fifteenth day of the seventh month, when you have gathered in the fruit of the land, you shall keep a feast to the LORD seven days: on the first day shall be a sabbath, and on the eighth day shall be a sabbath. And you shall take you on the first day the boughs of goodly trees, branches of palm trees, and the boughs of thick trees, and willows of the brook; and you shall rejoice before the LORD your God seven days. And you shall keep it a feast to the LORD seven days in the year. It shall be a statute for ever in your generations: you shall celebrate it in the seventh month. (Leviticus 23:39-41)

Sukkot is celebrated for 7 days. It's like a community camp-out as they party and fellowship together. They march carrying a lulav consisting of three different types of tree branches and a citrus fruit (like a lemon). In ancient times they would wave their lulavs and march around the altar once each day and seven times on the seventh day, praying "Hosanna" ('Jah save'). The 7th day, the priests blew trumpets and the people sang God 'praises' from Psalms 113-118 (the Great *Hallel*).

After Nehemiah's return to Jerusalem, the people celebrate *Sukkot* for the first time in 1,000 years. On *Rosh Hashanah*, Ezra read Torah from a tower for six hours, while other teachers helped explain it to the people in the crowd. The people wept, worshiped, and celebrated. On the 15th day they made lulavs and made booths to live in for seven days, and on the eighth day had a solemn assembly. (Nehemiah 8:14-18)

Jesus is our Covering (*Sukkah*) and the Holy Spirit is our "Living Water"

The 8th day celebrates having crossed the Red Sea under God's protective covering to safety on the other side. On the 8th day of the feast, the high priest drew water from Siloam, which means "gently flowing waters," with a golden vase. Flowing waters are also called living waters because you can safely drink from them. Another priest had a silver pitcher of wine. A flute player, called "the pierced one," led the procession. After the other priests have sacrificed the required animals for the day, the high priest would pour the water onto the altar, and the other priest would pour the wine. This represented Christ's pierced heart gushing water and blood together to atone for our sins. Jesus is a 'covering' or *sukkah* to those who believe.

> *In the last day, that great day of the feast, Jesus stood and cried, saying, If any man thirst, let him come to me, and drink. He that believes on me, as the scripture has said, out of his belly shall flow rivers of living water. (But this spoke he of the Spirit, which they that believe on him should receive: for the Holy Ghost was not yet given; because that Jesus was not yet glorified.) (John 7:37-39)*

The future temple of the Lord given in Ezekiel 40-44 has a river flowing from its throne with healing water and healing trees on either side of it.

Jesus will pour out Judgment upon the Wicked at His Coming

During *Sukkot* Ezekiel 38-39 and Zechariah 14 are read which concern Christ's second coming. More on "*that day*" in the chapter on the 'Day of the LORD'.

> *For in my jealousy and in the fire of my wrath have I spoken, Surely **in that day** there shall be a great shaking in the land of Israel; So that the fishes of the sea, and the fowls of the heaven, and the beasts of the field, and all creeping things that creep on the earth, and all the men that are on the face of the earth, shall shake at my presence, and the mountains shall be thrown down, and the steep places shall fall, and every wall shall fall to the ground. And I will call for a sword against him throughout all my mountains, said the Lord GOD: every man's sword shall be against his brother. And I will plead against him with pestilence and with blood; and I will rain on him, and on his bands, and on the many people that are with him, an overflowing rain, and great hailstones, fire, and brimstone. Thus will I magnify myself, and sanctify myself; and I will be known in the eyes of many nations, and they shall know that I am the LORD. (Ezekiel 38:19-23)*

> *And it shall come to pass **in that day**, that I will seek to destroy all the nations that come against Jerusalem. (Zechariah 12:9)*

> *Then shall the LORD go forth, and fight against those nations, as when he fought in the day of battle. And his feet shall stand **in that day** on the mount of Olives, which is before Jerusalem on the east, and the mount of Olives shall split in the middle thereof toward the east and toward the west, and there shall be a very great valley; and half of the mountain shall remove toward the north, and half of it toward the south. And you shall flee to the valley of the mountains; for the valley of the mountains shall reach to Azal: yes, you shall flee, like as you fled from before the earthquake in the days of Uzziah king of Judah: and the LORD my God shall come, and all the saints with you. And it shall come to pass **in that day**, that the light shall not be clear, nor dark: But it shall be **one day** which shall be known to the LORD, not day, nor night: but it shall come to pass, that at evening time it shall be light. And it shall be **in that day**, that <u>living waters shall go out from Jerusalem</u>; half of them toward the former sea, and half of them toward the hinder sea: in summer and*

*in winter shall it be. And the LORD shall be king over all the earth: **in that day** shall there be one LORD, and his name one. (Zechariah 14:3-9)*

King Jesus will Rule the Nations in Peace during the Millennium

*Sing and rejoice, O daughter of Zion: for, see, I come, and I will dwell in the middle of you, said the LORD. And many nations shall be joined to the LORD **in that day**, and shall be my people: and I will dwell in the middle of you, and you shall know that the LORD of hosts has sent me to you. And the LORD shall inherit Judah his portion in the holy land, and shall choose Jerusalem again. (Zechariah 2:10-12)*

At the end of the 1,000 years, after the Great White Throne judgment when Satan and death and all wicked are cast into the lake of fire, then eternity without rebellion begins. It is the 8th day of Tabernacles when God's Spirit covers the globe and righteousness, peace and joy never end.

Summary of Jesus' Partial Fulfillment of Fall Feasts

Tishri 1: Jesus is born in Bethlehem to the sound of trumpets acknowledging the King is born. [More on this in the chapter on Biblical Astronomy.]

Tishri 10: Jesus' sinless death made atonement for us in the Holy of Holies, splitting its veil (Mark 15:38), and providing us direct access to our Father through His Holy Spirit.

Tishri 15-21: Jesus 'tabernacled' with us as God in the flesh.

Tishri 22: Jesus breathed on His disciples to receive the Holy Spirit. Jesus left so He could send us His Holy Spirit to be our Comforter and Teacher (John 16:7).

Summary of Jesus' Future Fulfillment of Fall Feasts

The following will be fleshed out in the remainder of the book.

Tishri 1-2: The long, "great and terrible Day of the Lord" lasts for two days. King Jesus and those resurrected and raptured do battle with Christ against armies of Antichrist. Antichrist/Beast and the False Prophet are cast into lake of fire, and the wicked are judged. The righteous are taken to the bridal chamber called "New Jerusalem" for seven days of a wedding feast with Jesus, and are rewarded. The wicked and the earth are destroyed by fire, and it is terra-formed again by God in six days (Tishri 3-9).

Tishri 10: The earth has been redeemed and returned to its Edenic state. The millennial reign of King Jesus begins. The raptured righteous return to earth in their restored bodies, and some saints return to earth in their immortal bodies, and all praise God in humble awe.

After *Yom Kippur*, the next few days are spent making booths.

Tishri 15-21: The righteous live in booths, and begin planning cities. Millennial reign.

Tishri 22: The earthly New Jerusalem descends from heaven with the Temple of the Lord described in Ezekiel 40-47. After the 1,000 years and the Great White Throne judgment, then eternity without rebellion begins.

Ten Toes & Ten Horns

Daniel answered and said, Blessed be the name of God for ever and ever: for wisdom and might are his: And he changes the times and the seasons: he removes kings, and sets up kings: he gives wisdom to the wise, and knowledge to them that know understanding: He reveals the deep and secret things: he knows what is in the darkness, and the light dwells with him.
(Daniel 2:20-22)

Israel's Babylonian Exile

A brief overview of Israel's history from the creation to the Hebrews' exodus (1490 BC) and wandering in the wilderness was provided in the first few chapters. Joshua led them into the promised land of Canaan, and then the twelve tribes of their patriarch, Israel, named their newly conquered country Israel. Israel was led by judges (Samson being the last to 1155 BC) and priests (Eli and Samuel to 1095 BC). Then Israel was led by three kings, each for forty years: Saul, David, and Solomon (975 BC), who built a temple to God in Jerusalem before the kingdom was divided. The northern kingdom of ten tribes retained the name Israel, and the southern kingdom of two tribes was referred to as Judah, the larger of the two. The years of Judah's exile in the empire of Babylon in the following outline are Before Christ (BC).

Israel's History	Daniel's History
734-732 Ten tribes taken to Assyria by Tiglath-Pileser	
729-724 More taken to Assyria by Shalmaneser & Sargon	
716-715 Last wave taken to Assyria & Media by Sargon	
605 Two tribes (Judah and Benjamin) taken to Babylon	605 Daniel taken as a teenager
597 Ezekiel & 10,000 deported from Jerusalem	
586 Jerusalem & Temple burned	554 Daniel thrown into lion's den
538 Babylon surrenders to Cyrus, the Persian	
536 Zerubbabel restores altar of temple in Jerusalem	
535 Temple foundation laid, but work stops	534 Daniel finishes his book
520 Temple work resumed	
516 Temple finished & dedicated	
473 Esther is queen of Persia	
467 More exiles return to Jerusalem with Ezra	
454 Nehemiah rebuilds walls of Jerusalem	
333 Alexander the Great conquers Darius III	

Awake, Bride

Daniel's Babylonian Exile and Book

In 605 Babylon conquered Jerusalem and the two remaining tribes (house of Judah), and Daniel and his teen-age friends found themselves being trained for its high court a year later. Daniel describes it in Hebrew in the first chapter of his book.

In the third year of the reign of Jehoiakim king of Judah came Nebuchadnezzar king of Babylon to Jerusalem, and besieged it. And the king spoke to Ashpenaz the master of his eunuchs, that he should bring certain of the children of Israel, and of the king's seed, and of the princes; Children in whom was no blemish, but well favored, and skillful in all wisdom, and cunning in knowledge, and understanding science, and such as had ability in them to stand in the king's palace, and whom they might teach the learning and the tongue of the Chaldeans. (Daniel 1:1, 3-4)

Daniel learned the language of Aramaic, and the next six chapters of Daniel are written in that business language of the Babylonian Empire. So Daniel 2-7 are written in the language of the Gentiles because they deal specifically with the Gentiles; and Daniel 8-12 are written in Hebrew because they deal specifically with Israel. The book is not chronological, but divided as to its intended audience. This study is about toes and horns, chapters 2 and 7 respectively (though horns are also mentioned in chapter 8), and concern the Gentiles.

The dream of the statue consisting of 4 metals (Daniel 2) and the vision of 4 beasts representing world empires (Daniel 7) were given to the Gentiles; they are often wrongly interpreted as representing the same kingdoms. The 4 metal kingdoms of the statue are those Gentile empires which persecute the Hebrews until Christ's first coming. The 4 beasts are those Gentile empires which persecute Jews prior to Christ's second coming.

Nebuchadnezzar's Statue Dream (Daniel 2)

In the second year of Nebuchadnezzar's reign, he had a dream so frightening he is ready to kill all his wise men because they can not tell him what it was or interpret it. Daniel reasons with the king's captain sent to slay him to give him some time to give the king what he wants. Daniel asks his three buddies to pray that God would reveal the dream and its interpretation to him that night, and God does. It is an outline of the empires who will persecute the Hebrews until Christ's first coming, and how they will be destroyed by Christ's kingdom.

*You, O king, saw, and behold a great image. <u>This image's head was of fine gold, his breast and his arms of silver, his belly and his thighs of brass, His legs of iron, his feet part of iron and part of clay.</u> You saw till that a **stone** was cut out without hands, which smote the image on his feet that were of iron and clay, and **broke them to pieces**. Then was the iron, the clay, the brass, the silver, and the gold, broken to pieces together, that no place was found for them: and the **stone** that smote the image became a great mountain, and **filled the whole earth**. This is the* *dream; and we will tell the interpretation thereof before the king. You, O king, are a king of kings: for the God of heaven has given you a kingdom, power, and strength, and glory. . . . And after you shall arise another kingdom inferior to you, and another third kingdom of brass, which shall bear rule over all the earth. And the fourth kingdom shall be strong as iron. And whereas you saw the feet and toes, part of potters' clay, and part of iron, the kingdom shall be divided; but there shall be in it of the strength of the iron, for as much as you saw the iron mixed with miry clay. (Daniel 2:31-41 edited)*

Daniel lived to see the Persians and Medes (silver arms and chest of statue) overtake the Babylonian empire, and he continued to serve in their courts. Though Cyrus gave the decree for Jews to return to Judah, Daniel remained in Babylon. Then Alexander the Great (of Greece, the brass belly and thighs) conquered the area. And finally the Romans (legs and feet of iron) conquered it. Then Jesus, our Rock and our Cornerstone, lived and died and resurrected. Christ's kingdom became great. Constantine declared Christianity the religion of the Roman empire in 324 AD, and within 150 years, the Roman empire ceased to exist.

Ten Toes and Ten Caesars

And the fourth kingdom shall be strong as iron: for as much as iron breaks in pieces and subdues all things: and as iron that breaks all these, shall it break in pieces and bruise. And as the toes of the feet were part of iron, and part of clay, so the kingdom shall be partly strong, and partly broken. And whereas you saw iron mixed with miry clay, they shall mingle themselves with the seed of men: but they shall not join one to another, even as iron is not mixed with clay. <u>*And in the days of these kings*</u> **shall the God of heaven set up a kingdom, which shall never be destroyed: and the kingdom shall not be left to other people, but it shall break in pieces and consume all these kingdoms, and it shall stand for ever.** *For as much as you saw that the stone was cut out of the mountain without hands, and that it broke in pieces the iron, the brass, the clay, the silver, and the gold; the great God has made known to the king what shall come to pass hereafter: and the dream is certain, and the interpretation thereof sure. (Daniel 2:40-45 edited)*

Rome attempted to absorb all cultures and all gods, consuming the other kingdoms. But the Jews and the Christians would not accept their polytheism. Jesus was born into a Roman occupied country and He established His Kingdom in the midst of it. Historians record the persecution of Christians by ten different caesars; not nine or twelve, but ten. These persecutions span 250 years from Nero to Diocletian in the 'year of our Lord' *Anno Domini* (AD).

Ten Persecutions

Nero 64-68	Maximin 235-237
Domitian 95-96	Decius 250-256
Trajan 100-115	Valerian 257-260
Aurelius 168-171	Aurelian 276
Severus 203-210	Diocletian 303-310

These ten caesars ("*kings*") are the ten toes of the statue in Daniel 2 who "*break in pieces and bruise*". They correlate with the "*ten days*" or periods of tribulation prophesied for the Church in Revelation 2.

> *And to the angel of the church in Smyrna write; These things said the first and the last, which was dead, and is alive; Fear none of those things which you shall suffer: behold, the devil shall cast some of you into prison, that you may be tried; and you shall have <u>tribulation ten days</u>: be you faithful to death, and I will give you a crown of life. (Revelation 2:8, 10)*

Notice there is no mention of a little toe rising up and claiming anything in Nebuchadnezzar's vision of the statue. There is no end-time antichrist character in this dream, though these kingdoms and the ten toes were definitely against Christ and God.

The Stone (Jesus) of the Kingdom which shall Never Be Destroyed

> *And as they heard these things, he added and spoke a parable, because he was near to Jerusalem, and because they thought that the kingdom of God should immediately appear. He said therefore, A certain nobleman went into a far country to receive for himself a kingdom, and to return. And he called his <u>ten</u> servants, and delivered them <u>ten</u> pounds, and said to them, Occupy till I come. (Luke 19:11-13)*

Jesus taught His disciples that His Kingdom would not be obvious immediately, and He did so using a parable with 'tens'. Jesus taught that His Kingdom would start small and grow to be enormous and fill the earth (Matthew 13:31-32).

Rome divided into East and West in 305 AD. In 306 Constantine was proclaimed a Roman Emperor by his troops, and took over Britain, Gaul, Spain, and Germania provinces. Constantine conquered in the sign of the cross in 313, and declared "religious toleration" except towards Judaism. Jews and all who participated in Jewish rituals were still heavily taxed throughout the empire because of their revolt in 66 AD. In 324 Constantine declared Christianity the only religion of the Roman Empire.

The Stone is Jesus (Isaiah 28:16; Psalms 118:22), and the believers who obey Him exhibit His Kingdom on earth. The Roman Empire no longer existed by 476 AD; Christianity crushed the Roman Empire. So, except for Christ's Kingdom never being destroyed, the statue prophecy is fulfilled. The Bride should not be looking for a revived Roman Empire of ten nations. But the Bride should be looking for ten nations of a beast.

By 640 AD a new religion was claiming the lands of the old Roman Empire. Those who did not convert to Islam were taxed and subjugated, or executed.

Daniel's Visions of Four Beasts (Daniel 7)

Daniel spoke and said, I saw in my vision by night, and, behold, the four winds of the heaven strove on the great sea. And four great beasts came up from the sea, diverse one from another. The first was like a lion, and had eagle's wings: I beheld till the wings thereof were plucked, and it was lifted up from the earth, and made stand on the feet as a man, and a man's heart was given to it. And behold another beast, a second, like to a bear, and it raised up itself on one side, and it had three ribs in the mouth of it between the teeth of it: and they said thus to it, Arise, devour much flesh. After this I beheld, and see another, like a leopard, which had on the back of it four wings of a fowl; the beast had also four heads; and dominion was given to it. After this I saw in the night visions, and behold a fourth beast, dreadful and terrible, and strong exceedingly; and it had great iron teeth: it devoured and broke in pieces, and stamped the residue with the feet of it: and it was diverse from all the beasts that were before it; and it had ten horns. . . . As concerning the rest of the beasts, they had their dominion taken away: yet their lives were prolonged for a season and time. . . .These great beasts, which are four, are <u>four kings</u>, which shall arise out of the earth. **But the saints of the most High shall take the kingdom, and possess the kingdom for ever, even for ever and ever.** *Then I would know the truth of the fourth beast, which was diverse from all the others, exceeding dreadful, whose teeth were of iron, and his nails of brass; which devoured, broke in pieces, and stamped the residue with his feet;* (Daniel 7:2-7, 12, 17-19)

These 4 beast empires are the world powers which persecute Jews prior to Christ's second coming. [My thanks to James Lloyd of Christian Media Network for this insight.] The winged lion represents England. In 1189 AD at the coronation of <u>Richard the</u> <u>**Lion**hearted</u>, unexpected persecution of the Jews broke out in England. Most Jewish houses in London were burned, and many Jews killed. All possessions of the Jews were claimed by the Crown. Richard's successor relieved the Jews of more than 8 million marks. England lost it's American colonies (eagle wings) in 1783.

Then the Russian **bear** came devouring much flesh in 1880. "Between 1929 and 1953 the state created by <u>Lenin and set in motion by Stalin</u> deprived 21.5 million Soviet citizens of their lives," stated Dmitri Volkogonov. Many Jews fled to Israel.

Germany began its persecution of Jews in 1933 and killed six million Jews by the end of WWII. Germans regarded the panther as an exceptional animal, which is also called a **leopard**. After <u>Hitler's</u> defeat Germany was controlled by four (wings) commanders. Again, many Jews fled to Israel. God may have been using these beasts to drive His Hebrew children home to Israel.

For I will take you from among the heathen, and gather you out of all countries, and will bring you into your own land. (Ezekiel 36:24)

The **ten-horned monster** is a Muslim conglomerate which has persecuted Jews. PLO (Palestinian Liberation Organization) attacks, or *intifadas*, began in the 1970's. Muslims control one fourth of the earth and have a quarter of the world's population. And a "little horn" will arise to lead them.

On September 11, 2001, even Americans had to recognize the rising power of Islam; and by September 2008, America ceased to be the world power. Though Russia seeks to be large and in-charge again (and it does still have a large Muslim population even after all the -'istan' secessions); it will be the Muslim nations which will dominate. But Russia, Britain, and Germany will still have roles to play.

The Fourth Beast is the Beast of the Sea

*And I stood on the sand of the sea, and saw a beast rise up out of the sea, having seven heads and ten horns, and on his horns ten crowns, and on his heads the name of blasphemy. And the beast which I saw was like to a **leopard**, and his feet were as the feet of a **bear**, and his mouth as the mouth of a **lion**: and the dragon gave him his power, and his seat, and great authority. . . . And they worshipped the dragon which gave power to the beast: and they worshipped the beast, saying, Who is like to the beast? who is able to make war with him? And there was given to him a mouth speaking great things and blasphemies; and power was given to him to continue forty and two months. . . . And it was given to him to make war with the saints, and to overcome them: and power was given him over all kindreds, and tongues, and nations. And all that dwell on the earth shall worship him, whose names are not written in the book of life of the Lamb slain from the foundation of the world. (Revelation 13:1-2, 4-5, 7-8)*

Leopard is like Germany

The end-time body of the beast is like Nazi Germany, determined to extinguish all Jews while using propaganda and threats to keep the rest of the world from interfering. Muslim nations, especially Iran, still have close ties to Germany.

The swastika came to be identified as "the oldest Aryan symbol" by several writers in the late 19th century. *Aryan* means 'noble'. In the 1930's Shah Reza Pahlavi admired Hitler and the concept of the Aryan master race. In 1935, the Shah changed the name of Persia to Iran. In Persian '*Iran*' means "land of Aryans".

The Allies disrupted their relations after WWII, but by 1970 West Germany was the European country with the largest Iranian expatriate community. In a speech during a "World without Zionism" conference on 10/26/2005, Ahmadinejad, President of Iran, stated, "Our dear Imam said that the occupying regime must be wiped off the map and this was a very wise statement. We cannot compromise over the issue of Palestine." The Imam he referred to was Ayatollah Khomeni.

"It's 1938 and Iran is Germany. And Iran is racing to arm itself with atomic bombs," Netanyahu told delegates to the annual United Jewish Communities General Assembly, "Believe him and stop him." {Peter Hirschberg, Haaretz Correspondent 11/14/2006}

"Iran has said it would respond to any attack by targeting U.S. interests and America's ally Israel, as well as closing the Strait of Hormuz, a vital route for world oil supplies." On November 12, 2008 it successfully tested a two-staged missile with a range of 1200 miles, able to reach Israel.

Bear Feet of Russia

Russia is providing military transport and arms to the middle east below cost or as gifts. According to the 9/1/2007 Global Politician report by Natalya Hmelik, "President Vladimir Putin also offered Mr. Abbas support in a form of 50 armored personnel vehicles for his security forces" as humanitarian aid. Hmelik's report continued:

"The United Arab Emirates have in service about 1,000 Russian-made armored personnel carriers. . . . Now Russia sells missiles to Damascus and Tehran, upgrades Syrian Air Forces' fighters MiG-21 (Fishbed), MiG-23 (Flogger) and MiG-29 (Fulcrum) bought in the Soviet Union. Russian-made advanced anti-tank guided missiles Kornet and RPG-29 (Vampire) grenade launchers sold to Syria were used by Hezbollah terrorist organisation against Israel during the last summer conflict in the South Lebanon. Earlier this year Moscow started supplying to Damascus a batch of the Buk-M2 (SA-17 Grizzly) air defense systems worth at least $200m. . . . Before 2001, Moscow supplied Tehran with two air regiments of MiG-29 fighters and Su-24 (fencer) bombers, three diesel subs 877 EKM (Kilo), several divisions of S-200 (SA-5) surface-to-air missile systems; established license production of T-72 main battle tanks, armoured personnel carriers BMP-2 and Kornet missiles. After a short break, in November 2005, Russia signed $1bn contract to supply the Tehran regime with 29 surface-to-air missile systems Tor-M1 (SA-15 Gauntlet) and a consignment of military boats, and upgrade Iran's Soviet-made bombers and fighter jets."

"Cooperation between Turkey and Russia is the key to solving our problems," Putin said after the World Economic Forum on January 30, 2009.

Mouthpiece of Britain (BBC)

Britain has largely succumbed to Islam. It has sanctioned Sharia courts for its Muslim population, by reclassifying these formerly illegal courts as tribunal hearings, making their judgments legally binding on cases involving divorce, financial disputes, and even domestic violence. A breakdown of programming from the BBC's Religion and Ethics department reveals that since 2001, the BBC made 41 faith programs on Islam, compared

Awake, Bride

with just five on Hinduism and one on Sikhism (Jerome Taylor for the *Independent* on September 8, 2008).

The beast of the sea has seven heads, but it still has ten horns with crowns signifying ten kings. With the understanding that the prophecy regarding the ten toes of the Roman Empire was fulfilled, and the clue that the whore who rides the beast is called "mystery Babylon" (Revelation 17:3-5), it is likely the seven heads of state and ten kings of the beast will be found in Muslim countries located in the ancient Babylonian empire.

The beast has seven heads, but ten horns. The seven heads of nations could be Egypt, Saudi Arabia, Jordan, Iraq, Iran, Turkey, and Syria. These countries, in part or in whole, were in the Babylonian empire. The extra three horns could be the Muslim leaders of Hamas, Hezbollah, and the PLO. But there are other possibilities.

The Arab League

The Arab League was founded in Cairo in 1945 by Egypt, Iraq, Lebanon, Saudi Arabia, Syria, Jordan, and Yemen (who joined within months of founding). So it began with seven countries.

All members of Arab League are also members of the Organization of the Islamic Conference. Other members in order of their joining are: Libya, Sudan, Morocco, Tunisia, Kuwait, Algeria, United Arab Emirates (UAE), Bahrain, Qatar, Oman, Mauritania, Somalia, Palestine, Djibouti, Comorros, Eritrea, Venezuela, and India. [India attended as an observer in March of 2005 and 2006, and supported the Arab League's desire to reduce Israel back to pre-1967 borders. In December 2006, they were hit by a tsunami. God has ways of punishing countries who seek Israel's harm.] Of the Arab league nations, India is the fourth largest producer of iron, and may provide the beast with its bite (and nuclear know-how). Though India still imports some copper, it is the second largest producer of brass products in Asia. No wonder the Arab League invited them to join.

The Arab League initiated the creation of an organization representing the Palestinian people. Palestine Liberation Organization (PLO). The PLO was founded by a meeting of 422 Palestinian national figures in Jerusalem in May 1964 following an earlier decision of the Arab League; its goal was the liberation of Palestine from the Jews through armed struggle (*jihad*).

Of the Arab League nations, Jordan, Saudi Arabia, Morocco, and Bahrain are kingdoms and they call their leader by the title 'king'; but except for Jordan, they are seen as dictators by the world. In the monarchies of Kuwait and Qatar, their leaders are called 'emir', a title of nobility. A president heads the UAE, and a sultan in Oman. Sudan's form of government is declared as a 'dictatorship'. Libya has a unique name for their form of government which means 'ruled by the masses', but it is well known as a dictatorship. Egypt declares itself to be a "semi-presidential republic" but is seen as a dictatorship. Though Hugo Chavez in Venezuela is also a dictator, his country is not near the middle east. The other countries have various forms of government, or no government at all (transitional government) as in Somalia and Eritrea. Formally, the other leaders of the Arab

League have declared themselves to be republics or constitutionally placed into power. Iraq might be playing the western political game until the combat troops are pulled out in August 2010.

A list of the ten kings of the Arab League would include Egypt and cancel tiny Bahrain (which has an area of 253 sq. miles). Ten horns/kings of the Arab League are the leaders of Jordan, Saudi Arabia, Morocco, Kuwait, Qatar, UAE, Oman, Sudan, Libya, and Egypt. Though theses Arab League nations are likely candidates for the ten horns/kings, there are other possible combinations of Muslim nations which should be considered.

Ten Horns are Ten Kings; Three Get Uprooted

After this I saw in the night visions, and behold a fourth beast, dreadful and terrible, and strong exceedingly; and it had great iron teeth: it devoured and broke in pieces, and stamped the residue with the feet of it: and it was diverse from all the beasts that were before it; and it had ten horns. I considered the horns, and, behold, there came up among them another little horn, before whom there were three of the first horns plucked up by the roots: and, behold, in this horn were eyes like the eyes of man, and a mouth speaking great things. . . . The fourth beast shall be the fourth kingdom on earth, which shall be diverse from all kingdoms, and shall devour the whole earth, and shall tread it down, and break it in pieces. And the ten horns out of this kingdom are ten kings that shall arise: and another shall rise after them; and he shall be diverse from the first, and he shall subdue three kings. And he shall speak great words against the most High, and shall wear out the saints of the most High, and think to change times and laws: and they shall be given into his hand until a time and times and the dividing of time. But the judgment shall sit, and they shall take away his dominion, to consume and to destroy it to the end. (Daniel 7:7-8, 23-26)

The kingdom of Islam is diverse from the other kingdoms in that the first three empires had one king ruling at a time; whereas Islam has many kings. As noted in the first chapter, Islam uses a strict lunar calendar, and they also impose Sharia law. The phrase "*time and times and the dividing of time*" (see Revelation 12:14) signals the little horn will be active during the Great Tribulation. To better understand which three kings the little horn might uproot, we need to understand the different sects of Islam.

The Wahhabis believe Allah has a physical body and sits on a throne, and is a unique unity. They insist on hatred and violence toward Muslims and non-Muslims who disagree with them. The House of Saud, which rules Saudi Arabia, funds the indoctrination of other Muslims into this sect. In order to remain in good standing as a Muslim, they also fund jihadists. [Osama bin Laden is of the House of Saud.] Kuwait and United Arab Emirates are also Wahhabis. Those countries border Saudi Arabia on the Arabian Peninsula, as do Qatar, Oman, and Yemen.

The Shia, predominantly Iran with large populations in Iraq and Afghanistan, believe the descendants of Mohammed (Imams) have special political and religious power over the people. The Sunnis believe Mohammed's generals and their descendants hold such power. They also believe Allah does not resemble his creation in any way, and to imagine him in a form is idolatry. Yet they pray to saints to aid their prayers, which the Wahhabis consider idolatry. The Sunni sect is the largest with dozens of national adherents. The little horn has several possible groups of three nations to uproot.

But a more likely group of three Muslim nations the little horn would have to remove, are those who have peace treaties with Israel. Egypt signed a peace treaty in 1979, and Jordan did in 1994. The third most likely candidate is Syria. On December 18, 2008, Ehud Olmert said that "a peace treaty between Israel and Syria is feasible." Olmert told a conference of the Institute for National Security Studies at Tel Aviv University, "A peace treaty would lower the possibility of war, break the strategic ties between Damascus and Teheran, lead to the expulsion of the Islamic Jihad and Hamas headquarters from Syria, and would stop the cash flow to Hizbullah." Syria might use 'peace' as a ploy to invade Israel.

Confederation of ten tribes who sought to wipe out Israel

Power is given to the beast for 3 1/2 years to *"wear out the saints of the most High"* (Daniel 7:25), which is the same as 42 months *"to make war with the saints, and to overcome them: and power was given him over all kindreds, and tongues, and nations"* (Revelation 13:7). These are prophetic 360 day years, totaling 1,260 days (Revelation 11:3; 12:6). This beast shall *"shall devour the whole earth, and shall tread it down, and break it in pieces"* (Daniel 7:23). Though the ultimate goal of Islam is world domination, their immediate objective is the extermination of the Jewish people from the land of Israel.

This is nothing new. In an attempt to deny God's existence, His enemies seek to wipe out His people. The following is a Psalm of Asaph. Asaph was a Levite who was one of the leaders of king David's choir (1 Chronicles 6:39), a skilled in musician, and a "seer" or prophet (2 Chronicles 29:30).

> *Keep not you silence, O God: hold not your peace, and be not still, O God. For, see, your enemies make a tumult: and they that hate you have lifted up the head. They have taken crafty counsel against your people, and consulted against your hidden ones.* <u>*They have said, Come, and let us cut them off from being a nation; that the name of Israel may be no more in remembrance.*</u> *For they have consulted together with one consent: they are confederate against you: The tabernacles of Edom, and the Ishmaelites; of Moab, and the Hagarenes; Gebal, and Ammon, and Amalek; the Philistines with the inhabitants of Tyre; Assur also is joined with them: they have helped the children of Lot. Selah. Do to them as to the Midianites; as to Sisera, as to Jabin, at the brook of Kison: Which perished at Endor: they became as dung for the earth. Make their nobles like Oreb, and like Zeeb: yes, all their princes as Zebah, and as Zalmunna: Who said, Let us take to ourselves the houses of God in*

possession. O my God, make them like a wheel; as the stubble before the wind. As the fire burns a wood, and as the flame sets the mountains on fire; So persecute them with your tempest, and make them afraid with your storm. Fill their faces with shame; that they may seek your name, O LORD. Let them be confounded and troubled for ever; yes, let them be put to shame, and perish: That men may know that you, whose name alone is JEHOVAH, are the most high over all the earth. (Psalm 83:1-18)

Some Bible commentators say this prophetic psalm was fulfilled during the reign of Jehoshaphat when Ammon, Moab, and those of mount Seir came to cast them out of their inheritance (2 Chronicles 20:10-12). But others say this particular confederation of nations never attacked Israel in Biblical history. All these tribes and the city of Tyre bordered Israel, only the city of Assur was distant.

Edom (in Jordan)	Ammon (in Jordan)
Ishmaelites (Egypt, Saudia Arabia and Iraq)	Amalek (in Jordan)
Moab (in Jordan)	Philistines (in Gaza Strip)
Hagarenes (Saudi Arabia and Jordan)	Tyre (in Lebanon)
Gebal (in Lebanon)	Assur (in northern Iraq)

The "children of Lot" are Edom and Moab from Lot's incestuous relations with his daughters after the destruction of Sodom and Gomorrah. Sisera and Jabin were located in Hazor (Judges 4:2), on the southwest tip of Hula Lake which is due north of the Sea of Galilee. Oreb, Zeeb, Zebah, and Zalmunna were Ishmaelite kings of Midian (Judges 8:3-5) located in the Arabian Peninsula. When Asaph wrote this psalm, the city of Assur was the capital of the waning Assyrian empire; "the Assyrian" was equated with an antichrist in prophecy. This Muslim confederation of nations attacked Israel in 1967, and God shamed them in the Six-Day War. The main aggressors were Egypt, Jordan, and Syria, but the following nations contributed troops and arms: Iraq, Saudi Arabia, Sudan, Tunisia, Morocco, and Algeria.

The movie *Against All Odds* documents how the Arabs in the Six-Day War were "confused and troubled" by supernatural occurrences such as freak "winds" and "storms" or of seeing angels and hearing voices which either paralyzed them or caused them to run in fear. Psalm 83 has been fulfilled, and it gives clarity to the immediate goal of the beast, as well as to the foundation of its worship.

Israel's Enemies are MOON-otheistic

Then Zebah and Zalmunna said, Rise you, and fall on us: for as the man is, so is his strength. And Gideon arose, and slew Zebah and Zalmunna, and took away the <u>ornaments</u> that were on their camels' necks. Then the men of Israel said to Gideon, Rule you over us, both you, and your son, and your son's son also: for you have *delivered us from the hand of Midian. And Gideon said to them, I will not rule over you, neither shall my son rule over you: the LORD shall rule over you. And Gideon said to them, I would desire a request of you, that you would give me every man the earrings of his prey. (For they had golden earrings, because they were Ishmaelites.) (Judges 8:21-24)*

In that day the Lord will take away the bravery of their tinkling ornaments about their feet, and their cauls, and their <u>round tires like the moon</u> (Isaiah 3:18)

Zebah and Zalmunna's ornaments are *sah-har-one'*; a round pendant for the neck, a round tire like the moon. Most Muslim flags contain a waxing crescent moon and the morning star (Venus); the root of their religion. Midian is now Saudi Arabia, and the heart of moon worship is Mecca. Nimrod, "a mighty hunter *against* the LORD" built the cities of Assur and Babel from whence came the Assyrians and Babylonians. The religious system he implemented was that of worshiping the moon and stars with the aide of cult prostitutes. In Isaiah's prophecy against the king of Babylon, he refers to him as *heilel ben-shachar* which is translated "morning star, son of dawn" or "Lucifer, son of the morning" (Isaiah 14:12). *Heilel* can also be translated as brightness. *Hilal*, an Arabic term, refers to the bright waxing crescent when it becomes visible to a normal observer by the naked-eye; which is how they determine their lunar months.

How are you fallen from heaven, O Lucifer, son of the morning! how are you cut down to the ground, which did weaken the nations! For you have said in your heart, I will ascend into heaven, I will exalt my throne above the stars of God. (Isaiah 14:12-13a)

Worship of the moon-god was always the dominant religion of Mesopotamia. The moon-god was worshiped by praying toward Mecca several times a day, making an annual pilgrimage to the Kabah (the black cubic structure in Mecca) which was a temple of the moon-god, running around the Kabah seven times, caressing an idol of a black stone set in the wall of the Kabah, making animal sacrifices, fasting for the month which begins and ends with the crescent moon, gathering on Fridays for prayers, etc.. These were pagan rites practiced by the Arabs long before Mohammed was born. The black stone is a meteorite, a "fallen star" much like Satan "fell" from heaven (also Revelation 12:3-4).

A temple of the moon-god in Babylon was excavated in Ur (Abram's birthplace) by Sir Leonard Woolley. Besides moon symbols, Woolley also found the symbols of bulls and tripods (pyramids) used in moon worship. Harran (in Turkey) was also noted for its devotion to the moon-god. In the 1950's a major temple to the moon-god was excavated at Hazer in Palestine and at Marib in Yemen. Two idols of the moon god were found. Each was a statue of a man sitting upon a throne with a crescent moon carved on his chest. Several smaller statues were also found which were identified by their inscriptions as the "daughters" of the moon-god. The moon-god's name 'Sin' is a part of such Arabic geography as 'Mt. Sinai' and the 'wilderness of Sin'. Though the name of the moon-god was

Sin, his title was *al-ilah*, i.e. 'the deity', meaning that he was the chief among the gods. Inscription of *al-ilah* was found on an idol with crescent moon and star symbols. While they worshiped 360 gods at the Kabah in Mecca, the moon-god was chief deity. Al-ilah was eventually compressed to Allah. The feminine form, 'Allat', represented one of Allah's daughters, and was the consort of the moon-god *Bel* in Nippur. 'Sanballat', in the book of Nehemiah, is the combination of Sin and Allat.

Digging up Prophetic Treasures

The Dead Sea Scrolls were discovered in 1947, just as the modern state of Israel was being formed. Just before war broke out between Israel and the Hezbollah in July 2006, another miraculous archaeological revelation was given. A bulldozer uncovered a Latin prayer book in Ireland on July 20, 2006. It was opened to Psalm 83, the prophetic psalm of Asaph. Hezbollah had launched Katusha rockets into Israel on July 12th, and a few days later kidnapped two Israeli soldiers; thus began the Lebanon War of July, 2006. Though it was not an all out war as in 1967, it was still a moon-otheistic confederation fighting towards Israel's extinction.

Summary

Nebuchadnezzar's dream of the statue consisting of 4 metals (Daniel 2) and Daniel's vision of 4 beasts representing world empires (Daniel 7) were written to and about Gentile empires. The 4 metals of the statue represent those Gentile empires which persecute the Hebrews until Christ's first coming. The 4 beasts represent those Gentile empires which persecute Jews prior to Christ's second coming.

The 4 metal empires were Babylonian (gold), Medes/Persian (silver), Greek (brass), and Roman (iron and clay). The ten caesars are the ten toes of the statue which each led a historically documented persecution against Christians. That statue was completely destroyed by Christianity, and the entire prophecy fulfilled. There will be no revived Roman empire.

The 4 beast empires were Britain (lion), Russia (bear), Germany (leopard), and the Muslim confederation (a ten-horned monster). Daniel's fourth beast correlates with John's "beast of the sea" which retains aspects of the prior three beasts. The body of the Muslim confederation is like Nazi Germany, determined to extinguish the Jews. It receives arms and armored transport from Russia (feet), and the BBC (mouth) promotes the cause of Islam over the airwaves.

The beast has seven heads, but ten horns. The seven nations which founded the Arab League were Egypt, Saudi Arabia, Jordan, Iraq, Lebanon, Syria, and Yemen. The extra three horns could be the Muslim leaders of Hamas, Hezbollah, and the PLO. When a "little horn" arises to lead the Muslim confederation for 1,260 days during the Great Tribulation, he will uproot three of the horns; likely those who have peace treaties with Israel. Egypt signed a peace treaty in 1979, and Jordan did in 1994. The third most likely candidate is Syria.

Awake, Bride

The Biblical and archaeological religion of Israel's enemies in the middle east is moon worship. Allah is the revised name of the moon-god, Sin. God prophesied through Asaph that a group of ten tribes which surrounded Israel would attack but be confounded by God, and Psalm 83 was fulfilled during the Six-Day War in 1967. Near the end of the 3 1/2 years Israel will be surrounded by enemies again, but Jesus will come to her rescue.

Resurrections & Rapture

But when you make a feast, call the poor, the maimed, the lame, the blind: And you shall be blessed; for they cannot recompense you: for you shall be recompensed at the resurrection of the just. (Luke 14:13-14)

The Jews were familiar with the resurrection of the righteous (Job 14:14 and Ezekiel 37:12-14). During the month of Elul they fast and repent of sins, and during the following ten 'days of awe' they seek God earnestly to be written in the book of the righteous. Resurrection is *anastasis* in Greek, from a root meaning 'to stand up', or literally 'to stand up again', raised to life, or rising again.

Resurrected People in the Bible

The following people in the Bible were resurrected:
- The widow's son by Elijah (1 Kings 17:19-24)
- A man whose body had been placed in Elisha's tomb (2 Kings 13:21)
- Lazarus by Jesus Christ (John 11:43-44)
- The ruler's daughter by Jesus Christ (Matthew 9:23-26)
- Eutychus by Paul after a fall from a third-floor window (Acts 20:9-10)
- Tabitha by Peter (Acts 9:36-43)

For I know that my redeemer lives, and that he shall stand at the latter day on the earth: And though after my skin worms destroy this body, yet in my flesh shall I see God. (Job 19:25-26)

Elijah was raptured and Moses was resurrected. They returned to earth in their glorified bodies to talk with Jesus. So to in the millennium, both those resurrected and raptured will be with Christ on earth.

And after six days Jesus takes Peter, James, and John his brother, and brings them up into an high mountain apart, And was transfigured before them: and his face did shine as the sun, and his raiment was white as the light. And, behold, there appeared to them Moses and Elias talking with him. (Matthew 17:1-3)

Resurrection On Third Day

After two days will he revive us: in the third day he will raise us up, and we shall live in his sight. (Hosea 6:2)

The Jews believed in a bodily resurrection on the latter/last day, and Hosea prophesied it would be on the third day.

For I delivered to you first of all that which I also received, how that Christ died for our sins according to the scriptures; And that he was buried, and that he rose again the third day according to the scriptures: (I Corinthians 15:3-4)

And it came to pass, that after three days they found him in the temple, (Luke 2:46a) This was a situational prophecy of Joseph and Mary representing all those seeking the Messiah would find the 'temple' of Christ's body when He rose from the grave after three days.

Jesus' Teaching on the Resurrection

Jesus answered and said to them, Destroy this temple, and in three days I will raise it up. Then said the Jews, Forty and six years was this temple in building, and will you raise it up in three days? But he spoke of the temple of his body. When therefore he was risen from the dead, his disciples remembered that he had said this to them; and they believed the scripture, and the word which Jesus had said. (John 2:19-22)

And he said to them, Go you, and tell that fox, Behold, I cast out devils, and I do cures to day and to morrow, and the third day I shall be perfected. (Luke 13:32)

Jesus spoke repeatedly of being in control of His death and resurrection (Matthew 12:40 and Mark 8:31), so much so that even His enemies were aware He taught He would rise again after three days (Matthew 27:63). But Jesus not only taught about His own bodily resurrection, but the bodily resurrection of all the righteous, and not just on the last day.

Jesus tells the story of the rich man and Lazarus. He states that Lazarus went to Abraham's bosom (paradise) when he died, but to the rich man *"Abraham said, Son, remember that you in your lifetime received your good things, and likewise Lazarus evil things: but now he is comforted, and you are tormented"* (Luke 16:25). The rich man pleaded for Abraham to send Lazarus to warn his brothers. *"And he said to him, If they hear not Moses and the prophets, neither will they be persuaded, <u>though one rose from the dead</u>"* (Luke 16:25).

In Jesus' day there were two main branches of Judaism. The Sadducees denied the resurrection (Luke 20:27), but the Pharisees believed in the resurrection and angels. The

Sadducees posed a question to Jesus regarding whose wife a women would be in the resurrection after she had seven husbands on earth. Jesus replied:

But they which shall be accounted worthy to obtain that world, and the resurrection from the dead, <u>neither marry, nor are given in marriage: Neither can they die any more: for they are equal to the angels; and are the children of God, being the children of the resurrection.</u> Now that the dead are raised, even Moses showed at the bush, when he calls the Lord the God of Abraham, and the God of Isaac, and the God of Jacob. For he is not a God of the dead, but of the living: for all live to him. (Luke 20:35-38)

That 'world' is *aeon*, or age, referring to Christ's 1,000 year reign on earth. Jesus defined worthiness, immortality, and the absence of marriage as characteristics of "*the children of the resurrection*". Those resurrected saints on earth during the millennium will not marry or have sex. Those that live to Him never cease living to Him. Jesus said during one of the feasts in Jerusalem (most likely First Fruits), . . .

Truly, truly, I say to you, He that hears my word, and believes on him that sent me, has everlasting life, and shall not come into condemnation; but is passed from death to life. Truly, truly, I say to you, <u>The hour is coming, and now is, when the dead shall hear the voice of the Son of God: and they that hear shall live</u>. For as the Father has life in himself; so has he given to the Son to have life in himself; And has given him authority to execute judgment also, because he is the Son of man. Marvel not at this: for the hour is coming, in the which all that are in the graves shall hear his voice, And shall come forth; they that have done good, to the resurrection of life; and they that have done evil, to the resurrection of damnation" (John 5:24-29).

The fulfillment of Jesus calling His sheep in Jerusalem out of their graves occurred on First Fruits after His crucifixion (Matthew 27:52-53). During the Feast of Dedication the next year, John records Jesus as the good Shepherd proclaiming, "*My sheep hear my voice, and I know them, and they follow me: And I give to them eternal life*" (John 10:27-28a). Then near the end of Christ's ministry He tells the parable of the rich man and Lazarus, and a few days later, Jesus raised Lazarus from the dead.

Then said Martha to Jesus, Lord, if you had been here, my brother had not died. But I know, that even now, whatever you will ask of God, God will give it you. Jesus said to her, Your brother shall rise again. Martha said to him, I know that he shall rise again in the resurrection at the last day. <u>Jesus said to her, I am the resurrection, and the life: he that believes in me, though he were dead, yet shall he live: And whoever lives and believes in me shall never die.</u> Believe you this? She said to him, Yes, Lord: I believe that you are the Christ, the Son of God, which should come into the world. (John 11:21-27)

Martha had the typical Jewish mindset that the resurrection would occur on the last day. But since Jesus is the resurrection, He brings back to life at any time He chooses. And He chose to resurrect Lazarus on that day. The followers of Jesus who have His resurrection life within them have the power to resurrect people as God chooses (John 14:12 and Mark 16:15-20).

But there is also a resurrection on the last day. *"They that have done good"* (John 5:29) and those who believe in Jesus, the *Christ* (anointed one, Messiah), the Son of God will share in His life now and in His resurrection. And those that live to Him never cease living to Him. And those who are counted worthy will obtain the edenic world that is to come in an immortal body.

Jesus Placed Resurrection After the Great Tribulation

The First Fruits harvest took place when Jesus resurrected from the dead, but there is a final harvest which He often described.

> *But he that received seed into the good ground is he that hears the word, and understands it; which also bears fruit, and brings forth, some an hundred times, some sixty, some thirty. Another parable put he forth to them, saying, The kingdom of heaven is likened to a man which sowed good seed in his field: But while men slept, his enemy came and sowed tares among the wheat, and went his way. But when the blade was sprung up, and brought forth fruit, then appeared the tares also. So the servants of the householder came and said to him, Sir, did not you sow good seed in your field? from where then has it tares? He said to them, An enemy has done this. The servants said to him, Will you then that we go and gather them up? But he said, No; lest while you gather up the tares, you root up also the wheat with them. <u>Let both grow together until the harvest: and in the time of harvest I will say to the reapers, Gather you together first the tares, and bind them in bundles to burn them: but gather the wheat into my barn</u>. . . . He answered and said to them, He that sows the good seed is the Son of man; The field is the world; the good seed are the children of the kingdom; but the tares are the children of the wicked one; The enemy that sowed them is the devil; <u>the harvest is the end of the world</u>; and the reapers are the angels. As therefore the tares are gathered and burned in the fire; so shall it be in the end of this world. The Son of man shall send forth his angels, and they shall gather out of his kingdom all things that offend, and them which do iniquity; And shall cast them into a furnace of fire: there shall be wailing and gnashing of teeth. Then shall the righteous shine forth as the sun in the kingdom of their Father. Who has ears to hear, let him hear. (Matthew 13:23-30, 37-43)*

Why is there wickedness in the world? *"An enemy has done this."* Why doesn't God remove the wicked? He will, but He's giving time for the righteous to mature since our lives are intertwined with theirs. According to Jesus, the good and the bad dwell together until the harvest at the end of the world. Then the wicked will be burned, but the righteous will be taken to God's 'barn'. He later states that the duration of the Great Tribulation is shortened for the sake of the elect (believers).

> *<u>For then shall be great tribulation, such as was not since the beginning of the world to this time, no, nor ever shall be. And except those days should be shortened, there should no flesh be saved: but for the elect's sake those days shall be shortened</u>. . . .Immediately after the tribulation of those days shall the sun be darkened, and the moon shall not give her light, and the stars shall fall from heaven, and the powers of the heavens shall be shaken: And then shall appear the sign of the Son of man in heaven: and then shall all the tribes of the earth mourn, and they shall see the Son of man coming in the **clouds** of heaven with power and great glory. And he shall send his **angels** with a great sound of a **trumpet**, and they shall gather together his elect from the four winds, from one end of heaven to the other. (Matthew 24:21-22, 29-31)*

According to Jesus, immediately after the Great Tribulation there are cataclysmic signs in the heavens just prior to His appearance and our resurrection and rapture.

> *And when he had spoken these things, while they beheld, he was taken up; and a **cloud** received him out of their sight. And while they looked steadfastly toward heaven as he went up, behold, two men stood by them in white apparel; Which also said, You men of Galilee, why stand you gazing up into heaven? <u>this same Jesus, which is taken up from you into heaven, shall so come in like manner as you have seen him go into heaven.</u> (Acts 1:9-11)*

> *And he shall send Jesus Christ, which before was preached to you: <u>Whom the heaven must receive until the times of restitution of all things,</u> which God has spoken by the mouth of all his holy prophets since the world began. (Acts 3:20-21)*

According to Peter, Jesus must remain in heaven until the "*restitution of all things*". Jesus ascended into heaven with clouds and angels, and He will return with clouds and angels and a trumpet blast, and there will be restitution.

Paul's Teaching on the Resurrection

Paul's teaching on the resurrection is extensive, and we will just look at a few key scriptures. Paul elaborates profusely upon our death in Jesus so that we can live for Him and with Him.

> *For you are dead, and your life is hid with Christ in God. When Christ, who is our life, shall appear, then shall you also appear with him in glory. (Colossians 3:3-4)*

> *That I may know him, and the power of his resurrection, and the fellowship of his sufferings, being made conformable to his death; If by any means I might attain to the resurrection of the dead. (Philippians 3:10-11)*

Awake, Bride

Paul uses the analogies of our death and resurrection in Christ as being buried with Him in baptism and raised up, being like a seed planted in the ground and sprouting up, being naked then fully clothed, and several others.

*Therefore we are **buried** with him by baptism into death: that like as Christ was raised up from the dead by the glory of the Father, even so we also should walk in newness of life. For if we have been **planted** together in the likeness of his death, we shall be also in the likeness of his resurrection." (Romans 6:4-5)*

*But some man will say, How are the dead raised up? and with what body do they come? You fool, that which you sow is not quickened, except it die: And that which you sow, you sow not that body that shall be, but bore grain, it may chance of wheat, or of some other grain: But God gives it a body as it has pleased him, and to every seed his own body. All flesh is not the same flesh: but there is one kind of flesh of men, another flesh of beasts, another of fishes, and another of birds. There are also celestial bodies, and bodies terrestrial: but the glory of the celestial is one, and the glory of the terrestrial is another. There is one glory of the sun, and another glory of the moon, and another glory of the stars: for one star differs from another star in glory. So also is the resurrection of the dead. It is **sown** in corruption; it is raised in incorruption: It is sown in dishonor; it is raised in glory: it is sown in weakness; it is raised in power: It is sown a natural body; it is raised a spiritual body. There is a natural body, and there is a spiritual body. And so it is written, The first man Adam was made a living soul; the last Adam was made a quickening spirit. However, that was not first which is spiritual, but that which is natural; and afterward that which is spiritual. The first man is of the earth, earthy; the second man is the Lord from heaven. As is the earthy, such are they also that are earthy: and as is the heavenly, such are they also that are heavenly. And as we have borne the image of the earthy, we shall also bear the image of the heavenly. Now this I say, brothers, that flesh and blood cannot inherit the kingdom of God; neither does corruption inherit incorruption. (I Corinthians 15:35-50)*

*For we know that if our earthly house of this tabernacle were dissolved, we have a building of God, an house not made with hands, eternal in the heavens. For in this we groan, earnestly desiring to be **clothed** on with our house which is from heaven: If so be that being clothed we shall not be found naked. For we that are in this tabernacle do groan, being burdened: not for that we would be unclothed, but clothed on, that mortality might be swallowed up of life. Now he that has worked us for the selfsame thing is God, who also has given to us <u>the earnest of the Spirit</u>. Therefore we are always confident, knowing that, whilst we are at home in the body, we are absent from the Lord: (For we walk by faith, not by sight:) We are confident, I say, and willing rather <u>to be absent from the body, and to be present with the Lord</u>. Why we labor, that, whether present or absent, we may be accepted* *of him. For we must all appear before the judgment seat of Christ; that every one may receive the things done in his body, according to that he has done, whether it be good or bad. Knowing therefore the terror of the Lord, we persuade men; but we are made manifest to God; and I trust also are made manifest in your consciences. (2 Corinthians 5:1-11)*

God's Holy Spirit indwelling us is the 'security deposit' guaranteeing our new immortal body. There is no 'soul sleep'; once a believer's natural body dies, he/she is present with Jesus in an immortal body. But all people will appear before Christ's judgment seat regarding the things done in our natural bodies.

Order of Resurrections

And I saw thrones, and they sat on them, and judgment was given to them: and I saw the souls of them that were beheaded for the witness of Jesus, and for the word of God, and which had not worshipped the beast, neither his image, neither had received his mark on their foreheads, or in their hands; and they lived and reigned with Christ a thousand years. But the rest of the dead lived not again until the thousand years were finished. This is the first resurrection. <u>Blessed and holy is he that has part in the first resurrection: on such the second death has no power, but they shall be priests of God and of Christ, and shall reign with him a thousand years.</u> (Revelation 20:4-6)

And I saw a great white throne, and him that sat on it, from whose face the earth and the heaven fled away; and there was found no place for them. And I saw the dead, small and great, stand before God; and the books were opened: and another book was opened, which is the book of life: and the dead were judged out of those things which were written in the books, according to their works. And the sea gave up the dead which were in it; and death and hell delivered up the dead which were in them: and they were judged every man according to their works. And death and hell were cast into the lake of fire. <u>This is the second death. And whoever was not found written in the book of life was cast into the lake of fire.</u> (Revelation 20:11-15)

There is good reason to be in the first resurrection, even if it costs you your life to obtain it.

Women received their dead raised to life again: and others were tortured, not accepting deliverance; that they might obtain a better resurrection. (Hebrews 11:35)

Paul puts these resurrections in order for us beginning with the First Fruits harvest at the end of Christ's first coming, and then the resurrection of the dead saints and the rapture of those alive at the beginning of His second coming (also in 1 Thessalonians 4:14-18).

> *But every man in his own **order**: <u>Christ the first fruits</u>; afterward they that are Christ's at his coming. Then comes the end, when he shall have delivered up the kingdom to God, even the Father; when he shall have put down all rule and all authority and power. For he must reign, till he has put all enemies under his feet. The last enemy that shall be destroyed is death. . . . Behold, I show you a mystery; We shall not all sleep, but we shall all be changed, In a moment, in the twinkling of an eye, at the last trump: for the trumpet shall sound, and <u>the dead shall be raised incorruptible, and we shall be changed</u>. For this corruptible must put on incorruption, and this mortal must put on immortality. (1 Cor. 15:23-26, 51-53)*

There is just a blink of an eye in time when the dead are raised and the living saints are changed, not years. The only separation is in the order, and the resurrection comes before the rapture. Putting it all together, the following is the order of resurrections:

The original resurrection at Christ's 1st coming
    Jesus Christ, on the day of First Fruits
    Those saints in graves in Jerusalem
Christ's 2nd coming
    The 1st Resurrection of dead saints
    Rapture (*change*) of those saints alive
2nd Resurrection after Millennial Reign
    Great White Throne Judgment
    2nd Death

Rapture

> *Blessed be the God and Father of our Lord Jesus Christ, which according to his abundant mercy has begotten us again to a lively hope by the resurrection of Jesus Christ from the dead, To an <u>inheritance incorruptible</u>, and undefiled, and that fades not away, reserved in heaven for you, <u>Who are kept by the power of God through faith to salvation ready to be revealed in the last time.</u> Wherein you greatly rejoice, though now for a season, if need be, you are in heaviness through manifold temptations: That the trial of your faith, being much more precious than of gold that perishes, though it be tried with fire, might be found to praise and honor and glory at the appearing of Jesus Christ. (1 Peter 1:3-7)*

Saints go through temptations and trials until the appearing of Jesus Christ. The saints go through the Great Tribulation, and then when Jesus appears, the resurrection and rapture occur in that order. "*Inheritance incorruptible*" is the resurrection. The rapture is the "*salvation ready to be revealed*". To place the rapture before the resurrection is to twist what Paul clearly wrote to the Christians in Thessalonica.

*For if we believe that Jesus died and rose again, even so **them also which sleep in Jesus will God bring with him**. For this we say to you by the word of the Lord, that <u>we which are alive and remain to the coming of the Lord shall not prevent [precede] them which are asleep</u>. For the Lord himself shall descend from heaven with a shout, with the voice of the archangel, and with the trump of God: and <u>the dead in Christ shall rise first: Then we which are alive and remain shall be caught up together with them in the **clouds**, to meet the Lord in the air: and so shall we ever be with the Lord</u>. Why comfort one another with these words. (1 Thess. 4:14-18 clarification added)*

God will bring the resurrected saints with Him. They will not come out of the ground, but already have their resurrection bodies in heaven and will *rise* (stand up) with Jesus at His coming. They were raised up first into immortal bodies, then we who are alive will be caught up into the clouds and forever be with Jesus, and be "*changed*" into our immortal bodies as well. 'Changed' is *allasso*, meaning 'to make different', or new; like the new heavens and new earth.

*Now this I say, brothers, that flesh and blood cannot inherit the kingdom of God; neither does corruption inherit incorruption. Behold, I show you a mystery; <u>We shall not all sleep, but we shall all be **changed**, In a moment, in the twinkling of an eye, at the last trump: for the trumpet shall sound, and the dead shall be raised incorruptible, and we shall be **changed**</u>. For this corruptible must put on incorruption, and this mortal must put on immortality. (1 Corinthians 15:50-53)*

*And, You, Lord, in the beginning have laid the foundation of the earth; and the heavens are the works of your hands: They shall perish; but you remain; and <u>they all shall wax old as does a garment; And as a clothing shall you fold them up, and they shall be **changed**</u>: but you are the same, and your years shall not fail. (Hebrews 1:10-12)*

The marriage vow is valid until a spouse dies (1 Cor. 7:39). Since those who were raptured did not die, their marriage vows will still be valid. Jesus said, "in the resurrection they neither marry, nor are given in marriage" (Matthew 22:30). It may be that in the millennium, raptured married couples will be able to have sex and produce mortal, but long-lived, children (Isaiah 65:20, 23).

Enoch and Elijah

The first person recorded in Scripture to have been raptured is Enoch. "*And Enoch walked with God: and he was not; for God took him*" (Genesis 5:24). The second person to be raptured was Elijah, and all the prophets knew it would happen that day. There is a scriptural precedent for foreknowledge of the exact day of rapture.

Awake, Bride

> *And it came to pass, <u>when the LORD would take up Elijah into heaven by a whirlwind</u>, that Elijah went with Elisha from Gilgal. . . And the sons of the prophets that were at Bethel came forth to Elisha, and said to him, <u>Know you that the LORD will take away your master from your head to day? And he said, Yes, I know it; hold you your peace.</u> . . . And the sons of the prophets that were at Jericho came to Elisha, and said to him, <u>Know you that the LORD will take away your master from your head to day? And he answered, Yes, I know it; hold you your peace.</u> . . . Elijah said to Elisha, Ask what I shall do for you, <u>before I be taken away from you</u>. And Elisha said, I pray you, let a double portion of your spirit be on me. And he said, You have asked a hard thing: nevertheless, <u>if you see me when I am taken from you</u>, it shall be so to you; but if not, it shall not be so. And it came to pass, as they still went on, and talked, that, behold, there appeared a chariot of fire, and horses of fire, and parted them both asunder; and <u>Elijah went up by a whirlwind into heaven</u>. (2 Kings 2:1-11 edited)*

A whirlwind may or may not have clouds associated with it, but when Christ returns to rapture His Bride, there will definitely be clouds.

> *The word of the LORD came again to me, saying, Son of man, prophesy and say, Thus said the Lord GOD; Howl you, Woe worth the day! For the day is near, even the day of the LORD is near, **a cloudy day**; it shall be the time of the heathen. (Ezekiel 30:1-2)*

Caught up to Meet Jesus

The phrase "*caught up*" was translated into the Latin Vulgate as *rapturo*, which means to seize by force, and from it we get the words 'rapture' and 'rape'. Definitely not the picture a Bride or Groom wants to promote. But the Greek word *harpazo* has similar connotations: to seize or take by force (as soldiers did to Jesus and Paul), to pluck or to pull, or to catch away. It is the last definition which is most fitting to the transport we will encounter, much as Jesus did at His ascension (Revelation 12:5). How we get transported to Jesus is not as important as actually meeting Him. 'Meet' (*apentesis*) means to officially welcome a newly arriving dignitary. Jesus used this word in the parable of the virgins who "*went forth to meet the bridegroom*" (Matthew 25:1); a more suitable picture for the Bride welcoming King Jesus.

"Taken" to Jesus

> *But as the days of Noe were, so shall also the coming of the Son of man be. For as in the days that were before the flood they were eating and drinking, marrying and giving in marriage, until the day that Noe entered into the ark, And knew not until the flood came, and took them all away; so shall also the coming of the Son of man be. Then shall two be in the field; the one shall be <u>taken</u>, and the other left. Two*

women shall be grinding at the mill; the one shall be <u>taken</u>, and the other left. (Matthew 24:37-41)

Noah's world was acting as if everything was normal. When Noah's flood *'took'* the wicked away, that word is *airo*, and means to take or put away. But 'taken' is *paralambano* meaning "'to receive near', associate with oneself (in any familiar or intimate act or relation); receive, take unto, take with" (*Strong's*). The same Greek word is used by Jesus and translated *'receive'* in the following verse.

And if I go and prepare a place for you, I will come again, and <u>receive</u> you to myself; that where I am, there you may be also. (John 14:3)

It is Christ's Bride who are taken away from the wicked and received by Jesus. Until that day, we await Christ's return, His appearing, and His revealing. In Luke's version, Jesus gives a stern warning not to look back at your old life like Lot's wife, and lose eternal life. He also emphasized the destruction of the wicked on the day of the Lord.

For as the lightning, that lightens out of the one part under heaven, shines to the other part under heaven; so shall also the Son of man be in his day. . . . And as it was in the days of Noe, so shall it be also in the days of the Son of man. They did eat, they drank, they married wives, they were given in marriage, until the day that Noe entered into the ark, and the flood came, and destroyed them all. Likewise also as it was in the days of Lot; they did eat, they drank, they bought, they sold, they planted, they built; But the same day that Lot went out of Sodom it rained fire and brimstone from heaven, and destroyed them all. Even thus shall it be in the day when the Son of man is revealed. <u>In that day, he which shall be on the housetop, and his stuff in the house, let him not come down to take it away: and he that is in the field, let him likewise not return back. Remember Lot's wife. Whoever shall seek to save his life shall lose it; and whoever shall lose his life shall preserve it</u>. I tell you, in that night there shall be two men in one bed; the one shall be taken, and the other shall be left. Two women shall be grinding together; the one shall be taken, and the other left. Two men shall be in the field; the one shall be taken, and the other left. And they answered and said to him, Where, Lord? And he said to them, Wherever the body is, thither will the eagles be gathered together. (Luke 17:24-37)

Jesus also answered His disciples' question that His coming would be as obvious as vultures circling a corpse.

Christ's Return, the Second Coming

Jesus described His coming like lightning that streaks across the sky (Matthew 24:27). The description in Thessalonians includes clouds, as did His ascension (Acts 1:9-11). The *'coming'* is *parousia* in Greek meaning advent, return, coming, or presence. During Jesus' time, it also had the connotation of the arrival of a King.

> *For what is our hope, or joy, or crown of rejoicing? Are not even you in the presence of our Lord Jesus Christ at his coming? (1 Thessalonians 2:19)*
>
> *And now, little children, abide in him; that, when he shall appear, we may have confidence, and not be ashamed before him at his coming. (1 John 2:28)*

Christ's Appearing, "that Blessed Hope"

> *For the grace of God that brings salvation has appeared to all men, Teaching us that, denying ungodliness and worldly lusts, we should live soberly, righteously, and godly, in this present world; <u>Looking for that blessed hope, and the glorious appearing of the great God and our Savior Jesus Christ</u>. (Titus 2:11-13)*

'Appeared' and 'appearing' are *epiphaneia* (from which we get 'epiphany') and means brightness and a manifestation, that is, an advent of Christ (past or future). This passage as well as 1 Timothy 2:14-15 command us to live righteously as we await Christ's appearing, because our works will also make an appearance on that day and be judged (1 Corinthians 3:11-15) and rewarded.

> *I charge you therefore before God, and the Lord Jesus Christ, who shall judge the quick and the dead at his appearing and his kingdom; Preach the word; be instant in season, out of season; reprove, rebuke, exhort with all long-suffering and doctrine. . . . I have fought a good fight, I have finished my course, I have kept the faith: From now on there is laid up for me a crown of righteousness, which the Lord, the righteous judge, shall give me at that day: and not to me only, but to all them also that love his appearing. (2 Timothy 4:1-2, 7-8)*

Christ's Revelation, the Apocalypse

> *Seeing it is a righteous thing with God to recompense tribulation to them that trouble you; And to you who are troubled rest with us, when the Lord Jesus shall be revealed from heaven with his mighty angels, In flaming fire taking vengeance on them that know not God, and that obey not the gospel of our Lord Jesus Christ: Who shall be punished with everlasting destruction from the presence of the Lord, and from the glory of his power; When he shall come to be glorified in his saints, and to be admired in all them that believe (because our testimony among you was believed) in that day. (2 Thessalonians 1:6-10)*

The Greek *apokalusis* translated revealed and revelation is where we get the word 'apocalypse'. There is a consistent theme of tribulation of the righteous prior to Christ's revelation, and judgment upon the wicked at His revealing. Christian's have been encountering persecution and tribulation since the time of Christ. But our faith's motivation is Jesus' love of us and our love of Jesus.

Who are kept by the power of God through faith to salvation ready to be revealed in the last time. Wherein you greatly rejoice, though now for a season, if need be, you are in heaviness through manifold temptations: That the trial of your faith, being much more precious than of gold that perishes, though it be tried with fire, might be found to praise and honor and glory at the appearing of Jesus Christ: Whom having not seen, you love; in whom, though now you see him not, yet believing, you rejoice with joy unspeakable and full of glory: Receiving the end of your faith, even the salvation of your souls. . . . Why gird up the loins of your mind, be sober, and hope to the end for the grace that is to be brought to you at the revelation of Jesus Christ; As obedient children, not fashioning yourselves according to the former lusts in your ignorance: But as he which has called you is holy, so be you holy in all manner of conversation. (1 Peter 1:5-9, 13-15)

And from Jesus Christ, who is the faithful witness, and the first begotten of the dead, and the prince of the kings of the earth. To him that loved us, and washed us from our sins in his own blood, And has made us kings and priests to God and his Father; to him be glory and dominion for ever and ever. Amen. (Revelation 1:5-6)

From pre-trib. to post-trib.

I know a post-tribulation rapture is a very bitter pill for many to swallow. Thoughts beginning, "How could a loving God . . ." immediately come to mind. We've been taught that the Bride would be raptured before the Great Tribulation began.

The pre-tribulation rapture theory wasn't contrived until 500 AD. It was a Catholic invention first appearing under the name pseudo-Ephraim, and later promoted by Jesuit priests to keep Protestants from calling the Pope, the Antichrist. They deduced if a rapture of the church occurs before the Antichrist declares himself deity in the Temple, they could no longer accuse the pope of being That Wicked One. It was popularized by John Darby in the early 1840's.

In 1830 *Principles of Geology* was written by Charles Lyell espousing the new idea that the great canyons were produced over periods of thousands of years (uniformitarianism) instead of at the cataclysm of Noah's flood. These new 'geologists' continued to attack every historical fact of Holy Scripture including fulfilled prophecies. In 1886, Rev. E. B. Pusey published nine lectures titled *Daniel, the Prophet*, upholding creation and the traditional view that Daniel's seventy week prophecy was fulfilled in Christ's first coming, and there was no future period of seven years.

In 1873 a Greek document was discovered titled *Didache*, which means "The Teaching". The longer title is "The Teaching of the Twelve Apostles". The last chapter of the *Didache* deals with end-times and correlates with Matthew 24:29-31. [This English translation is by Charles Hoole.]

16:6 <u>And then shall appear the signs of the truth; first the sign of the appearance in heaven, then the sign of the sound of the trumpet, and thirdly the resurrection of the dead</u>
16:7 -- not of all, but as it has been said, "The Lord shall come and all his saints with him";
16:8 then shall the world behold the Lord coming on the clouds of heaven.

Eusebius quotes the Didache in 324 AD. Most scholars believe it was written in the first century and truly contains The Teaching of the Apostles. The *Didache* is not inspired, but is valuable as an early church document which showed what the apostles taught. But we have a "*more sure word*" (2 Peter 1:19-21).

Tribulation is NOT God's Wrath

The wrath of God is for unbelievers. But that doesn't mean believers are completely unaffected as God's wrath is poured out upon unbelievers. When God saved Noah and seven others on the ark, they spent 100 years of their lives building that ark while being ridiculed and scorned by the unbelievers who were wicked, corrupt, and violent (Genesis 6:5, 11-14). They spent 150 days on turbulent seas, and the remainder of the year cooped up with smelly animals waiting for the ground to dry. Then they had to build and do everything from scratch by themselves. Noah's family demonstrated a lot of obedient preparation beforehand, and trust in God's love and provision during and after the flood.

When God brought out Lot and his daughters before He destroyed Sodom and Gomorrah, they lost their home, and their wife/mother, and their livelihood. They suffered trials and tribulations in the process of God pouring out His wrath upon unbelievers.

For if God spared not the angels that sinned, but cast them down to hell, and delivered them into chains of darkness, to be reserved to judgment; And spared not the old world, but saved Noah the eighth person, a preacher of righteousness, bringing in the flood on the world of the ungodly; And turning the cities of Sodom and Gomorrha into ashes condemned them with an overthrow, making them an ensample to those that after should live ungodly; And delivered just Lot, vexed with the filthy conversation of the wicked: (For that righteous man dwelling among them, in seeing and hearing, vexed his righteous soul from day to day with their unlawful deeds;) <u>The Lord knows how to deliver the godly out of temptations, and to reserve the unjust to the day of judgment to be punished</u>. (2 Peter 2:4-9)

These godly ones were taken out of the path of God's judgment upon unbelievers (Jude 1:6-7), but they suffered great loss in the process prior to, during, and after the judgment. And we know these things are written to prepare us so that we don't lose heart in the process. "*For whatever things were written aforetime were written for our learning, that we through patience and comfort of the scriptures might have hope*" (Romans 15:4).

Moses and the Hebrew slaves lived through ten plagues until they were delivered and they saw their enemies destroyed. For seven days the bloody Nile river stank of rotting fish, and then heaps of dead frogs stank. Then the lice came, but then God made a distinction between the Hebrews in Goshen and the Egyptians (Exodus 8:22-23), and the flies and remaining plagues did not touch His chosen people. The Great Tribulation will be similar with God making a distinction between believers and unbelievers. God kept Moses and the Hebrews safe while He poured out His wrath upon the Egyptians, and Moses wrote a promise from the Lord regarding similar situations in the future.

> *When you are in <u>tribulation</u>, and all these things are come on you, <u>even in the latter days</u>, if you turn to the LORD your God, and shall be obedient to his voice; (For the LORD your God is a merciful God;) he will not forsake you, neither destroy you, nor forget the covenant of your fathers which he swore to them. (Deuteronomy 4:30-31)*

Summary

The doctrine that the Church will not go through God's wrath poured out upon unbelievers on the earth is a false teaching; both the Old and New Testaments state otherwise. The resurrection of the dead occurs seconds prior to the rapture of those still alive at Christ's coming. There is only one second coming of Christ, and hence, only one rapture. There is scriptural precedence for knowing the exact day of rapture.

> *I charge you therefore before God, and the <u>Lord Jesus Christ, who shall judge the quick and the dead at his appearing and his kingdom</u>;* **Preach** *the word; be instant in season, out of season;* **reprove, rebuke, exhort** <u>*with all long-suffering and doctrine.*</u> *For the time will come when they will not endure sound doctrine; but after their own lusts shall they heap to themselves teachers, having itching ears; And they shall turn away their ears from the truth, and shall be turned to fables. But* **watch** *you in all things,* **endure** *afflictions, do the* **work** *of an evangelist, make full proof of your ministry. (2 Timothy 4:1-5)*

Correct doctrine is vital. If you really care for someone, you will put your relationship at risk in order for them to understand the truth of God's Word and Christ's coming judgment. Christians may lose their faith when they find themselves going through the Great Tribulation. They may give up hope in the promise of the Lord's coming, and choose to worship the Beast instead, especially when choosing not to worship the Beast will mean their death. That's when belief in a physical resurrection with Jesus is really put to the test. And Scripture promises that those martyred during the Great Tribulation will reign with Christ 1,000 years (Rev. 20:4-6).

Time-line of the "Last Days"

Vertical AD time-line spans "three days" in which "*a thousand years as one day*":

First Fruits Resurrection of Jesus Christ and saints in Jerusalem (33 AD)
                1,000 years (one day)
                1,000 years (two days)
Christ's 2nd coming and 1st Resurrection of dead saints and rapture of those saints alive
                1,000 years Millennial Reign (three days)
2nd Resurrection of all dead, the Great White Throne Judgment and the 2nd Death

70 X 7
(Daniel 9)

Then came Peter to him, and said, Lord, how oft shall my brother sin against me, and I forgive him? till seven times? Jesus saith unto him, I say not unto thee, Until seven times: but, Until seventy times seven. (Matthew 18:21-22)

In Greek, seven and seventy just refer to the numbers. In Hebrew, seven is *sheh'-bah*, meaning the number, or seven times; but by implication, a week, and a sacred full period. A related word for taking an oath, *shaw-bah'* means to be complete, to seven oneself, that is, to swear as if by repeating a declaration seven times. *Shib-eem'* is seventy in Hebrew. "*Seventy times seven*" and "*seventy weeks*" refer to the prophecy regarding the forgiveness of Israel's sins through the coming Messiah in Daniel 9. Jesus used the prophetic number of "*seventy times seven*" to let Peter know He was the fulfillment of punishment for sins. To better understand that prophecy, we need to look at what Daniel was studying.

In the first year of Darius the son of Ahasuerus, of the seed of the Medes, which was made king over the realm of the Chaldeans; In the first year of his reign I Daniel understood by books the number of the years, whereof the word of the LORD came to Jeremiah the prophet, that he would accomplish seventy years in the desolations of Jerusalem. And I set my face to the Lord God, to seek by prayer and supplications, with fasting, and sackcloth, and ashes. (Daniel 9:1-3)

The first year of Darius, the Mede, as ruler of the city of Babylon was 538 BC. Daniel and his friends had been deported to Babylon in 605 BC as teen-agers, so 67 years had passed since Jeremiah's prophecy in the first year of Nebuchadnezzar. Daniel was in his seventies or eighties and came to realize there were only three more years left until Jeremiah's prophecy was fulfilled. He might live long enough to go home to Jerusalem.

Jeremiah's Seventy Year Prophecy

*And this whole land shall be a desolation, and an astonishment; and these nations shall serve the king of Babylon **seventy years**. (Jeremiah 25:11-12) For thus said the LORD, That after **seventy years** be accomplished at Babylon I will visit you, and perform my good word toward you, in causing you to return to this place. (Jeremiah 29:10)*

Daniel kept praying and studying and seeking truth. After reading the scroll of Jeremiah, he opened the Torah scrolls, the first five books of the Bible.

Yes, all Israel have transgressed your law, even by departing, that they might not obey your voice; <u>therefore the curse is poured on us, and the oath that is written in the law of Moses</u> the servant of God, because we have sinned against him. And he has confirmed his words, which he spoke against us, and against our judges that judged us, by bringing on us a great evil: for under the whole heaven has not been done as has been done on Jerusalem. <u>As it is written in the law of Moses, all this evil is come on us</u>: yet made we not our prayer before the LORD our God, that we might turn from our iniquities, and understand your truth. (Daniel 9:11-14)

By reading the oath that was written in the law of Moses, he understood God's people were being punished for their sins. And on behalf of his people he repented. Like much prophetic understanding of today, one has to look backward in order to see forward.

Punished Sevenfold for Sins

*And the LORD said to him, Therefore whoever slays Cain, vengeance shall be taken on him **sevenfold**. And the LORD set a mark on Cain, lest any finding him should kill him.(Genesis 4:15)*

*And Lamech said to his wives, Adah and Zillah, Hear my voice; you wives of Lamech, listen to my speech: for I have slain a man to my wounding, and a young man to my hurt. If Cain shall be avenged sevenfold, truly Lamech **seventy and sevenfold**.(Genesis 4:23-24)*

The precedence for being punished sevenfold, or seven times, for sins was established very early with individuals. It is further exemplified in God's dealings with Israel. God did not make idle threats through Moses, but prophecies of how they would be punished for breaking His covenant, which was often followed immediately by deliverance.

And if you shall despise my statutes, or if your soul abhor my judgments, so that you will not do all my commandments, but that you break my covenant: I also will do this to you; I will even appoint over you terror, consumption, and the burning ague, that shall consume the eyes, and cause sorrow of heart: and you shall sow your seed in vain, for your enemies shall eat it. And I will set my face against you, and you shall be slain before your enemies: they that hate you shall reign over you; and you shall flee when none pursues you. (Leviticus 26:15-18)

This was fulfilled after Israel endured 7 years of pillaging and oppression by the Midianites, but God sent Gideon to deliver them (Judges 6).

And if you will not yet for all this listen to me, then <u>I will punish you seven times more for your sins.</u> And I will break the pride of your power; and I will make your *heaven as iron, and your earth as brass: And your strength shall be spent in vain: for your land shall not yield her increase, neither shall the trees of the land yield their fruits. (Leviticus 26:18-20)*

For three and a half years (half of seven) Elijah prayed that it would not rain (James 5:17) to demonstrate God's power and authority to king Ahab (I Kings 17-19). God proved his point on Mount Carmel when He sent fire from heaven to consume Elijah's soaking wet offering. Elijah later found Elisha and discipled him.

*And if you walk contrary to me, and will not listen to me; I will bring <u>seven times more plagues on you according to your sins</u>. I will also send wild beasts among you, **which shall rob you of your children**, and destroy your cattle, and make you few in number; and your high ways shall be desolate. (Leviticus 26:21-22)*

Some children were mocking Elisha, and he cursed them, and a bear came out of the woods and ate 42 of them (2 Kings 2:23-24). Plague, *nega*, can mean a blow (infliction) or a spot (leprosy).

*And if you will not be reformed by me by these things, but will walk contrary to me; Then will I also walk contrary to you, and <u>will punish you yet seven times for your sins.</u> And I will bring a **sword** on you, that shall avenge the quarrel of my covenant: and when you are gathered together within your cities, I will send the pestilence among you; and you shall be delivered into the hand of the enemy. (Leviticus 26:23-25)*

God brought Shishak (Sheshonk) from Egypt to humble king Rehoboam who had forsaken Jehovah (2 Chronicles 12:5-9). Shishak conquered the outlying cities, and took away the treasures of Jerusalem and made them a vassal state.

*And when I have broken the staff of your bread, ten women shall bake your bread in one oven, and they shall deliver you your bread again by weight: and you shall eat, and not be satisfied. And if you will not for all this listen to me, but walk contrary to me; Then I will walk contrary to you also in fury; and I, even I, <u>will chastise you seven times for your sins.</u> And **you shall eat the flesh of your sons**, and the flesh of your daughters shall you eat. (Leviticus 26:26-29)*

Syria attacked Israel during the days of Elisha. They laid siege to Samaria creating such a famine that women boiled and ate their children, but the lepers of the gate were the first to discover God had vanquished their enemies (2 Kings 6-7).

*And I will destroy your high places, and cut down your images, and cast your carcasses on the carcasses of your idols, and my soul shall abhor you. And <u>I will make your cities waste, and bring your **sanctuaries** to desolation</u>, and I will not smell the smell of your sweet odors. And I will bring the land into desolation: and your enemies which dwell therein shall be astonished at it. And I will scatter you* *among the heathen, and will draw out a sword after you: and your land shall be desolate, and your cities waste. <u>Then shall the land enjoy her sabbaths, as long as it lies desolate</u>, and you be in your enemies' land; even then shall the land rest, and enjoy her sabbaths. As long as it lies desolate it shall rest; because it did not rest in your sabbaths, when you dwelled on it. And on them that are left alive of you I will send a faintness into their hearts in the lands of their enemies; and the sound of a shaken leaf shall chase them; and they shall flee, as fleeing from a sword; and they shall fall when none pursues. And they shall fall one on another, as it were before a sword, when none pursues: and you shall have no power to stand before your enemies. And you shall perish among the heathen, and the land of your enemies shall eat you up. And they that are left of you shall pine away in their iniquity in your enemies' lands; and also in the iniquities of their fathers shall they pine away with them. (Leviticus 26:30-39)*

Even before there were any sanctuaries (plural, not just one) in Israel, God foretells they will be built and destroyed due to Israel's sins. Israel was not obedient in allowing the land to rest each seventh year. Trusting God to provide double manna on the 6th day for the 7th day was a easier than trusting God to double the harvest in the 6th year and not sow in the 7th year.

Assyria attacked the northern tribes of Israel and deported them. Tiglath-Pileser III deported Israelis to northern Assyria during 734-732 BC. Shalmaneser V and Sargon II deported Israelis to the areas surrounding Gozam (and the river Gozan) and Nineveh during 729-724 BC. Sargon II deported another wave of Israelis to Persia (Media) during 716-715 BC. Shalmaneser V deported a final wave of Israelis to the cities of Halah and Habor, the river Gozan, and the cities of Media in 702 BC (2 Kings 17:6). Then in 605 BC Nebuchadnezzar's armies deported choice children of Judah and Benjamin to Babylon along with Jehoiakim's family.

> 734-702 Ten tribes deported to Assyria
> 605 Choice children and Jehoiakim's family deported to Babylon
> 597 Babylonian siege of Jerusalem; Ezekiel & 10,000 deported
> 586 Jerusalem & Temple burned
> 538 Babylon surrenders to Cyrus

If they shall confess their iniquity, and the iniquity of their fathers, with their trespass which they trespassed against me, and that also they have walked contrary to me; And that I also have walked contrary to them, and <u>have brought them into the land of their enemies</u>; if then their uncircumcised hearts be humbled, and they then accept of the punishment of their iniquity: Then will I remember my covenant with Jacob, and also my covenant with Isaac, and also my covenant with Abraham will I remember; and I will remember the land. (Leviticus 26:27-42)

Jesus is the New Covenant

If God's people would confess their iniquity and accept the punishment of their iniquity, then God would remember His covenant with them, and provide a new covenant. As Daniel continued to read in Jeremiah, he would have read the following:

*Behold, the days come, said the LORD, that I will make a **new covenant** with the house of Israel, and with the house of Judah: Not according to the covenant that I made with their fathers in the day that I took them by the hand to bring them out of the land of Egypt; which my covenant they broke, although I was an husband to them, said the LORD: <u>But this shall be **the covenant** that I will make with the house of Israel; After those days, said the LORD, I will put my law in their inward parts, and write it in their hearts; and will be their God, and they shall be my people.</u> (Jeremiah 31:31-33)*

The Messiah is that new covenant. Before He died Jesus took the cup of redemption at Passover and told His disciples, *"this is my blood of the new testament, which is shed for many for the remission of sins"* (Matthew 26:28). The word 'covenant' in the passages above and below is *b'reeth*, from the root word 'to create'; but it means cutting, as a compact made by passing between cut pieces of flesh. The first covenant (*b'reeth*) God made was with Noah (Genesis 6:18; 9:9-13), and the sign of His promise was the rainbow. The signs of God's new covenant would be His Spirit within them teaching them His truth, and miracles of sight to the blind and deliverance from darkness; Light within and without.

*Behold my servant, whom I uphold; my elect, in whom my soul delights; I have put my spirit on him: he shall bring forth judgment to the Gentiles. . . . I the LORD have called you in righteousness, and will hold your hand, and will keep you, and <u>give you for a **covenant** of the people</u>, for a light of the Gentiles; To open the blind eyes, to bring out the prisoners from the prison, and them that sit in darkness out of the prison house. (Isaiah 42:1, 6-7)*

Daniel was fasting in sackcloth and ashes, repenting and interceding for his people. He was not seeking a prophecy, he was seeking to be obedient to the prophecy that was in the midst of being fulfilled in the next three years if his people would acknowledge their sin and accept their just punishment.

O Lord, hear; O Lord, forgive; O Lord, listen and do; defer not, for your own sake, O my God: for your city and your people are called by your name. And <u>whiles I was speaking, and praying, and confessing my sin and the sin of my people Israel</u>, and presenting my supplication before the LORD my God for the holy mountain of my God; Yes, whiles I was speaking in prayer, even <u>the man Gabriel</u>, whom I had seen in the vision at the beginning, being caused to fly swiftly, touched me about the time of the evening oblation. And he informed me, and talked with me, and <u>said, O Daniel, I am now come forth to give you skill and understanding</u>. At the beginning *of your supplications the commandment came forth, and I am come to show you; for you are greatly beloved: therefore understand the matter, and consider the vision. (Daniel 9:19-23)*

In response to Daniel's humble confession regarding Jeremiah's prophecy of 70 years of punishment, God sent the angel Gabriel to encourage him and give him a new vision of 70 weeks which would fulfill all of Israel's punishment.

Daniel's 70 Week Prophecy

*Seventy weeks are determined on your people and on your holy city, to finish the transgression, and to make an end of sins, and to make reconciliation for iniquity, and to bring in everlasting righteousness, and to seal up the vision and prophecy, and to anoint the most Holy. Know therefore and understand, that from the going forth of the commandment to restore and to build Jerusalem to the Messiah the Prince shall be seven weeks, and three score and two weeks: the street shall be built again, and the wall, even in troublous times. And after three score and two weeks shall Messiah be **cut off**, but not for himself: and the people of the prince that shall come shall destroy the city and the sanctuary; and the end thereof shall be with a flood, and to the end of the war desolations are determined. And he shall confirm the **covenant** with many for one week: and in the middle of the week he shall cause the sacrifice and the oblation to cease, and for the overspreading of abominations he shall make it desolate, even until the consummation, and that determined shall be poured on the desolate. (Daniel 9:24-27)*

When it says *"after threescore and two weeks"*, that also implies after the initial seven weeks as well. The phrase *"cut off"* in Hebrew is *kawrath*, meaning to cut, specifically to **covenant**; that is, to make an alliance or bargain, originally by cutting flesh and passing between the pieces as God did with Abram (Genesis 15). Jesus was also the sin offering (Leviticus 5:6 and Isaiah 53:10). 'Covenant' is *b'reeth*, from a sense of cutting, meaning a compact. Thereby the Messiah who is to be *"cut off"* is linked with the person making the covenant; otherwise Daniel would have used a different word which simply meant to die. Daniel would have read of death prior to a new covenant in the Torah. 'He' is the Messiah who will prevail as the new covenant. [This is the traditional interpretation which was held until 'scientific' theologians, duped by evolution, began to attack the historicity of the Bible. See introduction to "Daniel the Prophet" by E. B. Pusey, 1886.] The word to 'confirm' the covenant is *gawbar*, meaning to be strong, to prevail, to be great, and to be valiant. Jesus gave His life willingly; it was a complete victory.

The first time God made a covenant, He 'cut off' the people.

And I will establish my covenant [b'reeth] with you, neither shall all flesh be cut off [kawrath] any more by the waters of a flood; neither shall there any more be a flood to destroy the earth. (Genesis 9:11 with additions)

Christ's Sacrifice is New Covenant

*Blotting out the handwriting of ordinances that was against us, which was contrary to us, and took it out of the way, nailing it to his cross; And having spoiled principalities and powers, he made a show of them openly, **triumphing** over them in it. (Colossians 2:14-15)*

Because Christ's atonement was the final one needed on God's mercy seat of the ark of the **covenant**, the veil before the ark of the covenant was rent in two (Mark 15:37-38); and the "*oblations ceased*" because the priests dared not enter the Temple (Hebrews 9).

The Purposes of the Prophecy

Seventy weeks are determined on your people and on your holy city, to finish the transgression, and to make an end of sins, and to make reconciliation for iniquity, and to bring in everlasting righteousness, and to seal up the vision and prophecy, and to anoint the most Holy. (Daniel 9:24)

This prophecy concerns Jews and Jerusalem. 'Transgression' is *pesha*, which can be translated national revolt or rebellion. "*To finish the transgression*" could mean to end their sinful practice of going after other gods. One way to end national rebellion is to remove the nation. Jesus predicted the end of the Temple and Jerusalem within a generation, which both occurred in 70 AD, and the diaspora (dispersion of Jews) followed. After their revolt, the Romans laid a heavy tax on Jews throughout the empire, so many Jews fled to far-away countries.

Jesus' atonement for our sins on the cross and His resurrection fulfilled "*to make an end of sins, and to make reconciliation for iniquity, and to bring in everlasting righteousness*". 'Seal' is *kawtham*, meaning to close, mark, or end in "*to seal up the vision and prophecy*". Jesus fulfilled hundreds of prophecies regarding His first coming. "*To anoint the most Holy*" refers to Jesus Himself. Messiah was anointed before His death (Mark 14:3-9); and as High Priest, He sent believers His Holy Spirit.

To foretell of the Antichrist and the Great Tribulation is not listed in the purposes. To have a peace treaty with the nation of Israel is not a purpose since this prophecy specifies it has to do with the city of Jerusalem, not the land of Israel. This prophecy has been misinterpreted to imply a seven year treaty with Israel which is broken after three and a half years by the Antichrist.

In 1830 *Principles of Geology* was written by Charles Lyell espousing the new idea that the great canyons were produced over periods of thousands of years (uniformitarianism) instead of at the cataclysm of Noah's flood. These new 'geologists' continued to attack every historical fact of Holy Scripture including fulfilled prophecies. In 1886, Rev. E. B. Pusey published nine lectures titled *Daniel, the Prophet*, upholding creation and the traditional view that Daniel's seventy week prophecy was fulfilled in Christ's first coming, and there was no future period of seven years.

God's Commandment Marks Prophecy's Beginning

At the beginning of your supplications the commandment came forth, and I am come to show you; for you are greatly beloved: therefore understand the matter, and consider the vision. Know therefore and understand, that from the going forth of the commandment to restore and to build Jerusalem to the Messiah the Prince shall be seven weeks, and three score and two weeks: the street shall be built again, and the wall, even in troublous times.(Daniel 9:23, 25)

'Commandment' in these verses is the Hebrew word *dabar*, meaning word, matter or cause, and can be translated decree. Throughout the book of Daniel it is ascribed to words spoken by God and angels. In Daniel 9:23 it is ascribed to the angel giving him understanding. When Daniel refers to a decree of Nebuchadnezzar, he uses the Chaldean word *teh-ame* (*te-em* in Hebrew). The same is true of Ezra: the commandment of God is *dabar*, and the commandments of men are *te-em*.

And the elders of the Jews built, and they prospered through the prophesying of Haggai the prophet and Zechariah the son of Iddo. And they built, and finished it, according to the commandment [dabar] *of the God of Israel, and according to the commandment* [te-em] *of Cyrus, and Darius, and Artaxerxes king of Persia. (Ezra 6:14 clarification added)*

The Decrees of Men are Noteworthy

Cyrus

That confirms the word of his servant, and performs the counsel of his messengers; that said to Jerusalem, You shall be inhabited; and to the cities of Judah, You shall be built, and I will raise up the decayed places thereof: That said to the deep, Be dry, and I will dry up your rivers: <u>*That said of Cyrus, He is my shepherd, and shall perform all my pleasure: even saying to Jerusalem, You shall be built; and to the temple, Your foundation shall be laid.*</u> *(Isaiah 44:27-28)*

I have raised him [Cyrus] *up in righteousness, and I will direct all his ways: he shall build my city, and he shall let go my captives, not for price nor reward, said the LORD of hosts. (Isaiah 45:13)*

Isaiah prophesied about Cyrus 150 years before he was born. Daniel interpreted Nebuchadnezzar's dream about the Medes and Persians (Cyrus) conquering the Babylonian kingdom 67 years in advance. Cyrus defeats Babylon in 538 BC, and made his decree to rebuild the Temple in Jerusalem in 535 BC.

And them that had escaped from the sword carried he away to Babylon; where they were servants to him and his sons until the reign of the kingdom of Persia: To fulfill *the word of the LORD by the mouth of Jeremiah, until the land had enjoyed her sabbaths: for as long as she lay desolate she kept sabbath, to fulfill three score and ten years. Now in the first year of Cyrus king of Persia, that the word of the LORD spoken by the mouth of Jeremiah might be accomplished, the LORD stirred up the spirit of Cyrus king of Persia, that he made a proclamation throughout all his kingdom, and put it also in writing, saying, <u>Thus said Cyrus king of Persia, All the kingdoms of the earth has the LORD God of heaven given me; and he has charged me to build him an house in Jerusalem, which is in Judah.</u> Who is there among you of all his people? The LORD his God be with him, and let him go up. (2 Chronicles 36:20-23)*

Darius Hytaspes I

Ezra (6:3-12) records a divine decree was issued by God in the 2nd year of Darius I (519 BC) commanding Joshua and Zerubabbel to restart construction on the Temple and Jerusalem. These divine commands were witnessed by the two prophets Haggai (Haggai 1:1 - 2:9) and Zechariah.

Therefore thus said the LORD; I am returned to Jerusalem with mercies: my house shall be built in it, said the LORD of hosts, and a line shall be stretched forth on Jerusalem. (Zechariah 1:16)

Artaxerxes Longimanus

Ezra (7:12-26) records a decree by Artaxerxes Longimanus in his seventh year (467 BC) to provide articles for the Temple. Nehemiah (2:4-9) records a decree to rebuild Jerusalem by Artaxerxes Longimanus in his 20th year (454 BC). Thucydides stated Artaxerxes began to reign with his father in Xerxes' 12th year, when Artaxerxes was 16 years old. [See Hengstenberg's *Messianic Predictions in the Prophets*, p.222-240.]

Rulers of Persia	Leaders in Jerusalem
Cyrus 539-530	Zerubbabel, governor 535-515
Darius, the Mede 538	Haggai, prophet 535-513
Cambyses II 529-522	Zechariah, prophet 535-513
	Jeshua, high priest 515-483
Darius I Hystaspis 521-486	Joiakim, high priest 483-458
Xerxes 486-475	
Artaxerxes 474-424	Ezra, governor 467-455
(9 years as co-king with Xerxes)	
	Nehemiah, governor 454-443
Darius II Nothus 423-404	Ezra, priest 454-443

Nehemiah and Ezra worked together with the people to "*rebuild*" Jerusalem. In only 52 days the wall was completed (Neh. 6:15). For twelve years (Nehemiah 13:6) they labored. In the thirteenth year Nehemiah returned and gave many commands in order to "*restore*" the proper function of the city. It may have been another 36 years until the roads ("*street*") of commerce were reestablished, for a total of 49 years ("*seven weeks*"). Then after another 434 years (62 weeks), for a total of 483 years, "*Messiah the Prince*" is baptized.

Artaxerxes decree in his 20th year to Nehemiah to rebuild the wall of Jerusalem was in the year 454 BC, and 483 years later comes "*Messiah the Prince*". It is not unreasonable for man's decree and God's commandment to coincide. [Using Hebrew regnal years from Tishri to Tishri would begin each reign in the seventh month of the previous year. Hence Artaxerxes' reign would be 475/474 to 425/424. His 20th year would be 455/454. Then 483-455=28 and then add a year because there was no zero year, and come to 29 AD.]

69 Weeks until Messiah the Prince

> *Know therefore and understand, that from the going forth of the commandment to restore and to build Jerusalem to the Messiah the Prince shall be seven weeks, and three score and two weeks: the street shall be built again, and the wall, even in troublous times. And after three score and two weeks shall Messiah be cut off, but not for himself. (Daniel 9:25-26a)* $69 \times 7 = 483$. $483 - 454 = 29$.

The fifteenth year of the reign of Tiberius Caesar was 29 AD. God publicly declared Jesus His Son, the Prince, at His baptism; and the Holy Spirit descended upon Him, anointing Jesus as Messiah (Matthew 3:16-17).

> *Now in the fifteenth year of the reign of Tiberius Caesar, Pontius Pilate being governor of Judaea, and Herod being tetrarch of Galilee, . . . and Caiaphas being the high priests, the word of God came to John the son of Zacharias in the wilderness. . . . Now when all the people were baptized, it came to pass, that Jesus also being baptized, and praying, the heaven was opened, And the Holy Ghost descended in a bodily shape like a dove on him, and a voice came from heaven, which said, You are my beloved Son; in you I am well pleased. (Luke 3:1-2, 21-22)*

Jesus immediately fasts for 40 days after his baptism (Matthew 4:1-2). It was customary to fast 40 days starting on the first day of Elul, which then makes Yom Kippur the fortieth day. The 15th year of Tiberius Caesar was 29 AD. Therefore I surmise Jesus was baptized on Elul 1, 29 AD. After Christ's baptism, John proclaims the purpose of Messiah the Prince as "*the Lamb of God, which takes away the sin of the world*" (John 1:29). Jesus, the covenant, would be "cut off" in the middle of the 70th week, three and a half years later on Passover, April 3, 33 AD. [Pilate's desire to appease Herod Antipas (Luke 23:12) after being accused of not being Caesar's friend (John 19:12) required Christ's crucifixion to be after the death of Sejanus in 31 AD.]

The Second Half of the 70th Week

> *...and the people of the prince that shall come shall destroy the city and the sanctuary; and <u>the end thereof</u> shall be with a flood, and <u>to the end</u> of the war desolations are determined. ... and for the overspreading of abominations he shall make it desolate, <u>even until the consummation</u>, and that determined shall be poured on the desolate. (Daniel 9:26-27 edited)*

Immediately after Christ's death there was no war or destruction of the sanctuary or desolations. But note the underlined phrases which hint of its delay. Moses prophesied desolations and the destruction of sanctuaries because Israel disobeyed God's commands and followed after idols (Leviticus 26), so the war and destruction of the city and sanctuary were already determined because of the 'overspreading' (extremity) of their abominations. Jesus added a time frame of a generation to this prophecy, and concluded with a new prophecy regarding His second coming.

> *Why you be witnesses to yourselves, that you are the children of them which killed the prophets. <u>Fill you up then the measure of your fathers.</u> You serpents, you <u>generation of vipers</u>, how can you escape the damnation of hell? Why, behold, I send to you prophets, and wise men, and scribes: and some of them you shall kill and crucify; and some of them shall you whip in your synagogues, and persecute them from city to city: That on you may come all the righteous blood shed on the earth, from the blood of righteous Abel to the blood of Zacharias son of Barachias, whom you slew between the temple and the altar. Truly I say to you, **All these things** shall come on <u>this generation.</u> O Jerusalem, Jerusalem, you that kill the prophets, and stone them which are sent to you, how often would I have gathered your children together, even as a hen gathers her chickens under her wings, and you would not! Behold, <u>your house is left to you desolate.</u> For I say to you, You shall not see me from now on, till you shall say, Blessed is he that comes in the name of the Lord. (Matthew 23:31-39)*

> *And Jesus went out, and departed from the temple: and his disciples came to him for to show him the buildings of the temple. And Jesus said to them, See you not **all these things**? truly I say to you, **There shall not be left here one stone on another, that shall not be thrown down.** And as he sat on the mount of Olives, the disciples came to him privately, saying, Tell us, when shall **these things** be? and what shall be the sign of your coming, and of the end of the world? ...Now learn a parable of the fig tree; When his branch is yet tender, and puts forth leaves, you know that summer is near: So likewise you, when you shall see **all these things**, know that **it** is near, even at the doors. Truly I say to you, <u>This generation</u> shall not pass, till **all these things** be fulfilled. (Matthew 24:1-3, 32-34)*

Of the Temple buildings, not one stone was left on another because the fire which destroyed the buildings also melted the gold, and so the gold was removed from each of the stones. Jesus used the phrase "*all these things*" to include the Temple buildings and the Temple's destruction and desolation upon that generation. For people born after the flood and the tower of Babel, a generation was forty years (Numbers 32:13). Jerusalem and the Temple were destroyed in 70 AD, and Jesus was crucified in 33 AD (70 - 33 = 37); which was within that generation to whom He spoke. [See the time-line in the Appendix.]

The First Jewish-Roman War (66 - 73 AD)

On Pentecost, Peter exhorted the Jews to "Save yourselves from this untoward generation" (Acts 2:40b). Thirty years later, Emperor Nero led the first persecution of Christians after blaming the great fire of Rome on them in the summer of 64 AD. The summer of 67 AD Peter and Paul were martyred in Rome. The Jewish rebellion began and ended at Masada on the Dead Sea. In August of 66, Jewish revolutionaries overtook the Roman garrison of Masada. In 73 the Jews committed suicide during the Roman siege of Masada rather than be captured. But most of the battles took place far from Masada.

According to historians Flavius Josephus and James Ussher, the Jewish revolt began at Caesarea in 66 AD. It was provoked by Greeks sacrificing birds in front of a local synagogue while the Greek-speaking Roman garrison sat and watched. The son of the high priest ceased sacrifices for Nero at the Temple, and led a successful attack against the Roman garrison stationed in Jerusalem. Cestius Gallus, the legate of Syria, brought 30,000 reinforcements and burned the city of Lydda to restore order. During the feast of tabernacles he marched toward Jerusalem, but was met and soundly defeated by the Jews at the Beth Horon. After more reinforcements arrived, he attacked Jerusalem, and was close to success when he suddenly retreated to Antipatris. Elated with victory, the Jews appointed Josephus (then Joseph, son of Gorion) to command troops in Galilee.

Emperor Nero appointed general Vespasian to replace Gallus and crush the Jewish rebellion. Vespasian made Caesarea his headquarters, and with his son Titus and 60,000 professional soldiers in the Spring of 67, he began to methodically attack the coast and Galilee. By 68 AD Jewish resistance in the north had been crushed.

Joseph was captured the summer of 67 at Jotapata after a siege of forty-seven days. Joseph predicted that Vespasian would become emperor. He was not believed, and spent the next two years in chains in the Roman camp, during which time he began to write about the war. After Nero's death in 68, four emperors died in quick succession and Vespasian became emperor himself in 69. Joseph was freed and adopted into Vespasian's family, the Flavians, and so he became Flavius Josephus.

Before he left for Rome, Vespasian placed his son Titus in charge with four legions. He laid siege to Jerusalem during Passover, which trapped many more people inside than the city could normally provide with food and water. Many who tried to escape were killed or sold into slavery. The Romans annihilated a million in Jerusalem who did not escape, and destroyed the Temple on August 10, 70 AD.

And when you shall see Jerusalem compassed with armies, then know that the desolation thereof is near. Then let them which are in Judaea flee to the mountains; and let them which are in the middle of it depart out; and let not them that are in the countries enter thereinto. <u>For these be the days of vengeance, that all things which are written may be fulfilled.</u> But woe to them that are with child, and to them that give suck, in those days! for there shall be great distress in the land, and wrath on this people. And they shall fall by the edge of the sword, and shall be led away captive into all nations: and Jerusalem shall be trodden down of the Gentiles, until the times of the Gentiles be fulfilled. . . . Truly I say to you, This generation shall not pass away, till all be fulfilled. (Luke 21:20-24, 32)

The word for 'vengeance' is *ekdikesis* which means punishment. These desolations of war upon the Jews and Jerusalem were determined as punishment because of their sins. The desolations of war of the last half of the 70th week was from March/April 67 when Vespasian's troops fought against the Judeans in Galilee to the Temple's destruction on (9th of Av) August 10, 70 AD. This Temple's destruction was on the same exact day the first Temple was destroyed by the Babylonians in 586 BC. Thus was the punishment for past sins completed and the 70 week prophecy of Daniel fulfilled, including a notable detail.

The People of the Prince that shall Come

. . .and <u>the people of the prince that shall come shall destroy the city and the sanctuary</u>; and the end thereof shall be with a flood, and to the end of the war desolations are determined. . . . and for the overspreading of abominations he shall make it desolate, even until the consummation, and that determined shall be poured on the desolate. (Daniel 9:26-27 edited)

Titus led four legions against Jerusalem: V, X, XII, XV. The fifth was composed of Greeks from Bulgaria/Romania. The tenth was composed of Syrians based in Jerusalem. The twelfth and fifteenth legions were composed of Syrians based in Turkey. The people who destroyed the Temple and Jerusalem were mostly Syrians. Titus was born in Rome, and could be called a 'prince' since his father had became emperor. But the *"prince that shall come"* is actually a prophecy within a prophecy; he will be of "*the people*" who "*destroy the city and the sanctuary*".

The *"prince that shall come"* would be Syrian. In the Old Testament prophets, their nemesis is often called "the Assyrian". It was the Assyrians who captured the northern 10 tribes of Israel prior to Babylon capturing Judah in 605. Daniel prophesied of two other abominations which cause desolation, one of which being caused by an army. In the chapter on "Abominations", the leader of that army is the king (former prince) of Syria. Antiochus IV, king of Syria, was a prince who came into Jerusalem with his army and defiled the sanctuary and the city according to other prophecies in Daniel 230 years before the Syrian troops of Titus destroyed it. Antiochus IV was "*the prince that shall come*".

Summary

Daniel recognized he and his people were enduring a prophesied seventy years of banishment for their sins, and that it was almost over. As he studied about this in Jeremiah and the Torah, and repented on behalf of his people, God gave him a new prophecy of a period of seventy weeks for His people and Jerusalem to complete all punishment and forgive all sin. God's command to start the 490 year period corresponds with king Artaxerxes decree in his 20th year to Nehemiah to rebuild Jerusalem. After 483 years Jesus is baptized and declared to be God's anointed Son, the Messiah and Prince; and the Lamb of God, the new covenant. Jesus ministered during the first half of the 70th week, and then was "*cut off*" as the new 'covenant'. The last half of the 70th week occurred within that generation, beginning with Vespasian troops attacking Israel's northern coast and Galilee in the spring of 67 AD, and ending with the siege and destruction of Jerusalem and its Temple in the summer of 70 AD. The entire 70 weeks prophecy has been fulfilled, including its clue regarding the "*prince that shall come*" being Syrian.

Therefore, Christ's Bride should not be anticipating any seven year treaty with Israel nor a seven year period of tribulation.

609 BC	Jehoiakim began to rule Judah (Jeremiah 25:1, 11-12)
605 BC	Jeremiah prophesied Judah would be in captivity for seventy years.
605 BC	Daniel and his friends taken as captives to Babylon. (Daniel 1:1-2)
538 BC	Cyrus conquered Babylonian Empire.
538 BC	Daniel understood from Jeremiah's prophecy that three years were left.
535 BC	Cyrus made his decree to rebuild the Temple in Jerusalem.
519 BC	Darius I commanded Joshua and Zerubabbel to restart Temple construction.
467 BC	Artaxerxes decreed provision of articles for the Temple.
454 BC	Artaxerxes decreed rebuilding of Jerusalem.
453 BC	Wall and gates of Jerusalem rebuilt under Nehemiah in "troublous times"
405 BC	Roads of commerce from Jerusalem restored "*seven weeks*" after 454 decree.
29 AD	After "*three score and two weeks*" or 483 - 454 = 29
29 AD	"*Messiah*" Yeshua, the Son ("*Prince*") of God, was baptized and announced.
33 AD	"*Messiah*" Yeshua was "*cut off*" 3 1/2 years into the seventieth week.
67 AD	Vespasian began squashing Jewish rebellion for next 3 1/2 years.
70 AD	Within a "*generation*" "*desolation*" came to the Temple and Jerusalem.

Prophetic Devolution of the Greek Empire
(Daniel 11)

Also I in the first year of Darius the Mede, even I, stood to confirm and to strengthen him. And now will I show you the truth. (Daniel 11:1-2a)

Because Daniel's prophecies were so intricate and accurate, many scholars deny the fact that he lived during the period of Judah's deportation to Babylon, and say he was merely an historian writing in the first century before Christ. Daniel 11 is a prophetic, political narrative of the history leading up to the time of Messiah. Daniel 9 is the prophetic, religious narrative of the time leading up to and including Messiah and the Temple's destruction. Between is the chapter which records Gabriel's spiritual narrative during Daniel's agonizing three weeks of prayer and fasting. The geo-political background of Daniel 11 is necessary for understanding both fulfilled and yet to be fulfilled prophecies.

Behold, there shall stand up yet three kings in Persia; and the fourth shall be far richer than they all: and by his strength through his riches he shall stir up all against the realm of Grecia. And a mighty king shall stand up, that shall rule with great dominion, and do according to his will. (Daniel 11:2b-3)

Darius, the Mede, was ruling Babylon under Cyrus. The next three kings of Persia were Cyrus' son, Cambyses (529-522 BC), then Darius I Hystaspis (521-486 BC), and then Xerxes (486-475 BC).

Herodotus, an historian who lived in that time, wrote that Xerxes' army amounted to five millions, two hundred and eighty-three thousand, two hundred and twenty men. Besides these, the Carthaginians furnished him with an army of three hundred thousand men, and a fleet of two hundred ships. He led an army against the Greeks of eight hundred thousand men, and twelve hundred and seven ships, with three banks of rowers each. As he marched along, he obliged all the people of the countries through which he passed to join him. Justin wrote, "He had so great an abundance of riches in his kingdom, that although rivers were dried up by his numerous armies, yet his wealth remained unexhausted."

Over 100 years later, a mighty king of Greece did arise. Alexander was tutored by Aristotle. In 338 BC at eighteen he showed himself a valiant warrior in a battle led by his father, king Philip. Two years later, Philip was assassinated, and Alexander became king of Macedon (Greece). The next year Alexander began conquests to extend the boundaries of his kingdom, and by the time he died in 322 BC, he had conquered most of the world known to the Greeks and had earned the title Alexander the Great.

Greek Empire Divided

And when he shall stand up, his kingdom shall be broken, and shall be divided toward the four winds of heaven; and not to his posterity, nor according to his dominion which he ruled: for his kingdom shall be plucked up, even for others beside those. (Daniel 11:4)

From Alexander's death in 323 until 301 BC there were four wars fought over succession which eventually settled into the four kingdoms of Greece, Thrace (Turkey), Syria, and Egypt. Ptolemy became king of Egypt and made the southern kingdom strong. In 320 BC he entered Jerusalem and added Judah to his realm. Seleucus Nicator built up Syria. Syria became the stronger of the two kingdoms. Antioch became Syria's capital, and kings used it in their names. Antiochus I was surnamed Soter, which means Saviour, by the appreciative Gauls (who later became the Galatians).

Egypt and Syria

Ptolemy, king of Egypt, was king of the south. Seleucus I, king of Syria, was king of the north.

And the king of the south [Ptolemy I] shall be strong, and one of his princes [Ptoelmy II]; and he shall be strong above him, and have dominion; his dominion shall be a great dominion. And in the end of years they shall join themselves together; for the king's daughter of the south [Berenice]shall come to the king of the north [Antiochus II] to make an agreement: but she shall not retain the power of the arm; neither shall he stand, nor his arm: but she shall be given up, and they that brought her, and he that begat her, and he that strengthened her in these times. But out of a branch of her roots [Ptolemy III]shall one stand up in his estate, which shall come with an army, and shall enter into the fortress of the king of the north, and shall deal against them, and shall prevail: And shall also carry captives into Egypt their gods, with their princes, and with their precious vessels of silver and of gold; and he shall continue more years than the king of the north. So the king of the south shall come into his kingdom, and shall return into his own land. (Daniel 11:5-9 edited with additions)

To conclude an alliance of peace, Ptolemy II Philadelphus compelled Antiochus II (Theos) of Syria to put aside his own wife, Laodice, and marry his daughter, Berenice. But when Ptolemy died two years later, Antiochus abandoned his Egyptian wife and took back Laodice. In order to gain her revenge, Laodice first had her husband murdered, then brought Bernice and her son by Antiochus to Antioch in Syria, and had them slain.

[Ptolemy II invited 72 Jews to translate the Torah into Greek, which is why it's called the Septuagint (70).] Ptolemy II Philadelphus was succeeded by Ptolemy III Euergetes, *"a branch of her roots,"* Berenice's brother. Ptolemy III invaded and made strong inroads into the Syrian power, laying low all they had built to avenge the murder of his sister. He took people and 40,000 talents of silver and gold vessels.

Seleucus II Callinicus reigned in Syria from 247-226 BC and conducted an unsuccessful expedition against Egypt. His sons, Seleucus III (227-224), and Antiochus III the Great (224-187), jointly continued their father's campaign against Egypt. Seleucus came to an untimely end, but Antiochus III continued to make great and rapid conquests. He defeated the Egyptians at Sidon and was able to penetrate as far south as to attack the Egyptian *"fortress"* at Gaza. Antiochus III took over Palestine in 195 BC.

Antiochus III

But his sons shall be stirred up, and shall assemble a multitude of great forces: and one shall certainly come, and overflow, and pass through: then shall he return, and be stirred up, even to his fortress. And the king of the south [Ptolemy IV] shall be moved with choler, and shall come forth and fight with him, even with the king of the north [Antiochus III]: and he shall set forth a great multitude; but the multitude shall be given into his hand. And when he has taken away the multitude, his heart shall be lifted up; and he shall cast down many ten thousands: but he shall not be strengthened by it. For the king of the north shall return, and shall set forth a multitude greater than the former, and shall certainly come after certain years with a great army and with much riches. And in those times there shall many stand up against the king of the south: also the robbers of your people [Tobias] shall exalt themselves to establish the vision; but they shall fall. So the king of the north shall come, and cast up a mount, and take the most fenced cities: and the arms of the south shall not withstand, neither his chosen people, neither shall there be any strength to withstand. But he that comes against him shall do according to his own will, and none shall stand before him: and he shall stand in the glorious land [Israel], which by his hand shall be consumed. He shall also set his face to enter with the strength of his whole kingdom, and upright ones with him; thus shall he do: and he shall give him the daughter of women [Cleopatra I], corrupting her: but she shall not stand on his side, neither be for him. (Daniel 11:10-17 edited with additions)

Ptolemy IV gathered 73,000 men and 73 elephants. However the army of Antiochus III was even greater -- 72,000 infantry, 6,000 horsemen and 102 elephants -- and at first gained the advantage, but too soon abandoned caution and sought to plunder an enemy not fully conquered and the Egyptian king was victorious. However as Ptolemy was so much addicted to luxurious living, it was of little concern to him to utilize his success to the full and he was not *"strengthened"* by his victory.

Some years later, Antiochus III the Great raised a greater army, and securing better equipment, attained some of the success of his first efforts because the king of Egypt offered no opposition, and after his death various uprisings materially weakened the

Egyptian power and broke it by internal dissension. In Daniel 11:15-16 Antiochus III drove the Egyptians back to Sidon, defeating *"the most fenced cities"*. Liberating the Jews from Egypt, he released them from all taxes for three years, and afterwards from one third of the taxes.

Antiochus III gives his daughter Cleopatra to Ptolemy V for "peace", but instructs her to destroy Egypt (but she didn't). Antiochus III proceeds to attack Greece, but is encountered by Roman armies and defeated in 190, and dies in 187 BC. Cleopatra gives birth to Ptolemy VI and VII and Cleopatra II. [It is Cleopatra VII who has a fling with Marc Antony.]

After this shall he [Antiochus III] turn his face to the isles, and shall take many: but a prince [Scipio] for his own behalf shall cause the reproach offered by him to cease; without his own reproach he shall cause it to turn on him. Then he [Antiochus III] shall turn his face toward the fort [Magnesia] of his own land: but he shall stumble and fall, and not be found. Then shall stand up in his estate a raiser of taxes in the glory of the kingdom: but within few days he shall be destroyed, neither in anger, nor in battle. (Daniel 11:18-20 edited with additions)

Not content with acquiring Egypt, Antiochus III next sought to gain control of the Greek islands. By 196 BC he had a foothold in Thrace which called forth the active resistance of Rome. Lucius Scipio defeated his attack on Thermopylae, beat his commanders in two naval battles as he retreated, and beat him at his own fort in the Battle of Magnesia (190 BC). Scipio administered such a sound defeat that the *"reproach"* or presumptuous boastings of the Syrian were silenced once and for all. Yet Scipio achieved his victory without repaying Antiochus with like boasting -- *"without his own reproach"*.

In his humiliation, Antiochus turned to *"the fort of his own land"* where no trouble or defeat could befall him. So disheartened did he become, in fact, his end was still more ignominious: he *"shall stumble and fall and be found no more"*. History once again vindicated God's foreknowledge of what will be, and constituted sure proof He could also control what He foreknew.

Seleucus IV Philopater (187-176 BC) succeeded Antiochus. Only what bears upon the fortune of Israel is told about this Syrian king who had to pay Rome an enormous annual tribute of 1,000 talents. To this end he sent a *"raiser of taxes"*, probably Heliodorus (II Maccabees 7), to appropriate the rich treasures of the Temple at Jerusalem.

[I have found the historical books of 1 & 2 Maccabees most helpful in filling in historical details. They are included in the Apocrypha in Catholic Bibles, but since the Apocrypha also includes fanciful stories, it is rightly excluded from the Protestant Holy Bible. Christians and non-Christians both agree the books of Maccabees are historically accurate. The author of the books is unknown, but was likely a Jew who lived through the events described or had primary sources available.]

Antiochus IV

> *And in his estate shall stand up a vile person* [Antiochus IV], *to whom they shall not give the honor of the kingdom: but he shall come in peaceably, and obtain the kingdom by flatteries. And with the arms of a flood shall they be overflowed from before him, and shall be broken; yes, also the prince of the covenant* [Jason, the high priest]. *And after the league made with him* [Ptolemy IV] *he* [Antiochus IV and for the next six male pronouns] *shall work deceitfully: for he shall come up, and shall become strong with a small people. He shall enter peaceably even on the fattest places of the province; and he shall do that which his fathers have not done, nor his fathers' fathers; he shall scatter among them the prey, and spoil, and riches: yes, and he shall forecast his devices against the strong holds, even for a time. And he shall stir up his power and his courage against the king of the south with a great army; and the king of the south* [Ptolemy IV and next two male pronouns] *shall be stirred up to battle with a very great and mighty army; but he shall not stand: for they shall forecast devices against him. (Daniel 11:21-25 edited with additions)*

Jason was the high priest of Jerusalem (175-171 B.C.) who encouraged his countrymen to accept Hellenistic ways of life. He allowed Antiochus IV the privilege of authorizing the appointment of future high priests. He allowed the building of a gymnasium in Jerusalem.

The next two paragraphs were gleaned from the Bible commentary (1831) of Adam Clarke. Antiochus IV was at Athens, on his way from Rome, when his father died; and Heliodorus had declared himself king, as had several others. But Antiochus came in peaceably, for he obtained the kingdom by flatteries. He flattered Eumenes, king of Pergamus, and Attalus his brother, and got their assistance. He flattered the Romans, and sent ambassadors to court their favour, and pay them the arrears of the tribute. He flattered the Syrians, and gained their concurrence; and as he flattered the Syrians, so they flattered him, giving him the epithet of Epiphanes-the Illustrious. But he was a vile person, for Polybius says of him,"He ate and drank with the meanest fellows, singing debauched songs."

"*He shall stir up his power*": Antiochus marched against Ptolemy IV, the king of the south, with a great army; and the Egyptian generals had raised a mighty force. But the Egyptian army was defeated. The next campaign Antiochus had greater success; he took Memphis, and made himself master of all Egypt, except Alexandria, (I Maccabees 1:16-19). Ptolemy Macron gave up Cyprus to Antiochus; and the Alexandrians were led to renounce their allegiance to Ptolemy Philometer, and took his younger brother, and made him king in his stead.

Antiochus returned with great riches through Israel to Syria on his way home from Egypt, but antagonistic against the covenant people and their destiny, he plundered the Temple in passing (II Maccabees 5; I Maccabees 1:20ff).

> *Yes, they that feed of the portion of his meat shall destroy him, and his army shall overflow: and many shall fall down slain. And both of these kings' hearts shall be to do mischief, and they shall speak lies at one table; but it shall not prosper: for yet the end shall be at the time appointed. Then shall he return into his land with great riches; and <u>his heart shall be against the holy covenant; and he shall do exploits, and return to his own land</u>. At the time appointed he shall return, and come toward the south; but it shall not be as the former, or as the latter. For the ships of Chittim shall come against him: therefore he shall be grieved, and return, and have <u>indignation against the holy covenant</u>: so shall he do; he shall even return, and have intelligence with them that forsake the holy covenant. <u>And arms shall stand on his part, and they shall pollute the sanctuary of strength, and shall take away the daily sacrifice, and they shall place the **abomination that makes desolate**. And such as do wickedly against the covenant shall he corrupt by flatteries</u>: but the people that do know their God shall be strong, and do exploits. And they that understand among the people shall instruct many: yet they shall fall by the sword, and by flame, by captivity, and by spoil, many days. (Daniel 11:26-33)*

The next three paragraphs were gleaned from the Bible commentary (1831) of Adam Clarke. They who ate his meat betrayed him, so that he was defeated. When Antiochus came to Memphis, he and Philometer had frequent conferences and spoke lies to each other; Antiochus, professed great friendship to his nephew, yet in his heart designed to ruin the kingdom by fomenting the discords which already subsisted between the two brothers. On the other hand, Philometer spoke lies, determined to join his brother against their deceitful uncle. Neither succeeded in his object.

Ships from Chittim took a Roman Senator to Alexandria where he drew a circle about Antiochus and curtly told him he must agree to withdraw his troops before he stepped out of the circle, else meet the Romans in war. Antiochus agreed to withdraw from Egypt immediately with great spoils. That circle became better known as 'the line in the sand'.

En route, Antiochus brought a great army against Jerusalem; took it by storm; he boiled swine's flesh, and sprinkled the temple and the altar with the broth; broke into the holy of holies; took away the golden vessels and other sacred treasures, to the value of one thousand eight hundred talents. This *"abomination that makes desolate"* is also referred to as the *"transgression of desolation"* in Daniel 8:13.

60,000 Slain; 40,000 Enslaved

"Now when there was gone forth a false rumour, as though Antiochus had been dead, Jason took at the least a thousand men, and suddenly made an assault upon the city [Jerusalem] . . . Now when this that was done came to the king's ear, he thought that Judea had revolted: whereupon removing out of Egypt in a furious mind, he took the city by force of arms, And commanded his men of war not to spare such as they met, and to slay such as went up upon the houses. Thus there was killing of young and old, making away of men, women, and children, slaying of virgins and infants. And there were destroyed within the space of three whole days fourscore thousand, whereof forty thousand were slain in the conflict; and no fewer sold than slain." (II Maccabees 5:5a,11-14)

"Lysias chose Ptolemy the son of Dorymenes, and Nicanor and Gorgias, mighty men among the friends of the king, and sent with them forty thousand infantry and seven thousand cavalry to go into the land of Judah and destroy it, as the king had commanded. so they departed with their entire force, and when they arrived they encamped near Emmaus in the plain. When the traders of the region heard what was said to them, they took silver and gold in immense amounts, and fetters, and went to the camp to get the sons of Israel for slaves. And forces from Syria and the land of the Philistines joined with them." (I Maccabees 3:38-41)

And they that understand among the people shall instruct many: yet they shall fall by the <u>sword</u>, and by <u>flame</u>, by <u>captivity</u>, and by <u>spoil</u>, many days. (Daniel 11:33)

"And after two years fully expired the king sent his chief collector of tribute unto the cities of Juda, who came unto Jerusalem with a great multitude, And spake peaceable words unto them, but all was deceit: for when they had given him credence, he fell suddenly upon the city, and **smote** it very sore, and destroyed much people of Israel. And when he had taken the **spoils** of the city, he set it on **fire**, and pulled down the houses and walls thereof on every side. But the women and children took they **captive**, and possessed the cattle. Then builded they the city of David with a great and strong wall, and with mighty towers, and made it a strong hold for them." (I Maccabees 1:29-33)

"So when Antiochus had carried out of the temple a thousand and eight hundred talents, he departed in all haste unto Antiochia, weening in his pride to make the land navigable, and the sea passable by foot: such was the haughtiness of his mind. And he left governors to vex the nation: at Jerusalem, Philip, for his country a Phrygian, and for manners more barbarous than he that set him there; And at Garizim, Andronicus; and besides, Menelaus, who worse than all the rest bare an heavy hand over the citizens, having a malicious mind against his countrymen the Jews. He sent also that detestable ringleader Apollonius with an army of two and twenty thousand, commanding him to slay all those that were in their best age, and to sell the women and the younger sort: Who coming to Jerusalem, and pretending peace, did forbear till the holy day of the sabbath, when taking the Jews keeping holy day, he commanded his men to arm themselves. And so he slew all them that were gone to the celebrating of the sabbath, and running through the city with weapons slew great multitudes." (II Maccabees 5:21-26)

Antiochus IV worshiped Zeus/Jupiter

In Greece, Zeus watched over the famous Olympic games, of which wrestling was a primary sport. All athletes performed in the nude (*gymnos* means naked; hence the name *gymnasium*). Antiochus IV built a gymnasium in Jerusalem and forced the priests to strip and wrestle in his attempt to 'hellenize' the Jews (make them accept Greek culture). Zeus was known as Jupiter in Roman mythology. In both he was the king of the gods and led their warriors to victory.

> *And the king shall do according to his will; and he shall exalt himself, and magnify himself above every god, and shall speak marvelous things against the God of gods, and shall prosper till the indignation be accomplished: for that that is determined shall be done. <u>Neither shall he regard the God of his fathers, nor the desire of women, nor regard any god: for he shall magnify himself above all. But in his estate shall he honor the God of forces: and a god whom his fathers knew not shall he honor with gold, and silver, and with precious stones, and pleasant things.</u> Thus shall he do in the most strong holds with a strange god, whom he shall acknowledge and increase with glory: and he shall cause them to rule over many, and shall divide the land for gain. (Daniel 11:36-39)*

Antiochus introduced worship of Roman Zeus (Jupiter Olympius to the Greeks) which his fathers had not known. Because of his father, Antiochus was held hostage in Rome for several years, and thus learned to admire Zeus. He tricked his older brother into taking his place as hostage, and then took the kingdom of Syria which was rightfully his to rule.

"Not long after this the king sent an old man of Athens to compel the Jews to depart from the laws of their fathers, and not to live after the laws of God: And to pollute also the temple in Jerusalem, and to call it the temple of Jupiter Olympius; and that in Garizim, of Jupiter the Defender of strangers, as they did desire that dwelt in the place. The coming in of this mischief was sore and grievous to the people: For the temple was filled with riot and reveling by the Gentiles, who dallied with harlots, and had to do with women within the circuit of the holy places, and besides that brought in things that were not lawful. The altar also was filled with profane things, which the law forbiddeth. Neither was it lawful for a man to keep sabbath days or ancient fasts, or to profess himself at all to be a Jew." (II Maccabees 6:1-6)

"Nor the desire of women nor any god" refers to the worship of female deities. The primary female deity was Venus, who was known by many names like Nanea.

"For when the leader was come into Persia, and the army with him that seemed invincible, they were slain in the temple of Nanea by the deceit of Nanea's priests. For Antiochus, as though he would marry her, came into the place, and his friends that were with him, to receive money in name of a dowry. Which when the priests of Nanea had set forth, and he was entered with a small company into the compass of the temple, they shut the temple as soon as Antiochus was come in: And opening a privy door of the roof, they threw stones like thunderbolts, and struck down the captain, hewed them in pieces, smote off their heads and cast them to those that were without." (II Maccabees 1:13-16)

Like many of today who keep pressuring Israel to divide its land and capital, Antiochus did *"divide the land for gain"*.

"Lysias was to send a force against them to wipe out and destroy the strength of Israel and the remnant of Jerusalem; he was to banish the memory of them from the place, settle aliens in all their territory, and <u>distribute their land</u>." (I Maccabees 3:35-36)

Proud Antiochus IV is Humbled before his Death

And at the time of the end shall the king of the south push at him: and the king of the north shall come against him like a whirlwind, with chariots, and with horsemen, and with many ships; and he shall enter into the countries, and shall overflow and pass over. He shall enter also into the glorious land, and many countries shall be overthrown: <u>but these shall escape out of his hand, even Edom, and Moab, and the chief of the children of Ammon</u>. He shall stretch forth his hand also on the countries: and the land of Egypt shall not escape. But he shall have power over the treasures of gold and of silver, and over all the precious things of Egypt: <u>and the Libyans and the Ethiopians shall be at his steps</u>. But tidings out of the east and out of the north shall trouble him: therefore he shall go forth with great fury to destroy, and utterly to make away many. And he shall plant the tabernacles of his palace between the seas in the glorious holy mountain; yet he shall come to his end, and none shall help him. (Daniel 11:40-45)

Edom, Moab, and Ammon were in league with Antiochus against the Jews. Antiochus had hired Libyan and Ethiopian mercenaries. Though he did not attack Egypt again, by his threats and show of power he plundered their treasures.

After the battle of Beth-Horon: "Then Judas and his brothers began to be feared, and terror fell upon the Gentiles round about them. His fame reached the king, and the Gentiles talked of the battles of Judas. When king Antiochus heard these reports, he was greatly angered; and he sent and gathered all the forces of his kingdom, a very strong army." (I Maccabees 3:25-27)

Antiochus headed east to Susa, hoping to plunder there as well, but meets his end. 40,000 of his troops under the command of Lysias pitch their tents (tabernacles) in Emmaus, halfway between Jerusalem and the Mediterranean Sea.

"Howbeit he nothing at all ceased from his bragging, but still was filled with pride, breathing out fire in his rage against the Jews, and commanding to haste the journey: but it came to pass that he fell down from his chariot, carried violently; so that having a sore fall, all the members of his body were much pained. And thus he that a little afore _thought he might command the waves of the sea,_ (so proud was he beyond the condition of man) _and weigh the high mountains in a balance_, was now cast on the ground, and carried in an horselitter, shewing forth unto all the manifest power of God. So that the worms rose up out of the body of this wicked man, and whiles he lived in sorrow and pain, his flesh fell away, and the filthiness of his smell was noisome to all his army. And the man, that thought a little afore _he could reach to the stars of heaven_, no man could endure to carry for his intolerable stink. Here therefore, being plagued, he began to leave off his great pride, and to come to the knowledge of himself by the scourge of God, his pain increasing every moment. And when he himself could not abide his own smell, he said these words, It is meet to be subject unto God, and that a man that is mortal should not proudly think of himself if he were God." (II Maccabees 9:7-12)

Time-line of Antiochus IV

170: He killed 60,000 in Judah and sold 40,000 as slaves. He took all the gold and silver from the Temple. He sacrificed a pig on the altar, boiled the meat and forced priests to eat it; those who refused had their tongues cut out.

169: Antiochus built a navy (against the terms of the Peace of Apamea his father signed) and conquered Cyprus and large parts of Egypt and presented himself as protector of Ptolemy VI against his relatives Ptolemy VIII and Cleopatra II.

168: Roman pressure forced Antiochus to stop attack of Egypt. He sent Apollonius with army of 22,000 to collect tribute from Jerusalem. His army kill and capture many, plunder the city and burn it.

167: Antiochus forbad sacrifices, circumcision and other Jewish laws; they were to worship idols and eat pork, or be killed. An idol of Zeus was placed on the altar. Scrolls were burned; their owners, killed.

165: Antiochus captured Artaxias, capital of Armenia.

164: Antiochus' attack on Susa failed. He got reports of Israel and bragged he would make Jerusalem a graveyard of Jews but became ill after being thrown from his chariot. He repented, and sought to restore to the Jews all he had taken, and to let them worship God freely. He died a of a painful, stinky bowel disease.

Antiochus IV began terrorizing Jerusalem's Temple in spring 170, and died in Nov/Dec 164 after writing letters of apology for doing so: a period of 6 2/3 years. 2300 days = 6 2/3 years (6.66) using the 360 day calendar.

The Maccabees

> *Now when they [Syrians] shall fall, they [Jews] shall be helped with a little help [Maccabees]: but many shall join to them with flatteries. And some of them of understanding shall fall, to try them, and to purge, and to make them white, even to the time of the end: because it is yet for a time appointed. (Daniel 11:34-35 edited with additions)*

The Maccabees are a Judean family who stood up to the atrocities of Antiochus Epiphanes. The father was Mattathias, and he had five sons.

"Moreover king Antiochus wrote to his whole kingdom, that all should be one people, And every one should leave his laws: so all the heathen agreed according to the commandment of the king. Yea, many also of the Israelites consented to his religion, and sacrificed unto idols, and profaned the sabbath. . . . And whosoever would not do according to the commandment of the king, he said, he should die. In the selfsame manner wrote he to his whole kingdom, and appointed overseers over all the people, commanding the cities of Juda to sacrifice, city by city." (I Maccabees 1:41-43, 50-51)

"Then Mattathias spake with a loud voice, Though all the nations that are under the king's dominion obey him, and fall away every one from the religion of their fathers, and give consent to his commandments: Yet will I and my sons and my brethren walk in the covenant of our fathers." Mattathias had five sons: Joannan, Simon, Judas, Eleazar, and Jonathan." (I Maccabees 2:19-20)

Mattathias organized open resistance in 167-166, and with his son and successor Judas the Maccabee (hammer) defeated two large and well-equipped armies of Antiochus. Antiochus was busy fighting against the Parthians. He gave Lysias instructions to send a large army against the Jews and exterminate them utterly. But the generals Ptolemæus, Nicanor, and Gorgias, whom Lysias dispatched with large armies against Judah, were defeated one after the other (166-165), and compelled to take refuge upon Philistine soil. Lysias himself (165) was forced to flee to Antioch, having been completely routed by the victorious Jews. Antiochus died shortly thereafter in Persia in 164.

Battles

Judas divided his 600 men into 4 groups and wiped out 2,000 men of Apollonia in Wadi Haramia, and Judas took Apollonia's sword. At Beth Horon, Judas killed 800 men, and the rest fled into Philistia.

After Beth-Horon, "Then began the fear of Judas and his brethren, and an exceeding great dread, to fall upon the nations round about them: Insomuch as his fame came unto the king, and all nations talked of the battles of Judas" (I Maccabees 3:25-26).

At the Battle of Emmaus, Judas and his men killed 3,000 out of the 27,000 men whom Lysias sent under the command of Gorgias and Nicanor, and they dropped their weapons as they fled "unto Gazera, and unto the plains of Idumea, and Azotus, and Jamnia" (I Maccabees 4:15). Their weapons included javelins, spears, swords, shields, battering rams, and ballistas.

Two years later at Beth Zur, Judas killed 5,000 out of Lysias' 65,000 men, and Lysias' men dropped their shields and weapons and ran.

At Beth Zechariah, Lysias returned with 50,000 better trained mercenaries and 32 elephants which caused Judas to retreat.

When Judas went to Gilead, he killed 8,000 of the army of Timotheus, and killed all the men in Bosora, Casphon, Maked, Bosor, and Ephron, and all the Arabians in Raphon. While he was busy there, his brother Simon was defeating the enemy in the Galilee all the way to Arbatta and the coast city of Ptolemais (Acco). Judas and Simon brought the women and children back to Judah, and then took Hebron and Maspha (Mispah). Judas died at Elasa.

Time-line of the Maccabees

167: Mattathias and his sons (the Maccabees) fought the Syrians and destroyed their altars. Cleansing of the temple in Jerusalem began.

166: Judas Maccabeus led a successful revolt with 6,000 men; routing and killing over 20,000 of the enemy and apostates.

165: Judas routed an army of 65,000, killing 5,000. Judas captured Jerusalem, and had the priests cleanse and rededicate the Temple (on the 25th of Kislev) and they celebrated for 8 days (Hanukkah).

164: Countries around Israel killed the Jews in their lands. Antiochus died, but one of his generals continued to fight the Jews. The armies of Judas killed 70,000 of them.

163: The Jews killed 26,000 who attacked Jerusalem, and 100,000 in other battles throughout Judah.

The descendants of the Maccabees, the Hasmoneans, ruled Judah until Herod the Great.

The Hasmoneans

The prophet Micah takes up where Daniel left off after Antiochus IV, and foretells the rulers of Judah until Christ is born in Bethlehem.

But you, Bethlehem Ephratah, though you be little among the thousands of Judah, yet out of you shall he come forth to me that is to be ruler in Israel; whose goings forth have been from of old, from everlasting. Therefore will he give them up, until the time that she which travails has brought forth: then the remnant of his brothers shall return to the children of Israel. And he shall stand and feed in the strength of the LORD, in the majesty of the name of the LORD his God; and they shall abide: for now shall he be great to the ends of the earth. And this man shall be the peace, when the Assyrian [Antiochus IV]shall come into our land [Judah]: and when he shall tread in our palaces, <u>*then shall we raise against him seven shepherds, and eight principal men.*</u> *And they shall waste the land of Assyria with the sword, and the land of Nimrod in the entrances thereof: thus shall he deliver us from the Assyrian, when he comes into our land, and when he treads within our borders. And the remnant of Jacob shall be in the middle of many people as a dew from the LORD, as the showers on the grass, that tarries not for man, nor waits for the sons of men. (Micah 5:2-7 edited with additions)*

Mattathias, his five sons, and Hyrcanus, the son of Simon make seven Maccabees. Eight princes of the Hasmonean family began with Aristobulus, and ended with Herod, who was married to Mariamne. The Maccabees and the Hasmoneans ruled Judah until Messiah was born.

<u>Seven Shepherds</u>
Maccabees (hammers)
Mattathias 168-167
Jonnan
Simon 144-135
Judas 167- 161
Eleazar
Jonathan 161-144
Hyrcanus, Simon' son 135-104

<u>Eight Principle Men</u>
Aristobulus 104-103
Alexander Janraeus 103-76
Alexandra 76-67
Hyrcanus II 67-66
Aristobulus II 66-63
Hyrcanus II 63-40
Antigorus 40-37
Herod the Great 37-1

Eleazar died in the Battle of Beth Zechariah valiantly attacking and killing an elephant from underneath, but then was crushed to death. Jonnan was not the ruling type.

Alexander ruled from 103 to 76. Alexander reconquered much of ancient Israel which had existed under King David's reign. But he had made the Pharisees his enemies, which he sought to correct in his will with directions to his wife. Salome Alexandra abided by his wishes and allowed the Pharisees to direct matters of state until Hyrcanus II took the throne. He and Aristobulus appealed to Rome, and Rome restored Hyrcanus II to the throne in 63. So it's actually 7 men, one of whom rules twice.

Herod, was not a Jew, He was Idumean (from Edom). Herod defeated Antigorus and then married his teenage niece, Mariamne, which helped to secure him a claim to the throne and gain some Jewish favor because she was Hasmonean. However, Herod already had a wife, Doris, and a young son, Antipater III, and chose to banish them both. King Herod ordered boys aged two and under killed in 3 BC when Christ was born in Bethlehem. He died in 1 BC (not 4 BC).

Summary

Daniel's amazing prophecy in chapter 11 reads like a docu-drama of the tug-o-war between Egypt and Syria. They often used Israel as a battle ground or a means of quick cash. The stronger of the kings is **bold**.

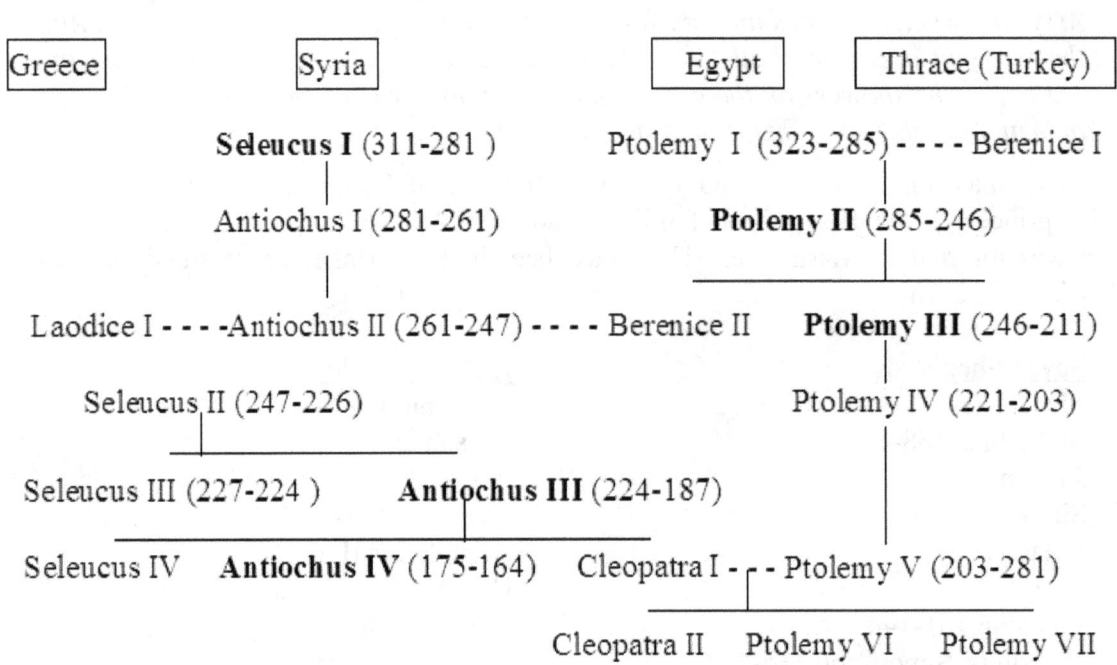

The Maccabees defeated the troops of Antiochus IV, and reasserted the sovereignty of Judea. Their descendants, the Hasmoneans, continued to rule over Judea until Jesus was born, though under empirical Rome.

Biblical Astronomy

And God said, Let there be lights in the firmament of the heaven to divide the day from the night; and let them be for signs, and for seasons, and for days, and years: (Genesis 1:14)

Thus said the LORD, Learn not the way of the heathen, and be not dismayed at the signs of heaven; for the heathen are dismayed at them. (Jeremiah 10:2)

God created the stars for signs and seasons, and for days and years. Just because the heathen have corrupted their good uses doesn't mean we should discount them. The original constellations proclaimed the glory of God and His plan for mankind including the virgin birth (Virgo) and the Southern Cross. The zodiac is like a belt in the night sky upon which twelve main constellations rest. Each zodiac constellation is associated with three other constellations (*decans*) near it which help tell its story. *Zodiac* means 'the way', and it proclaims the way of salvation. E. W. Bullinger wrote a book about the original meanings titled *The Witness of the Stars* which can be read for free on-line at http://philologos.org/__eb-tws/.

Can you bind the sweet influences of Pleiades, or loose the bands of Orion? Can you bring forth Mazzaroth in his season? or can you guide Arcturus with his sons? (Job 38:31-32)

Job is considered the oldest book of the Bible, likely written during the ice age which followed Noah's flood since it has so many references to snow and ice (Job 6:16, 9:30, 24:19, and 37:6). So the names of the Pleiades and Orion and other certain constellations have been with us for millennia.

Beth Alpha is a 6th century synagogue located at the base of Mount Gilboa. Beth Alpha's mosaic floor was created with three panels: the Holy Ark, the zodiac, and the story of the sacrifice of Issac. In Hebrew, the zodiac is called *mazzaroth*. The Hebrew names replace the Latin ones with which we are familiar. For example, instead of Sagittarius for the archer, there is the Hebrew word for 'bow'.

This mazzaroth begins due east with the first month of the Hebrew year, Nisan. Aries, a lamb, corresponds with this Spring month in which Passover is celebrated. Going counterclockwise, Taurus represents the second month of Iyar. Continuing in order until due west is the seventh month of Tishri, represented by Virgo, when the Virgin Mary gave birth to the second Adam (Jesus). It is the birth of Jesus on September 11, (Tishri 1, Rosh Hashanah), 3 BC that this chapter will address.

12 Tribes Linked to 12 Constellations

And Jacob called to his sons, and said, Gather yourselves together, that I may tell you that which shall befall you in the last days. Gather yourselves together, and hear, you sons of Jacob; and listen to Israel your father. (Genesis 49:1-2)

Before Jacob/Israel died, he spoke blessings and prophecies over his sons. Clyde Ferguson associates the 12 constellations of the zodiac with these descriptions of the 12 sons of Israel in *The Stars and the Bible* (pp.13-15).

1. REUBEN was "Unstable (pouring out) as waters" likened to AQUARIUS, represented as a man pouring waters from an urn.
2. SIMEON and LEVI were brothers called "the united brethren" likened to GEMINI, the Twins.
3. JUDAH *"is a lion's whelp"* likened to LEO, the lion.
4. ZEBULUN *"shall be for an haven of ships"* likened to CANCER, the crab. The Latin and Greek words for Cancer mean 'to hold' or 'encircle'.
5. ISSACHAR *"is a strong ass"* or *ox*, both used in husbandry, likened to TAURUS, the Bull.
6. and 7. DAN *"shall be a serpent by the way, an adder in the path, that bites the horse heels."* The space occupied by SCORPIO and LIBRA, has the constellation Ophiochus, the snake holder, towering above them. The snake is named Serpens. In ancient zodiacs, Ophiochus is the 13th constellation. Libra, the scales of justice, is better linked to *"Dan shall judge his people."* Dan, the serpent, is not listed as a tribe of the 144,000 in Revelation 7, neither is Ephraim because God held these two tribes responsible for leading the 10 tribes into idolatry (1 Kings 12:26-33; Jer. 7:15).
8. GAD was *"A troop"*. *Gad* reversed is *dag*, a fish, the sign PISCES. Pisces is two fish bound together, representing the Jews and Gentiles bound together in the love of Christ.
9. ASHER: *"His bread shall be fat"* likened to VIRGO, who is generally represented as holding wheat.
10. NAPHTALI *"is a hind let loose"*; a mountain gazelle. Israel's national animal is the mountain gazelle. *Naphtali* means struggle, but the end of the name by itself, *taleh*, means a lamb likened to ARIES. According to the rabbis, Aries is the sign for the Jewish people as a whole.
11. JOSEPH, *"his bow stayed in strength"* likened to SAGITTARIUS, the *archer* or *bowman*; commonly represented with his bow bent in full strength with the arrow drawn up to the head.
12. BENJAMIN *"shall shred as a wolf"*. CAPRICORN on the Egyptian sphere was represented by a goat led by Pan with a wolf's head.

Lion of Judah

*Judah, you are he whom your brothers shall praise: your hand shall be in the neck of your enemies; your father's children shall bow down before you. Judah is a **lion's** whelp: from the prey, my son, you are gone up: he stooped down, he couched as a **lion**, and as an old **lion**; who shall rouse him up? The scepter shall not depart from Judah, nor a lawgiver from between his feet [regel], until Shiloh come; and to him shall the gathering of the people be. Binding his foal to the vine, and his ass's colt to the choice vine; he washed his garments in wine, and his clothes in the blood of grapes: His eyes shall be red with wine, and his teeth white with milk. (Genesis 49:8-11)*

Regel in Hebrew means foot, and the star Regulus in the foot of *Leo* (Latin for '**lion**') is the brightest star of that constellation. *Regulus* means 'kingly' in Latin. In all ancient documents it is known as the "king star". King Jesus rode into Israel, the chosen vine, on the "foal of a donkey". "*From the prey*" of wicked men who crucified Him, He ascended into heaven ("*you are gone up*") three days later. Jesus will come down again and pounce like a lion upon the wicked. And as "*the Ancient of Days*," King Jesus will judge those who reject Him as King. Jesus is pure as milk in His bloody destruction of the wicked. "*And he was clothed with a clothing dipped in blood: and his name is called The Word of God. . . . and he treads the wine press of the fierceness and wrath of Almighty God*" (Rev. 19:13, 15b). "*Behold, the Lion of the tribe of Juda, the Root of David, has prevailed to open the book, and to loose the seven seals thereof*" (Rev. 5:5b). Only the Judge of the earth has the right to take the wedding contract and break its seals. Jesus was descended from Judah through king David's line.

Daniel, the Astronomer

*And in all matters of wisdom and understanding, that the king inquired of them, he found them ten times better than all the magicians and **astrologers** that were in all his realm. (Daniel 1:20)*

*There is a man in your kingdom, in whom is the spirit of the holy gods; and in the days of your father light and understanding and wisdom, like the wisdom of the gods, was found in him; whom the king Nebuchadnezzar your father, the king, I say, your father, made master of the magicians, **astrologers**, Chaldeans, and soothsayers. (Daniel 5:11)*

Daniel was the chief astronomer of Babylon. Chaldeans were known for astrology and magic, to the point we called them 'magi'. But a group who accepted the truths Daniel told them became devoted to His God, forbade idols, and lived morally. They took his prophecies about the 70 weeks of the Messiah seriously; understanding it concerned

Daniel's people, the tribe of Judah (the lion), and Jerusalem. If the Messiah was to come onto the scene 483 years after the decree to restore and rebuild Jerusalem and be *"cut off"* 3 ½ years later, they'd be wise to look for His birth at least a generation (40 years) earlier.

The Chaldean Magi

The Chaldean royal astronomers had the book of Daniel and were aware of the decrees of the Persian kings regarding the Jews. And many Jews still lived in the lands of their exile who could tell them the proper age for a Jewish rabbi to begin his ministry of teaching others would be between the ages of 30 to 40. So the astronomers likely began watching the skies after only 443 years had passed (483-40=443). From Artaxerxes' decree in 455 BC, that would be 12 BC (455-443=12).

He delivers and rescues, and he works signs and wonders in heaven and in earth, who has delivered Daniel from the power of the lions. (Daniel 6:27)

Halley's comet passed Earth in 12 BC. A comet also appeared in both 5 and 4 BC, recorded by the Chinese. There was a very close conjunction of Jupiter and Saturn in the constellation of Pisces in 7 BC. [Many use this year because of the incorrect dating of Herod's death in 4 BC. Josephus records a full lunar eclipse prior to Herod's death before Passover, and that occurred in 1 BC.] These were important precursors to something monumental about to take place, but the royal astronomers knew Regulus was the 'king star', and that's the one they would be watching.

He tells the number of the stars; he calls them all by their names. (Psalms 147:4)

Jesus' Birth

And there appeared a great wonder in heaven; a woman clothed with the sun, and the moon under her feet, and on her head a <u>crown of twelve stars</u>: And she being with child cried, travailing in birth, and pained to be delivered. (Revelation 12:1-2)

Of the twelve constellations in the zodiac, Virgo is the largest. The sun takes 44 days to pass through Virgo, from late summer to the autumn equinox. Many of the stories associated with Virgo involve a king or male god who dies and is reborn again in the spring. In Egypt, Virgo was called *Aspolio*, which means 'the Seed'.

"In 3 BC the constellation Virgo clothed with the sun as it entered the mid-body in its ecliptic course had the moon under her feet on one day only - Wednesday, September 11th. This configuration was visible in the Palestine area between 6:18 P.M. and 7:39 P.M. (sunset) on that day. During these 81 minutes, Jesus Christ was born" (*Jesus Christ, Our Promised Seed* by Victor Paul Wierwille).

The 13 stars of Virgo include the bright star Spica ('Seed of wheat'). <u>The constellation of Coma is the crown of twelve stars above the virgin's head.</u> Coma means 'The Desired One', and shows a woman with infant: *"the desire of all nations shall come"* (Haggai 2:7)

September 11, 3 BC fell on the first day of the month of Tishri - "Rosh Hashanah" or New Year's Day. It is the feast day of blowing of trumpets to celebrate the king's coronation. Since it is the only feast on a new moon, shouts of *mikkodesh*, 'it is consecrated', would have been heard. It is a tradition that the first day of the first year was the day that the first Adam was formed, and it was the birthday of the second Adam as well. That first Adam sinned. Yet a Redeemer was promised who would crush Satan's head, and so Hebrews would read about the miraculous birth of Isaac and how God redeemed his life with a ram caught in a thicket. Therefore a ram's horn, *shofar*, is blown in memory of God's past redemption looking forward to the hope of His final redemption of mankind.

There was a combined census and oath of allegiance to Caesar Augustus in 3 BC. This corresponded with the 750th anniversary of the founding of Rome and with the 25th anniversary of the reign of Augustus.

Magi make their Observations

Jupiter is the fourth brightest object in the heaven after the sun, moon, and Venus. Jupiter is the royal planet. As royal astronomers, the magi were dedicated to watching the sky for signs regarding kings and would have expected this planet to be involved with Regulus in Messiah's birth.

Jupiter's Retrograde Creates a Crown

Aug. 12, 3 BC	Jupiter and Venus were in conjunction in Leo, and the magi would be noting their observations of the activity of Jupiter, the king planet.
Sept. 14, 3 BC	(Days of Awe) Jupiter and Regulus were in conjunction in Leo.
Feb. 17, 2 BC	(Purim) After stopping in its path on Dec 1, 3 BC and beginning its annual retrogression backward, Jupiter and Regulus came into conjunction in Leo.
May 8, 2 BC	(Pentecost) After once again heading forward, Jupiter and Regulus were in conjunction in Leo.
June 17, 2 BC	Jupiter and Venus were in conjunction in Leo.

The Hebrew name for Jupiter is *ssedeq*, meaning righteousness. Melchi<u>zedek</u> means king of righteousness. Venus and Jesus are both called the *"morning star"*. Venus and Jupiter are the two brightest objects in the night sky after the Moon. On August 12, 3 BC the two planets almost seemed to touch. And on June 17, 2 BC again — people in Babylon would have seen the two planets merge into one in the west toward Judea. Because Jupiter's orbital path is so far from ours, it appears to go backwards as we orbit the sun, which is called retrograde. During the year between August 12th and June 17th, Jupiter made an elliptical shape (a crown) around Regulus in Leo.

Aug. 24, 2 BC   The massing of planets Jupiter, Mars, and Mercury, with Venus in Leo, are remarkable, but the conjunction of Jupiter and Mars resembled a <u>scepter between the feet</u> of Leo. This culminated a year of royal signs, to the point the magi would leave for Jerusalem to find the Messiah of Judah, King of the Jews.

Magi Visit Herod

Sept. - Nov., 2 B.C. Jupiter is too close to the sun to be seen as the magi travel.

Matthew 2:1-8 summary: When the magi arrived in Jerusalem a few months after their departure, they started asking, *"Where is He born King of the Jews?"* This stirred up all Jerusalem, and when Herod heard of it, he had the scribes find out what the Scripture said, and they told him a 'Governor' will be born in Bethlehem. Herod privately called the magi in to see him and inquired the exact time they saw the royal Jupiter star announced His coming, and the magi gave the August 12, 3 BC date according to their calendars. So the *"young child"* must be at least one year and three months old. To be safe, Herod later had all the boys two years and under killed.

Magi Visit Jesus at his House

When they had heard the king, they departed; and, see, the star, which they saw in the east, went before them, till it came and stood over where the young child was. When they saw the star, they rejoiced with exceeding great joy. And when they were come into the house, they saw the young child with Mary his mother, and fell down, and worshipped him: and when they had opened their treasures, they presented to him gifts; gold, and frankincense and myrrh. And being warned of God in a dream that they should not return to Herod, they departed into their own country another way. (Matthew 2:9-12)

"Stood over" is when a star reaches its second stationary point that evening. The planet Jupiter began to be seen crossing the meridian, the "high point," by December 4, at 6:09 a.m. Jupiter continued to rise four minutes earlier each day. By December 24, Jupiter crossed the meridian at 4:44 a.m. The exact day is unknown when the Magi presented their gifts during December when Jupiter "stood above" where Jesus was. It may have been Dec. 4th. But I'd like to think their giving gifts to Christ coincided with Hannukah that year. After the magi departed, then the angel of the Lord appeared to Joseph and told him to take his family to Egypt. God could have used an angel to direct the magi as angels are His *"fiery messengers"*, but God chose to use a star.

Dec. 22-29, 2 BC (Hannukah) Magi likely presented gifts before departing for Persia without seeing Herod. Jesus' family left for Egypt.

Jan. 9, 1 BC A full lunar eclipse preceded Herod's death before Passover.

Revelation 12

Mary giving birth to Jesus

And there appeared a great wonder in heaven; a woman clothed with the sun, and the moon under her feet, and on her head a crown of twelve stars: And she being with child cried, travailing in birth, and pained to be delivered. And there appeared *another wonder in heaven; and behold a great red dragon, having seven heads and ten horns, and seven crowns on his heads. And his tail drew the third part of the stars of heaven, and did cast them to the earth: and the dragon stood before the woman which was ready to be delivered, for to devour her child as soon as it was born. And she brought forth a man child, who was to <u>rule all nations</u> with a <u>rod of iron</u>: and her child was caught up to God, and to his throne. And the woman fled into the wilderness, where she has a place prepared of God, that they should feed her there a thousand two hundred and three score days. And there was war in heaven: Michael and his angels fought against the dragon; and the dragon fought and his angels, (Revelation 12:1-8)*

The woman is the virgin Mary who gives birth to Jesus. Satan tried to kill Jesus as a baby (Rev. 12:4b) through king Herod. We know that Joseph and Mary fled with infant Jesus to Egypt. According to this scripture, they lived and were cared for in Egypt for 1,260 days, or 3 ½ years using the 360-day calendar. There was a large Jewish population in Egypt which likely took them in as the refugees they were. As a second fulfillment of "*I called my son out of Egypt*," (Hosea 11:1; Matthew 2:15) they returned and settled in Nazareth. Jesus was resurrected and ascended into heaven ("*caught up to God*") and sits at the right hand of His Father.

Yet have I set my <u>king</u> on my holy hill of Zion. I will declare the decree: the LORD has said to me, You are my Son; this day have I begotten you. Ask of me, and I shall give you the heathen for your inheritance, and the uttermost parts of the earth for your possession. <u>You shall break them with a rod of iron;</u> you shall dash them in pieces like a potter's vessel. (Psalm 2:6-9)

Satan accusing and persecuting Jews and Christians

Much like Daniel 10 describes the angelic spiritual battle in the middle of two similar prophecies in Daniel 9 and 11, the interlude of Michael fighting Satan in Revelation 12:7-11, separates the first prophecy about a woman who fled to a wilderness with a second one.

And I heard a loud voice saying in heaven, Now is come salvation, and strength, and the kingdom of our God, and the power of his Christ: for the accuser of our brothers is cast down, which accused them before our God day and night. And they overcame him by the blood of the Lamb, and by the word of their testimony; and they loved not their lives to the death. Therefore rejoice, you heavens, and you that dwell in them. Woe to the inhabitants of the earth and of the sea! for the devil is come down to you, having great wrath, because he knows that he has but a short time. And when the dragon saw that he was cast to the earth, he persecuted the woman which brought forth the man child. (Revelation 12:10-13)

The kingdom of our God and of His Christ has been persecuted throughout the ages. The Spanish Inquisition brings to mind those who were accused day and night, but

Protestants held onto their faith in Jesus and Jews held onto their faith in Jehovah even as they were exiled, tortured, and martyred. Sephardic Jews are those who lived in Spain and Portugal. Ferdinand and Isabella made the Alhambra Decree on March 31, 1492 ordering the conversion or expulsion of Jews from the Kingdom of Spain by July 31st of that year. Thousands were killed, hundreds of thousands left, and tens of thousands were baptized into the Catholic church (*conversos*). This has been confirmed using Y chromosome DNA testing which indicated that around 20% of Spanish men today have direct patrilineal descent from Sephardic Jews (University of Leicester and Pompeu Fara University, 2008). Christopher Columbus set sail for the New World three days after the Alhambra Decree deadline, which has caused some to consider he may have been a *converso*.

Christ's Bride is Protected in America for 3 1/2 Centuries

And to the woman were given <u>two wings of a great eagle</u>, that she might fly into the <u>wilderness</u>, into her place, where she is nourished for a time, and times, and half a time, from the face of the serpent. And the serpent cast out of his mouth water as a flood after the woman, that he might cause her to be carried away of the flood. And the earth helped the woman, and the earth opened her mouth, and swallowed up the flood which the dragon cast out of his mouth. And the dragon was wroth with the woman, and went to make war with the remnant of her seed, which keep the commandments of God, and have the testimony of Jesus Christ. (Rev. 12:14-17)

Beginning in Revelation 12:14 and through the next chapter, the animals of Daniel's fourth beast (Daniel 7) come back into play, beginning with the eagle wings which were plucked from the lion. These were the American colonies detached from the lion of England. A group of Puritans settled Jamestown in 1611; the same year the King James Bible was published back in England. America was still known as "the wilderness" for the next two hundred years.

In this case, "*time, times, and half a time*" equal 350 years. 2000 - 350 = 1650. From 1650-1726 the first wave of Jewish immigration came to the American colonies. The Jewish population rose to ten thousand. [According to US Census Bureau, the total population of colonies in 1650 was 4,700, and in 1720 it was 466,200.]

From 1630-1650 the Puritans tried to establish a new Parliamentary system in England established on the sure foundation of Biblical Christianity. They won the civil war and installed Oliver Cromwell. In 1656, Cromwell allowed Jews to establish a Jewish Cemetery, and to have protection during prayers, but not to worship publicly. This was the end of the expulsion of the Jews from England. But the Puritans of England were grossly disappointed in Cromwell and the Parliament they set up, and continued to immigrate to America by the thousands.

Satan sent a flood of people to America's shores to try to water down the kingdom of God through the influx of foreigners with foreign beliefs, but America became a melting pot which allowed for cultural differences while maintaining the high ideals of Christianity (at least until the 1900's). So Satan sought to destroy Christians and Jews elsewhere around the globe.

Satan and the Stars

> . . . *Therefore rejoice, you heavens, and you that dwell in them. Woe to the inhabitants of the earth and of the sea! for <u>the devil is come down to you, having great wrath, because he knows that he has but a short time. And when the dragon saw that he was cast to the earth, he persecuted the woman which brought forth the man child.</u> And to the woman were given two wings of a great eagle, that she might fly into the wilderness, into her place, where she is nourished for a time, and times, and half a time, from the face of the serpent. And the serpent cast out of his mouth water as a flood after the woman, that he might cause her to be carried away of the flood. And the earth helped the woman, and the earth opened her mouth, and swallowed up the flood which the dragon cast out of his mouth. And <u>the dragon was wroth with the woman, and went to make war with the remnant of her seed, which keep the commandments of God, and have the testimony of Jesus Christ.</u> (Revelation 12:3-17 edited)*

In Revelation 12, Satan is interchangeably called devil, red dragon, great dragon, and serpent. Overall Satan is a deceiver who does not prevail, though for a short season during the Great Tribulation it will look like he's winning.

Satan's constellations tell his story in several acts. Draco takes Satan from the throne room of God to offering a throne to Jesus if He would worship him. As the seraph who contained the north star which pointed all towards worshiping God in heaven, Satan was thrown out of heaven, but continued to hold the north star in Draco. Hydra is the sea-serpent who pours out a flood of persecution after the woman, Virgo. Cetus is the seven-headed leviathan who persecutes Jews (the lamb of Aries) and Christ's bride (the enthroned woman, Cassiopeia), but the 'breaker" (Perseus) stops Cetus. Serpens is the serpent being held back by Michael (Ophiochus) and is bound for 1,000 years. Satan and his ilk eventually end up in the fire (Eridanus).

Draco

> *And there was war in heaven: Michael and his angels fought against the **dragon**; and the dragon fought and his angels, And prevailed not; neither was their place found any more in heaven. And the great dragon was cast out, that old **serpent**, called the Devil, and Satan, which deceives the whole world: he was cast out into the earth, and his angels were cast out with him. (Revelation 12:7-9)*

The seraphs around God's throne who cry "*Holy, holy, holy*" are serpentine in appearance with wings and many eyes. (Isaiah 6:2-3). *Seraph* comes from a root word for 'burning' and the copper color; (figuratively) a fiery or poisonous serpent. With his long tail you can visualize him sweeping a third of the stars/angels away from God's Presence with him.

> *And his tail drew the third part of the stars of heaven, and did cast them to the earth. (Revelation 12:4)*

Like the Little Dipper (Ursa Minor), Draco is always visible in the northern hemisphere. It's a very long constellation, and its long body seems to enfold the Little Dipper. Due to the precession of the Earth, Draco's brightest star Thuban was the pole star approximately 4600 years ago. It would have seemed to ancient sky watchers that the Earth revolved around Draco.

The Dragon/Satan, wants to be pre-eminent again, and seeks to destroy the One who will rule and reign, Jesus, the man-child. But he missed Him as a baby, and thought he had Him on the cross, so now he pursues and persecutes his people in an effort to wipe out the Jews so none will be around to say, "*Blessed is he who comes in the name of the Lord*" to hasten His return.

Hydra

There is another long serpent in the sky. It is a sea-serpent close to Virgo and capable of trying to consume her with a flood. Draco missed his chance of destroying Jesus, so now sea-serpent Hydra is going after His remnant on earth issuing a flood from its mouth.

> *And <u>the serpent cast out of his mouth water as a flood after the woman, that he might cause her to be carried away of the flood.</u> And the earth helped the woman, and the earth opened her mouth, and swallowed up the flood which the dragon cast out of his mouth. And the dragon was wroth with the woman, and went to make war with the remnant of her seed, which keep the commandments of God, and have the testimony of Jesus Christ. (Revelation 12:3-17 edited)*

Hydra represents the "*beast of the sea*". Just above Hydra are the constellations Corax with 7 stars and Crater with 10 stars corresponding to 7 heads & 10 horns. (Rev. 12:3b)

In Greek myth, the second labor of Heracles was to kill Hydra. It was no easy task because the Hydra had 9 heads (but it is often pictured with only 7, one of which was <u>immortal</u>). During the battle each time Heracles cut off a head two more heads sprouted in its place. Heracles was losing the battle until he took a torch and burned each neck as he cut off the head. Finally the Hydra only had its <u>single immortal head</u> remaining. Heracles cut it off and buried it.

> *A beast rise up out of the sea, <u>having seven heads and ten horns,</u> and on his horns ten crowns, and on his heads the name of blasphemy. . . . And I saw <u>one of his heads as it were wounded to death; and his deadly wound was healed;</u> and all the world wondered after the beast. (Revelation 13:1b-3)*

According to E.E. Bullinger, "It is pictured as *the female serpent (Hydra)*, the mother and author of all evil. *Hydra* has the significant meaning, *he is abhorred*!" The constellation Crater (Cup) is connected to Hydra. Again, Bullinger noted, "The Cup is wide and deep, and fastened on by the stars to the very body of the writhing serpent. The same stars which are in the foot of the Cup form part of the body of Hydra, and are reckoned as belonging to both constellations."

> *So he carried me away in the spirit into the wilderness: and I saw a woman sit on a scarlet colored beast, full of names of **blasphemy**, <u>having seven heads and ten horns</u>. And the woman was arrayed in purple and scarlet color, and decked with gold and precious stones and pearls, having a golden <u>cup</u> in her hand full of abominations and filthiness of her fornication: And on her forehead was a name written, MYSTERY, BABYLON THE GREAT, THE MOTHER OF HARLOTS AND ABOMINATIONS OF THE EARTH. (Revelation 17:3-5)*

Cetus (Leviathan)

According to Strong's Concordance, leviathan was a symbol of Babylon. The constellation of Cetus is pictured like a gnarwhal. The brightest star in Cetus is is named *Menikar*, and means 'the bound or chained enemy'. The star in its neck is named *Mira*, which means 'the rebel'.

> *All that the enemy has done wickedly in the sanctuary. Your enemies roar in the middle of your congregations; they set up their ensigns for signs. . . .They have cast fire into your sanctuary, they have defiled by casting down the dwelling place of your name to the ground. They said in their hearts, Let us destroy them together: they have burned up all the synagogues of God in the land. . . .O God, how long shall the adversary reproach? shall the enemy **blaspheme** your name for ever? . . .You did divide the sea by your strength: you <u>brake the heads of the dragons</u> in the waters. You <u>brake the heads of leviathan</u> in pieces, and gave him to be meat to the people inhabiting the wilderness. . . .Remember this, that the enemy has reproached, O LORD, and that the foolish people have **blasphemed** your name. O deliver not the soul of your turtledove to the multitude of the wicked: . . . for the dark places of the earth are full of the habitations of cruelty. O let not the oppressed return ashamed: let the poor and needy praise your name. Arise, O God. (Psalm 74:3-22 edited)*

The foolish people who blasphemed Jehovah's Name in the past, continue to do so in the present. They have cast down the Temple Mount and have erected their own insignia to their god, Allah. The Muslims pursue the destruction of the Hebrew people and their synagogues around the world.

Perseus, the breaker, is the constellation with the sword who cuts off the head of this creature. A star in that head is called *Algol*, which means 'demon star'. Ancient skywatchers thought it was cursed because its brightness changes. That's because Algol is the most famous eclipsing binary star.

> *Can you draw out <u>leviathan</u> with an hook? . . . his teeth are terrible round about. His scales are his pride, shut up together as with a close seal. . . . Out of his mouth go burning lamps, and sparks of fire leap out. Out of his nostrils goes smoke, as out of a seething pot or caldron. His breath kindles coals, and a flame goes out of his mouth. . . . His heart is as firm as a stone; . . . He esteems iron as straw, and brass as rotten wood. . . . He makes the deep to boil like a pot: he makes the sea like a pot of ointment. He makes a path to shine after him; one would think the deep to be hoary. On earth there is not his like, who is made without fear. He beholds all high things: he is a king over all the children of pride. (Job 41:1-34 edited)*

Leviathan is a fire-breathing dragon who leaves a shining wake. Leviathan terrorizes the world. Satan is proud of his beauty (Ezekiel 25:3; 28:12); he is the king of the prideful.

Serpens

Another snake constellation which plagues Virgo is Serpens. The constellations Bootes, Virgo, and Serpens represent Joseph, Mary and Herod, as well as Adam, Eve and the Serpent in Eden. "*Satan, the deceiver of the whole world*" (Revelation 12:9).

> *And the LORD God said to the serpent, . . . I will put enmity between you and the woman, and between your seed and her seed; it shall bruise your head, and you shall bruise his heel. (Genesis 3:14-15 edited)*

There's also an ancient constellation called Serpentarius who destroys the serpent which is striving for the crown (Corona). Today he's called *Ophiuchus* (the serpent held). And being close to Virgo, he is also known as her Seed. Ophiuchus' foot is crushing the head of Scorpio at the red star Antares, while it tries to sting his heel.

> *And he said to them, I beheld Satan as lightning fall from heaven. Behold, I give to you power to tread on serpents and scorpions, and over all the power of the enemy: and nothing shall by any means hurt you. (Luke 10:18-19)*

The Judgment

Taurus and his decans provide the picture of final judgment in the sky. Taurus, the rushing bull, is composed of over 100 stars, including the the Pleiades in its neck. *Pleiades* means 'the congregation of the judge'. Jesus comes to judge the earth as victorious king pictured as Orion stepping upon Lepus, a snake. To His sheep, Jesus is the shepherd, Auriga; but the wicked will be cast into the fire of Eridanus.

> *For the indignation of the LORD is on all nations, and his fury on all their armies: he has utterly destroyed them, he has delivered them to the slaughter. . . . And all the host of heaven shall be dissolved, and the heavens shall be rolled together as a*

scroll: and all their host shall fall down,. . . For my sword shall be bathed in heaven: behold, it shall come down on Idumea, and on the people of my curse, to judgment. . . . And the unicorns shall come down with them, and the bullocks with the bulls; and their land shall be soaked with blood, and their dust made fat with fatness. <u>For it is the day of the LORD's vengeance, and the year of recompenses for the controversy of Zion. And the streams thereof shall be turned into pitch,</u> and the dust thereof into brimstone, and the land thereof shall become burning pitch. It shall not be quenched night nor day; the smoke thereof shall go up for ever: (Isaiah 34:2-10 edited)

Job said God made "*Arcturus, Orion, and Pleiades, and the chambers of the south*" (Job 9:9). Orion was spelled Oarion, from the Hebrew root which means 'light'. His Egyptian name is *Ha-ga-t*, meaning 'this is he who triumphs'. Orion's brightest star is named *Betelgeuz*, which means 'the coming of the branch' (Malachi 3:2). The next brightest star is named *Rigel* which means 'the foot that crusheth'. The star called *Saiph* means 'bruised', and is the very word used in Genesis 3:15. Like Ophiuchus, Orion has one leg *bruised*; while, with the other, he is *crushing* the enemy under foot. The star called *Bellatrix* means 'quickly coming', or 'swiftly destroying'.

Summary

God created the stars and gave them names to help us understand His plan of salvation. The twelve sons of Israel are represented by the constellations of the zodiac; most importantly Naphtali which is represented by the lamb of Aries for the nation of Israel, and Judah represented by Leo. Jesus was born of a virgin while Virgo had the moon under her feet and Coma of twelve stars on her head, on Tishri 1, 3 BC. Daniel was an astronomer who trained the astronomers of the east who passed on this knowledge so that their descendants ("*wise men from the east*") recognized the birth of the King of the Jews during very specific and spectacular astronomical events.

Jews and Christians have been protected in America for 350 years ("*time, times, and half a time*"). The "short" 3 1/2 years of the Great Tribulation began when Michael released Satan (2 Thess. 2:6-9).

And at that time shall <u>Michael</u> stand up, the great prince which stands for the children of your people: and there shall be a time of trouble, such as never was since there was a nation even to that same time: and at that time your people shall be delivered, every one that shall be found written in the book. And many of them that sleep in the dust of the earth shall awake, some to everlasting life, and some to shame and everlasting contempt. And they that be wise shall shine as the brightness of the firmament; and they that turn many to righteousness as the stars for ever and ever. But you, O Daniel, shut up the words, and seal the book, even to the time of the end: many shall run to and fro, and knowledge shall be increased. . . .How long shall it be to the end of these wonders? And I heard . . . that it shall be for a <u>time,</u>

times, and an half; and when he shall have accomplished to scatter the power of the holy people, all these things shall be finished. (Daniel 12:1-7 edited)

Satan has many representations in the constellations, none of which are victorious. And all the believers he kills "*shall awake to everlasting life*" when Jesus comes again. Christ's Bride should watch the sky with hope, not fear.

And there shall be signs in the sun, and in the moon, and in the stars; and on the earth distress of nations, with perplexity; the sea and the waves roaring; Men's hearts failing them for fear, and for looking after those things which are coming on the earth: for the powers of heaven shall be shaken. And then shall they see the Son of man coming in a cloud with power and great glory. And when these things begin to come to pass, then look up, and lift up your heads; for your redemption draws near. (Luke 21:25-28)

One Third of Heavenly Light Will Be Darkened

And the third angel sounded, and there fell a great star from heaven, burning as it were a lamp, and it fell on the third part of the rivers, and on the fountains of waters; And the name of the star is called Wormwood: and the third part of the waters became wormwood; and many men died of the waters, because they were made bitter. And the fourth angel sounded, and the third part of the sun was smitten, and the third part of the moon, and the third part of the stars; so as the third part of them was darkened, and the day shone not for a third part of it, and the night likewise. (Revelation 8:10-12)

'Wormwood' is *apsinthos*, meaning bitter. A great fiery star, or comet, falls upon a third of the fresh water sources, bringing death to those who drink its bitter waters. Being given bitter water to drink was a judgment of God (Jeremiah 8:14, 9:13-15) for forsaking Him (Deut. 29:17-20). Scientists Prinn and Fegley theorized in 1987 that a comet's collision with Earth might produce acid rain from the "heat shock" during entry.

'Smitten' is *plesso*, meaning to flatten or pound as a potter does. Sunspots were first observed by Galileo, and records kept in 1749. Continuous records of sunspots have been kept since 1849. When the magnetic sunspots reverse polarity, a new cycle begins; this happens on average every eleven years. Solar cycle 23 began October 1996. Though four small reverse sunspots heralded the weak beginning of solar cycle 24. Five sunspots of polarity for cycle 23 appeared after April fool's day in 2009, making it one of the longest cycles at 12.6 years. Long, less active solar cycles indicate a less bright sun and cooler earth. Between cycle 22 and 23 the global temperature dropped two degrees. The last "mini Ice Age" of 1650-1700 had very few sunspots, and that's where Cliverd (2007) and other scientists predict we are heading. Yet along with the sun's darkness, an angel will also scorch men with fire and heat (Rev. 16:8-9). There are, and will be, signs in the sun.

Israel

*Give ear, O Shepherd of Israel,
you that lead Joseph like a flock;
you that dwell between the cherubim,
shine forth. (Psalm 80:1)*

Israel's past, present and future are rich and deep and full of miracles. God calls Himself their Shepherd and Husband as well as their Savior. Thousands of Messianic Jews in Israel are crying out for the return of their Messiah, and He will answer their cry.

Descendants of Shem (Semites) and Eber (Hebrew)

Noah's three sons, Ham, Shem, and Japheth, had sons whose names have been traced to the geographic areas in which they lived. Bill Cooper's extensive research on tracing Biblical lineages is in his book, *After the Flood*. From my map in the Appendix you can see Ham's sons migrated to Africa, the land of (K)Ham, but Cush remained in Mesopotamia, and Canaan occupied what is now the land of Israel. Japheth's sons migrated north, "by Jove," surrounding the Black and Caspian Seas. Shem's sons largely remained in Mesopotamia, except for Lud who ventured into north Africa.

These are the generations of Shem: Shem was an hundred years old, and begat Arphaxad two years after the flood: And Shem lived after he begat Arphaxad five hundred years, and begat sons and daughters. And Arphaxad begat Salah: . . . And Salah begat Eber: . . .And Eber begat Peleg: And Eber begat Peleg . . . And Peleg begat Reu: . . . And Reu begat Serug: . . . And Serug begat Nahor: . . . And Nahor begat Terah:. . .And Terah begat Abram, Nahor, and Haran. . . .Haran begat Lot. (Genesis 11:10-22 edited)

Though I have deleted the information about how long each man lived before he begat his first son, great men like Bishop James Ussher have used that information to provide us with Biblical time-lines which are tremendous aides in history and prophecy. After the flood, there were only two generations before people built the Tower of Babel and God gave them their different languages. Hebrew was the language of Eber and all his descendants.

Awake, Bride

Ancient People of Mesopotamia and Egypt Worshiped the Moon-god

The moon-god was called Nanna and Sin. The moon-god was originally depicted as a man who had a beard made of lapis lazuli and who rode on a winged bull (Babylon). His symbols are the crescent moon, the bull, and a tripod (pyramid shape).

In Mizraim, ancient Egypt, the Apis bull votive offering had a sun disc on its head. But a prospective new Apis bull was required to have **a white crescent** on one side of its body or a white triangle on its forehead, signifying its unique character and its acceptance by the moon-god.

"The Old Testament constantly rebuked the worship of the moon-god (see: Deut. 4:19;17:3; II Kings. 21:3,5; 23:5; Jer. 8:2; 19:13; Zeph. 1:5, etc.) When Israel fell into idolatry, it was usually the cult of the moon-god. Everywhere in the ancient world, the symbol of the crescent moon can be found on seal impressions, steles, pottery, amulets, clay tablets, cylinders, weights, earrings, necklaces, wall murals, etc. In Tel-el-Obeid (ruins of Tower of Babel), a copper calf was found with a crescent moon on its forehead. An idol with the body of a bull and the head of man has a crescent moon inlaid on its forehead with shells. In Ur, the Stela of Ur-Nammu has the crescent symbol placed at the top of the register of gods because the moon-god was the head of the gods. Even bread was baked in the form of a crescent as an act of devotion to the moon-god. The Ur of the Chaldees was so devoted to the moon-god that it was sometimes called Nannar in tablets from that time period." [http://www.yeshua.co.uk]

Abram/Abraham (great father)

God wanted to get Abram and his family out of Ur and away from moon-god worship. They traveled north between the two rivers, until they reached Haran in what is now southern Turkey.

And Abram and Nahor took them wives: the name of Abram's wife was Sarai; ... But Sarai was barren; she had no child. And Terah took Abram his son, and Lot the son of Haran his son's son, and Sarai his daughter in law, his son Abram's wife; and they went forth with them from Ur of the Chaldees, to go into the land of Canaan; and they came to Haran, and dwelled there. (Genesis 11:29-31 edited)

Then from Haran, Abram and Sarai took his nephew Lot and headed south. Because of their large herds they needed to separate, and Lot chose the lush fields of the Jordan valley near Sodom and Gomorrah. And God gave Abram a promise that his seed would own all that land he could see (Genesis 13:14-18), the "*whole land of Canaan*" (Genesis 17:8), and God clarified the boundaries between the Nile and the Euphrates.

> *In the same day the LORD made a covenant with Abram, saying, To your seed have I given this land, from the river of Egypt to the great river, the river Euphrates: (Genesis 15:18)*

This land included the area known as the 'fertile crescent' west of the Euphrates. The Fertile Crescent had to be conquered by every empire because it contained the travel routes between Africa and Asia and the North. At this point Abram, age 85, and Sarai, age 75, still had no children. Through Sarah's maid, Hagar, Abraham had a son named Ishmael the following year. When he was 99, God commanded Abraham and every male in his household to be circumcised, and He changed their names to Abraham and Sarah and promised them a son. The next year (Abram, age 100, and Sarai, age 90) Isaac was born. About twenty years later Abraham and Isaac go up Mount Moriah (what would become the Temple Mount) and God provided a ram for the offering, but knows Abraham was willing to give up his "only" son (Genesis 22). But the promise of land to his seed also came with a prophecy of struggle and servitude.

Strangers in Egypt

> *And he said to Abram, Know of a surety that your seed shall be a stranger in a land that is not their's, and <u>shall serve them; and they shall afflict them</u> four hundred years; And also that nation, whom they shall serve, will I judge: and afterward shall they come out with great substance. . . . But in the fourth generation they shall come here again: for the iniquity of the Amorites is not yet full. (Gen. 15:13-14, 16)*

> *Now to Abraham and his seed were the promises made. He said not, And to seeds, as of many; but as of one, And to your seed, which is Christ. And this I say, that the covenant, that was confirmed before of God in Christ, the law, which was four hundred and thirty years after, cannot cancel, that it should make the promise of none effect. For if the inheritance be of the law, it is no more of promise: but God gave it to Abraham by promise. (Galatians 3:16-18)*

Isaac married Rebekah who gave birth to twins, Esau and Jacob. Jacob wrestled with the Angel of the LORD who changed his name from Jacob ('deceiver') to Israel ('prevailer' or 'prince of God'). Jacob/Israel had 12 sons, including Joseph, who became the patriarchs of the tribes of Israel. From God's calling Abram out of Ur to when Jacob takes his whole family to join Joseph in Egypt is 215 years. From Jacob's move to Egypt until the Exodus was 215 years. It was only about the last 100 years of their time in Egypt that the Hebrews were enslaved and afflicted.

Moses and the Exodus

> *But when the time of the promise drew near, which God had sworn to Abraham, <u>the people grew and multiplied in Egypt, Till another king arose, which knew not</u>*

*<u>Joseph. The same dealt subtly with our kindred, . . . so that they cast out their young children, to the end they might not live. In which time Moses was born</u>, . . . Pharaoh's daughter took him up, and nourished him for her own son. And Moses was learned in all the wisdom of the Egyptians, and was mighty in words and in deeds. And when he was full forty years old, it came into his heart to visit his brothers the children of Israel. And seeing one of them suffer wrong, he defended him,. . . and smote the Egyptian: For he supposed his brothers would have understood how that God by his hand would deliver them: but they understood not. . . . Then fled Moses and was a stranger in the land of Madian, where he begat two sons. And when forty years were expired, there appeared to him in the wilderness of mount Sina an angel of the Lord in a flame of fire in a bush. . . . and as he drew near to behold it, the voice of the LORD came to him, Saying, I am the God of your fathers, the God of Abraham, and the God of Isaac, and the God of Jacob. . . . Put off your shoes from your feet: for the place where you stand is holy ground. I have seen, <u>I have seen the affliction of my people which is in Egypt</u>, and I have heard their groaning, and am come down to deliver them. And now come, I will send you into Egypt. . . . <u>He brought them out, after that he had showed wonders and signs in the land of Egypt, and in the Red sea, and in the wilderness forty years.</u> This is that Moses, which said to the children of Israel, A **prophet** shall the Lord your God raise up to you of your brothers, like to me; him shall you hear. This is he, that was in the church in the wilderness with the angel which spoke to him in the mount Sina, and with our fathers: who received the lively oracles to give to us: To whom our fathers would not obey, but thrust him from them, and in their hearts turned back again into Egypt, Saying to Aaron, Make us gods to go before us: for as for this Moses, which brought us out of the land of Egypt, we know not what is become of him. And they made a calf in those days, and offered sacrifice to the idol, and rejoiced in the works of their own hands. <u>Then God turned, and gave them up to worship the host of heaven</u>; as it is written in the book of the prophets, O you house of Israel, have you offered to me slain beasts and sacrifices by the space of forty years in the wilderness? Yes, you took up the tabernacle of Moloch, and the star of your god Remphan, figures which you made to worship them: and I will carry you away beyond Babylon. (Acts 7:17-43 edited)*

The Exodus coincides with Passover, and the giving of the Law on Mount Sinai coincides with Pentecost (Feast of Weeks). Though it was only an eleven day trip from Mount Horeb/Sinai in Arabia to Kadesh-barnea in Canaan (Deuteronomy 1:2), their fear and disobedience cost them forty years in the desert. But Moses foretold of a prophet from whom they would hear God's Word. They resorted to worship of the moon-god bull so popular in Egypt. The true God who created the moon, sun, and stars had brought them out of bondage with mighty miracles, but it did not wrest their hearts from bondage to idolatry, even that which demanded child sacrifice (Moloch).

12 Tribes

After Moses died, God now had a miracle generation which had grown up living upon manna and wearing clothes and shoes which never wore out, who had been trained to worship Him alone. Joshua took them into the Promised Land of Canaan to destroy the idol worshipers there. But first, God did another crossing of water miracle, over the Jordan river at flood stage on dry ground, which would propel them into their new future. God performed this miracle on the 10th of Nisan, which was the day of selecting the Passover lamb. Joshua is the Hebrew form of the name Jesus, thus alluding to the future "Lamb of God" who would miraculously and prophetically be "cut off" as the river had been, to provide access to God's Promised Land of eternal life: *"cut off [kawrath] before [in the face of] the ark of the covenant [b'reeth]."*

> *And it came to pass, when all the people were clean passed over Jordan, that the LORD spoke to Joshua, saying, Take you twelve men out of the people, out of every tribe a man, And command you them, saying, Take you hence out of the middle of Jordan, out of the place where the priests' feet stood firm, twelve stones, and you shall carry them over with you, and leave them in the lodging place, where you shall lodge this night. . . . That this may be a sign among you, that when your children ask their fathers in time to come, saying, What mean you by these stones? Then you shall answer them, That the waters of Jordan were <u>cut off</u> before the ark of the **covenant** of the LORD; when it passed over Jordan, the waters of Jordan were <u>cut off:</u> and these stones shall be for a memorial to the children of Israel for ever. . . .On that day the LORD magnified Joshua in the sight of all Israel; and they feared him, as they feared Moses, all the days of his life. And the LORD spoke to Joshua, saying, Command the priests that bear the ark of the testimony, that they come up out of Jordan. Joshua therefore commanded the priests, saying, Come you up out of Jordan. And it came to pass, when the priests that bore the ark of the covenant of the LORD were come up out of the middle of Jordan, and the soles of the priests' feet were lifted up to the dry land, that the waters of Jordan returned to their place, and flowed over all his banks, as they did before. And the people came up out of Jordan on the tenth day of the first month, and encamped in Gilgal, in the east border of Jericho. And those <u>twelve stones</u>, which they took out of Jordan, did Joshua pitch in Gilgal. And he spoke to the children of Israel, saying, When your children shall ask their fathers in time to come, saying, What mean these stones? Then you shall let your children know, saying, Israel came over this Jordan on dry land. For the LORD your God dried up the waters of Jordan from before you, until you were passed over, as the LORD your God did to the Red sea, which he dried up from before us, until we were gone over: That all the people of the earth might know the hand of the LORD, that it is mighty: that you might fear the LORD your God for ever. (Joshua 4:1-24 edited)*

Awake, Bride

The twelve tribes had a bit of transformation when Jacob/Israel adopted Joseph's two sons, Ephraim and Manasseh as his own (Genesis 48:5). Then God chose the tribe of Levi as His possession, and gave them cities instead of a tract of land to inhabit. So the twelve sons of Jacob morphed into the following twelve tribes of Israel when they came into their land: Reuben, Simeon, Judah, Zebulun, Issachar, Dan, Gad, Asher, Naphtali, Benjamin, Ephraim and Manasseh (Numbers 34-35).

Judges/Kings

But after Joshua and that miracle generation died . . .

there arose another generation after them, which knew not the LORD, nor yet the works which he had done for Israel. And the children of Israel did evil in the sight of the LORD, and served Baalim: . . . And <u>they forsook the LORD, and served Baal and Ashtaroth</u>. And the anger of the LORD was hot against Israel, and he delivered them into the hands of spoilers that spoiled them, and he sold them into the hands of their enemies round about, so that they could not any longer stand before their enemies. . . . Nevertheless the LORD raised up judges, which delivered them out of the hand of those that spoiled them. And yet they would not listen to their judges, but they went a whoring after other gods, and bowed themselves to them: . . . And when the LORD raised them up judges, then the LORD was with the judge, and delivered them out of the hand of their enemies all the days of the judge: for it repented the LORD because of their groanings by reason of them that oppressed them and vexed them. And it came to pass, when the judge was dead, that they returned, and <u>corrupted themselves more than their fathers</u>, in following other gods to serve them, and to bow down to them; they ceased not from their own doings, nor from their stubborn way. (Judges 2:10-19 edited)

For 450 years Israel was led by judges. Caleb's younger brother, Othniel, judged for 40 years (Judges 3:11) as did Deborah (Judges 5:31) and Gideon (Judges 8:28). Samson judged Israel for 20 years (Judges 15:20).

Then Paul stood up, and beckoning with his hand said, Men of Israel, and you that fear God, give audience. The God of this people of Israel chose our fathers, and exalted the people when they dwelled as strangers in the land of Egypt, and with an high arm brought he them out of it. And about the time of forty years suffered he their manners in the wilderness. And when he had destroyed seven nations in the land of Chanaan, he divided their land to them by lot. And after that <u>he gave to them judges about the space of four hundred and fifty years, until Samuel the prophet.</u> (Acts 13:16-20)

The last 'judge' was Eli, the priest, who judged Israel for forty years while Samuel served in the Tabernacle (1 Samuel 4:16-18). Then God made another transition.

Prophets and Kings

God raised up Samuel, the prophet, who inspired Israel to give up their idols and return to the living God. But the people cried out to have a king like the other nations, rejecting God as their King (1 Samuel 8). And God began to use prophets and kings to lead His people. Samuel anointed Saul as Israel's first king. David desired to build God a temple, but it was his son, Solomon, who built the first Temple. Each of the first three kings of Israel all ruled for forty years: Saul (Acts 13:21), David (2 Samuel 5:4 and 1 Kings 2:11), and Solomon (1 Kings 11:42). After Solomon, the kingdom of Israel was divided into two 'houses' or nations; the house of Israel (ten tribes) and the house of Judah (two tribes). The southern two tribes are Judah and Benjamin, but because Benjamin was so small, it was usually referred to as Judah. The northern ten tribes are known as the house of Israel. After the division, Jehoash was the first king of Israel (2 Kings 12:1) and Joash was the first king of Judah (2 Chronicles 24:1)

It is under the reign of Ahaz that the people of the southern tribes are first called Jews (2 Kings 16:6).

Southern 2 tribes	Northern 10 tribes
king Uzziah; prophet Isaiah	king Jeroboam; prophets Jonah, Amos, Hosea
kings Jotham, Ahaz, Hezekiah prophets Isaiah, Micah, Hosea	king Hoshea -->taken into Assyria 722 BC
king Josiah; prophets Nahum, Zephaniah	--
king Jehoiakim; prophets Habakkuk, Daniel	---> taken into Babylon 605 BC
king Jehoichin; prophet Ezekiel	---> taken into Babylon 597 BC
king Zedekiah; prophet Jeremiah	---> taken into Babylon 588 BC

You therefore, son of man, prophesy, and smite your hands together. and let the sword be doubled <u>the third time</u>, the sword of the slain: it is the sword of the great men that are slain, which enters into their privy chambers. (Ezekiel 21:14 regarding Babylon in v19 coming against Jerusalem three times)

Israel and Judah are in exile. Solomon's Temple and Jerusalem are destroyed by fire in 586 BC. Nebuchadnezzar and the Babylonian empire are large and in charge, but he becomes proud, and God humbles him (Daniel 4:16-37).

Daniel

Daniel explains his deportation as a youth and how he learned the language of Aramaic, the business language of the Babylonian Empire, in Daniel 1. Daniel 2-7 are written in the language of the Gentiles because they deal specifically with the Gentiles; and Daniel 8-12 are written in Hebrew because they deal specifically with Israel. The book is not chronological, but divided as to its intended audience. An outline of Daniel chapters 2-12 follows:

Daniel 2-7 in Aramaic	Daniel 8-12 in Hebrew
2 Statue vision	8 Ram and Goat
3 Bow to gold statue	9 Seventy weeks
4 Great tree to stump	10 Vision of Christ
5 Writing on the wall	11 Syria and Egypt
6 Darius / Lion's den	12 Great Tribulation
7 Four beasts	

Daniel 8 prophesied the Medes/Persians (ram with two horns) would conquer the Babylonians, but the description of the actual takeover with *"the writing on the wall"* is in Daniel 5 (538 BC).

Judah's Return from Exile

Beginning with king Cyrus, the Persian, the Jewish exiles return in waves to Judah. The first group returns with Zerubbabel by the decree of Cyrus; the second group with Ezra, and the third group with Nehemiah under the decrees of Artaxerxes.

Rulers of Persia	Leaders in Jerusalem
Cyrus 539-530	Zerubbabel, governor 536-515
Darius, the Mede 538	Haggai, prophet 536-513
Cambyses II 529-522	Zechariah, prophet 536-513
	Jeshua, high priest 515-483
Darius I Hystaspis 521-486	Joiakim, high priest 483-458
Xerxes 486-475	
Artaxerxes 474-424	Ezra, governor 467-455
	Nehemiah, governor 454-443
Darius II Nothus 423-404	
Darius III Codomannus 380-330	

Alexander, the Great Conquered Darius III in 333 BC

Alexander's troops were outnumbered 2 to 1 at the Battle of Issus in southern Anatolia (Turkey), but routed their enemies. Alexander went on to conquer Tyre and Egypt, which is why Darius III tentatively held onto the remains of his kingdom until 330.

In one of Daniel's visions, he sees Alexander the Great as the "*notable horn*" of the goat of Greece which defeats the two-horned ram of the Medes and Persians.

Then I lifted up my eyes, and saw, and, behold, there stood before the river a ram which had two horns: and the two horns were high; but one was higher than the other, and the higher came up last. I saw the ram pushing westward, and northward, and southward; so that no beasts might stand before him, neither was there any that could deliver out of his hand; but he did according to his will, and *became great. And as I was considering, behold, an he goat came from the west on the face of the whole earth, and touched not the ground: and the goat had a <u>notable horn</u> between his eyes. And he came to the ram that had two horns, which I had seen standing before the river, and ran to him in the fury of his power. And I saw him come close to the ram, and he was moved with choler against him, and smote the ram, and broke his two horns: and there was no power in the ram to stand before him, but he cast him down to the ground, and stamped on him: and there was none that could deliver the ram out of his hand. Therefore the he goat waxed very great: and when he was strong, the great horn was broken; and for it came up four notable ones toward the four winds of heaven. . . . The ram which you saw having two horns are the kings of Media and Persia. And <u>the rough goat is the king of Grecia: and the great horn that is between his eyes is the first king</u>. Now that being broken, whereas four stood up for it, **four** kingdoms shall stand up out of the nation, but not in his power. (Daniel 8:3-8, 20-22 edited)*

After Alexander's death in 323 BC, his four generals divided up the kingdom, and Seleucus took Syria. Daniel 11 prophetically described the devolution of the Greek empire. The Seleucids of Syria took over Israel in 198 BC. Syria was eventually ruled by Antiochus Epiphanes. The Maccabeans led a successful revolt against his Syrian armies and cleansed and rededicated the temple, which is commemorated in Hanukkah. The descendants of the Maccabees ruled until Christ's birth under Herod the Great (who married into their Hasmonean family). Within a generation of Christ's death, the Temple was destroyed (70 AD) and the Jews scattered throughout the earth. Israel ceased to be a nation even though many Jews remained in the land the Romans renamed Palestine. The Romans placed a tax upon anyone performing Jewish rituals throughout their empire, so many Jews traveled to other continents.

Thus the empires in Nebuchadnezzar's metal statue (Daniel 2) took their turns at persecuting the Jews prior to Messiah's first coming: Babylonians, Medes/Persians, Grecians, and Romans. Jews continued to be persecuted in the lands to which they fled, and so many became crypto-Jews, or hidden-Jews. But God provided a safe haven for Jews in America for 350 years (1650-2000).

Zionists Create a Jewish Homeland

In the late 1800's Americans were praying and providing for a future state of the Jewish people. The plight of the Russian Jews immigrating to America touched the hearts of Christians like D. L. Moody and William Blackstone who held a conference and wrote a petition to restore Palestine to Jews.

It read, in part: "Why shall not the powers which under the treaty of Berlin, in 1878, gave Bulgaria to the Bulgarians and Servia to the Servians now give Palestine back to the Jews?…These provinces, as well as Romania, Montenegro, and Greece, were wrested from the Turks and given to their natural owners. Does not Palestine as rightfully belong to the Jews?"

Theodor Herzl, a Jew in Hungary, wrote a book titled *Jewish State* in 1896, and promoted the concept of Zionism, the reestablishment of a homeland for the Jewish people. When WWI began, Europe was already looking at how to carve up the Ottoman Empire. In 1917, a key letter from the British Foreign Office was sent to Lord Rothschild, a leader of the British Jewish community, known as the Balfour Declaration.

> "His Majesty's Government view with favour the establishment in Palestine of a national home for the Jewish people, and will use their best endeavours to facilitate the achievement of this object, it being clearly understood that nothing shall be done which may prejudice the civil and religious rights of existing non-Jewish communities in Palestine, or the rights and political status enjoyed by Jews in any other country."

"The international community, including the emerging Arab nations, recognized Israel at the 1919 Paris Peace Conference, which was held by the victorious Allies in order to settle international questions after the 1918 armistice ended World War I. The head of the Arab delegation, Emir Feisal, great-grandfather of Abdallah, the future king of Jordan, agreed that 'Palestine' would be the Jewish homeland. Feisal accepted the British Balfour Declaration of Nov. 2, 1917, which afforded recognition to a Jewish national homeland, and agreed with the Zionist delegation, stating, "All such measures shall be adopted as we afford the fullest guarantee of carrying into effect the British Government's Balfour Declaration." Emir Feisal confirmed this determination in a March 3, 1919 letter to Harvard Law Professor, and later US Supreme Court Justice, Felix Frankfurter, to whom he wrote: "Our deputation here in Paris is fully acquainted with the proposals submitted by the Zionist organization to the Peace Conference, and we regard them as modest and proper. We will do our best, insofar as we are concerned, to help them through. We will wish the Jews a most hearty welcome home." In exchange for Arab recognition of Israel, the Allied powers, in 1919, agreed to the eventual sovereignty of almost 20 Arab states, covering vast oil-rich lands, after a period of mandatory oversight by European powers. The Europeans would proceed to draw the borders of their respective mandates and, in essence, create the system of Arab states that would emerge out of the remnants of the old Turkish Ottoman Empire. In 1922, a couple of years after the Conference, in a land for peace deal, the British would split Mandatory Palestine into an Arab and a Jewish Mandate using the Jordan River as the line of demarcation. The Arabs were granted East Palestine, or Transjordan, which would later become Arab Jordan while West Palestine, or Cis-Jordan, would become the Jewish National homeland of Israel." (by Chuck Morse April 14, 2006)

The League of Nations made Palestine a British mandate in 1922. The Jews were called Palestinians then, and they accounted for 11% of the population. Later in 1922, the British made the TransJordan an Arab State. So the world already provided an Arab state from Jewish lands; it's called the nation of Jordan. It was the king of Jordan who kicked out Arafat and his violent troublemakers, who then eventually moved to Palestine and began to call themselves Palestinians, trying to convince the world to give them yet another state carved out of Israel's lands.

During WWII the British ruled Palestine with Jerusalem as its capital. Jews came to Israel by droves. But the Temple Mount was controlled by the Muslims.

Daniel's Visions of Four Beasts (Daniel 7)

Daniel spoke and said, I saw in my vision by night, and, behold, the four winds of the heaven strove on the great sea. And four great beasts came up from the sea, diverse one from another. The first was like a lion, and had eagle's wings: I beheld till the wings thereof were plucked, and it was lifted up from the earth, and made stand on the feet as a man, and a man's heart was given to it. And behold another beast, a second, like to a bear, and it raised up itself on one side, and it had three ribs in the mouth of it between the teeth of it: and they said thus to it, Arise, devour much flesh. After this I beheld, and see another, like a leopard, which had on the back of it four wings of a fowl; the beast had also four heads; and dominion was given to it. After this I saw in the night visions, and behold a fourth beast, dreadful and terrible, and strong exceedingly; and it had great iron teeth: it devoured and broke in pieces, and stamped the residue with the feet of it: and it was diverse from all the beasts that were before it; and it had ten horns. . . . As concerning the rest of the beasts, they had their dominion taken away: yet their lives were prolonged for a season and time. . . .These great beasts, which are four, are four kings, which shall arise out of the earth. But the saints of the most High shall take the kingdom, and possess the kingdom for ever, even for ever and ever. (Daniel 7:2-7, 12, 17-18 edited)

These 4 beast empires are the world powers which persecute Jews prior to Christ's second coming. [My thanks to James Lloyd of Christian Media Network for this insight.] The winged lion represents England. In 1189 AD at the coronation of Richard the **Lion**hearted, unexpected persecution of the Jews broke out in England. Most Jewish houses in London were burned, and many Jews killed. All possessions of the Jews were claimed by the Crown. Richard's successor took more than 8 million marks from the Jews. England lost it's American colonies ("*eagle wings*") in 1783.

Then the Russian **bear** came devouring much flesh in 1880. "Between 1929 and 1953 the state created by Lenin and set in motion by Stalin deprived 21.5 million Soviet citizens of their lives," stated Dmitri Volkogonov. Many Jews fled to Palestine.

Germany began its persecution of Jews in 1933 and killed six million Jews by the end of WWII. Germans regarded the panther as an exceptional animal, which is also called a **leopard**. After Hitler's defeat, Germany was divided into four sectors ("*wings*") which were controlled by four commanders ("*heads*"). The Four Power Agreement on Berlin was signed September 3, 1971 by the allied powers: United States, Soviet Union, United Kingdom, and France. A *Russian* general controlled the Eastern zone, a *British* general commanded the Northwestern zone, a *French* general ran the Southwestern zone, and an *American* general administered the western zone.

Again, many Jews fled to Palestine. God may have been using these beasts to drive His Hebrew children home to Israel.

For I will take you from among the heathen, and gather you out of all countries, and will bring you into your own land. (Ezekiel 36:24)

Aliyahs

The Hebrew word *aliyah* means 'ascent', and refers to the return of Jews to their land. The first, second, and third aliyahs were mostly Jews coming from Russia; the fourth aliyah was mostly Jews coming from Poland and Hungary. The fifth aliyah of the 1930's brought over 250,000 Jews from Germany. Then the British made it illegal for the Jews to immigrate as a concession to Germany, but still many came.

1881	First Aliyah	
1904-1914	Second Aliyah	40,000 Jews
1919-1923	Third Aliyah	50,000 Jews
1924-1929	Fourth Aliyah	50,000 Jews
1929-1939	Fifth Aliyah	250,000 Jews

From 1940-1944 Aliyah Bet secretly brought in Jews during WWII. By the end of WWII, Jews accounted for 33% of the population of Palestine. In just 22 years Jews had tripled their population in Palestine.

Israel Miraculously became a Nation in 1948

Before she travailed, she brought forth; before her pain came, she was delivered of a man child. Who has heard such a thing? who has seen such things? Shall the earth be made to bring forth in one day? or <u>shall a nation be born at once</u>? for as soon as Zion travailed, she brought forth her children. Shall I bring to the birth, and not cause to bring forth? said the LORD: shall I cause to bring forth, and shut the womb? said your God. Rejoice you with Jerusalem, and be glad with her, all you that love her: rejoice for joy with her, all you that mourn for her: . . .And when you see this, your heart shall rejoice, and your bones shall flourish like an herb:

and the hand of the LORD shall be known toward his servants, and his indignation toward his enemies. (Isaiah 66:7-14 edited)

The Dead Sea Scrolls were discovered in 1947, and photographed in February 1948. Arab protests erupted in March. On May 14, 1948, one day before the end of the British Mandate, the Jewish Agency proclaimed independence, naming their country Israel. She became a nation, and then "*her pain came*". The next day five Arab countries invaded Israel: Egypt, Syria, Jordan, Lebanon and Iraq. The Arab-Israeli War lasted a year. The 1949 Armistice Agreements created temporary borders. Jordan annexed the West Bank and East Jerusalem, and Egypt controlled the Gaza Strip. There was rejoicing and mourning specifically over Jerusalem; the Muslims controlled the east side including the Temple Mount.

In 1948 the Soviet Union immediately recognized the new state of Israel. The population of Israel rose from 800,000 to two million between 1948 and 1958. During that period, Israel was frequently attacked by Egyptian-sponsored Muslims in the Gaza Strip, and no nation cared. But when Egypt nationalized the Suez Canal in 1956, France and the United Kingdom secretly created a plan with Israel to recapture the Sinai Peninsula which was successful, but then the United States and the Soviet Union required Israel to retreat from it for guarantees of shipping rights. Egyptian President Nasser began to call for Arabs to unite and plan Israel's destruction.

Six-Day War of 1967 (retaking of Jerusalem and Temple Mount)

Syria often shelled Israeli villages from bases in the Golan Heights. This escalated to an air battle in April 1967, and Israel shot down six of Syria's MiG fighter planes (gifts from the Soviet Union). On May 12th, the Soviet Union provided Nasser false intelligence of Israel's plans for an imminent attack on Syria. Nasser sent Egyptian troops into the de-militarized Sinai buffer area beginning May 14th. On May 23rd Nasser closed the Straits of Tiran, which blockaded Israel's only access to the Indian Ocean.

Israel countered by sending troops to the Sinai, and then led a "pre-emptive" air attack. The Israeli air force destroyed most of the Egyptian and other allied Arab air forces on the ground. Egypt had 100,000 troops in the Sinai. Syria had 75,000 troops. Jordan had 55,000 troops, 300 tanks, plus 100 Iraqi tanks and an infantry division. The Israeli army had a total strength, including reservists, of 264,000.

The 1967 War was a watershed event in the history of Israel and the Middle East. In just six days Israel regained the Sinai Peninsula, Gaza Strip, Golan Heights, and West Bank; but most importantly, they took back Jerusalem and the Temple Mount. After Israel won the war they were pressured into giving up over 80% of their land. Under Russian threat, Israel returned the Temple Mount to Muslim authorities (Waqf), and the Golan Heights to Syria for supposed peace. Israel also returned the Sinai Peninsula to Egypt for peace. Israel kept the West Bank.

Yom Kippur War of 1973

On October 6, 1973 on Yom Kippur, Egypt and Syria led a surprise attack against Israel. Algeria, Libya, Kuwait, Jordan and Lebanon all pledged their support for the Arab offensive. Israel was outnumbered three to two in immediately available man-power, three to two in tanks and two to one in combat aircraft against the combined forces of Egypt and Syria. And Israel beat them, but not before incurring 6,000 casualties.

Fourth Beast Stomps Upon Jews

After this I saw in the night visions, and behold a fourth beast, dreadful and terrible, and strong exceedingly; and it had great iron teeth: it devoured and broke in pieces, and <u>stamped the residue with the feet</u> of it: and it was diverse from all the beasts that were before it; and it had ten horns. . . . Thus he said, The fourth beast shall be the fourth kingdom on earth, which shall be diverse from all kingdoms, and shall devour the whole earth, and shall tread it down, and break it in pieces. (Daniel 7:7, 23)

The **ten-horned monster** is a Muslim conglomerate which continues to persecute non-Muslims, and Jews particularly. PLO (Palestinian Liberation Organization) attacks, or *intifadas*, began in Israel in the 1970's and continue. Hezbollah attacks Israel from the north, and Hamas attacks from the south. The moon-worshipers have trodden upon the Jews and the Temple Mount for over a thousand years.

Then I heard one saint speaking, and another saint said to that certain saint which spoke, How long shall be the vision concerning the daily sacrifice, and the transgression of desolation, to give both the sanctuary and the host <u>to be trodden under foot</u>? And he said to me, To two thousand and three hundred days; then shall the sanctuary be cleansed. (Daniel 8:13-14)

The "Fullness" of Its Time

*The ram which you saw having two horns are the kings of Media and Persia. And the rough goat is the king of Grecia: and the great horn that is between his eyes is the first king. Now that being broken, whereas four stood up for it, four kingdoms shall stand up out of the nation, but not in his power. And in the latter time of their kingdom, when the **<u>transgressors</u>** <u>are come to the full</u>, a king of fierce countenance, and understanding dark sentences, shall stand up. (Daniel 8:20-23)*

'Transgressors' is *paw-shah'* which means 'rush on' via expansion and 'break away' from just authority; that is, trespass, apostatize, quarrel, offend, rebel, or revolt. The Muslims have "broken away" from the former USSR and have expanded their territories. They have brought down good governments and begun wars around the world to expand Islam. After Alexander's death, his kingdom was split between his four generals. From one of their kingdoms (Syria) will emerge *"a king of fierce countenance"*, a "little horn" *"when the transgressors come to the full"*.

Muslims now control one fourth of the earth and have a quarter of the world's population. According to Revelation 6:8, the rider of the pale horse is given power "*over the fourth part of the earth*" to kill, and his name is Death. Muslims are quoted saying, "We love death like you love life." The transgressors have come to the full, and it's time for the "little horn" to emerge and lead the forth beast in the Great Tribulation.

The fullness of transgressors is not to be confused with the fullness of the Gentiles, though I believe both have reached their fullness. Within the last two decades, thousands of Jews have come to believe Jesus is their Messiah, and now there are dozens of Messianic groups in Israel.

> *For I would not, brothers, that you should be ignorant of this mystery, lest you should be wise in your own conceits; that blindness in part is happened to Israel, until the <u>fullness of the Gentiles</u> be come in. And so all Israel shall be saved: as it is written, There shall come out of Sion the Deliverer, and shall turn away ungodliness from Jacob: (Romans 11:25-26)*

Sealing of 144,000 Hebrews

God will "seal" 144,000 Hebrews; only 12,000 of which will be from the tribe of Judah (which is listed first), the rest will be from the lost tribes of the house of Israel (Revelation 7:2-8; 14:3-5). Dan and Ephraim are excluded from the twelve tribes sealed in Revelation because they allowed king Jeroboam to establish worship of golden calves in their territories (1 Kings 12:26-33). Ephraim is replaced with the "tribe of Joseph". Within the last twenty years, groups of crypto-Jews have come out of hundreds and thousands of years of hiding to declare they have remained faithful to the one true God. Some groups prove their lineage through careful genealogies, while others through DNA testing.

It is not unusual for God to hide His people. When wicked Jezebel was persecuting His prophets, God had Obadiah hide 100 of them in caves (1 Kings 18:4), and God kept 7,000 faithful who refused to worship her wicked Baal (1 Kings 19:18). So even though these 144,000 will be sealed, it does not necessarily mean it will be done openly; God may choose to keep them hidden for their safety. Or He may place a visible mark on their foreheads which will keep them from taking the mark of the beast.

To be "sealed" by God is to be given His Holy Spirit after trusting in Jesus Christ for salvation. Note this is done in "*the fullness of times . . . until the redemption*" of Christ's second coming. The Jews are called the "first-fruits" because they trusted in Christ first, and many Jews rose from their graves in Jerusalem when Jesus rose from His (Matthew 27:52-53).

> *That in the dispensation of the <u>fullness of times</u> he might gather together in one all things in Christ, both which are in heaven, and which are on earth; even in him: In*

*whom also we have obtained an inheritance, being predestinated according to the purpose of him who works all things after the counsel of his own will: That we should be to the praise of his glory, who **first** trusted in Christ. In whom you also trusted, after that you heard the word of truth, the gospel of your salvation: in whom also after that you believed, you were **sealed** with that holy Spirit of promise, Which is the earnest of our inheritance <u>until the redemption</u> of the purchased possession, to the praise of his glory. (Ephesians 1:10-14)*

Future War Against Israel by "All Nations"

Nations continue to pressure Israel to divide its land and its capital, and to give away more land for false peace. Israelis can't have peace with people who want to exterminate them. Israel will eventually stand up and defend itself in a way that so incenses the other nations that they will all come against Israel at the battle of Armageddon.

For, behold, in those days, and in that time, when I shall bring again the captivity of Judah and Jerusalem, <u>I will also gather all nations, and will bring them down into the valley of Jehoshaphat</u>, and will plead with them there for my people and for my heritage Israel, whom they have scattered among the nations, and parted my land. (Joel 3:1-2)

"*Those days*" refers back to Joel 2 and the days of the LORD's second coming at the blowing of the trumpet (Rosh Hashanah is celebrated for two days) when the sun is dark and the moon is red. There is no actual "*valley of Jehosaphat*" in Israel. *Jehosaphat* means "Jehovah judges". The place where God intends to draw all the kings of the world so that He may judge for what they've done to Jews and Israel is Har Megiddo, Mount Megiddo ("*Armageddon*" in Revelation 16:12-16). Note God gathers "*all nations*", not the nations listed in Ezekiel 38.

Future Return of House of Israel

Though the house of Judah has been restored to the land in fulfillment of prophecy, there is yet a greater restoration of the house of Israel yet to come.

And, you son of man, thus said the Lord GOD; Speak to every feathered fowl, and to every beast of the field, Assemble yourselves, and come; gather yourselves on every side to my sacrifice that I do sacrifice for you, even a great sacrifice on the mountains of Israel, that you may eat flesh, and drink blood. You shall eat the flesh of the mighty, and drink the blood of the princes of the earth, . . .So the house of Israel shall know that I am the LORD their God from that day and forward. And the heathen shall know that the house of Israel went into captivity for their iniquity: because they trespassed against me, therefore hid I my face from them, and gave them into the hand of their enemies: so fell they all by the sword. According to their uncleanness and according to their transgressions have I done to them, and hid my face from them. Therefore thus said the Lord GOD; Now will I bring again the captivity of Jacob, and have mercy on the whole house of Israel, and will be jealous for my holy name; After that they have borne their shame, and all their trespasses whereby they have trespassed against me, when they dwelled safely in their land, and none made them afraid. <u>*When I have brought them again from the people, and gathered them out of their enemies' lands, and am sanctified in them in the sight of many nations; Then shall they know that I am the LORD their God, which caused them to be led into captivity among the heathen: but I have gathered them to their own land, and have left none of them any more there.*</u> *Neither will I hide my face any more from them: for I have poured out my spirit on the house of Israel, said the Lord GOD. (Ezekiel 39:17-18, 22-29)*

After the battle of Megiddo, God will restore all Hebrews to their land. "*. . . blindness in part is happened to Israel, until the fullness of the Gentiles be come in. And so <u>all Israel shall be saved</u>*" (Romans 11:25b-26).

Summary

After Noah's flood, Shem's descendants settled in Mesopotamia. God chose Abram and promised him the "*whole land of Canaan*" between the Nile and the Euphrates, but the promise of land to his seed also came with a prophecy of struggle until the iniquity of the Amorites was full (Genesis 15:16). [There is a pattern of the promise withheld until the transgressions of others have reached fullness.]

Israel, the prince of God, married Leah and Rachel (and two concubines) and had 12 sons, who became the patriarchs of the 12 tribes of Israel. The eleven jealous brothers sold Joseph into slavery for twenty pieces of silver to Egypt, but he became their redeemer during the famine, and the entire clan moved to Goshen. About four generations later God gave the Hebrews another deliverer named Moses.

The Exodus from Egypt coincides with Passover, the crossing of the Red Sea with First Fruits, and the giving of the Law on Mount Sinai with Pentecost (Feast of Weeks). After Moses died, Joshua took the Hebrews across the Jordan river into the Promised Land of Canaan to destroy the idol worshipers there. But they did not eradicate all the idol worshipers.

After Joshua and that generation died the people of Israel were led by judges for 450 years. The people rejected God as their King, and God used prophets and kings to lead His people. The kingdom of Israel was divided into two after 120 years. The northern house of Israel was taken into exile by the Assyrians from 734 to 715 BC in three waves, and the southern house of Judah was taken into exile by Babylonians from 605 to 588 BC also in three waves. Solomon's Temple and Jerusalem were destroyed by fire in 586 BC.

Daniel recognized the exile was punishment for sin, and that it was almost over. The Jewish exiles returned in waves to Judah from 536 to 454 BC by Persian decrees. Daniel also knew through visions that after the Persians would come the Greeks. Alexander the

Great conquered Darius III of Persia in 333 BC. Daniel predicted the decline of the Grecian empire (Daniel 11) until it was conquered by the Romans (Daniel 2). Daniel's seventy week prophecy (Daniel 9) predicted the destruction of the Temple and Jerusalem after Messiah was "cut off". Jews dispersed and time passed.

In the late 1800's people began to seek a future state for the Jewish people. In 1917 the British Balfour Declaration brought it closer to reality. The League of Nations made Palestine a British mandate in 1922, and Jews accounted for 11% of the population. Many Jews fled to Palestine to escape Russian and German pogroms against them. By the end of WWII, Jews accounted for 33% of the population of Palestine, tripling their population in 22 years.

Israel miraculously became a Nation in 1948. The next day five Arab countries began a war which lasted a year. The population of Israel rose from 800,000 to two million between 1948 and 1958. During that period, Israel was frequently attacked by Muslims which escalated until the 1967 War. In just six days Israel regained the Sinai Peninsula, Gaza Strip, Golan Heights, and West Bank; but most importantly, they took back Jerusalem and the Temple Mount. Under pressure Israel returned all the land it had won except the West Bank. Israel was attacked by Muslim nations again on Yom Kippur in 1973.

Daniel's fourth beast represents a Muslim conglomerate which continues to tread upon Israel. Muslims have reached their "fullness" of a fourth of the earth in which they have power to kill, and a "little horn" (caliph) should soon arise to lead the beast and begin the Great Tribulation. Prior to this God will seal 144,000 Hebrews with His Holy Spirit.

Nations will continue to pressure Israel to divide its land and its capital, and to give away more land for false peace. Israelis can't have peace with people who want to exterminate them. Israel will eventually stand up and defend itself in a way that so incenses the other nations that they will all come against Israel at the battle of Armageddon. After the battle in the valley of Mount Megiddo, God will restore all Hebrews to their land.

The Gentile church does not replace Israel; instead, Gentile believers in Yeshua are placed into Israel, adopted into God's family. Israel is often referred to as an olive tree. And we Gentiles *"were grafted in among them, and with them partake of the root and fatness of the olive tree"* (Romans 11:17).

> *For if you were cut out of the olive tree which is wild by nature, and were grafted contrary to nature into a good olive tree: . . . that blindness in part is happened to Israel, until the fullness of the Gentiles be come in. And so all Israel shall be saved: . . . As concerning the gospel, they are enemies for your sakes: but as touching the election, they are beloved for the father's sakes. For the gifts and calling of God are without repentance. (Romans 11:24-29 edited)*

The fullness of the Gentiles has come in, and the blinders have been removed from Hebrew people who are coming to faith in Jesus as their Messiah by the thousands. There is yet time for many Jews and Gentiles to trust in the Lord Jesus Christ for their salvation, so we should be about our Father's business.

Abominations

And you have seen their abominations, and their idols, wood and stone, silver and gold, which were among them. (Deuteronomy 29:17)

There are several words translated as 'abomination'. The one in the verse above is *shikkoots*, meaning disgusting, filthy, detestable, and especially idolatrous. Our God is a jealous God. Jesus paid our bride price with His life-blood; thus He requires and deserves our complete affection. We are not to go whoring after other gods or idols.

When people talk about the "abomination of desolation" you should ask them, which one? God prophesied several desolations upon the Hebrews for their disobedience in the wilderness (Leviticus 26:21-43). 'Desolation' is *shamem* meaning to stun or stupefy, devastate or be astonished, be destitute, destroyed, or laid waste. Jesus specified, "*When you therefore shall see the abomination of desolation, spoken of by Daniel the prophet, stand in the holy place*" (Matthew 24:15). But again we need to ask, "Which one?"

"Abominations of Desolation" in Daniel

Seventy weeks are determined on your people and on your holy city . . . And after threescore and two weeks shall <u>Messiah</u> be cut off, but not for himself: and the people of the prince that shall come shall destroy the city and the sanctuary; and the end thereof shall be with a flood, **and unto the end of the war desolations are determined.** *And <u>he</u> shall confirm the covenant with many for one week: and in the midst of the week <u>he</u> shall cause the sacrifice and the oblation to cease, and **for the overspreading of abominations <u>he</u> shall make it desolate**, even until the consummation, and that determined shall be poured upon the desolate. (Daniel 9:24-27 edited)*

And <u>arms</u> shall stand on his part, and <u>they</u> shall pollute the sanctuary of strength, and shall take away the daily sacrifice, and <u>they</u> shall place the abomination that makes desolate. (Daniel 11:31)

***And from the time that the daily sacrifice shall be taken away, and the abomination that makes desolate set up**, there shall be a thousand two hundred and ninety days. Blessed is he that waits, and comes to the thousand three hundred and five and thirty days. (Daniel 12:11-12)*

Note the differences of pronouns or lack thereof between the three. Taken out of context they are rather difficult to understand. In the first verse it is 'because of' or 'due to' the over-spreading of abominations that he will make it desolate and an individual is referenced. In the second, an army pollutes the sanctuary, takes away the daily sacrifice, and places the abomination that makes desolate. In the third verse, an abomination that makes desolate is "*set up*". We'll begin with the army that pollutes the sanctuary, takes away the daily sacrifice, and places the abomination that makes desolate, because it's also responsible for a fourth "*transgression of desolation*".

Antiochus IV Epiphanes

In one of Daniel's visions, he sees Alexander the Great as the great horn of the goat of Greece.

> *Therefore the he goat waxed very great: and when he was strong, the* <u>great horn</u> *was broken; and for it came up four notable ones toward the four winds of heaven. And out of one of them came forth a little horn, which waxed exceeding great, toward the south, and toward the east, and toward the pleasant land. And it waxed great, even to the host of heaven; and it cast down some of the host and of the stars to the ground, and stamped on them. Yes, he magnified himself even to the prince of the host, and by him the daily sacrifice was taken away, and the place of the sanctuary was cast down. And an host was given him against the daily sacrifice by reason of transgression, and it cast down the truth to the ground; and it practiced, and prospered. Then I heard one saint speaking, and another saint said to that certain saint which spoke, How long shall be the vision concerning the daily sacrifice, and the* **transgression of desolation**, *to give both the sanctuary and the host to be trodden under foot? And he said to me, To two thousand and three hundred days; then shall the sanctuary be cleansed. (Daniel 8:8-14)*

'Transgression' is *pesha* which means revolt, rebellion, or trespass. 'Host' is *tsaba* which means a mass of people or an army. 2300 days = 6 2/3 years (6.66) using a 360 day year.

After Alexander's death in 323 BC, his four generals divided up the kingdom, and Seleucus took Syria. The Seleucids of Syria took over Israel in 198 BC. Syria was eventually ruled by Antiochus Epiphanes ('shining one'), but the Jews called him Antiochus Epimanes ('mad one'). This "little horn" invaded Egypt with his Syrian army in 170 and again in 168 BC (each time going through Israel). He had a pig sacrificed in the temple to Zeus on Kislev 15, 167 BC, and tried to get the Jews to eat the meat; they were tortured for refusing and burnt on the altar (II Maccabees 6 and 7).

> "Moreover king Antiochus wrote to his whole kingdom, that all should be one people, And every one should leave his laws: so all the heathen agreed according to the commandment of the king. Yea, many also of the Israelites consented to his

religion, and sacrificed unto idols, and profaned the sabbath. For the king had sent letters by messengers unto Jerusalem and the cities of Juda that they should follow the strange laws of the land, And <u>forbid burnt offerings, and sacrifice, and drink offerings, in the temple; and that they should profane the sabbaths and festival days: And pollute the sanctuary and holy people: Set up altars, and groves, and chapels of idols, and sacrifice swine's flesh, and unclean beasts: That they should also leave their children uncircumcised, and make their souls abominable with all manner of uncleanness and profanation: To the end they might forget the law, and change all the ordinances. And whosoever would not do according to the commandment of the king, he said, he should die.</u> In the selfsame manner wrote he to his whole kingdom, and appointed overseers over all the people, commanding the cities of Juda to sacrifice, city by city. Then many of the people were gathered unto them, to wit every one that forsook the law; and so they committed evils in the land; And drove the Israelites into secret places, even wheresoever they could flee for succour. Now the fifteenth day of the month Casleu, in the hundred forty and fifth year, they set up the **abomination of desolation** upon the altar, and builded idol altars throughout the cities of Juda on every side; And burnt incense at the doors of their houses, and in the streets. And when they had <u>rent in pieces the books of the law which they found, they burnt them with fire</u>." (I Maccabees 1:41-56)

Josephus states Antiochus held Jerusalem for 3½ years. He decided to exterminate the Jews, but mysteriously died en route in November/December of 164 BC after writing letters of apology to the Jews for his plans to do so. Antiochus IV had been terrorizing Jerusalem for 6 2/3 years. The Maccabeans led a successful revolt against his Syrian armies and cleansed and rededicated the temple, which is commemorated in Hanukkah and foretold in Ezekiel.

Therefore say, Thus said the Lord GOD; Although I have cast them far off among the heathen, and although I have scattered them among the countries, yet will I be to them as a little sanctuary in the countries where they shall come. Therefore say, Thus said the Lord GOD; I will even gather you from the people, and assemble you out of the countries where you have been scattered, and I will give you the land of Israel. And they shall come thither, and <u>they shall take away all the detestable things thereof and all the abominations thereof from there. And I will give them one heart, and I will put a new spirit within you</u>; and I will take the stony heart out of their flesh, and will give them an heart of flesh: That they may walk in my statutes, and keep my ordinances, and do them: and they shall be my people, and I will be their God. But as for them whose heart walks after the heart of their detestable things and their abominations, I will recompense their way on their own heads, said the Lord GOD. (Ezekiel 11:16-21)

Therefore the second 'abomination of desolation' verse (Daniel 11:31) was fulfilled before Christ was born by the armies of Antiochus Epiphanes. To understand the first one, we need more background information.

How Jesus "Fills Up" Israel's Punishments of Desolations

*And if you walk contrary to me, and will not listen to me; I will bring seven times more plagues on you according to your sins. I will also send wild beasts among you, which shall rob you of your children, and destroy your cattle, and make you few in number; and your high ways shall be **desolate**. . . . And I will make your cities waste, <u>and bring your sanctuaries to **desolation**</u>, and I will not smell the smell of your sweet odors. And I will bring the land into **desolation**: and your enemies which dwell therein shall be astonished at it. And I will scatter you among the heathen, and will draw out a sword after you: and your land shall be **desolate**, and your cities waste. Then shall the land enjoy her sabbaths, as long as it lies **desolate**, and you be in your enemies' land; even then shall the land rest, and enjoy her sabbaths. As long as it lies **desolate** it shall rest; because it did not rest in your sabbaths, when you dwelled on it. . . .The land also shall be left of them, and shall enjoy her sabbaths, while she lies **desolate** without them: and they shall accept of the punishment of their iniquity: because, even because they despised my judgments, and because their soul abhorred my statutes. (Leviticus 26:21-43 edited)*

Seven is used as a period of punishment, and the word desolate/desolation appears 7 times in this chapter. It's appropriate since part of their disobedience concerned ignoring God's laws concerning the 'sabbath' (a period of seven). Chapter 9 of Daniel contains the famous 70 weeks prophecy regarding the coming of Messiah, but at the beginning of that chapter Daniel refers to his revelation stemming from his study of Jeremiah and the Law of Moses. Because the Hebrews refused to enter the Promised Land when God commanded them, God prophesied to them about the future punishments which would come upon them.

*In the first year of his reign I Daniel understood by books the number of the years, whereof the word of the LORD came to Jeremiah the prophet, that he would accomplish seventy years in the desolations of Jerusalem. . . . As it is written in the law of Moses, all this evil is come on us: yet made we not our prayer before the LORD our God, that we might turn from our iniquities, and understand your truth. Therefore has the <u>LORD</u> **watched on the evil, and brought it on us**: for the LORD our God is righteous in all his works which he does: for we obeyed not his voice. . . . Seventy weeks are determined on your people and on your holy city . . . And after threescore and two weeks shall <u>Messiah</u> be cut off, but not for himself: and the people of the prince that shall come **shall destroy the city and the sanctuary**; and the end thereof shall be with a flood, **and unto the end of the war desolations are determined.** And <u>he</u> shall confirm the covenant with many for one week: and in the* *midst of the week **he** shall cause the sacrifice and the oblation to cease, and **for the overspreading of abominations he shall make it desolate**, even until the consummation, and that determined shall be poured upon the desolate. (Daniel 9:2, 13-14, 24-27 edited)*

When Messiah came, it was to complete **their** punishment and desolations, and then to be "*cut off*" for **their** salvation. Jesus taught this punishment would be completed within forty years (a generation).

*And when you shall see Jerusalem **compassed** with **armies**, then know that the desolation thereof is near. Then let them which are in Judaea flee to the mountains; and let them which are in the middle of it depart out; and let not them that are in the countries enter thereinto. <u>For these be the days of vengeance, that all things which are written may be fulfilled.</u> But woe to them that are with child, and to them that give suck, in those days! for there shall be great distress in the land, and wrath on this people. And they shall fall by the edge of the sword, and shall be led away captive into all nations: and Jerusalem shall be trodden down of the Gentiles, until the times of the Gentiles be fulfilled. . . . Truly I say to you, <u>This generation shall not pass away, till all be fulfilled</u>. (Luke 21:20-24, 32)*

The word for 'vengeance' is *ekdikesis* which means punishment. These desolations of war upon the Jews and Jerusalem were determined as punishment because of their sins back when the Hebrews refused to go into the promised land (Leviticus 26). The desolations of war of the last half of the 70th week (Daniel 9:24-27) was from March/April 67 when Vespasian's troops fought against the Judeans in Galilee to the Temple's destruction on (9th of Av) August 29, 70 AD. Besides Leviticus and Daniel, this destruction was also foretold in Psalms using similar wording (in bold):

*Why should I fear in the days of evil, when the iniquity of my heels [supplanters or **enemies**] shall **compass** me about? (Psalm 49:5 edited with additions)*

Titus tried to protect the Temple, but a fire started in adjoining buildings which eventually destroyed the Temple and melted its gold. The stones were cast down and picked apart to retrieve the gold. This destruction of the second Temple was on the same exact day that Solomon's Temple was destroyed by the Babylonians in 586 BC. Thus was the first punishment of 70 years prophesied by Jeremiah for past sins linked to the 70 week prophecy of Daniel.

The second Temple's destruction fulfills the Messiah's prophecy as well as the completion *"for the overspreading of abominations"* in Daniel's 70th week (Daniel 9). The first 'abomination of desolation' verse in Daniel was fulfilled by Jesus within a generation of His being the covenant "*cut off*" on the cross.

Daniel's Last "Abomination of Desolation"

In Matthew 24:15 Jesus prophesied of a future fulfillment of Daniel's "abomination of desolation". The False Prophet will declare himself god in the Temple Complex.

*When you therefore shall see the abomination of desolation, spoken of by Daniel the prophet, **stand in the holy place**, (whoever reads, let him understand:) Then let them which be in Judaea flee into the mountains: Let him which is on the housetop not come down to take any thing out of his house: Neither let him which is in the field return back to take his clothes. And woe to them that are with child, and to them that give suck in those days! But pray you that your flight be not in the winter, neither on the sabbath day: For then shall be <u>great tribulation</u>, such as was not since the beginning of the world to this time, no, nor ever shall be. And except those days should be shortened, there should no flesh be saved: but for the elect's sake <u>those days shall be shortened</u>. (Matthew 24:15-22)*

Some might say that this passage is just like the one in Luke 21 which was already fulfilled. But that passage specified the destruction of Jerusalem for the fulfillment of previously written punishment: "*And when you shall see Jerusalem compassed with armies, then know that the desolation thereof is near*" (Luke 15:2). But the Matthew passage is at the time of the Great Tribulation, when the "*abomination of desolation*" will "*stand in the holy place*". 'Stand' is *histemi* in Greek, meaning abide, continue, covenant, establish, hold up, lay, stand forth and set up. The Greek word meaning 'to place' (*tithemi*) was not used.

*And from the time that the daily sacrifice shall be taken away, and the abomination that makes desolate **set up**, there shall be a thousand two hundred and ninety days. Blessed is he that waits, and comes to the thousand three hundred and five and thirty days. (Daniel 12:11-12)*

'Set up' is *nawthan* in Hebrew, meaning many things based upon the root 'to give'; put, make, bestow, deliver, lay up, perform, place, render, set forth, etc. It is the same as the word "*place*" in the second abomination verse: "*And arms shall stand on his part, and they shall pollute the sanctuary of strength, and shall take away the daily sacrifice, and they shall **place** the abomination that makes desolate*" (Daniel 11:31). After polluting the sanctuary with pig's blood, Antiochus Epiphanes **placed** a statue of Zeus on the altar.

So we are looking for something "*set up*" in the "*holy place*" to fulfill this prophecy. When the holy of holies of the Temple are referred to in Hebrews 9, it's called the *hagion*. When the Temple Mount is referred to as the "*holy place*" in Acts (6:13; 21:28) it's called *hagios topos;* and it is this phrase used by Jesus in Matthew 24:15. Another Temple does not need to be built for this "*abomination of desolation spoken of by Daniel*" to occur on the Temple Mount.

The Temple Mount is Holy because Jehovah Placed His NAME There

Then there shall be a place which the LORD your God shall choose to cause his name to dwell there; thither shall you bring all that I command you; your burnt offerings, and your sacrifices, your tithes, and the heave offering of your hand, and all your choice vows which you vow to the LORD: . . . Take heed to yourself that you offer not your burnt offerings in every place that you see: But in the place which the LORD shall choose in one of your tribes, there you shall offer your burnt offerings, and there you shall do all that I command you. (Deut. 12:11, 13-14)

And it came to pass, when Solomon had finished the building of the house of the LORD, and the king's house, and all Solomon's desire which he was pleased to do, That the LORD appeared to Solomon . . . And the LORD said to him, I have heard your prayer and your supplication, that you have made before me: I have hallowed this house, which you have built, to put my name there for ever; and my eyes and my heart shall be there perpetually. (1 Kings 9:1-3 edited)

People and places are holy because God has set them apart for His special use. And Jehovah has chosen Jerusalem (2 Chronicles 6:6; 33:4). Thayer's Greek definition of *Jerusalem* is "set ye double peace". But because of sin, God removed His people and the Temple for a season (2 Kings 21:7; 23:27). Daniel prophesied the holy people would be completely scattered from Jerusalem.

It shall be for a time, times, and an half; and when he shall have accomplished to scatter the power of the holy people, all these things shall be finished. (Daniel 12:7b)

Emperor Hadrian (117-138 AD) Fulfilled Daniel 12:7

Emperor Hadrian sought peace through multiculturalism and pantheism, but Jews refused to worship other gods. He began to pass laws to undermine their religion, and even outlawed circumcision. Hadrian had an enlarged square platform built on top of Mount Moriah to cover all remains of the Temple so that the place of the Temple could not be identified. In his sixteenth year, 132, the Romans built an abomination on the Temple Mount by building a temple to Jupiter. The Jews, under Simon Bar Khokhab and Akiba ben Joseph, rose up against the Romans. But by the end of the war three and a half years later in 136, the Jews were banished from Jerusalem on pain of death. 580,000 Jews were killed and 50 fortified towns and 985 villages razed; and thenceforth, the land became desolate. Hadrian ceremonially burned the Torah scroll on the Temple Mount. He attempted to erase all memory of Judea by renaming the province *Syria Palaestina* after the Philistines, and renaming Jerusalem *Aelia Capitolina*.

> *How long shall it be to the end of these wonders? . . . and swore by him that lives for ever that it shall be for a time, times, and an half; and when he shall have accomplished to scatter the power of the holy people, all these things shall be finished. (Daniel 12:6b and 7b)*

Hadrian fulfilled this prophecy regarding the "*time, times, and an half . . . to scatter the power of the holy people.*" Even after the siege and burning of Jerusalem in 70 AD, Jews still returned to their beloved capital and the remains of the Temple. After Hadrian, the Jews stayed away for hundreds of years. Hadrian did "*set up*" an abomination on the Temple Mount, and the war did last three and a half years in seeming accordance with "*time, times and half a time*" which is used in Revelation, but he was just an antichrist, not the Antichrist. The reasons are as follows: the years given regarding the Antichrist's abomination being "*set up*" are given at the end of the Daniel 12, the phrase in Revelation correlates to 350 years, not 3 1/2 years; and Hadrian was more interested in worshiping his dead homosexual lover than in seeking worship for himself.

Al-Aqsa Masjid Mosque Complex

After the Jews and Romans had been defeated, a different people who worshiped a different God built another abomination on Hadrian's square, likely using the foundations of his Roman temple. This Muslim complex covers the Jewish Temple Mount, and the Muslims have control over all aspects of it. It includes the Al-Aqsa Mosque and the Dome of the Rock. Al-Aqsa was built upon Solomon's place of prayer by Omar/Umar, since it was the southern portion of the Temple Mount closest to Mecca. The Dome of the Rock is where Muslims "say" Mohammed came by night in a dream and went from there on a horse to heaven. Jerusalem is never mentioned in the Koran. When I see a postcard with their looming domes, I think, "what an abomination".

> *But when you shall see the abomination of desolation, spoken of by Daniel the prophet, **standing where it ought not**, (let him that reads understand,) then let them that be in Judaea flee to the mountains (Mark 13:14)*

The parallel verse in Mark echoes the same theme: Daniel's abomination of desolation "*standing where it ought not*". These Muslim shrines should not stand upon God's holy place in Jerusalem where an angel kept Abraham from slaying Isaac, and the destroying angel stopped God's plague against Israel during David's reign, and where the first and second Temples stood.

The Temple Mount is controlled by the Waqf who are Hashemites of Jordan. They dug under the Temple Mount and cast the precious remnants of Jewish archaeological heritage like mere debris into the Kidron valley. The Muslims have tried to expunge the Name of Jehovah from the Temple Mount.

> *Remember your congregation, which you have purchased of old; the rod of your inheritance, which you have redeemed; <u>this mount Zion, wherein you have dwelled</u>.*

Abominations

*Lift up your feet to the perpetual <u>desolations; even all that the enemy has done wickedly in the sanctuary</u>. Your enemies roar in the middle of your congregations; they **set up** their ensigns for signs. . . . They have cast fire into your sanctuary, <u>they have defiled by casting down the dwelling place of your name to the ground</u>. They said in their hearts, Let us destroy them together: they have burned up all the synagogues of God in the land. We see not our signs: there is no more any prophet: neither is there among us any that knows how long. O God, how long shall the adversary reproach? shall the enemy blaspheme your name for ever? . . .Remember this, that the enemy has reproached, O LORD, and that the foolish people have blasphemed your name. (Psalm 74:2-18 edited)*

'Set up' is *soom/seem,* meaning call [a name], change, charge, commit, determine, disguise, dispose, hold, impute, mark, name, paint, place, preserve, purpose, rehearse, reward, tread down, and overturn. 'Ensigns' and 'signs' are *oth*, meaning a signal as a flag, beacon, monument, omen, prodigy, evidence, mark, or token. 'Desolations' is *mashshuah* meaning destruction (Ps. 73:18). The Muslims have changed the name and purpose of the Temple Mount and placed their golden dome as a beacon of the destruction of Jehovah's presence there.

After Israel turned Nablus (Shechem) over to the Palestinians, Muslims began to desecrate Joseph's tomb in 1999 with hammers, then they painted its dome green (for Islam), and they eventually destroyed it by fire in 2001 to erect a mosque in its place.

Prophetic Time-line of "abomination of desolation spoken of by Daniel"

And from the time that the daily sacrifice shall be taken away, and the abomination that makes desolate set up, there shall be a thousand two hundred and ninety days. Blessed is he that waits, and comes to the thousand three hundred and five and thirty days. (Daniel 12:11-12)

The angel talking to Daniel gave specific times until the end as well as the action which starts the clock, which is when the daily sacrifice is taken away and **the abomination that makes desolate set up.** Then there is a period of 1,290 'days' when something major happens, followed by a "blessing" 45 'days' later; totaling 1,335 days. Prophetic 'days' in Daniel are often equal to a year. God gave Daniel the 70 weeks prophecy which accurately foretold the year of Messiah being "cut off" at His first coming; it is reasonable to believe God also gave Daniel prophecies regarding the year of Messiah's second coming, "*that blessed hope*".

In 614 the Persians captured Jerusalem and allowed the Jews to reestablish the daily sacrifice on the Temple mount (only lasting 3 years). In 632 Mohammed dies saying, "Destroy the Jews until the end." When Mohammed's followers captured Jerusalem in 638, they expelled the Jews from the city.

Awake, Bride

Possible Time-line from Mohammed's Deathbed Death-wish for the Jews

632 Mohammed dies saying "destroy the Jews until the end" and Muslims capture Jerusalem in 638. 638 + 1,290 = 1922.

1922 League of Nations make the Palestine Mandate: "All responsibility in connection with the Holy Places and religious buildings or sites in Palestine, including that of preserving existing rights and of <u>securing free access to the Holy Places</u>, religious buildings and sites and the free exercise of worship, while ensuring the requirements of public order and decorum, is assumed by the Mandatory, who shall be responsible solely to the League of Nations in all matters connected herewith" (Article 13). 632 + 1,335 = 1967

1967 Jews regain control of Jerusalem after 6-day war which began June 5, 1967.

Jerusalem Day, is officially the 28th of Iyar. On the 28th of Iyar, Samuel the prophet passed away. When King David re-conquered the Land of Israel, Jerusalem was in the hands of the Jebusites. In the last chapter of 2 Samuel is the story of David numbering Israel and choosing pestilence for his sin. The plague was stopped at the threshing floor of Arunuah, and David built an altar and sacrificed there, and it would be the place of Solomon's temple on the 28th of Iyar. Jews retook the Temple Mount in 1967 on the same day David built an altar there.

Possible Time-line from Al-Aqsa Mosque "set up" on Temple Mount

677 Al-Aqsa Mosque construction began between 670 and 674. The first, clearest testimony of seeing the completed wooden Al-Aqsa Mosque on the Temple site is from Gaullic bishop Arculf who lived in Palestine between 679 and 682, who described the new mosque as a rectangular wooden structure, built over ruins and capable of holding 3000 worshipers (*Medieval Jerusalem and Islamic Worship* by Amikam Elad). Umar began clearing the rubble of the Temple site in 638 and recited a prayer in what he understood to be the "sanctuary of David". The date for the completion of the Al-Aqsa Mosque is unclear; it's between 674 and 679. I chose 677 because it works. 677 + 1,290 = 1967.

1967 Jews regain control of Jerusalem after 6-day war. Though the Jews recaptured Jerusalem, the abomination of the Muslim structures on the Temple Mount remained.
677 + 1,335 = 2012.

2012 Messiah Jesus begins His kingdom reign of 1,000 years.

Possible Time-line from Dome of the Rock construction started on Temple Mount

687 Dome of the Rock construction started upon the Temple site as noted by Caliph Abd al-Malik ibn Marwan who began writing letters in 685, and saw his engineer Raja ibn Haywah begin construction this year upon the 50 sq. ft. flat uprising of rock towards which the Jews prayed and made sacrifices. Two years earlier Caliph Abd al Malik ibn Marwan commanded a structure to be built over the area to keep the rain and chill off. The range for the beginning and completion of the Dome of the Rock is from 685 to 692 AD. But many view 687 as its first year of construction. 687 +1,290 = 1977

1977 Egyptian President Anwar Sadat recognizes Israel. In November, Sadat visited Israel and began talks with Begin, resulting in the Camp David Accords and the Egypt-Israel Peace Treaty. Earlier in the year Menachem Begin stated, "If I become the Prime Minister, I will open the Temple Mount to Jews. I will not fear the reactions of the Christians and Moslems" (but he did not). 687 + 1,335 = 2022.

2022 Messiah Jesus begins His kingdom reign of 1,000 years.

Possible Time-line from Dome of the Rock completion on Temple Mount

691 Dome of the Rock completed upon the Temple site. 691 +1,290 = 1981

1981, June 7, Israel destroyed Iraq's nuclear reactor. Prime minister Menachem Begin resorts to military means only after diplomacy failed. 691 + 1,335 = 2026

2026 Messiah Jesus begins His kingdom reign of 1,000 years.

These time-line possibilities are interesting, but Daniel gave us another prophecy to help us arrive at a correct year for Christ's second coming. Daniel's prophecies regarding the year of Messiah's first coming and being cut off were accurate, so we can have confidence in his prophetic year for Messiah's second coming.

Another Important End-Time Start Date from Daniel 8

In the third year of the reign of king Belshazzar a vision appeared to me, . . . a ram which had two horns . . . became great. And as I was considering, behold, an he goat came from the west . . . and the goat had a notable horn between his eyes. And he came to the ram that had two horns, which I had seen standing before the river, and ran to him in the fury of his power. And I saw him come close to the ram, and he was moved with choler against him, and smote the ram, and broke his two horns: and there was no power in the ram to stand before him, but he cast him down to the ground, and stamped on him: and there was none that could deliver the ram out of his hand. Therefore the he goat waxed very great: and when he was strong, the great horn was broken; and for it came up four notable ones toward the four winds of heaven. And out of one of them came forth a little horn, which waxed exceeding great, toward the south, and toward the east, and toward the pleasant land. And it waxed great, even to the host of heaven; and it cast down some of the host and of the stars to the ground, and stamped on them. Yes, he magnified himself even to the prince of the host, and by him the daily sacrifice was taken away, and the place of the sanctuary was cast down. And an host was given him against the daily sacrifice by reason of transgression, and it cast down the truth to the ground; and it practiced, and prospered. <u>Then I heard one saint speaking, and another saint said to that certain saint which spoke, How long shall be the vision concerning the daily sacrifice, and the transgression of desolation, to give both the sanctuary and the</u>

host to be trodden under foot? And he said to me, To two thousand and three hundred days; then shall the sanctuary be cleansed. . . . *And he said, Behold, I will make you know what shall be in the last end of the indignation: for at the time appointed the end shall be. The ram which you saw having two horns are the kings of Media and Persia. And the rough goat is the king of Grecia: and the great horn that is between his eyes is the first king. Now that being broken, whereas four stood up for it, four kingdoms shall stand up out of the nation, but not in his power. And in the latter time of their kingdom, when the transgressors are come to the full, a king of fierce countenance, and understanding dark sentences, shall stand up. And his power shall be mighty, but not by his own power: and he shall destroy wonderfully, and shall prosper, and practice, and shall destroy the mighty and the holy people. And through his policy also he shall cause craft to prosper in his hand; and he shall magnify himself in his heart, and by peace shall destroy many: he shall also stand up against the Prince of princes; but he shall be broken without hand. And the vision of the evening and the morning which was told is true: why shut you up the vision; for it shall be for many days. (Daniel 8:1-26 edited)*

Note the similarities between the wording of this passage and Daniel 12:11-12. The possible start dates for the 2300 years ('days') within this chapter are as follows:
538 BC the ram became great, and one horn, Darius the Mede, is now king of Babylon;
333 BC the goat conquered the ram; Alexander conquered Darius III Codomannus;
323 BC when four notable horns came from the goat; Alexander dies suddenly
     and his four generals rule fourths of his kingdom; and
167 BC when the "little horn" stopped the daily sacrifice;
     Antiochus Epiphanes stopped Temple sacrifice.

Subtracting the above dates from the 2300 years we arrive at the following:
2300 - 538 = 1762 which was too early for end-time prophecies regarding Israel
     because it hadn't been made a country again until 1948.
2300 - 333 = 1967 Jews recaptured Jerusalem and the Temple Mount in the 6-day war.
2300 - 323 = 1977 Egyptian President Anwar Sadat recognizes Israel; the first Arab head of state to do so. In November, Sadat visited Israel and began talks with Begin, resulting in the Camp David Accords and the Egypt-Israel Peace Treaty. Earlier in the year Menachem Begin stated, "If I become the Prime Minister, I will open the Temple Mount to Jews. I will not fear the reactions of the Christians and Moslems" (but he did not).
2300 - 167 = 2133 and some future event in Israel.

The year 2133 seems too far in the future considering the four horsemen have already galloped across the globe. Using 323, the year of Alexander's death corresponds with the beginning of construction on the Dome of the Rock in 687 from Daniel 12, but it leads to little of significance in 1977 in Israel and certainly nothing of importance with the Temple

Mount. But using 333 when Alexander conquered the Persians yields the important year of 1967, and it corresponds with the "setting up" of the first Muslim abomination on the Temple Mount in 677 from Daniel 12. [See the appendix for the time-line.]

Best Time-line is from Al-Aqsa Mosque "set up" on Temple Mount

333 BC the goat conquered the ram; Alexander conquered Darius III Codomannus. From Daniel 8 we get the following: 2300 - 333 = 1967.

677 The date for the completion of the Al-Aqsa Mosque is between 674 and 679. I chose 677 because it yields the 1967 year. 677 + 1,290 = 1967.

1967 Jews regain control of Jerusalem after 6-day war. Though the Jews recaptured Jerusalem, the abomination of the Muslim structures on the Temple Mount remained. 677 + 1,335 = 2012.

2012 Those waiting and "*looking for that blessed hope*" will see "*the glorious appearing of our Savior Jesus Christ*" (Titus 2:13). Christ will cleanse His Temple Mount in order to build His Temple upon it, described in the last chapters of Ezekiel, and begin His kingdom reign of 1,000 years.

Mayans

Yes, I know 2012 is the same year of the Mayan doomsday on the winter solstice, Dec. 21, 2012. I did not try to find scripture which would support that date. I place Jesus' return on the evening of His birth on the Feast of Trumpets, which would be September 16, 2012, because of Daniel's prophecies in chapters 8 and 12. Astronomers from the east correctly ascertained the year of Christ's first coming, so it is not unreasonable that astronomers in the west correctly predicted the year of Christ's second coming. But since neither group was aware of the importance of Hebrew feasts, they did not know the correct day.

From the feast studies you see why Jesus will return on Rosh Hashanah in 2012. Counting backwards, 1260 days prior is April 6, 2009. So I would expect the final "*abomination of desolation*" soon after by "*a king of fierce countenance, and understanding dark sentence*" who "*shall **stand up***". "*He shall also **stand up** against the Prince of princes.*" Both times 'stand up' in Hebrew is *amad*, meaning appoint, arise, confirm, place, raise up, remain, or stand fast. '*Ahmad*' in Persian means Mohammed or virtue; *Ahmadinejad* means Mohammed's race or virtuous race.

Sit in the Temple

Like Lucifer, "*he shall magnify himself in his heart,*" and consider himself equal to God. In Isaiah, the king of Babylon is called Lucifer (*haylel*, which means brightness). But though he will "*stand up*" against Jesus, this antichrist will do so sitting down. His desire is to sit on the Temple Mount as God.

> *How are you fallen from heaven, O Lucifer, son of the morning! how are you cut down to the ground, which did weaken the nations! For <u>you have said in your heart, I will ascend into heaven, I will exalt my throne above the stars of God: **I will sit**</u>*

> ***also on the mount of the congregation***, *in the sides of the north: I will ascend above the heights of the clouds;* ***I will be like the most High****. (Isaiah 14:12-14)*
>
> *Now we beseech you, brothers, by the coming of our Lord Jesus Christ, and by our gathering together to him, That you be not soon shaken in mind, or be troubled, neither by spirit, nor by word, nor by letter as from us, as that the day of Christ is at hand. Let no man deceive you by any means: for that day shall not come, except there come a falling away first, and* ***that man of sin be revealed, the son of perdition; Who opposes and exalts himself above all that is called God, or that is worshipped****;* **so that he as God sits in the temple of God, showing himself that he is God.** *Remember you not, that, when I was yet with you, I told you these things? And now you know what withholds that he might be revealed in his time. For the mystery of iniquity does already work: only he who now lets will let, until he be taken out of the way. And* ***then shall that Wicked be revealed****, whom the Lord shall consume with the spirit of his mouth, and shall destroy with the brightness of his coming: Even him,* ***whose coming is after the working of Satan with all power and signs and lying wonders, And with all delusion of unrighteousness in them that perish;*** *because they received not the love of the truth, that they might be saved. And for this cause God shall send them strong delusion, that they should believe a lie: That they all might be damned who believed not the truth, but had pleasure in unrighteousness. (2 Thessalonians 2:1-12)*

The Temple in Jerusalem was known as *hieron*, which is a word built upon the first part of the city's name *Jerusalem*, which means 'to teach peace'; *salem* being peace. This word is used in the Gospels and Acts and once in 1 Corinthians 9:13. A common word for dwelling or tent, *naos*, was also used to refer to the Temple as well as other places, like the shrine of Diana (Acts 19:24). It is this more general word, *naos*, which is used in this passage. 'God' is *Theos,* which is also used for pagan gods. So the "*temple of God*" he sits in could be either of the Muslim shrines on the Temple Mount.

The Muslims are waiting for their savior called the Mahdi, whom the Bible refers to as the "little horn" and "mouth" of the Beast, and Christians call the Antichrist. This Beast/Mahdi will be supported by the False Prophet who will perform miraculous signs and proclaim himself god on the Temple Mount in one of the shrines. At the end of the Great Tribulation, Jesus will destroy this False Prophet with the 'brightness' (*epiphaneia*) of His coming.

Summary

Three times Daniel mentions the abomination of desolation.

Seventy weeks are determined on your people and on your holy city . . . And after threescore and two weeks shall <u>Messiah</u> be cut off, but not for himself: and the people of the prince that shall come **shall destroy the city and the sanctuary***; and the end thereof shall be with a flood,* **and unto the end of the war desolations are determined.** *And <u>he</u> shall confirm the covenant with many for one week: and in the midst of the week <u>he</u> shall cause the sacrifice and the oblation to cease, and* **for the overspreading of abominations <u>he</u> shall make it desolate***, even until the consummation, and that determined shall be poured upon the desolate. (Daniel 9:24-27 edited)* Jesus was "*cut off*" in 33 AD, and Titus destroyed the Temple and Jerusalem in 70 AD. Antiochus Epiphanes IV of Syria was the "*prince that shall come*"; he came in 167 BC.

And <u>arms</u> shall stand on his part, and <u>they</u> shall pollute the sanctuary of strength, and shall take away the daily sacrifice, and <u>they</u> shall place the abomination that makes desolate. (Daniel 11:31) Antiochus Epiphanes IV and his Syrian army fulfilled this in 167 BC.

And from the time that the daily sacrifice shall be taken away, and the abomination that makes desolate set up*, there shall be a thousand two hundred and ninety days. Blessed is he that waits, and comes to the thousand three hundred and five and thirty days. (Daniel 12:11-12 edited)* This is the passage referred to by Jesus as to be fulfilled in the Great Tribulation. These numbers coupled with the numbers from Daniel 8, lead to the year 2012 for Christ's second coming.

333 BC the goat conquered the ram; Alexander conquered Darius III Codomannus. From Daniel 8 we get the following: 2300 - 333 = 1967.

677 The date for the completion of the Al-Aqsa Mosque is between 674 and 679. I chose 677 because it yields the 1967 year. 677 + 1,290 = 1967.

1967 Jews regain control of Jerusalem after 6-day war. Though the Jews recaptured Jerusalem, the abomination of the Muslim structures on the Temple Mount remained. 677 + 1,335 = 2012.

2012 Those waiting and "*looking for that blessed hope*" will see "*the glorious appearing of our Savior Jesus Christ*" (Titus 2:13) on His birthday, Tishri 1, Rosh Hashanah.

Three and a half prophetic years is 1,260 days. Remember that Rosh Hashanah begins at sundown on Sept. 16, 2012 with the rest of the 'day' following on the 17th. Counting backwards from Sunday, Sept. 16th we arrive at Monday, April 6, 2009 for the beginning of the Great Tribulation.

How should the Bride respond to all this prophetic stuff?

*Many shall be purified, and made white, and tried; but the wicked shall do wickedly: and none of the wicked shall understand; but the <u>wise</u> shall understand. And from the time that the daily sacrifice shall be taken away, and the abomination that makes desolate set up, there shall be a thousand two hundred and ninety days. Blessed is he that **waits**, and comes to the thousand three hundred and five and thirty days. (Daniel 12:10-12)*

Christ's bride should seek to "*understand*" prophecy in order to prepare for the future without fear. As always, that includes proclaiming the gospel and living by the power of the Holy Spirit. And the Bride is to "wait" and to "come". 'Waits' is *chakah*, (from a primitive root with the idea of engraving or piercing as was done to life-long slaves); meaning properly to adhere to; long, tarry, or wait. 'Comes' is *naga*, (from a primitive root 'to touch'); meaning 'lay the hand upon', or reach, draw near, get up, happen, join, near, or touch. The Bride is to draw near to her Bridegroom spiritually as well as in service; both born of love and hope.

*Oh that you would tear the heavens, that you would come down, that the mountains might quake at your presence, as when fire kindles the brushwood, and the fire causes the waters to boil; to make your name known to your adversaries, that the nations may tremble at your presence! When you did terrible things which we didn't look for, you came down, the mountains quaked at your presence. For from of old men have not heard, nor perceived by the ear, neither has the eye seen a God besides you, who works for him who **waits** for him. (Isaiah 64:1-4)*

Be Wise and Work with God's Holy Spirit

And it shall come to pass afterward, that I will pour out my spirit on all flesh; and your sons and your daughters shall prophesy, your old men shall dream dreams, your young men shall see visions: And also on the servants and on the handmaids in those days will I pour out my spirit. . . . And it shall come to pass, that whoever shall call on the name of the LORD shall be delivered: for in mount Zion and in Jerusalem shall be deliverance, as the LORD has said, and in the remnant whom the LORD shall call. (Joel 2:28-32)

God is appearing to many unsaved Jews and Gentiles in their dreams; be prepared to answer their questions about Jesus and disciple them in His teachings. Ask God's Spirit to fill you and use you to bring many into His kingdom. Daniel wrote, "*they that be <u>wise</u> shall shine as the brightness of the firmament; and they that turn many to righteousness as the stars for ever and ever*" (Daniel 12:3).

Little Horn
with a Blasphemous Mouth

And there was given to him a mouth speaking great things and blasphemies; and power was given to him to continue forty and two months. (Revelation 13:5)

The blasphemous "*mouth*" is already in power and will "*continue*" to lead during the Great Tribulation. We will look at past 'little horns' and the Great Tribulation 'mouth'. Though John is the only Bible writer to use the word 'antichrist', he doesn't use it in the book of Revelation. An antichrist is opposed to Christ, and against Him. An antichrist is also a substitute instead of Christ. We will look at both: the Antichrist ("*little horn*") and an antichrist ("*false prophet*"). John referred to a future Antichrist as "*the antichrist*".

Antichrists

Little children, it is the last time: and as you have heard that [the] antichrist shall come, even now are there many antichrists; whereby we know that it is the last time. They went out from us, but they were not of us; for if they had been of us, they would no doubt have continued with us: but they went out, that they might be made manifest that they were not all of us. But you have an unction from the Holy One, and you know all things. I have not written to you because you know not the truth, but because you know it, and that no lie is of the truth. Who is a liar but he that denies that Jesus is the Christ? He is antichrist, that denies the Father and the Son. Whoever denies the Son, the same has not the Father: he that acknowledges the Son has the Father also. . . . These things have I written to you concerning them that seduce you. (1 John 2:18-23, 26 [original Greek word omitted by translator])

These "*antichrists*" came from the church denying that Jesus was the Messiah, the Son of God the Father. In the past, many have taught that the pope was the Antichrist. Catholics believe in the Father, Son and Holy Spirit. Though some of their doctrines are anti-Bible, they are not against Christ nor do they substitute a false Christ. Much of our eschatology (end-times doctrine) was derived from the early Christian fathers who were oppressed by the Roman Empire, and later oppressed by the Catholic church officiated from Rome. Park what you've learned previously to the side, and open your mind and spirit to what the Scriptures actually teach. You have "*an unction from the Holy One*" to discern who is an antichrist ("*false prophet*") as well as the Antichrist ("*little horn*").

Past and Future "Little horns"

It becomes clear from the descriptions of the "*little horn*" in Daniel 7 and 8 that it is a person who is against Christ, or an antichrist. The following passage describes a past antichrist and a future Antichrist to whom most prophecy books refer.

*Therefore the he goat waxed very great: and when he was strong, the great horn was broken; and for it came up four notable ones toward the four winds of heaven. And out of one of them came forth a **little horn**, which waxed exceeding great, toward the south, and toward the east, and toward the pleasant land. And it waxed great, even to the host of heaven; and it cast down some of the host and of the stars to the ground, and stamped on them. Yes, he magnified himself even to the prince of the host, and by him the daily sacrifice was taken away, and the place of the sanctuary was cast down. And an host was given him against the daily sacrifice by reason of transgression, and it cast down the truth to the ground; and it practiced, and prospered. . . .Gabriel, make this man to understand the vision. . . . And he said, Behold, I will make you know what <u>shall be in the last end of the indignation: for at the time appointed the end shall be.</u> The ram which you saw having two horns are the kings of Media and Persia. And the rough goat is the king of Grecia: and the great horn that is between his eyes is the first king. Now that being broken, whereas four stood up for it, four kingdoms shall stand up out of the nation, but not in his power. And <u>in the latter time of their kingdom, when the transgressors are come to the full</u>, **a king of fierce countenance**, and understanding dark sentences, shall stand up. And his power shall be mighty, but not by his own power: and he shall destroy wonderfully, and shall prosper, and practice, and shall destroy the mighty and the holy people. And through his policy also he shall cause craft to prosper in his hand; and he shall magnify himself in his heart, and by peace shall destroy many: he shall also stand up against the Prince of princes; but he shall be broken without hand. (Daniel 8:8-25 edited)*

Gabriel clarified that there were two separate fulfillments of this "*little horn*" prophecy. There was a "*little horn*" which followed from one of the four generals of Alexander the Great, and then there will be a "*little horn*" that arises "*in the last end of indignation*" (Great Tribulation) from "*their kingdom*" (Alexander's Grecian Empire) "*when the transgressors are come to the full.*" First we will look at the "*little horn*" of the past.

Syria's Antiochus IV Epiphanes

After Alexander's death in 323 BC his four generals fought over succession which eventually settled into the four kingdoms of Greece, Thrace (Turkey), Syria, and Egypt by 301 BC. Seleucus Nicator built up Syria until it became the largest and strongest of the kingdoms. Antioch became Syria's capital, and kings used it in their names. Antiochus IV reigned from 175-164 BC.

*Therefore the he goat waxed very great: and when he was strong, the great horn was broken; and for it came up four notable ones toward the four winds of heaven. And out of one of them came forth a little horn, which waxed exceeding great, toward the south, and toward the east, and toward the <u>pleasant land</u>. And it waxed great, even to the host of heaven; and it cast down some of the **host** and of the stars to the ground, and stamped on them. Yes, he magnified himself even to the prince of the **host**, and by him the daily sacrifice was taken away, and the place of the sanctuary was cast down. And an host was given him against the daily sacrifice by reason of transgression, and it cast down the truth to the ground; and it practiced, and prospered. . . . (Daniel 8:8-12)*

Antiochus IV went to war to expand his kingdom in all directions (Daniel 8:9), including the "*pleasant land*" of Israel. 'Host' means 'army', and this is how they occurred in history. In 170 BC while the real high priest, Jason, was abroad, a lapsed Jew named Menelaus bought the the office. Jason returned from Sparta and deposed Menelaus.

"Now when there was gone forth a false rumour, as though Antiochus had been dead, Jason took at the least a thousand men, and suddenly made an assault upon the city [Jerusalem] . . . Now when this that was done came to the king's ear, he thought that Judea had revolted: whereupon removing out of Egypt in a furious mind, he took the city by force of arms, And commanded his men of war not to spare such as they met, and to slay such as went up upon the houses. Thus there was killing of young and old, making away of men, women, and children, slaying of virgins and infants. And there were destroyed within the space of three whole days fourscore thousand, whereof forty thousand were slain in the conflict; and no fewer sold than slain." (II Maccabees 5:5a,11-14)

Jason, the high priest, was the "*prince of the host*" to which Antiochus magnified himself. He sacrificed a pig on the altar, boiled the meat and forced priests to eat it; those who refused had tongues cut out or worse. So "*by him the daily sacrifice was taken away, and the place of the sanctuary was cast down.*" The Temple was completely defiled and unable to be used. Antiochus IV also "*cast truth to the ground,*" literally tearing and burning the scrolls of the Law of God.

"Moreover king Antiochus wrote to his whole kingdom, that all should be one people, And every one should leave his laws: so all the heathen agreed according to the commandment of the king. Yea, many also of the Israelites consented to his religion, and sacrificed unto idols, and profaned the sabbath. For the king had sent letters by messengers unto Jerusalem and the cities of Juda that they should follow the strange laws of the land, And <u>forbid burnt offerings, and sacrifice, and drink offerings, in the temple; and that they should profane the sabbaths and festival days: And pollute the sanctuary and holy people: Set up altars, and groves, and chapels of idols, and sacrifice swine's flesh, and unclean beasts:</u> That they should also leave their children uncircumcised, and make their souls abominable with all manner of uncleanness and profanation: To the end they might forget the law, and change all the ordinances. And whosoever would not do according to the commandment of the king, he said, he should die. . . . Now the fifteenth day of the month Casleu, in the hundred forty and fifth year, they set up the abomination of desolation upon the altar, and builded idol altars throughout the cities of Juda on every side; And burnt incense at the doors of their houses, and in the streets. And when they had <u>rent in pieces the books of the law which they found, they burnt them with fire</u>. And whosoever was found with any the book of the testament, or if any committed to the law, the king's commandment was, that they should put him to death. Thus did they by their authority unto the Israelites every month, to as many as were found in the cities." (I Maccabees 1:41-51, 54-58)

Antiochus IV took all the gold and silver from the Temple, so he *"practiced and prospered"*. Antiochus IV did boast he could reach the stars of heaven, but he did not cast them down. Though he was killed *"without hand"*, both of those prophecies regard the future "Little horn". Antiochus did think he was God, but God humbled him before his death. Antiochus IV bragged he would make Jerusalem a graveyard of Jews but during his painful, stinky bowel disease, he repented, and sought to restore to the Jews all he had taken, and to let them worship God freely.

"Howbeit he nothing at all ceased from his bragging, but still was filled with pride, breathing out fire in his rage against the Jews, and commanding to haste the journey: but it came to pass that he fell down from his chariot, carried violently; so that having a sore fall, all the members of his body were much pained. And thus he that a little afore <u>thought he might command the waves of the sea</u>, (so proud was he beyond the condition of man) and <u>weigh the high mountains in a balance</u>, was now cast on the ground, and carried in an horselitter, shewing forth unto all the manifest power of God. So that the worms rose up out of the body of this wicked man, and whiles he lived in sorrow and pain, his flesh fell away, and the filthiness of his smell was noisome to all his army. And the man, that thought a little afore <u>he could reach to the stars of heaven</u>, no man could endure to carry for his intolerable stink. Here therefore, being plagued, he began to leave off his great pride, and to come to the knowledge of himself by the scourge of God, his pain increasing every moment. And when he himself could not abide his own smell, he said these words, It is meet to be subject unto God, and that a man that is mortal should not proudly think of himself if he were God." (II Maccabees 9:7-12)

Antiochus IV began terrorizing Jerusalem's Temple in spring 170, and died in Nov/Dec 164: a period of 6 2/3 years in accordance with Daniel 8:14. 2300 days = 6 2/3 years (6.66) using the 360 day calendar. The time period for this *"little horn"* to terrorize Judah is different from the time period the future "*little horn*" will terrorize the earth (1260 days, which is 42 months or 3 1/2 years).

The Assyrian

*And he shall stand and feed in the strength of the LORD, in the majesty of the name of the LORD his God; and they shall abide: for now shall he be great to the ends of the earth. And this man shall be the peace, when **the Assyrian** shall come into our land: and when he shall tread in our palaces, then shall we raise against him seven shepherds, and eight principal men. And they shall waste the land of Assyria with the sword, and the land of Nimrod in the entrances thereof: thus shall he deliver us from the Assyrian, when he comes into our land, and when he treads within our borders. (Micah 5:4-6)*

Hundreds of years before Alexander the Great, Micah and other prophets referred to this "little horn" as "*the Assyrian*". The Assyrians ruled the northern Mesopotamia before the Babylonians conquered them. The preceding passage specifically refers to Antiochus IV and the seven Maccabees that humiliated him by defeating his armies, and then eight of their relatives, Hasmoneans, who continued to keep them at bay.

For <u>through the voice of the LORD</u> shall the Assyrian be beaten down, which smote with a rod. (Isaiah 30:31)

This verse refers to the future "little horn" "*whom the Lord shall consume <u>with the spirit of his mouth</u>*" (2 Thessalonians 2:8). Isaiah and Micah prophesied to Judah while Amos and Hosea prophesied to Israel during the reign of the Assyrians. Many of the characteristics attributed to "*the Assyrian*" by these prophets are similar to those of the "little horn" and future Antichrist. Today the people who still occupy a great deal of the ancient Assyrian lands are called Kurds, and they would like to restore their own identity from Lebanon, Syria, eastern Turkey, and northern Iraq and Iran. Ezekiel prophesied to Judah during the Babylonian captivity, and again you can see prophecies for a "little horn" and a future satan-possessed Antichrist.

***The Assyrian** shall be his king, because they [Israel] refused to return [repent]. (Hosea 11:5 with additions)*

*And it came to pass . . . that the word of the LORD came to me, saying, Son of man, speak to Pharaoh king of Egypt, and to his multitude; Whom are you like in your greatness? Behold, **the Assyrian** was a cedar in Lebanon with fair branches, and with a shadowing shroud, and of an high stature; and his top was among the thick boughs. . . . All the fowls of heaven made their nests in his boughs, and under his branches did all the beasts of the field bring forth their young, and under his shadow dwelled all great nations. || Thus was he fair in his greatness, in the length of his branches: for his root was by great waters. The cedars in the garden of God* *could not hide him: the fir trees were not like his boughs, and the chestnut trees were not like his branches; nor any tree in the garden of God was like to him in his beauty. I have made him fair by the multitude of his branches: so that all the trees of Eden, that were in the garden of God, envied him. Therefore thus said the Lord GOD; Because you have lifted up yourself in height, and he has shot up his top among the thick boughs, and his heart is lifted up in his height;|| I have therefore delivered him into the hand of the mighty one of the heathen; he shall surely deal with him: I have driven him out for his wickedness. And strangers, the terrible of the nations, have cut him off, and have left him: . . . and all the people of the earth are gone down from his shadow, and have left him. . . .Thus said the Lord GOD; In the day when he went down to the grave I caused a mourning: . . . and I caused Lebanon to mourn for him, and all the trees of the field fainted for him. I made the nations to shake at the sound of his fall, when I cast him down to hell with them that descend into the pit: and all the trees of Eden, the choice and best of Lebanon, all that drink water, shall be comforted in the nether parts of the earth. They also went down into hell with him to them that be slain with the sword; and they that were his arm, that dwelled under his shadow in the middle of the heathen. To whom are you thus like in glory and in greatness among the trees of Eden? yet shall you be brought down with the trees of Eden to the nether parts of the earth: you shall lie in the middle of the uncircumcised with them that be slain by the sword. This is Pharaoh and all his multitude, said the Lord GOD. (Ezekiel 31:1-18 edited)*

The beginning of the passage refers to an Assyrian antichrist. The verses between the double bars refer to the satan-possessed Antichrist, but the rest of the passage seems to mix the two together. Rulers of the great world empires have dealt with Satan's pride of feeling equal to God. Satan doesn't just want people to be subjugated to him, he wants people to worship him as God, as Antiochus Epiphanes IV did.

Daniel's Description of the Antichrist ("*little horn*")

Pay careful attention to the context of Daniel's fourth beast and its "*little horn*".

After this I saw in the night visions, and behold a fourth beast, dreadful and terrible, and strong exceedingly; and it had great iron teeth: it devoured and broke in pieces, and stamped the residue with the feet of it: and it was diverse from all the beasts that were before it; and it had ten horns. I considered the horns, and, behold, there came up among them another **little horn**, *before whom there were three of the first horns plucked up by the roots: and, behold, in this* **horn** *were eyes like the eyes of man, and a mouth speaking great things. I beheld till the thrones were cast down, and the Ancient of days did sit, . . . A fiery stream issued and came forth from before him: thousand thousands ministered to him, and ten thousand times ten thousand stood before him: <u>the judgment was set, and the books were opened</u>. I beheld then because of the <u>voice of the great words which the</u>* **horn** *<u>spoke: I beheld</u>*

Little Horn with the Blasphemous Mouth

even till the beast was slain, and his body destroyed, and given to the burning flame. . . . These great beasts, which are four, are four kings, which shall arise out of the earth. But the saints of the most High shall take the kingdom, and possess the kingdom for ever, even for ever and ever. Then I would know the truth of the fourth beast, which was diverse from all the others, exceeding dreadful, whose teeth were of iron, and his nails of brass; which devoured, broke in pieces, and stamped the residue with his feet; And of the ten horns that were in his head, and of the **other** which came up, and before whom three fell; *even of that* **horn** *that had eyes, and a mouth that spoke very great things, whose look was more stout than his fellows.* I beheld, and *the same* **horn** *made war with the saints, and prevailed against them; Until the Ancient of days came, and judgment was given to the saints of the most High; and the time came that the saints possessed the kingdom*. Thus he said, The fourth beast shall be the fourth kingdom on earth, which shall be diverse from all kingdoms, and shall devour the whole earth, and shall tread it down, and break it in pieces. And the ten horns out of this kingdom are ten kings that shall arise: and **another** shall rise after them; and **he** shall be diverse from the first, and **he** shall subdue three kings. And **he** shall speak great words against the most High, and shall wear out the saints of the most High, and think to change times and laws: and *they shall be given into* **his** *hand until a time and times and the dividing of time. But the judgment shall sit, and they shall take away* **his** *dominion, to consume and to destroy it to the end*. And the kingdom and dominion, and the greatness of the kingdom under the whole heaven, shall be given to the people of the saints of the most High, whose kingdom is an everlasting kingdom, and all dominions shall serve and obey him. (Daniel 7:7-27 edited)*

The "*little horn*" will mentally wear out the saints using threats and deceit with hopes to create a Muslim world with Sharia law and the strict lunar calendar. This "*little horn*" will make war against the saints and prevail against them (also Rev. 13:7) because they are "*given into his hand*" during the Great Tribulation, clarifying Daniel's "*time and times and the dividing of time*". The phrase "*more stout than his fellows*" could allude to the following passage regarding the Assyrian.

Why it shall come to pass, that when the Lord has performed his whole work on mount Zion and on Jerusalem, I will punish the fruit of the **stout** *heart of the king of* **Assyria**, *and the glory of his high looks. For he said, By the strength of my hand I have done it, and by my wisdom; for I am prudent: and I have removed the bounds of the people, and have robbed their treasures, and I have put down the inhabitants like a valiant man: And my hand has found as a nest the riches of the people: and as one gathers eggs that are left, have I gathered all the earth; and there was none that moved the wing, or opened the mouth, or peeped. . . . Therefore thus said the Lord GOD of hosts, O my people that dwell in Zion, be not afraid of* **the Assyrian**: *he shall smite you with a rod, and shall lift up his staff against you, after the* *manner of Egypt. For yet a very little while, and the indignation shall cease, and my anger in their destruction. And the LORD of hosts shall stir up a whip for him according to the slaughter of Midian at the rock of Oreb: and as his rod was on the sea, so shall he lift it up after the manner of Egypt. And it shall come to pass <u>in that day, that his burden shall be taken away from off your shoulder, and his yoke from off your neck, and the yoke shall be destroyed because of the anointing</u>. (Isaiah 10:12-14, 24-27)*

'Stout' is *godel* from a root meaning to twist, enlarge and promote. He twists who he really is so that others believe in the larger image he promotes. He might begin to believe his own PR ('public relations') like Antiochus IV did. The Assyrian enslaved God's people, but God breaks their "*yoke*" of enslavement "*because of the anointing*" (which could also be translated "by the face of anointing" referring to Christ). The future Assyrian will be destroyed by the brightness of the coming of Jesus, the anointed (Christ).

Future "Little horn" with Blasphemous Mouth from the Sea

*Daniel saw in my vision by night . . . And four great beasts came up from the sea, diverse one from another. The first was like a <u>lion</u>, and had eagle's wings: . . . a second, like to a <u>bear</u>, . . . and see another, like a <u>leopard</u>, . . . and behold a fourth beast, dreadful and terrible, and strong exceedingly; and it had great iron teeth: it devoured and broke in pieces, and stamped the residue with the feet of it: and it was diverse from all the beasts that were before it; and it had ten horns. I considered the horns, and, behold, there came up among them another **little horn**, before whom there were three of the first horns plucked up by the roots: and, behold, in this horn were eyes like the eyes of man, and a **mouth** speaking great things. (Daniel 7:2-8 edited)*

*. . .a beast rise up out of the sea, having seven heads and ten horns, and on his horns ten crowns, and on his heads the name of blasphemy. And the beast which I saw was like to a <u>leopard</u>, and his feet were as the feet of a <u>bear</u>, and his mouth as the mouth of a <u>lion</u>: and the dragon gave him his power, and his seat, and great authority. And I saw one of his heads as it were wounded to death; and his deadly wound was healed: and all the world wondered after the beast. And they worshiped the dragon which gave power to the beast: and they worshiped the beast, saying, Who is like to the beast? who is able to make war with him? And there was given to him a **mouth** speaking great things and blasphemies; and power was given to him to continue forty and two months. And he opened his mouth in blasphemy against God, to blaspheme his name, and his tabernacle, and them that dwell in heaven. And it was given to him to make war with the saints, and to overcome them: and power was given him over all kindreds, and tongues, and nations. And all that dwell on the earth shall worship him, whose names are not written in the book of life of*

the Lamb slain from the foundation of the world. If any man have an ear, let him hear. (Revelation 13:1-9 edited)

There is a clear correlation between Daniel's fourth beast of the sea, and John's beast of the sea. In Daniel the lion, bear, and leopard were given in the order of their persecution of the Jews: England, Russia, and Germany. But in Revelation they are given in order of their influence and support of Islam's persecution of the Jews: Germany, Russia, and Britain. This Satan-empowered Muslim confederation makes war with the saints and overcomes them; hence all the martyrs during the Great Tribulation. And their Muslim Mahdi/Caliph will be given power over the whole world, and all who do not worship Jesus will worship him. 'Worship' here is *proskuneō,* meaning 'to kiss the hand towards'. Among Persians it meant to fall upon the knees and touch the forehead to the ground as an expression of reverence.

Though John does not mention a "little horn," he does mention its blasphemous mouth. The Greek word for 'mouth' (*stoma*) can also mean the edge of a sword or weapon. In both cases, the mouth speaks "*great things*" against God. Although John's beast already has the "*mouth of a lion*", another "**mouth**" is given to it. This Sunni 'mouth' is Al-Jazeera which has close ties to Al-Qaeda, the Muslim Brotherhood, and other Sunni terrorist groups. A weekly religious program is taught by Qaradawi, who is considered one of the most authoritative voices of Sunni Islam. Qaradawi has praised and defended suicide bombings against American and Israeli men, women and children.

"Little Horn" Rules After Ten Caliphs

*The fourth beast shall be the fourth kingdom on earth, which shall be diverse from all kingdoms, and shall devour the whole earth, and shall tread it down, and break it in pieces. And <u>the ten horns out of this kingdom are ten kings that shall arise: and another shall rise **after** them</u>; and he shall be diverse from the first, and he shall subdue three kings. (Daniel 7:23-24)*

The angel clarified that beasts are kingdoms, and horns are kings. The ten toes of the statue were ten caesars who persecuted Christians and Jews; the ten horns of the Beast of the Sea are ten caliphs who persecuted Christians and Jews. A *caliph* is a political head of state over all Muslim people and lands (a *caliphate*). The "little horn" shall arise **after** ten Muslim caliphs and be diverse from them, and will subdue three current kings. There have been over a hundred caliphs who reigned over various lands since Mohammed died, but there were ten famous ones before the Republic of Turkey ended the caliphate.

From the list given on Wikipedia, the ten famous caliphs are as follows:
- Abu Bakr (632-634)- He was the first successor of Mohammed.
- Umar ibn al-Khattab (634-644) - During his reign, the Islamic empire expanded to include Egypt, Jerusalem, and Persia.
- Uthman Ibn Affan (644-656)- The Quran was compiled under his direction.

- Ali ibn Abu Talib (656-661) - He was considered the first imam by Shias.
- Hasan ibn Ali (661-669) - He was considered as "rightly guided".
- Muawiyah I (661-680)- He was the first caliph of the Umayyad dynasty.
- Umar ibn AbdulAziz (717-720)- Umayyad was the sixth, true legitimate caliph.
- Harun al-Rashid (786-809)- Abbasid caliph during whose reign Baghdad became the world's prominent trade center. Harun is the subject of many stories in *One Thousand and One Nights*.
- Suleiman the Magnificent (1520-1566) - Early Ottoman Sultan during whose reign the Ottoman Empire reached its zenith.
- Abdul Hamid II (1876-1909) - The last Ottoman Sultan to rule the caliphate.

The Shia call their expectant end-time caliph the twelfth *imam* (religious leader) and the Mahdi ('guided one', savior of the world). Their twelfth, and last, imam was born in 869 but apparently never died, and will return and arise from a dry well ("*bottomless pit*" in Rev. 17:8) in Iran and appear with "Jesus" to bring peace to the world. The Muslim Mahdi is the Christian Antichrist.

Antichrist/Mahdi Rules After 7 Babylonian Moon Cult Dynasties

Although there are many similarities between Daniel's fourth beast and John's beast of the sea, there are some differences. Daniel spoke of the "Little horn" arising **after** the ten kings, whereas John speaks of ten kings having power at the same time with him.

And the ten horns which you saw are ten kings, which have received no kingdom as yet; but receive power as kings one hour with the beast. These have one mind, and shall give their power and strength to the beast. (Revelation 17:12-13)

Instead of following ten kings, John speaks of the Antichrist ruling **after** seven moon-worshiping dynasties.

And on her forehead was a name written, MYSTERY, BABYLON THE GREAT, THE MOTHER OF HARLOTS AND ABOMINATIONS OF THE EARTH. And I saw the woman drunken with the blood of the saints, and with the blood of the martyrs of Jesus: and when I saw her, I wondered with great admiration. And the angel said to me, Why did you marvel? I will tell you the mystery of the woman, and of the beast that carries her, which has the seven heads and ten horns. The beast that you saw was, and is not; and shall ascend out of the bottomless pit, and go into perdition: and they that dwell on the earth shall wonder, whose names were not written in the book of life from the foundation of the world, when they behold the beast that was, and is not, and yet is. And here is the mind which has wisdom. The seven heads are seven mountains, on which the woman sits. And there are seven kings: five are fallen, and one is, and the other is not yet come; and when he comes, he must continue a short space. And the beast that was, and is not, even he is the eighth, and is of the seven, and goes into perdition. (Revelation 17:5-11)

The "*mountains*" upon "*which the woman sits*" are 'seats' of power referred to as "*seven kings*". 'Kings' is *basileus* meaning 'power base'. The "*mystery*" of the power-base is Babylon. Nimrod founded Babel, in which worship of the moon-god began. Marduk (Merodach in Bible) further perverted it, as did his son Nebu (both were considered to be gods). In 2 Kings 17, Shalmaneser, king of Assyria, took Samaria and carried the northern tribes of Israel into Assyria, and replaced them with men from Babylon and other foreign cities who worshiped the moon-god and other pagan gods. Nabopolassar conquered the Assyrians in 612 BC making way for his son, Nebuchadnezzar to rule the Babylonian world. The last ruler of the Babylonian empire was Nabonidus who restored the temple of the moon-god at Harran. He was conquered by the Medes and Persians, who were conquered by the Greeks, who were conquered by the Romans. The Roman empire was completely conquered by 410 AD. Mohammed had a following from 613-632 AD (a "*short space*"), uniting Arabs. He had various successors, and one moved the capital of the caliphate to Baghdad in the 800's. Baghdad is 55 miles north of Babylon.

The seven dynasties which all controlled Babylon are as follows:
1. Sumerian - (Nimrod, then Marduk, then) Nebu
2. Assyrian - Shalmaneser
3. Babylonian - Nebucchadnezzar (to Nabonidas)
4. Mede & Persian - (Darius &) Cyrus
5. Macedonian (Greek) - Alexander
6. Roman - Caesar
7. Ottoman - Mohammed
8. Revived Muslim - Mahdi

And there are seven kings: five are fallen, and one is, and the other is not yet come; and when he comes, he must continue a short space. And the beast that was, and is not, even he is the eighth, and is of the seven, and goes into **perdition**. *(Revelation 17:10-11)*

John wrote Revelation between 95-96 AD; he died in 99. During his lifetime Rome ruled the world, which was the "*one is*". The five dynasties which were fallen were the Sumerian, Assyrian, Babylonian, Mede/Persian, and Macedonian. The one which had not yet come was the Ottoman.

The religious beast which has worshiped the moon-god since the days of Nimrod, is now called Islam. They call their savior the Mahdi, who is called 'Beast' in Revelation. The last Muslim empire was the Ottoman empire which lasted from 1299–1923. They backed Germany in WWI, and suffered partitioning after the war, bringing an end to their dynasty/caliphate. This is the head with the fatal wound which is healed (Rev.13:3). The eighth dynasty is of the seventh; both being Muslim. The eighth leader "*goes into perdition*" or destruction along with the "*son of perdition*," who is the False Prophet, or possibly the False Messiah. Judas, the original "*son of perdition*" once followed Christ.

*And the **beast** was taken, and with him the **false prophet** that worked miracles before him, with which he deceived them that had received the mark of the beast, and them that worshipped his image. These both were cast alive into a lake of fire burning with brimstone. (Revelation 19:20)*

False Prophet Sits as God in Temple

Jesus will not return until after "*the son of perdition*," "*that man of sin . . . that Wicked be revealed*" through his deity declaration on the Temple Mount. This antichrist opposes God and expects to be worshiped as God. The False Prophet's work is of Satan to deceive and delude "*with all power and signs and lying wonders*" to promote worship of the Beast.

*Now we beseech you, brothers, by the coming of our Lord Jesus Christ, and by our gathering together to him, That you be not soon shaken in mind, or be troubled, neither by spirit, nor by word, nor by letter as from us, as that the day of Christ is at hand. Let no man deceive you by any means: for that day shall not come, except there come a falling away first, and that man of sin be revealed, the son of **perdition**; Who opposes and exalts himself above all that is called God, or that is worshipped; so that he as God sits in the temple of God, showing himself that he is God. Remember you not, that, when I was yet with you, I told you these things? And now you know what withholds that he might be revealed in his time. For the mystery of iniquity does already work: only he who now lets will let, until he be taken out of the way. And then shall that Wicked be revealed, whom the Lord shall consume with the spirit of his mouth, and shall destroy with the brightness of his coming: **Even him**, whose coming is after the working of Satan with all power and signs and lying wonders, And with all delusion of unrighteousness in them that perish; because they received not the love of the truth, that they might be saved. And for this cause God shall send them strong delusion, that they should believe a lie: That they all might be damned who believed not the truth, but had pleasure in unrighteousness. (2 Thessalonians 2:1-12)*

The False Prophet will convince non-Christians to believe the lies of the False Messiah through the working of Satan and a "*strong delusion*" from God. These people refused salvation and truth, so now they will accept the lie and damnation. Interestingly, 'perdition' (*apoleia*) means the waste or destruction of vessels or money, according to Thayer.

The Temple in Jerusalem was known as *hieron*. A common word for dwelling or tent, *naos*, was also used to refer to the Temple as well as other shrines. It is this more general word, *naos*, which is used in this passage. 'God' is *Theos* which is also used for pagan gods. So the "*temple of God*" he sits in could be either of the Muslim shrines on the Temple Mount. Jesus told the Jews to pray it did not occur on a sabbath or during winter (Matthew 24:20), so the timing is not fixed. The Temple Mount is controlled by the Waqf who only allow Muslims to enter it, unless in a strictly controlled tour. John describes the False Prophet as follows:

> *He had two horns like a lamb, and he spoke as a dragon. And he exercises all the power of the first beast before him, and causes the earth and them which dwell therein to worship the first beast, whose deadly wound was healed. And he does great wonders, so that he makes fire come down from heaven on the earth in the sight of men, And deceives them that dwell on the earth by the means of those miracles which he had power to do in the sight of the beast; (Rev. 13:11b-14b)*

"False Prophet" also from Ancient Greek Empire

> *Gabriel, make this man to understand the vision. . . . And he said, Behold, I will make you know what <u>shall be in the last end of the indignation: for at the time appointed the end shall be.</u> The ram which you saw having two horns are the kings of Media and Persia. And the rough goat is the king of Grecia: and the great horn that is between his eyes is the first king. Now that being broken, whereas four stood up for it, four kingdoms shall stand up out of the nation, but not in his power. And <u>in the latter time of their kingdom, when the transgressors are come to the full,</u> a king of fierce countenance, and understanding dark sentences, shall **stand up**. (Daniel 8:16b-23 edited)*

Though the "*little horn*" of Antiochus IV is described earlier in chapter eight, it is not referenced here; but we have a clue a king shall **"stand up" (amad)**. 'Stand up' in Hebrew is *amad*, meaning appoint, arise, confirm, raise up or stand fast. 'Ahmad' in Persian means Mohammed or virtue; **Ahmad**inejad means Mohammed's race or virtuous race. A king will arise "*in the last end of indignation*" (Great Tribulation) from "*their kingdom*" (Alexander's Grecian Empire) "*when the transgressors are come to the full.*" Alexander's Empire extended throughout most of the known world of that time. It encompassed much of the 10x40 window, from 10°-40° latitude north. Today those countries are called Greece, Turkey, Syria, Lebanon, Israel, Egypt, Libya, Jordan, Iraq, Iran, Afghanistan, Pakistan, and Tajikistan, all of which are predominantly Muslim, except Greece and Israel. Muslims occupy one fourth of the earth and have one fourth of the world's population which is the criteria for the transgressors being full according to Revelation 6:8.

> *And in the latter time of their kingdom, when the transgressors are come to the full, **a king of fierce countenance**, and understanding dark sentences, shall stand up. And his power shall be mighty, but not by his own power: and he shall destroy wonderfully, and shall prosper, and practice, and <u>shall destroy the mighty and the holy people</u>. And through his policy also he shall cause craft to prosper in his hand; and he shall magnify himself in his heart, and <u>by peace shall destroy many</u>: he shall also **stand up** against the Prince of princes; but he shall be broken without hand. (Daniel 8:23-25)*

'Fierce' is *az*, meaning strong, vehement, and harsh. 'Countenance' is *pawneem*, meaning a face as the part that turns (two-faced), from a root that includes lying. 'Understanding' is *bene*, meaning cunning, intelligent, and eloquent. 'Dark sayings' is *kheedaw*, meaning puzzle, trick, conundrum or riddles. 'Be mighty' is *awtsam*, meaning to bind fast, to close (the eyes), to make numerous; or to crunch the bones. To "destroy wonderfully" includes destruction via miracles; this is an aspect of the False Prophet. Many Christians and Jews will continue to be slaughtered by Muslims through one-sided "peace" accords. 'Craft' is *meermaw*, meaning deceit and craftiness. The Antichrist will be an eloquent, vehement liar and trickster. He will defy Jesus, the Prince of princes, and lose.

In Islamic eschatology, *Qiyama*, Muslims believe their version of Jesus/Isa (False Prophet), will return bodily to defeat the bad al-Dajjal (False Messiah), who leads Muslims astray. Isa will tell people he did not die on the cross and Christianity is wrong, but Islam is true. Isa will support the militaristic Mahdi (Antichrist) in his world conquest for Islam.

Muslim Mahdi

The Muslim savior, al-Mahdi, will be a direct descendant of Mohammed. He will unite Muslims as one caliphate again and lead the army of black flags to conquer the Jews and establish a base at Jerusalem, but have his headquarters in Iraq.

Mohammed is quoted as having said, "Armies carrying black flags will come from Khurasan. No power will be able to stop them and they will finally reach Eela where they will erect flags." According to *Signs of Qiyamah*, 'Eela' is Baitul Maqdas, the holy house (Dome of the Rock) in Jerusalem. The land of Khurasan is the land of the Kurds which stretches from northern Iran and Iraq into eastern Turkey. But according to Shia eschatology, the Mahdi will arise from Khorassan, currently their north eastern province, which historically once covered parts of today's Afghanistan, Tadzhikistan, Turkmenistan and Uzbekistan as well.

Muslims believe the Mahdi will find the Ark of the Covenant and bring it to Jerusalem. He is also supposed to "discover" ancient biblical manuscripts which he uses to convert Jews and Christians to Islam. Muslims believe the Mahdi will have supernatural power over the wind, rain, and crops; and he will distribute wealth and be loved by all people.

Serpents from Dan

> *Yes, the stork in the heaven knows her <u>appointed times</u>; and the turtle and the crane and the swallow observe the time of their coming; but my people know not <u>the judgment of the LORD</u>. . . they have rejected the word of the LORD; and what wisdom is in them?. . . For they have healed the hurt of the daughter of my people slightly, saying, <u>Peace, peace; when there is no peace</u>. Were they ashamed when they had committed abomination? no, they were not at all ashamed, neither could they blush: therefore shall they fall among them that fall: <u>in the time of their</u>*

*visitation they shall be cast down, said the LORD. I will surely consume them, said the LORD: there shall be no grapes on the vine, nor figs on the fig tree, and the leaf shall fade; and the things that I have given them shall pass away from them. . . . We looked for peace, but no good came; and for a time of health, and behold trouble! The snorting of his horses was heard from **Dan**: the whole land trembled at the sound of the neighing of his strong ones; for they are come, and have devoured the land, and all that is in it; the city, and those that dwell therein. For, behold, I will send serpents, cockatrices, among you, which will not be charmed, and they shall bite you, said the LORD. When I would comfort myself against sorrow, my heart is faint in me. Behold the voice of the cry of the daughter of my people because of them that dwell in a far country: Is not the LORD in Zion? is not her king in her? Why have they provoked me to anger with their graven images, and with strange vanities? The harvest is past, the summer is ended, and we are not saved. (Jeremiah 8:7-20)*

'Charmed' is *lachash*. meaning to whisper an incantation, enchantment, or give oration. 'Serpent' is *nachash*. 'Bite' is *nashak*, meaning to strike, sting, or loan with high interest. 'Cockatrices' referred to enemies whose destructive power could not be counteracted by persuasion or other method.

This prophecy was fulfilled when the Babylonian cavalry came through the land of Dan to conquer Judah. Early church fathers like Irenaeus (180 AD) also attributed this passage to a future Antichrist, stating that he would arise from the tribe of Dan. Dan and Ephraim are excluded from the twelve tribes sealed in Revelation because they allowed king Jeroboam to establish worship of golden calves in their territories (1 Kings 12:26-33).

Possible Antichrists from Dan

Sayyid Muqtada al-Sadr is a possible candidate for the Antichrist. *Sayyid* is a title used among the Shia to denote direct descendants from Mohammed. Al-Sadr is a Shia cleric currently studying to be an ayatollah in Iran, but he was born in Baghdad, Iraq in 1973 of Lebanese (Dan's territory) ancestry. In Iraq he established the 60,000 man Mahdi Army whose uniform and flags are black. There is also a Black Banner Sunni army in Iraq. If he is able to combine and attack Jerusalem, it would fulfill several Muslim prophecies regarding their Mahdi (end-time savior). Though Sadr stood down his army in August 2008, in April 2009 he was holding talks with officials in Turkey who then changed the make-up of their cabinet to be pro-Islam.

Mahmoud Ahmadinejad is currently President of Iran (elections will be held June 12, 2009). His mother was a descendant of Mohammed. He was born Mahmoud Sabaghian, but his family changed their name when they moved to Tehran to pursue a better life. In January 2009, Mehdi Khazali wrote that the family of Iran's President changed their name because it was linked to Jewish ancestry. From 734 to 715 BC, three different kings deported the ten northern tribes (including Dan) to what is now Syria, northern Iraq, northern Iran, and Afghanistan. It would be no surprise if most Iranians had a link to Israeli ancestry. Ahmadinejad has no verified link to Dan.

Barack Hussein Obama, Jr. has genealogical roots to the tribe of Dan on his mother's side, and has possible roots to the tribe of Dan on his Kenyan father's side. A large remnant of the tribe of Dan currently lives in Ethiopia, Africa (Kenya lies directly south). Barack Obama attended both a Catholic school and a Muslim school for two years each as a child. During an interview Obama made a verbal slip and referred to "my Muslim faith". Obama is routinely called a messiah, and he has never denied being a messiah.

These three men are currently in positions of power and influence. The most likely scenario is that Muqtada al-Sadr is the Mahdi/Antichrist who is assisted by Mahmoud Ahmadinejad, the False Prophet bent on destruction. Barack Obama is a False Messiah (known as the al-Dajjal to Muslims) whom al-Sadr and Ahmadinejad seek to destroy.

Dan shall judge his people as one of the tribes of Israel. Dan shall be a serpent by the way, an adder in the path, that bites the horse heels, so that his rider shall fall backward. I have waited for your salvation, O LORD. (Genesis 49:16-18)

The first sentence could be translated, "Dan shall rule and overshadow his people, united tribes; he will rule as God." 'Serpent' is *nachash*, a hissing snake, from the verb meaning hiss, or whisper a (magic) spell generally used of enchanters. 'Bites' is *nashak*; Strong's translation is "to strike with a sting (as a serpent); figuratively, to oppress with interest on a loan: - bite, lend upon usury." The word 'adder' is *shephiphon*, which is nowhere else in the Bible; it was translated in the Vulgate as 'cerastes'. According to Clarke's Bible Commentary, the "*cerastes* has its name from **two little *horns*** upon its head, and is remarkable for the property here ascribed to the *shephiphon*." The root of the first part of *shephiphon* is *shuph* which means to bruise; and the word 'heels', are also used in Gen. 3:15 referring to satan, the serpent. 'Backward' can also mean behind or the West. The last sentence has three Hebrew words: qavah yeshua yehovah, which can be translated binding or twisting (salvation) Jesus, God. Jacob was prophesying an Antichrist and a False Prophet would come from Dan; two snakes, one of which has two little horns (Rev. 13:11).

This prophecy indicates we may be looking for two leaders to arise from the tribe of Dan which are deceptive talkers who seek to destroy the West (False Messiah): the blasphemous "*son of perdition (destruction)*" (2 Thess. 2:3) who is the False Prophet, and the "little horn" of the beast (Rev. 13:5), who is the Beast/Antichrist. Jeremiah and Daniel were contemporary prophets both speaking about lying leaders. "*Little horn*" is the name Daniel used for a future Antichrist; he also described the destroying False Prophet who 'stands up' (*amad*).

Son of Perdition/Destruction, False Prophet

*And in the latter time of their kingdom, when the transgressors are come to the full, a king of **fierce countenance**, and understanding dark sentences, shall stand up.*

*And his power shall be mighty, but not by his own power: and he <u>shall destroy wonderfully</u>, and shall prosper, and practice, and <u>shall destroy the mighty and the holy people</u>. And **through his policy** also he shall cause craft to prosper in his hand; and he shall magnify himself in his heart, and <u>by peace shall destroy many</u>: he shall also stand up against the Prince of princes; but he shall be broken without hand. (Daniel 8:23-25)*

The "*son of perdition*" is a destroyer. Mahmoud Ahmadinejad has consistently stated his goal is to create enough chaos to hasten the reign of the Mahdi, and has asserted that was why he was made president. When asked by the Ayatollah Khamenei, "What if he doesn't come by then [the end of your term]?" Ahmadinejad adamantly replied, "I assure you; I really believe this. He will come soon." [*Ahmadinejad: The Secret History of Iran's Radical Leader* by Kasra Naji, p.92] Ahmadinejad plans on quickly destroying Israel and slowly bringing the USA to its knees. He will destroy the holy and the mighty (Dan. 8:24).

*The LORD shall bring a nation against you from far, <u>from the end of the earth, as swift as the eagle flies</u>; a nation whose tongue you shall not understand; <u>A nation of **fierce countenance**, which shall not regard the person of the old, nor show favor to the young</u>: And he shall eat the fruit of your cattle, and the fruit of your land, until you be destroyed: (Deuteronomy 28:49-51a)*

Though this was true of the Roman legions who had eagles on their standards as they attacked Israel and destroyed Jerusalem, it is also true of America which has legalized euthanasia in several states, and has legalized abortion nationally, and is again promoting it internationally as well. On May 18, 2009 PM Netanyahu met with Pres. Obama. Obama said that within a year he would know if discussions/diplomacy had not worked with Iran, and then would consider sanctions. Sanctions have already failed. The next day Israel's air force held large-scale exercises simulating war with Iran in preparation for the real one. Obama's actions may have emboldened Iran's plans to destroy Israel. This passage is also true of Iran who, during their war with Iraq, sent children to the front lines to be martyred as they walked upon mines and were blown up.

False Messiahs

For before these days rose up Theudas, boasting himself to be somebody; to whom a number of men, about four hundred, joined themselves: who was slain; and all, as many as obeyed him, were scattered, and brought to nothing. After this man rose up Judas of Galilee in the days of the taxing, and drew away much people after him: he also perished; and all, even as many as obeyed him, were dispersed. (Acts 5:36-37)

Jesus warned His disciples sternly that false Christs would try to deceive them. Theudas (45 AD) claimed he parted the Jordan like Joshua did. An Egyptian prophet (52-58) claimed to bring down walls of Jerusalem. An anonymous prophet (59) promised people freedom if they followed him into the wilderness. Theudas and the Egyptian and the anonymous prophet and their bands were killed and dispersed by Roman procurators. Menahem, the son of Judas the Galilean (66), used Roman weapons to defend Masada until 74 AD. He dressed as a king and entered the temple with his men to 'worship', but the temple guard routed him and his men.

Summary

There are many antichrists; those who oppose Jesus and Father God. There have been particular antichrists like Antiochus IV. Antiochus IV meets the criterion for being "*the Assyrian*" and "*the prince that shall come,*" and the "*little horn*" of Daniel 8:8-14. Prophetic passages allude to the king of Babylon as a satan-possessed figure seeking to be worshiped as God. Scriptures direct us to look for two individuals from the tribe of Dan: the Beast, who is also called "*little horn*" and "*mouth,*" and the False Prophet.

Daniel refers to the Antichrist as "*little horn*" and John refers to him as the "*mouth*" who speaks great things against God. According to Daniel, he comes after ten kings (the Muslim caliphs). According to John, he comes after seven moon-worshiping dynasties (Sumerian through Ottoman). John clarifies that the Antichrist comes from the mystery religion of Babylon: moon-worship. The Antichrist and the Muslim Mahdi (twelfth *imam*) are the same character. John speaks of ten kings having power at the same time with the Antichrist for "*one hour*".

Christian eschatology specifies an antichrist who will proclaim himself to be God on the Temple Mount before Christ's second coming. Jesus will not return until after "*the son of perdition,*" "*that man of sin . . . that Wicked be revealed.*" This False Prophet's work is of Satan "*with all power and signs and lying wonders.*" At the end of the Great Tribulation, Jesus will destroy this False Prophet with the brightness of His coming on Sept. 16th, 2012, and cast him and the Beast into the lake of fire.

Who will declare himself to be god on the Temple Mount? Jesus warned there would be many false Christs and false prophets. Jesus commanded His disciples to pray that the "*abomination of desolation*" (Matthew 24:15-22) wouldn't take place on the sabbath or during winter. That means the date of the deity declaration on the Temple Mount is not set. I think it will occur after the withdrawal of troops from Iraq. Muqtada Sadr might declare himself to be the Mahdi (the Antichrist), Mahmoud Ahmadinejad might declare himself to be god's voice on earth (False Prophet), and/or Barack Obama might declare himself to be the Messiah (False Messiah). Together the three of them might gather at the Dome of the Rock to declare Israel is now a Palestinian state. It will be interesting to see what binding dates Obama's 'peace' plan establishes for Israel.

Gog
(Ezekiel 38-39)

Gog, and Magog, to gather them together to battle (Revelation 20:8b)

The purpose of this chapter is to show that Ezekiel 38 and 39 have been fulfilled and do not have a future fulfillment. The battle of Armageddon is with all the kings of the earth (Rev. 16:14-16), not just those countries listed in these two chapters of Ezekiel. Details of events in chapter seven on Antiochus IV will be fleshed out here.

Gog is a person, then a place, then a person, and then a place. But whether a person or a place, evil is associated with Gog.

And when the thousand years are expired, Satan shall be loosed out of his prison, And shall go out to deceive the nations which are in the four quarters of the earth, **Gog***, and Magog, to gather them together to battle: the number of whom is as the sand of the sea. And they went up on the breadth of the earth, and compassed the camp of the saints about, and the beloved city: and fire came down from God out of heaven, and devoured them. And the devil that deceived them was cast into the lake of fire and brimstone, where the beast and the false prophet are, and shall be tormented day and night for ever and ever. (Revelation 20:7-10)*

During the millennium, generations will be born who refuse to love and serve King Jesus. Satan will be loosed at the end and gather these unfaithful ones to his old stomping grounds of Gog and Magog and deceive them into attacking Jerusalem. Christ will destroy them quickly with fire and then toss the devil into the lake of fire to join his former comrades of 1,000 years prior. Knowing the final end of Gog, we will consider his beginning.

Gog was a Hebrew Man

The sons, I say, of Reuben the firstborn of Israel were, Hanoch, and Pallu, Hezron, and Carmi. The sons of Joel; Shemaiah his son, **Gog his son***, Shimei his son, Micah his son, Reaia his son, Baal his son, Beerah his son, whom Tilgathpilneser king of Assyria carried away captive: he was prince of the Reubenites. And his brothers by their families, when the genealogy of their generations was reckoned, were the chief, Jeiel, and Zechariah, And Bela the son of Azaz, the son of Shema, the son of Joel, who dwelled in Aroer, even to Nebo and Baalmeon:* <u>*And eastward he*</u>

> *inhabited to the entering in of the wilderness from the river Euphrates: because their cattle were multiplied in the land of Gilead. And in the days of Saul they made war with the Hagarites, who fell by their hand: and they dwelled in their tents throughout all the east land of Gilead. And the children of Gad dwelled over against them, in the <u>land of Bashan</u> to Salcah: . . . And they transgressed against the God of their fathers, and went a whoring after the gods of the people of the land, whom God destroyed before them. And the God of Israel stirred up the spirit of Pul king of Assyria, and the spirit of Tilgathpilneser king of Assyria, and he carried them away, even the Reubenites, and the Gadites, and the half tribe of Manasseh, and brought them to Halah, and Habor, and Hara, and to the river Gozan, to this day. (1 Chronicles 5:3-11, 25-26)*

The tribes of Reuben, Gad (land of Gilead), and the half tribe of Manasseh settled on this eastern side of the Jordan. Gog was of the tribe of Reuben. His descendants spread from Gilead to the Euphrates River because of their vast herds of cattle ("*the cows of Bashan*"). From 734 to 732 BC, Tiglath-pileser III deported northern tribes of Israel to what is now Syria and northern Iraq. According to Jamieson, Fausset, and Brown's *Commentary on the Whole Bible,* the first wave of exiles were even taken into upper Media (now Afghanistan). The year of "*this day*" in which the historian wrote was 450 BC, signifying they hadn't returned to Israel.

From Gog's Original Location to Deportation Location

There are three north-south routes through Israel: the Way of the Sea along the Mediterranean coast, the Way of the Passengers through the foothills to Jerusalem, and the King's Highway (Numbers 20:16-22) on the east of the Jordan River and the Dead Sea. All of these routes connect Assyria to Egypt. The kings of Assyria needed to clear these roads to be able to attack Egypt without resistance along the way. In 734 BC Assyrians came down the Way of the Sea, and the coastal tribes of Asher, Manasseh, and Ephraim were taken to Assyria by Tiglath-Pileser. For the next two years Tiglath-Pileser cleared the other two roads and took the rest of the ten northern tribes into exile.

> *In the days of Pekah king of Israel came Tiglathpileser king of Assyria, and took Ijon, and Abelbethmaachah, and Janoah, and Kedesh, and Hazor, and Gilead, and Galilee, all the land of Naphtali, and carried them captive to Assyria. (1 Kings 15:29)*

King Pekah was assassinated, and king Hoshea paid tribute to Tiglath-Pileser, but not to his son Shalmaneser V, who between 724-723 took more of the house of Israel into exile. The cities named in this verse were around ancient Lake Huleh north of the Sea of Galilee. The third wave of Israelites taken into Assyria and Media was between 716-715 by Shalmaneser's son, Sargon II.

Assur was the city from which the Assyrian Empire derived its name. The Assyrian Empire included lands beyond the Caspian Sea. In 732 BC Assyrian king Tiglath-pileser took 13,520 from Gog to live amidst the descendants of Japheth's sons: Tubal, Meshech, and Magog, between the Black and Caspian Seas [see map in Appendix]. Then he rebuilt the old Egyptian fort at Megiddo to protect the lands he just conquered. Twenty years later, Assyrian king Sennacherib, son of Sargon II, boasted of deporting 200,150 people from Israel to Assyria. Somehow throughout all these deportations, the tribe of Gog maintained its identity, and became associated with the ancient lands of Magog, Meshech and Tubal.

Ezekiel 38

About 100 years after the Assyrians deported the house of Israel, Ezekiel came on the scene as a prophet of Judah. He prophesied from about 595-575 BC when Jehoichin was king. He was deported to Babylon in 586 BC with thousands of others from the house of Judah. He was familiar with the lands of Assyria, but instead used the ancient Biblical names of the northern portions of it. Ezekiel named this future Assyrian leader, Gog. The prophecies of Gog fit Antiochus IV Epiphanes who fought against Israel from 170-164 BC.

And the word of the LORD came to me, saying, Son of man, set your face against Gog, the land of Magog, the chief prince of Meshech and Tubal, and prophesy against him, And say, Thus said the Lord GOD; Behold, I am against you, O Gog, the chief prince of Meshech and Tubal: And I will turn you back, and put hooks into your jaws, and I will bring you forth, and all your army, horses and horsemen, all of them clothed with all sorts of armor, even a great company with bucklers and shields, all of them handling swords: Persia, Ethiopia, and Libya with them; all of them with shield and helmet: Gomer, and all his bands; the house of Togarmah of the north quarters, and all his bands: and many people with you. Be you prepared, and prepare for yourself, you, and all your company that are assembled to you, and be you a guard to them. (Ezekiel 38:1-7)

Japheth's son Gomer dwelled above the Black Sea. Gomer's sons Ashchenaz, Riphath, and Togarmah, also lived around the Black Sea. A portion of Persia paid tribute to Antiochus IV, (I Maccabees 3:31). Ethiopia and Libya were auxiliaries of Antiochus: "*The Libyans and Ethiopians shall be at his steps*" (Daniel 11:43).

After many days you shall be visited: in the latter years you shall come into the land that is brought back from the sword, and is gathered out of many people, against the mountains of Israel, which have been always waste: but it is brought forth out of the nations, and they shall dwell safely all of them. (Ezekiel 38:8)

From 605 to 588 BC, Babylon deported the house of Judah. In 538 BC, Persian king Cyrus made a decree for the Jews to return to their homeland. The Jews were "*brought back from the sword, and gathered out of many people.*" But Gog would come upon them during a time when the Jews were safe and prosperous.

Antiochus IV Takes Great Spoil from Israel

*You shall ascend and come like a storm, you shall be like a cloud to cover the land, you, and all your bands, and many people with you. Thus said the Lord GOD; It shall also come to pass, that at the same time shall things come into your mind, and you shall think an evil thought: And you shall say, I will go up to the land of unwalled villages; I will go to them that are at rest, that dwell safely, all of them dwelling without walls, and having neither bars nor gates, To take a **spoil**, and to take a prey; to turn your hand on the desolate places that are now inhabited, and on the people that are gathered out of the nations, which have gotten **cattle** and goods, that dwell in the middle of the land. (Ezekiel 38:9-12)*

"And after two years fully expired the king sent his chief collector of tribute unto the cities of Juda, who came unto Jerusalem with a great multitude, And spake peaceable words unto them, but all was deceit: for when they had given him credence, he fell suddenly upon the city, and smote it very sore, and destroyed much people of Israel. And when he had taken the **spoils** of the city, he set it on fire, and pulled down the houses and walls thereof on every side. But the women and children took they captive, and possessed the **cattle**. Then builded they the city of David with a great and strong wall, and with mighty towers, and made it a strong hold for them." (I Maccabees 1:29-33)

*Sheba, and Dedan, and the merchants of Tarshish, with all the young lions thereof, shall say to you, Are you come to take a **spoil**? have you gathered your company to take a prey? to carry away <u>silver and gold</u>, to take away **cattle** and goods, to take a great **spoil**? Therefore, son of man, prophesy and say to Gog, Thus said the Lord GOD; In that day when my people of Israel dwells safely, shall you not know it? And you shall come from your place out of the north parts, you, and many people with you, all of them riding on horses, a great company, and a mighty army: And you shall come up against my people of Israel, as a cloud to cover the land; it shall be in the latter days, and I will bring you against my land, that the heathen may know me, when I shall be sanctified in you, O Gog, before their eyes. (Ezekiel 38:13-16)*

"And after that Antiochus had smitten Egypt, he returned again in the hundred forty and third year, and went up against Israel and Jerusalem with a great multitude, And entered proudly into the sanctuary, and took away the <u>golden</u> altar, and the candlestick of light, and all the vessels thereof, And the table of the shewbread, and the pouring vessels, and the vials. and the censers of <u>gold</u>, and the veil, and the crown, and the <u>golden</u> ornaments that were before the temple, all which he pulled off. He took also the <u>silver</u> and the <u>gold</u>, and the precious vessels: also he took the hidden treasures which he found. And when he had taken all away, he went into his own land, having made a great massacre, and spoken very proudly." (I Maccabees 1:20-24)

Antiochus boiled swine's flesh and killed an elderly scribe who refused to eat it (II Maccabees 6). He sprinkled the temple and the altar with the pig broth; then he broke into the holy of holies. "So when Antiochus had carried out of the temple a <u>thousand and eight hundred talents</u>, he departed in all haste unto Antiochia." (II Maccabees 5:21)

Slave Merchants at Slaughter of Emmaus

"Lysias chose Ptolemy the son of Dorymenes, and Nicanor and Gorgias, mighty men among the friends of the king, and sent with them forty thousand infantry and seven thousand cavalry to go into the land of Judah and destroy it, as the king had commanded. So they departed with their entire force, and when they arrived they encamped near Emmaus in the plain. <u>When the traders of the region heard what was said to them, they took silver and gold in immense amounts, and fetters, and went to the camp to get the sons of Israel for slaves</u>. And forces from Syria and the land of the Philistines joined with them." (I Macabbees 3:38-41)

Lysias was the general of the armies of Antiochus IV, and he appointed Ptolemy, Nicanor, and Gorgias as captains over 47,000 troops to annihilate Judah as their king had commanded. The slave merchants of Sheba and Dedan were from the eastern coast of the Arabian Peninsula. The Mediterranean Sea was called the Sea of Tarshish in ancient times, so merchants of Tarshish were those who traded along the coasts by ship. The slave traders were eager to make a profit off of Israel. And Lysias was eager to sell the Israelites to the merchants in order to obtain money to pay the mercenaries he hired from other countries.

"And there were destroyed within the space of three whole days fourscore thousand, whereof <u>forty thousand were slain in the conflict; and no fewer sold than slain</u>." (II Maccabees 5:14)

Gog, the Prophesied Assyrian

*Thus said the Lord GOD; Are you **he** of whom I have spoken in old time by my servants the prophets of Israel, which prophesied in those days many years that I would bring **you** against them? And it shall come to pass at the same time when Gog shall come against the land of Israel, said the Lord GOD, that my fury shall come up in my face. For in my jealousy and in the fire of my wrath have I spoken, Surely in that day there shall be a great shaking in the land of Israel; So that the fishes of the sea, and the fowls of the heaven, and the beasts of the field, and all creeping things that creep on the earth, and all the men that are on the face of the* *earth, shall shake at my presence, and the mountains shall be thrown down, and the steep places shall fall, and every wall shall fall to the ground. (Ezekiel 38:17-20)*

God is linking this prophecy against Gog with much earlier prophecies about the Assyrian. Ezekiel was contemporary with Daniel and Jeremiah. One hundred years earlier, Isaiah called this intruder the Assyrian. Prophets Hosea and Micah were Isaiah's contemporaries.

*When Israel was a child, then I loved him, and called my son out of Egypt. . . . He shall not return into the land of Egypt, and the **Assyrian** shall be his king, because they refused to return. And the sword shall abide on his cities, and shall consume his branches, and devour them, because of their own counsels. (Hosea 11:1, 5-6)*

*For thus said the Lord GOD, My people went down aforetime into Egypt to sojourn there; and the **Assyrian** oppressed them without cause. Now therefore, what have I here, said the LORD, that my people is taken away for nothing? they that rule over them make them to howl, said the LORD; and my name continually every day is blasphemed. (Isaiah 52:4)*

The prophet Ezekiel stated when Gog came against the land of Israel there would be a great earthquake. Israel has several north-south fault lines. One of them along the Dead Sea is called Serghaya. A paper published in 2003 in the *Geophysical Journal International* attributes the date of 170 BC to one of the wedges in the fault. The forty foot statue of Zeus and its temple collapsed in 170 BC in Olympia, Greece, even after surviving the earthquake of 226 BC which toppled the Colossus of Rhodes. The effect of shifting plates around the Mediterranean Sea is much like the "ring of fire" around the Pacific Ocean; when one plate shifts, it often causes others to shift as well. Antioch, the capital of Syria, did not start recording earthquakes until the one in 146 BC. It is likely the 170 BC earthquake in Greece had a counterpart in Israel. But this is only a partial fulfillment of the earthquake since "*all the men that are on the face of the earth, shall shake at my presence*" which will be fulfilled at Christ's second coming.

Time-line of Antiochus IV

170: He took all the gold and silver from the Temple. He sacrificed a pig on the altar, boiled the meat and forced priests to eat it; those who refused had tongues cut out. His armies killed 60,000 in Judah and sold 40,000 as slaves.

169: Antiochus built a navy and conquered Cyprus and large parts of Egypt.

168: Roman pressure forced Antiochus to stop the attack of Egypt. He sent Apollonius with an army of 22,000 to collect tribute from Jerusalem. They killed and captured many, plundered the city and burnt it.

167: Antiochus forbad sacrifices, circumcision and other Jewish laws; they were to worship idols and eat pork, or be killed. An idol of Zeus was placed on the altar. Scrolls were burned; their owners, killed. (I Maccabees 1:41-56)

165: Antiochus captured Artaxias, capital of Armenia.

164: Antiochus' attack on Susa failed. He got reports of Israel and bragged he would make Jerusalem a graveyard of Jews and hastened his chariot driver, but became ill after being thrown from his chariot. He repented, and sought to restore to the Jews all he had taken, and to let them worship God freely. He died of a bowel pestilence.

"But the Lord Almighty, the God of Isreal, smote him with an incurable and **invisible plague**: or as soon as he had spoken these words, a pain of the bowels that was remediless came upon him, and sore torments of the inner parts; And that most justly: for he had tormented other men's bowels with many and strange torments." (II Maccabees 9:5-6)

*And I will call for a <u>sword</u> against him throughout all my mountains, said the Lord GOD: every man's sword shall be against his brother. And I will plead against him with **pestilence** and with blood; and I will rain on him, and on his bands, and on the many people that are with him, an overflowing rain, and great hailstones, fire, and brimstone. Thus will I magnify myself, and sanctify myself; and I will be known in the eyes of many nations, and they shall know that I am the LORD. (Ezekiel 38:21-23)*

The sword God calls for against Gog is the Maccabees (hammers), a family in Judah who put Gog's armies to flight. Through God's mighty deliverance from the Assyrian, people will acknowledge Him as LORD.

The Maccabees

The tyranny of Antiochus IV aroused both the religious and the political consciousness of the Jews, which resulted in the revolution led by the Maccabees. The family was led by the father, Mattathias, who had five sons: Jonnan, Simon, Judas, Eleazar, and Jonathan. Mattathias, of the house of Asmon, was a priest. He organized open resistance in 167-166, and with his son and successor Judas the Maccabee (hammer), defeated two large and well-equipped armies of Antiochus. Antiochus was busy fighting against the Parthians. He gave Lysias instructions to send a large army against the Jews and exterminate them utterly. But the generals Ptolemæus, Nicanor, and Gorgias, whom Lysias dispatched with large armies against Judah, were defeated one after the other (166-165), and compelled to take refuge upon Philistine soil. Lysias himself (165) was forced to flee to Antioch, having been completely routed by the victorious Jews. Antiochus died shortly thereafter in Persia, 164.

Battles Led by the Maccabees

167: Mattathias and his sons (the Maccabees) fought the Syrians and destroyed their altars. Cleansing of the temple in Jerusalem began. At the Battle of Wadi Haramia, Judas divided his 600 men into four groups and wiped out 2,000 men of Apollonia in Wadi Haramia, and Judas took Apollonia's sword.

166: At the Battle of Beth Horon, Judas killed 800 men, and the rest fled into Philistia. At the Battle of Emmaus: Judas and his men killed 3,000 out of the 27,000 men whom Lysias sent under the command of Gorgias and Nicanor, as they fled "unto Gazera, and unto the plains of Idumea, and Azotus, and Jamnia," (I Maccabees 4:15). The weapons they abandoned included javelins, spears, swords, shields, battering rams, and ballistas. During this year, Judas Maccabeus led a successful revolt with 6,000 men; routing and killing over 20,000 of the enemy and apostates.

165: Judas routed an army of 65,000, killing 5,000. Judas captured Jerusalem, and had the priests cleanse and rededicate the Temple (the 25th of Kislev) and they celebrated for 8 days (Hanukkah).

164: Battle of Beth Zur: Judas killed 5,000 out of Lysias' 65,000 men, and Lysias' men dropped their shields and weapons and ran.

Battle of Beth Zechariah: Lysias returned with 50,000 better trained mercenaries and 32 elephants which cause Judas to retreat. Judas' younger brother, Eleazar thrust his sword underneath the lead elephant, killing the animal who then crushed him to death. Lysias retook Beth Zur.

Battle Arabattine: Jews killed 25,000. Countries around Israel killed the Jews in their lands. [In 164 alone, the armies of Judas killed 70,000 of their enemies.]

163: The Jews killed 26,000 who attacked Jerusalem. [For the last two years of the war (162-161), the Jews killed 100,000 in other battles throughout Judah.]

161: Battle of Adesa: 3,000 Jews killed 5,000 enemy troops, and the rest fled to Gazera, leaving their weapons behind them.

Battle of Capharsalama: Jews killed 5,000.

Battles in lands of Gilead and Galilee: Judas killed 8,000 of the army of Timotheus, and killed all the men in Bosora, Casphon, Maked, Bosor, and Ephron, and all the Arabians in Raphon. While he was busy there, his brother Simon defeated 3,000 of the enemy in the Galilee all the way to Arbatta and the coast city of Ptolemais (Acco). Judas and Simon brought the women and children back to Judah, and then took Hebron and Maspha (Mispah).

From Adasa to Gazera, Jews killed 35,000. Judas died at the next battle at Elasa.

Some of these battles were on the travel route of the passengers. The Jews killed over a quarter million troops sent against them from 167 to 161 BC.

Ezekiel 39

> *Therefore, you son of man, prophesy against Gog, and say, Thus said the Lord GOD; Behold, I am against you, O Gog, the chief prince of Meshech and Tubal: And I will turn you back, and <u>leave but the sixth part of you</u>, and will cause you to come up from the north parts, and will bring you on the mountains of Israel: (Ezekiel 39:1-2)*

The underlined portion could be translated "strike you with six plagues" as noted in Ezekiel 38:22 as pestilence, blood, an overflowing rain, great hailstones, fire, and brimstone. Or maybe the Syrians had 1.5 million troops prior to their engagement and were reduced by a sixth.

And I will smite your bow out of your left hand, and will cause your arrows to fall out of your right hand. You shall fall on the mountains of Israel, you, and all your bands, and the people that is with you: I will give you to the ravenous birds of every sort, and to the beasts of the field to be devoured. You shall fall on the open field: for I have spoken it, said the Lord GOD. (Ezekiel 39:3-5)

It is typical of a right-handed person to hold the bow with his left hand and draw the arrow with his right hand when shooting. It is interesting that Antiochus IV is pictured reclining with a bow in his left hand and an arrow in his right on the back (reverse) of a coin struck late in his reign.

The Syrian troops ("*Magog*") and their hired troops ("*dwell in isles*") fell in the mountains and valleys. The Maccabees used guerrilla warfare, often dividing their small numbers so as to surround a narrow passage in the hills and pick off the enemies, but they also won in open field battles.

And I will send a fire on Magog, and among them that dwell carelessly in the isles: and they shall know that I am the LORD. So will I make my holy name known in the middle of my people Israel; and I will not let them pollute my holy name any more: and the heathen shall know that I am the LORD, the Holy One in Israel. Behold, it is come, and it is done, said the Lord GOD; this is the day whereof I have spoken. (Ezekiel 39:6-8)

Israel has longingly awaited the day they would throw off the oppression of their enemies and live in accordance with God's laws in peace. And from 160 BC to 63 BC when Roman general Pompey entered the Temple, that was how they lived.

Israel Burned Abandoned Wooden Weaponry for Seven Years

And they that dwell in the cities of Israel shall go forth, and shall set on fire and burn the weapons, both the shields and the bucklers, the bows and the arrows, and the hand staves, and the spears, and they shall burn them with fire seven years: So that they shall take no wood out of the field, neither cut down any out of the forests; for they shall burn the weapons with fire: and they shall spoil those that spoiled them, and rob those that robbed them, said the Lord GOD. (Ezekiel 39:9-10)

What the Israelites could not use of the abandoned weapons and supplies of defeated Syrian troops, they used for fuel over the course of the seven year war. The bows, arrows, quivers, shields, bucklers, handstaves, and spears were found in vast amounts; especially when the mercenaries retreated, throwing away their arms. In Mariana's *History of Spain* (lib. xi., c. 24) he recounts that after the Spaniards had given that signal overthrow to the Saracens in AD 1212, they found such a vast quantity of lances, javelins, and such like, that they served them for four years for fuel.

"they shall spoil those that spoiled them"

"Wherefore Judas took their **spoils**, and Apollonius' sword also, and therewith he fought all his life long." (I Maccabees 3:12)

"Then Judas returned to **spoil** the tents, where they got much gold, and silver, and blue silk, and purple of the sea, and great riches. After this they went home, and sung a song of thanksgiving, and praised the Lord in heaven: because it is good, because his mercy endureth forever." (I Maccabees 4:23-24, after battle against Gorgias)

"Wherefore they thought to destroy the generation of Jacob that was among them, and thereupon they began to slay and destroy the people. Then Judas fought against the children of Esau in Idumea at Arabattine, because they besieged Gael: and he gave them a great overthrow, and abated their courage, and took their **spoils**." (I Maccabees 5:2-3)

"Hereupon Judas and his host turned suddenly by the way of the wilderness unto Bosora; and when he had won the city, he slew all the males with the edge of the sword, and took all their **spoils**, and burned the city with fire. . . . So Judas turned to Azotus in the land of the Philistines, and when he had pulled down their altars, and burned their carved images with fire, and **spoiled** their cities, he returned into the land of Judea." (I Maccabees 5:28 and 68)

"Now unto Simon were given three thousand men to go into Galilee, and unto Judas eight thousand men for the country of Galaad. Then went Simon into Galilee, where he fought many battles with the heathen, so that the heathen were discomfited by him. And he pursued them unto the gate of Ptolemais; and there were slain of the heathen about three thousand men, whose **spoils** he took. And those that were in Galilee, and in Arbattis, with their wives and their children, and all that they had, took he away with him and brought them into Judea with great joy."
(I Maccabees 5:20-23)

The tables were turned, and God enabled the Maccabees to spoil those who had spoiled them. But Antiochus IV continued to send captains and armies against the Jews, each captain thinking he wouldn't make the mistakes of the others, and would make a famous name for himself instead.

Battle of Emmaus: Jewish Victors instead of Slaves

Nicanor was such a captain. He knew of the guerrilla warfare of the Maccabees, and thought he could outfox them. So much so, that he announced to the slave merchants to get ready to buy Jewish slaves. Antiochus desperately needed money to pay his tribute to Rome, and Nicanor thought he could get it for him.

> "So Nicanor undertook to make so much money of the captive Jews, as should defray the tribute of two thousand talents, which the king was to pay to the Romans. Wherefore immediately he sent to the cities upon the sea coast, proclaiming a sale of the captive Jews, and promising that they should have fourscore and ten bodies for one talent, not expecting the vengeance that was to follow upon him from the Almighty God. . . . As for that most ungracious <u>Nicanor</u>, who had brought a thousand merchants to buy the Jews . . . he came like a fugitive servant . . . for that <u>his host was destroyed.</u> Thus he, that took upon him to make good to the Romans their tribute by means of captives in Jerusalem, told abroad, that the Jews had God to fight for them, and therefore they could not be hurt, because they followed the laws that he gave them." (II Maccabees 8: 10-11, 34-36 edited)

Valley of Passengers

And it shall come to pass in that day, that I will give to Gog a place there of graves in Israel, the valley of the passengers on the east of the sea: and it shall stop the noses of the passengers: and there shall they bury Gog and all his multitude: and they shall call it The valley of Hamongog. (Ezekiel 39:11)

'Valley' is *gevah*, meaning a gorge with lofty sides, or a narrow. It could describe a 'wadi', a river basin, as well. 'Passengers' is *abar*, meaning to cross over; used of any transition including over pass, pass over, or passage. 'Multitude' is *Hamon* (masc.) and *Hamonah* (fem.).

When Ezekiel referred to the Mediterranean Sea, he called it the "*great sea*" (four times in Ezek. 47, and once in 48:28). The writers of Numbers and Joshua also called it the "*great sea*". When Ezekiel used a word for the direction of east, he used *qadim,* but in the above verse he used "*qidmah,*" meaning front or former. A former or an 'ancient sea' north of the Sea of Galilee is now a very small lake called Huleh. The "*of the*" is added by the editor, it's not in the original. "*The noses*" is also added, but could be conveyed by the word 'muzzle' for "*stop*".

Recall there are three north-south routes through Israel: the Way of the Sea along the Mediterranean coast, the Way of the Passengers through the foothills to Jerusalem, and the King's Highway on the east of the Jordan River and the Dead Sea. The major crossroad cities which connect the routes are Megiddo and Hazor. [see map in Appendix] Hazor is just west of Lake Huleh and has a very broad valley which then narrows into a gorge along the Jordan through which is the Passenger's Way. Passengers could not avoid this crossing, and rotting bodies from a battle would surely make them put their hands over their noses.

> "As for Jonathan and his host, they pitched at the water of Gennesar [Sea of Galilee], from whence betimes in the morning they gat them to the **plain of** Nasor [**Hazor**]. And, behold, the host of strangers met them in the plain, who, having laid men in ambush for him in the mountains, came themselves over against him. So when they that lay in ambush rose out of their places and joined battle, all that were of Jonathan's side fled; Insomuch as there was not one of them left, except Mattathias the son of Absalom, and Judas the son of Calphi, the captains of the host. Then Jonathan rent his clothes, and cast earth upon his head, and prayed. Afterwards turning again to battle, he put them to flight, and so they ran away. Now when his own men that were fled saw this, they turned again unto him, and with him pursued them to Cades [**Kedesh**], even unto their own tents, and there they camped. So there were slain of the heathen that day about three thousand men: but Jonathan returned to Jerusalem." (1 Macabbees 11:68-74, edited with additions for clarification)

Burying for Seven Months

Those 3,000 were buried in the valley of Hazor, and the quarter million dead bodies were buried along the Valley of the Passengers, sometimes a bone at a time. The Jews had very strict laws regarding being defiled by touching a dead body (Numbers 9:7-10). A priest or Levite could not, but if they saw a human bone, they could set a marker for those who could bury it back in the valley of Hazor (Hamongog).

> *He that touches the dead body of any man shall be unclean seven days. He shall purify himself with it on the third day, and on the seventh day he shall be clean: but if he purify not himself the third day, then the seventh day he shall not be clean. Whoever touches the dead body of any man that is dead, and purifies not himself, defiles the tabernacle of the LORD; and that soul shall be cut off from Israel: because the water of separation was not sprinkled on him, he shall be unclean; his uncleanness is yet on him. . . .And whoever touches one that is slain with a sword in the open fields, or a dead body, or a bone of a man, or a grave, shall be unclean seven days. (Numbers 19:11-16 edited)*

During a seven year war, not all of the bodies are going to be buried immediately, and animal scavengers will come and feast upon the corpses. Neither were all the injured nor deserters found immediately. According to Clarke, "Many of the Syrian soldiers had secreted themselves in different places during the pursuit after the battle, where they died of their wounds, of hunger, and of fatigue; so that they were not all found and buried till *seven months* after the defeat of the Syrian army."

And <u>seven months shall the house of Israel be burying of them</u>, that they may cleanse the land. Yes, all the people of the land shall bury them; and it shall be to them a renown the day that I shall be glorified, said the Lord GOD. And they shall sever out men of continual employment, passing through the land to bury with the passengers those that remain on the face of the earth, to cleanse it: after the end of seven months shall they search. <u>And the passengers that pass through the land, when any sees a man's bone, then shall he set up a sign by it, till the buriers have buried it in the valley of Hamongog</u>. And also the name of the city shall be **Hamonah***. Thus shall they cleanse the land. || And, you son of man, thus said the Lord GOD; Speak to every feathered fowl, and to every beast of the field, Assemble yourselves, and come; gather yourselves on every side to my sacrifice that I do sacrifice for you, even a great sacrifice on the mountains of Israel, that you may eat flesh, and drink blood. You shall eat the flesh of the mighty, and drink the blood of the princes of the earth, of rams, of lambs, and of goats, of bullocks, all of them fatted calves of Bashan. And you shall eat fat till you be full, and drink blood till you be drunken, of my sacrifice which I have sacrificed for you. Thus you shall be filled at my table with horses and chariots, with mighty men, and with all men of war, said the Lord GOD. And I will set my glory among the heathen, and all the heathen shall see my judgment that I have executed, and my hand that I have laid on them. So the house of Israel shall know that I am the LORD their God from that day and forward. || (Ezekiel 39:12-22 with additions)*

Again we have a dual fulfillment between the double bars: one during the time of the reign of Antiochus IV, and another at the second coming of Messiah Jesus. Notice there are no chariots mentioned in the future, though horses are.

And he has on his clothing and on his thigh a name written, KING OF KINGS, AND LORD OF LORDS. And I saw an angel standing in the sun; and he cried with a loud voice, saying to all the fowls that fly in the middle of heaven, Come and gather yourselves together to the supper of the great God; That you may eat the flesh of kings, and the flesh of captains, and the flesh of mighty men, and the flesh of horses, and of them that sit on them, and the flesh of all men, both free and bond, both small and great. (Revelation 19:16-18)

Maccabees are Transition to Messiah

Other prophets saw the time when Israel would throw off its oppressors in anticipation of Messiah's birth. After the Temple's foundation was laid, Zechariah wrote the following:

Then lifted I up my eyes, and saw, and behold four horns. And I said to the angel that talked with me, What be these? And he answered me, These are the horns which have scattered Judah, [namely] Israel and Jerusalem. And the LORD showed me four carpenters. Then said I, What come these to do? And he spoke, saying,

> *These are the horns which have scattered Judah, so that no man did lift up his head: but these are come to fray them, to cast out the horns of the Gentiles, which lifted up their horn over the land of Judah to scatter it. (Zechariah 1:18-21 edited, [omitted by translator])*

Zechariah was born during the Babylonian exile, he wrote this after returning to Jerusalem under the decree of Cyrus, the Persian, and he later foretold of the Greek empire (Zech. 9:13). So it is unlikely this prophecy is about the four Gentile empires prior to Christ's first coming. 'Carpenters' is *kawrawsh*, meaning any workman who wields a tool in his craft. The four sons of Mattathias known as "hammers" were Simon, Judas, Eleazar, and Jonathan (Jonnan was not a leader). The four Gentile 'horns' or generals which they "frayed", or caused to fear, were Lysias, Gorgias and Nicanor, and Antiochus IV himself.

Isaiah particularly noted Galilee (where Simon and Jonathan obtained victories) and spoils and "*fuel of fire*".

> *Nevertheless the dimness shall not be such as was in her vexation, when at the first he lightly afflicted the land of Zebulun and the land of Naphtali, and afterward did more grievously afflict her by the way of the sea, beyond Jordan, in Galilee of the nations. The people that walked in darkness have seen a great light: they that dwell in the land of the shadow of death, on them has the light shined. You have multiplied the nation, and not increased the joy: they joy before you according to the joy in harvest, and as men rejoice when they divide the **spoil**. For you have broken the yoke of his burden, and the staff of his shoulder, the rod of his oppressor, as in the day of Midian. For every battle of the warrior is with confused noise, and garments rolled in blood; but this shall be with burning and <u>fuel of fire</u>. For to us a child is born, to us a son is given: and the government shall be on his shoulder: and his name shall be called Wonderful, Counselor, The mighty God, The everlasting Father, The Prince of Peace. (Isaiah 9:1-6)*

The Maccabees broke off the burden of the Syrians much as Midian did by allowing God to win miraculous battles with a few men by faith and cunning. After the seven Maccabees, eight of their family line, the Hasmoneans, continued to rule Israel.

> *When the **Assyrian** shall come into our land: and when he shall tread in our palaces, then shall <u>we raise against him seven shepherds, and eight principal men</u>. And they shall waste the land of Assyria with the sword, and the land of Nimrod in the entrances thereof: <u>thus shall he deliver us from the **Assyrian**, when he comes into our land</u>, and when he treads within our borders. And the remnant of Jacob shall be in the middle of many people as a dew from the LORD, as the showers on the grass, that tarries not for man, nor waits for the sons of men. And the remnant of Jacob shall be among the Gentiles in the middle of many people as a lion among the beasts of the forest, as a young lion among the flocks of sheep: who, if he go*

through, both treads down, and tears in pieces, and none can deliver. Your hand shall be lifted up on your adversaries, <u>and all your enemies shall be cut off</u>. (Micah 5:5b-9)

Maccabees	Hasmoneans
Mattathias 168-167	Aristobulus 104-103
Judas 167- 161	Alexander Jannaeus 103-76
Jonathan 161-144	Alexandra 76-67
Simon 144-135	Hyrcanus II 67-66
Hyrcanus, Simon's son 135-104	Aristobulus II 66-63
Jonnan	Hyrcanus II 63-40
Eleazar, killed in battle	Antigorus 40-37
	Herod the Great 37-1

Alexander Jannaeus was Aristobulus' brother. Alexander's wife, Salome Alexandra, reigned after him until their son, Hyrcanus II, took the throne. Then he and Aristobulus II appealed to Rome, and Rome restored Hyrcanus II to the throne in 63. So it's actually 7 men, one of whom rules twice.

Herod, was not a Jew, He was Idumean (from Edom). Herod defeated Antigorus and then married his teenage niece, Mariamne, which helped to secure him a claim to the throne and gain some Jewish favor because she was Hasmonean. However, Herod already had a wife, Doris, and a young son, Antipater III, and chose to banish them both. [King Herod executed Hyrcanus in 31 BC.] Herod ordered the slaughter of the innocents in Bethlehem when Christ was born in 3 BC.

Romans Come to Israel

In 64 BC Rome gave general Pompey jurisdiction of the Mediterranean and its coastlands 50 miles inland. He defeated the pirates swiftly. Then he deposed king Antiochus XIII of Syria. In 63 BC, he continued south to establish Roman rule in Phoenicia and Judea.

General Pompey came to Jerusalem to settle the civil war between brothers Hyrcanus II and Aristobulus II. With the assistance of Hyrcanus and a delegation of Pharisees, they besieged Jerusalem for three months, and took it from Aristobulus. Pompey entered the Holy of Holies to verify the Jews had no physical statue or image of their God in their temple, a truly radical thought to a Roman who worshiped many idols.

Return of the (Lost Tribes) "Whole House of Israel"

And the heathen shall know that the house of Israel went into captivity for their iniquity: because they trespassed against me, therefore hid I my face from them, and gave them into the hand of their enemies: so fell they all by the sword. According to their uncleanness and according to their transgressions have I done to *them, and hid my face from them. Therefore thus said the Lord GOD; Now <u>will I bring again the captivity of Jacob, and have mercy on the whole house of Israel,</u> and will be jealous for my holy name; After that they have borne their shame, and all their trespasses whereby they have trespassed against me, when they dwelled safely in their land, and none made them afraid. <u>When I have brought them again from the people, and gathered them out of their enemies' lands, and am sanctified in them in the sight of many nations;</u> Then shall they know that I am the LORD their God, which caused them to be led into captivity among the heathen: <u>but I have gathered them to their own land, and have left none of them any more there.</u> Neither will I hide my face any more from them: <u>for I have poured out my spirit on the house of Israel</u>, said the Lord GOD. (Ezekiel 39:23-29)*

This is part of the prophecy which wasn't fulfilled during the reign of Antiochus IV, but is currently in the process of being fulfilled beginning a couple decades ago. That God restored the nation of Israel after 1900 years was a major miracle. But now God is revealing the crypto-Israelites (ten lost tribes) who have been hidden in the world for 2,700 years, and even returning some of them to the land of Israel.

The following information is from the Jewish Voice Ministries "Lost Tribes" poster.
Asher is in Tunisia, Africa.
Dan is in Ethiopia, Africa. In 1991 Israel transported 14,500 Ethiopian Jews to Israel.
Levi is in Zimbabwe, Africa. Many in the Lemba tribe have a Y chromosome match
    for Cohanim (priests, descended from Aaron).
Issachar and Naphtali are in the -istans between Kazakhstan and Afghanistan.
    The descendants of Naphtali have been found along the silk road all the way to
    Kaifeng, China.
Reuben and Gad are in northern Afghanistan and Pakistan.
Ephraim and Simeon are in northwest Afghanistan.
    Four hill tribes of Afghanistan are called Reuveni, Gadun, Efredi, and Shinwari.
Manasseh: They traveled to China like Naphtali, but they eventually moved to India
    between what is now Myanmar and Bangladesh, and there are 1.5 million of them.
Whether King Jesus will return all of these to the land of Israel before or after He returns is uncertain, but He will not leave anyone behind.

Sealing of the 144,000

According to Revelation 7, the angels will seal 12,000 from each tribe who have remained faithful servants of God before the first of the seven trumpets is blown. (Dan and Ephraim are excluded because they allowed the worship of golden calves. 1 Kings 12) Whether the seal will be a visible or invisible mark on their foreheads is unclear. Over the span of 2,700 years these tribes have been forced to become Catholic, Muslim, Hindu, and/ or pagan; yet each has retained some vestige of their Hebrew heritage.

A further miracle is that 12,000 virgin men "*who are without fault*" are found among these tribes. After they are sealed, an angel will proclaim the gospel to the people on earth, again, prior to the first trumpet of judgment.

These are they which were not defiled with women; for they are virgins. These are they which follow the Lamb wherever he goes. These were redeemed from among men, being the first fruits to God and to the Lamb. And in their mouth was found no guile: for they are without fault before the throne of God. And I saw another angel fly in the middle of heaven, having the everlasting gospel to preach to them that dwell on the earth, and to every nation, and kindred, and tongue, and people, Saying with a loud voice, Fear God, and give glory to him; for the hour of his judgment is come: and worship him that made heaven, and earth, and the sea, and the fountains of waters. (Revelation 14:4-7)

Summary

The purpose of this chapter was to show that Ezekiel 38 and 39 have been fulfilled. All the kings of the earth will not be using wooden weapons at the battle of Armageddon, nor will there be seven years to burn them afterwards.

Gog was a Hebrew man of the tribe of Reuben. Because of his vast herds, his lands spread to the Euphrates and became known as the land of Gog. During several campaigns of Assyrian kings from 734-715 BC the ten northern tribes of Israel (including Reuben which contained Gog) were sent into exile in Assyria and Media. Somehow the tribe of Gog maintained its identity, and became associated with the ancient lands of Magog, Meshech and Tubal.

About 100 years after the Assyrians deported the house of Israel, Ezekiel prophesied about a future Assyrian leader named Gog. The prophecies of Gog fit Antiochus IV Epiphanes who fought against Israel from 170-164 BC.

In 170 BC Antiochus took all the gold and silver from the Temple. He sacrificed a pig on the altar, boiled the meat and forced priests to eat it; those who refused had their tongues cut out. In 167 BC Antiochus forbad sacrifices, circumcision and other Jewish laws; they were to worship idols and eat pork, or be killed. An idol of Zeus was placed on the altar. Scrolls were burned; their owners, killed. In 164 BC Antiochus died of a bowel pestilence.

Ezekiel also prophesied the destruction of Gog's armies and the burial Gog's multitudes (*Hamongog*) in Israel in "*the valley of the passengers*". This is located near Lake Huleh and the city of Hazor; a crossroads for the "way of the passengers" through the foothills to Jerusalem. Jonathan, one of the Maccabees, fought a battle against Syrian forces here. One of several battles throughout Israel and beyond in which the Jews killed over a quarter million troops sent against them from 167 to 161 BC, and burned the abandoned weapons during those seven years. For seven months afterwards, people were still finding bones of their attackers and marking them to be buried.

Awake, Bride

    After the seven Maccabees ruled Israel, eight of their family line, the Hasmoneans, continued to rule Israel in accordance with the prophecy in Micah 5:5b-9. Herod, was not a Jew, but he married his Hasmonean niece, which helped to secure him a claim to the throne. Herod ordered the slaughter of the innocents in Bethlehem after Christ was born in 3 BC. Thus bringing us to the first coming of Messiah.

    The last part of Ezekiel 39 contains prophecy about restoration of the "*whole house of Israel*" back to the land of Israel. These "lost tribes" have been revealed in the last two decades, and thousands have returned to Israel already. An angel will seal 12,000 faithful men from each before God gives humans one last chance to receive the gospel of Jesus before He begins the trumpets and vials of judgment which precede His second coming.

End-Times Overview
(Matthew 13-25)

These things I have spoken to you,
that in me you might have peace.
In the world you shall have tribulation:
but be of good cheer;
I have overcome the world.
(John 16:33)

The "*things*" Jesus spoke to His disciples concerned His own death as well as theirs. But Jesus had already chosen to be obedient to death on a cross, and so had already "*overcome*" (*nikao*; gained victory over) the world. Believers have been suffering persecution and tribulation since Jesus spoke this word to His twelve disciples, and we should "*be of good cheer*" (*tharseo*; encouraged) that our choice to obey our Father, even to death, has already given us the victory to endure any tribulation with grace and strength in our Lord Jesus Christ.

There is NO 7 Year Period of Tribulation

Tribulation is *thlipsis* in Greek, meaning pressure; affliction, anguish, burden, persecution, and trouble. Tribulation has been endured in the world since Adam and Eve's first sin. The chapter on 70 X 7 already showed that there is no future tribulation period of seven years; it is a false doctrine based upon an incorrect interpretation of the 70th week of Daniel which has already been fulfilled. Though Christians in America have not suffered much persecution, we too need to prepare ourselves for possible martyrdom as the Great Tribulation continues.

> *Saying, The Son of man must suffer many things, and be rejected of the elders and chief priests and scribes, and be slain, and be raised the third day. And he said to them all, If any man will come after me, let him deny himself, and take up his cross daily, and follow me. <u>For whoever will save his life shall lose it: but whoever will lose his life for my sake, the same shall save it.</u> For what is a man advantaged, if he gain the whole world, and lose himself, or be cast away? For whoever shall be ashamed of me and of my words, of him shall the Son of man be ashamed, when he shall come in his own glory, and in his Father's, and of the holy angels. (Luke 9:22-26)*

Confirming the souls of the disciples, and exhorting them to continue in the faith, and that we must through much tribulation enter into the kingdom of God. (Acts 14:22)

Tribulation (Romans 5:1-10) and persecution (2 Timothy 3:11-12) have been normal aspects of the Christian life for most Christians in the world throughout history. America and a few other places have been rarities. We should not be surprised when "*fiery trials*" and suffering come (1 Peter 4:12-19). Suffering tribulations of this world is NOT suffering God's wrath, as was concluded in the chapter of Resurrections and Rapture.

The purpose of this chapter is to present an overview of end-time events, particularly from the book of Matthew, and to create a framework for a time-line with that information. Jesus spoke of tribulation, great tribulation, resurrection and 'rapture', His coming in power, judgment, and His kingdom in heaven and on earth.

Kingdom of Heaven Parables

Jesus interspersed information about end-times and distinctions between believers and unbelievers in His parables in Matthew. The ending to several of the parables for unbelievers is "*cast him into outer darkness, there shall be weeping and gnashing of teeth*", or "*cast into hell*". The Jews believed in a literal, fiery hell, and understood clearly from these parables that they would go there if they did not accept Jesus as Messiah, the Son of God.

Believers	Matthew Parable	Unbelievers
Understands Word & bears its fruit	13:3-23 The Sower	Rootless & Fruitless
Good & just	13:47-50 The Dragnet	Bad & wicked
Receives children	18:1-20 Little Child & Lamb	Offends children
Forgiving	18:21-35 King's Accounts	Unforgiving
Like a child	19:13-15 Little Children	Unlike a child; not humble
Gives up possessions	19:16-30 Riches now & later	Possessed by things
Grateful for God's grace	20:1-16 Laborers first & last	Critical of God's grace
Obedient	21:28-32 Two sons	Disobedient
Accept the Son	21:33-46 Faithless Tenants	Reject the Son
Clothed with Christ	22:1-14 Wedding Invitation	Clothed with self

Some of these parables describe God's role and point of view, and others describe man's. Some describe the effects of God's kingdom on earth. Some describe duties or requirements for entrance into the kingdom of heaven. In the Mustard Seed and the Leaven (Matthew 13:31-33), Jesus speaks of the kingdom of heaven beginning small and having expansive growth. In the Treasure in the Field and the Pearl of Great Price (Matthew 13:44-46), Jesus speaks of giving all for the kingdom of heaven.

Wheat and Tares

This prophetic parable contains several insights. It also answers the question of why there is evil in the world and why it remains. There is evil because "*an enemy has done this*". Evil ones remain in the world, because to remove them would adversely effect the good ones.

*Another parable put he forth to them, saying, The kingdom of heaven is likened to a man which sowed good seed in his field: But while men slept, his enemy came and sowed tares among the wheat, and went his way. But when the blade was sprung up, and brought forth fruit, then appeared the tares also. So the servants of the householder came and said to him, Sir, did not you sow good seed in your field? from where then has it tares? He said to them, An enemy has done this. The servants said to him, Will you then that we go and gather them up? But he said, No; lest while you gather up the tares, you root up also the wheat with them. Let both grow together until the harvest: and in the time of harvest I will say to the reapers, Gather you together first the tares, and bind them in bundles to burn them: but gather the wheat into my barn. . . . He answered and said to them, He that sows the good seed is the Son of man; The field is the world; the good seed are the children of the kingdom; but the tares are the children of the wicked one; The enemy that sowed them is the devil; the harvest is the end of the world; and the <u>reapers are the angels</u>. As therefore the tares are gathered and burned in the **fire**; so shall it be in the end of this world. The Son of man shall send forth his angels, and they shall gather out of his kingdom all things that offend, and them which do iniquity; And shall cast them into a furnace of fire: there shall be wailing and gnashing of teeth. Then shall the righteous shine forth as the sun in the kingdom of their Father. Who has ears to hear, let him hear. (Matthew 13:24-30, 37-43 edited)*

Both good and evil grow together until the harvest. A group of wheat doesn't get plucked up early with the world ending twice. The harvest is at the end of the world, and the end of the world is with fire (2 Peter 3:10-12). God sends His angels to reap both the believers and unbelievers from the earth; the unbelievers are burned, and the believers are sheltered.

*And I looked, and behold a white cloud, and on the cloud one sat like to the Son of man, having on his head a golden crown, and in his hand a sharp sickle. And another <u>angel</u> came out of the temple, crying with a loud voice to him that sat on the cloud, Thrust in your sickle, and <u>reap</u>: for the time is come for you to reap; <u>for the harvest of the earth is ripe</u>. And he that sat on the cloud thrust in his sickle on the earth; and the earth was reaped. And another <u>angel</u> came out of the temple which is in heaven, he also <u>having a sharp sickle</u>. And another **angel** came out from the altar, which had power over **fire**; and cried with a loud cry to him that had the sharp sickle, saying, Thrust in your sharp sickle, and gather the clusters of the vine* *of the earth; for her grapes are fully ripe. And the angel thrust in his sickle into the earth, and gathered the vine of the earth, and cast it into the great wine press of the **wrath** of God. (Revelation 14:14-19)*

In Israel, barley is harvested in spring, but Jesus didn't use that crop in His end-time parable. Wheat is harvested in late spring/early summer, and grapes are harvested in the summer; both are eaten during the Feast of Tabernacles in Tishri, the month of Jesus' return. With the wheat harvest, the tares are bundled first to await their destruction. With the grape harvest, the good grapes are reaped first, and then the bad are cast into God's wine press of wrath by the angel over fire. Either way, fire awaits unbelievers.

There is a correlation between suffering for God's kingdom through enduring persecutions and tribulations now and obtaining glory later. Unbelievers will be punished for all the misery they've caused believers in this world.

*So that we ourselves glory in you in the churches of God for your patience and faith in all your persecutions and tribulations that you endure: Which is a manifest token of the righteous judgment of God, that you may be counted worthy of the kingdom of God, for which you also suffer: Seeing it is a righteous thing with God to recompense tribulation to them that trouble you; And to you who are troubled rest with us, when the Lord Jesus shall be revealed from heaven with his mighty <u>angels</u>, **In flaming fire taking vengeance on them that know not God, and that obey not the gospel of our Lord Jesus Christ: Who shall be punished with everlasting destruction from the presence of the Lord**, and from the glory of his power; <u>When he shall come to be glorified in his saints, and to be admired in all them that believe</u> (because our testimony among you was believed) <u>in that day</u>. (2 Thess. 1:4-10)*

Parables Regarding Israel

When Jesus rode into Jerusalem on a donkey, the people received him as Messiah, crying, "*Hosanna to the son of David: Blessed is he that comes in the name of the Lord; Hosanna in the highest*" (Matthew 21:9b). But the leaders rejected Him. Jesus told the unbelieving Jewish religious leaders to their faces that they were children of their father, the devil, and destined for hell and damnation. He also told them, "*That the publicans and the harlots go into the kingdom of God before you*" (Matthew 21:31c). He cursed the unfruitful fig tree which represented unbelieving Israel. He told the parable of the Prodigal Son (Matthew 21:28-32), hoping to reach some at an emotional level, but knowing there were those like the older brother who would refuse to celebrate His Father's grace for sinners who returned home. Jesus got personal in the parable of the Rented Vineyard (Matthew 21:33-46), prophesying that they would kill the Owner's Son in hopes of securing the vineyard for themselves.

> *Jesus said to them, Did you never read in the scriptures, The stone which the builders rejected, the same is become the head of the corner: this is the Lord's doing, and it is marvelous in our eyes? Therefore say I to you, The kingdom of God shall be taken from you, and given to a nation bringing forth the fruits thereof. And whoever shall fall on this **stone** shall be broken: but on whomsoever it shall fall, it will grind him to powder. And when the chief priests and Pharisees had heard his parables, they perceived that he spoke of them. (Matthew 22:42-45)*

Even the most hard-hearted Jews understood the meaning of His parables. Then Jesus prophesied concerning Jerusalem and the unbelieving Jews therein, that God would send an army to burn the city and kill those who rejected the Prince and the King's wedding invitation for Him (Matthew 22:7). At the coronation feast of Prince Solomon there were trumpets (1 Kings 3:39-41). Again, a wedding and a coronation point to Rosh Hashanah. Though they rejected their Messiah and their Temple would be destroyed, Jesus left them a promise of His return at their cry of acceptance of Him as Messiah.

> *Behold, your house is left to you desolate. For I say to you, You shall not see me from now on, till you shall say, <u>Blessed is he that comes in the name of the Lord</u>. (Matthew 23:38-39)*

Psalm 118 was sung after the Passover meal and during the Feast of Tabernacles (again pointing to His return in Tishri). It was the source for several of Christ's quotes during His last days. 'Hosanna' (*yashana* in Hebrew) means 'save, now'. The opening of the gates to the righteous is associated with Rosh Hashanah. "*The right hand of the LORD*" referred to God's Son, the Messiah, the Cornerstone, the "*light*" who would be bound and sacrificed to fulfill God's righteousness and provide mercy.

> *The LORD is my strength and song, and is become my salvation. The voice of rejoicing and salvation is in the tabernacles of the righteous: the right hand of the LORD does valiantly. The right hand of the LORD is exalted: the right hand of the LORD does valiantly. I shall not die, but live, and declare the works of the LORD. The LORD has chastened me sore: but he has not given me over to death. Open to me the gates of righteousness: I will go into them, and I will praise the LORD: This gate of the LORD, into which the righteous shall enter. I will praise you: for you have heard me, and are become my salvation. The **stone** which the builders refused is become the head stone of the corner. This is the LORD's doing; it is marvelous in our eyes. This is the day which the LORD has made; we will rejoice and be glad in it. Save [yasha] now [na], I beseech you, O LORD: O LORD, I beseech you, send now prosperity. <u>Blessed be he that comes in the name of the LORD</u>: we have blessed you out of the house of the LORD. God is the LORD, which has showed us light: bind the sacrifice with cords, even to the horns of the altar. You are my God, and I will praise you: you are my God, I will exalt you. O give thanks to the LORD; for he is good: for his mercy endures for ever. (Psalm 118:14-29 with additions)*

Singing Psalm 118 after the Passover meal and during the Feast of Tabernacles is a Jewish tradition. Jesus taught the Jewish people using parables, scriptures, and their traditions. The reason we Gentiles sometimes misunderstand Jesus' teachings, is because we don't know Jewish traditions. In Matthew 24-25, Jesus tells the Jews three times that no one knows the day or hour of His coming. Gentiles have misinterpreted that to mean we cannot know the day or hour of Christ's return.

Jesus Set the Day and the Hour of His Wedding

After the Hebrew wedding contract was accepted, the groom returned to his father's house to begin building an addition called the bridal chamber (John 14:2-3). Only when the father deemed the bridal chamber finished would he allow his son to leave at sunset to go get his bride. The groom's party would arrive with trumpets and a great noise, waking up the whole neighborhood to let them know he was "stealing" his bride and the wedding was about to take place (not your typical stealthy thief). The groom would escort his bride in grand procession back to his father's house where the wedding canopy and feast were ready for the ceremony. The new couple would consummate their marriage that night and remain in the bridal chamber for seven days, emerging to celebrate with guests (Genesis 29:26-28). Between the contract and the ceremony if someone asked the groom when the wedding would be, he would reply, "No one knows the day nor the hour, only my father knows."

Traditionally, the Hebrews believe Adam and Eve were created on Tishri 1, and God performed the first wedding ceremony; therefore Rosh Hashanah is associated with weddings. Also, to "not know the day or hour" was a tip to the Hebrews who celebrated Rosh Hashanah, because it's the only feast on a new moon. Since they had to wait for the signal fires to begin the celebration, they did "not know the day or hour"; so it was determined to celebrate the holiday for two days which were considered one long day.

Day and Hour of the Lord was Known Exactly

Based upon Elijah's rapture in 2 Kings 2:1-11, as noted in the chapter on Resurrections and Raptures, there is scriptural precedence for knowing the exact day of rapture. Also in that chapter, it was shown that the resurrection and the rapture both occur at Christ's second coming which is known as the Day of the Lord.

> *But of the times and the seasons, brothers, you have no need that I write to you. <u>For yourselves **know perfectly** that the day of the Lord so comes as a thief in the night.</u> For when they shall say, Peace and safety; then sudden destruction comes on them, as travail on a woman with child; and they shall not escape. <u>But you, brothers, are not in darkness, that that day should overtake you as a thief.</u> You are all the children of light, and the children of the day: we are not of the night, nor of darkness. Therefore let us not sleep, as do others; but let us watch and be sober. For they that sleep sleep in the night; and they that be drunken are drunken in the night. But let us, who are of the day, be sober, putting on the breastplate of faith*

and love; and for an helmet, the hope of salvation. For God has not appointed us to wrath, but to obtain salvation by our Lord Jesus Christ, Who died for us, that, whether we wake or sleep, we should live together with him. Why comfort yourselves together, and edify one another, even as also you do. . . . Prove all things; hold fast that which is good. Abstain from all appearance of evil. And the very God of peace sanctify you wholly; and <u>I pray God your whole spirit and soul and body be preserved blameless to the coming of our Lord Jesus Christ.</u> Faithful is he that calls you, who also will do it. (1 Thessalonians 5:1-24 edited)

'Perfectly' is *akribos*, meaning accurately, exactly, or diligently. The "*thief in the night*" (2 Peter 3:10) refers to our Lord Jesus when He returns on Rosh Hashanah to wed His Bride. It is the wicked who will be caught unaware at Christ's coming. Again, Christ's Bride is not appointed to God's wrath, but is to live a holy and pure life until the coming of our Lord Jesus Christ. Those members who have already died, currently live with Christ in their resurrected bodies, and we who are alive at His coming will join them.

*Heaven and earth shall pass away, but my words shall not pass away. But of that day and hour knows no man, no, not the angels of heaven, but my Father only. . . . Watch therefore: for you know not what hour your Lord does come. But know this, that <u>if the manager of the house had known in what watch the thief would come, he would have watched</u>, and would not have suffered his house to be broken up. Therefore be you also ready: **for in such an hour as you think not the Son of man comes.**" (Matthew 24:35-36, 42-44)*

Christians are to "*watch*" for Jesus in a way that we are not caught 'off guard' or 'overtaken' at His coming (Rev. 3:3). **But it won't be at the early evening hour they expect.** Jesus then tells them the time plainly in the next few verses of the wedding parable. "*While the bridegroom tarried, they all slumbered and slept. And at **midnight** there was a cry made, Behold, the bridegroom comes; go you out to meet him*" (Matthew 25:5-6). So they were to expect Jesus to return at midnight on Rosh Hashanah. Why didn't Jesus just say clearly, "I'm returning at midnight on Rosh Hashanah"? Likely for the same reason He never corrected anyone who thought He was born in Nazareth. He didn't want to provide His enemies with information to be used against Him or His Church.

Day and Hour and Year of our Lord's Return

From the studies in Daniel's abomination of desolation, the year 2012 is most plausible for Christ's return. Therefore, the return of Jesus Christ for His Bride will be at midnight on Rosh Hashanah, Tishri 1, which is Sunday, September 16, 2012. According to NASA, a new moon will occur at 2:11 A.M. that day.

Don't allow the many false predictions of the past keep you from recognizing the "appointed time" (*moed*) of the Lord's return.

Now let's see how all this fits into Jesus' other prophecies in Matthew 24-25.

Temple's Destruction in That Generation

Jesus' disciples asked Him two specific questions: when shall these things be? (referring to the Temple's destruction), and what shall be the sign of your coming and the end of the world? Jesus wove the answers to these questions in Matthew 24-25, but the first answer is fairly easy to pick out since Jesus repeated the key phrase "*all these things*" in His response.

*And Jesus went out, and departed from the temple: and his disciples came to him for to show him the buildings of the temple. And Jesus said to them, See you not **all these things**? truly I say to you, **There shall not be left here one stone on another, that shall not be thrown down**. And as he sat on the mount of Olives, the disciples came to him privately, saying, Tell us, when shall **these things** be? and what shall be the sign of your coming, and of the end of the world? And Jesus answered and said to them, Take heed that no man deceive you. For many shall come in my name, saying, I am Christ; and shall deceive many. And you shall hear of wars and rumors of wars: see that you be not troubled: for **all these things** must come to pass, but the end is not yet. . . . Now learn a parable of the fig tree; When his branch is yet tender, and puts forth leaves, you know that summer is near: So likewise you, when you shall see **all these things**, know that it is near, even at the doors. Truly I say to you, <u>This generation</u> shall not pass, till **all these things** be fulfilled. (Matthew 24:1-6, 32-34)*

Of the Temple buildings, not one stone was left on another because the fire which destroyed the buildings also melted the gold, and so the gold was removed from each of the stones. For people born after the flood and the tower of Babel, a generation was forty years (Numbers 32:13). Jerusalem and the Temple were destroyed in 70 AD, and Jesus was crucified in 33 AD (70 - 33 =37); which was within that generation to whom He spoke. Neither the fig tree parable here nor a generation is to be applied to the second question; they have already been fulfilled.

False Christs

The Jews who did not receive Jesus as Messiah were ready to receive someone, and several people obliged them. Theudas (45 AD) claimed he parted the Jordan like Joshua did. An Egyptian prophet (52-58) claimed to bring down walls of Jerusalem. An anonymous prophet (59) promised people freedom if they followed him into the wilderness. These three and their bands were killed and dispersed by Roman procurators. Menahem, the son of Judas the Galilean (66), used Roman weapons to defend Masada until 74 AD. He dressed as a king and entered the temple with his men to 'worship', but the temple guard routed him and his men. John of Gischala (67-70) began fighting Roman soldiers in Galilee and northern Israel. There were certainly wars and rumors of wars prior to the Temple's destruction, and Christ's disciples may have thought the world was coming to an end, but He told them it was not yet the end.

End-Times Overview

False Teachers in "Latter Times"

There were scoffers who denied the creation of the world and Noah's flood and questioned Christ's second coming in order to live their lustful lives with less guilt (2 Peter 3:3-12). Evolution is *"the lie"* which Paul wrote would be accompanied by *"strong delusion"* in the *"falling away"* from Biblical Christianity before *"that man of sin be revealed"* (2 Thess. 2:3-12) *Principles of Geology* was written by Charles Lyell in 1830 espousing the new idea that the great canyons around the world were not the after effects of a world-wide flood (cataclysmic), but the constant erosion over hundreds of thousands of years (uniformitarian). Until that time, creation and the cataclysm of Noah's flood were accepted facts. Charles Darwin took a copy of Lyell's book with him on the S.S. Beagle to the Galapagos Islands, leading to his harmful theories of evolution and the superiority of the white race. Evolution is a demonic doctrine that has eroded the faith of believers in their Creator and His Word. In American schools, evolution became the new religion.

> *Now the Spirit speaks expressly, that in the latter times some shall depart from the faith, giving heed to seducing spirits, and doctrines of devils; Speaking lies in hypocrisy; having their conscience seared with a hot iron (1 Timothy 4:1-2)*

Evolution led to much false teaching in the church (1 Timothy 6:20), which led to a lack of love and power in the church, and a resistance to the truth (2 Timothy 3:1-8). Theologians began attacking the historicity of the rest of the Bible, and questioned the long-held interpretations of Christ's second coming. John Darby promoted his pre-tribulation rapture theory in the 1840's. In 1886, E. B. Pusey compiled nine lectures in *Daniel the Prophet* with which he confronted these lies, but the lies have become accepted 'truths' in most 'churches' today.

As for the disciple's second question, *"What shall be the sign of your coming, and of the end of the world?"* Jesus answered it in several parts: signs preceding the rebirth of Israel, signs during the great tribulation, and several signs of His coming. A traditional Jewish literary technique was to write in a repetitive wave pattern: beginning, crest, end. The pattern is warning of deception, troubles, end.

Birth Pangs Prior to Israel's Birth

> *For nation shall rise against nation, and kingdom against kingdom: and there shall be famines, and pestilences, and earthquakes, in divers places. All these are the beginning of sorrows. Then shall they deliver you up to be afflicted, and shall kill you: and you shall be hated of all nations for my name's sake. And then shall many be offended, and shall betray one another, and shall hate one another. And many false prophets shall rise, and shall deceive many. And because iniquity shall abound, the love of many shall wax cold. But he that shall endure to the end, the same shall be saved. And this **gospel** of the kingdom shall be preached in all the world for a witness <u>to all nations; and then shall the end come</u>. (Matthew 24:7-14)*

Awake, Bride

In the first verse of the above passage, Jesus is describing hundreds of years of history, then makes a transition to "*the beginning of sorrows*" or travailing before a birth. The next portion points to the Inquisitions and particularly the Holocaust prior to the birth of Israel. Hitler considered himself a messiah who was ushering in the millennial reign (third *reich*). Iniquity increased, and love (*agape*) decreased. Those who persevere to the end shall be saved. God will make sure everyone has an opportunity to hear and to receive the gospel before the Great Tribulation.

> *And I saw another angel fly in the middle of heaven, having the everlasting **gospel** to preach to them that dwell on the earth, and to every nation, and kindred, and tongue, and people, Saying with a loud voice, Fear God, and give glory to him; for the hour of his judgment is come: and worship him that made heaven, and earth, and the sea, and the fountains of waters. (Revelation 14:6-7)*

Abomination of Desolation on Temple Mount

> *When you therefore shall see the abomination of desolation, spoken of by Daniel the prophet, stand in the holy place, (whoever reads, let him understand:) Then let them which be in Judaea flee into the mountains: Let him which is on the housetop not come down to take any thing out of his house: . . . But pray you that your flight be not in the winter, neither on the sabbath day: For then shall be great tribulation, such as was not since the beginning of the world to this time, no, nor ever shall be. And except those days should be shortened, there should no flesh be saved: but for the elect's sake those days shall be shortened. Then if any man shall say to you, See, here is Christ, or there; believe it not. For there shall arise false Christs, and false prophets, and shall show great signs and wonders; so that, if it were possible, they shall deceive the very elect. Behold, I have told you before. Why if they shall say to you, Behold, he is in the desert; go not forth: behold, he is in the secret chambers; believe it not. (Matthew 24:15-26 edited)*

'Read' is *anaginosko*, meaning to 'know again', to distinguish between, to recognize, to know accurately, or to acknowledge. 'Understand' is *noieo*, meaning to exercise the mind, observe, heed, comprehend, think or consider. The chapter on "Little Horn" should make it easier to recognize the Antichrist and the False Prophet when he declares he is god on the Temple Mount. The date of this announcement is not fixed and will have violent repercussions upon those in Israel, and so Jesus commanded His disciples to pray it would not be on a sabbath or during winter.

After the "*abomination of desolation*" Israel will have "*great tribulation*". The parallel passage in Mark 13:19 described it this way, "*For in those days shall be affliction.*" The Great Tribulation of 42 months/1,260 days of which John wrote in Rev. 11:2-3, started on April 6, 2009. The "*great tribulation*" Israel endures after the "*abomination of desolation*" occurs during the 3 ½ year Great Tribulation.

In the chapter on Abominations, it was determined that the prophecy to which Jesus refers here is the one in Daniel 12:11-12, which is associated with a false temple/shrine 'standing' on the Temple Mount which was part of the prediction of Christ second coming in 2012. It was also concluded that another Temple does not need to be built for this *"abomination of desolation spoken of by Daniel"* to occur on the Temple Mount.

I don't expect the False Prophet and/or False Messiah to declare himself God until after the US troops are pulled out of Iraq. So though the Great Tribulation has begun, and the Muslims will continue to control the Temple Mount for its duration of 42 months (Rev. 11:1-2); the declaration of deity may not be for several more months.

Deity Declaration After Apostasy

Now we beseech you, brothers, by the coming of our Lord Jesus Christ, and by our gathering together to him, That you be not soon shaken in mind, or be troubled, neither by spirit, nor by word, nor by letter as from us, as that the day of Christ is at hand. Let no man deceive you by any means: for that day shall not come, except there come a falling away first, and <u>that man of sin</u> be revealed, <u>the son of perdition</u>; Who opposes and exalts himself above all that is called God, or that is worshipped; so that he as God sits in the temple of God, showing himself that he is God. Remember you not, that, when I was yet with you, I told you these things? (2 Thessalonians 2:1-5)

Christ's second coming and our gathering together to him will not occur until after a *"falling away"* and the revealing of the *"son of perdition,"* the False Prophet. His declaration of deity on the Temple Mount won't occur until after a *"falling away"* (*apostasia*); a defection, a divorce, an apostasy. The word is used one other time in Acts 21:21 to *"forsake"* Moses. This refers to Christians abandoning their faith in Christ (1 Timothy 4:1). Entire denominations have left Biblical Christianity recently while others have so corrupted their doctrine or practice that real Christians can not associate with them.

But now I have written to you not to keep company, if any man <u>that is called a brother</u> be a fornicator, or covetous, or an idolater, or a reviler, or a drunkard, or an extortionist; with such an one no not to eat. (1 Corinthians 5:11)

Signs of Christ's Coming

Why if they shall say to you, Behold, he is in the desert; go not forth: behold, he is in the secret chambers; believe it not. <u>For as the lightning comes out of the east, and shines even to the west; so shall also the coming of the Son of man be</u>. For wherever the carcass is, there will the eagles be gathered together. Immediately after the tribulation of those days shall <u>the sun be darkened, and the moon shall not give her light, and the stars shall fall from heaven, and the powers of the heavens shall be shaken: And then shall appear the sign of the Son of man in heaven</u>: and *then shall all the tribes of the earth mourn, and <u>they shall see the Son of man coming in the clouds of heaven with power and great glory</u>. And he shall send his angels with a great sound of a trumpet, and they shall gather together his elect from the four winds, from one end of heaven to the other. (Matthew 24:26-31)*

Even the elect must guard themselves from deception and following the False Messiah. When Christ comes again, He won't be secluded as when He was a child. Jesus' second coming will be as obvious as knowing a corpse lies beneath where vultures circle. Jesus' appearance will light up the sky which has been darkened during the Great Tribulation, and there will be a meteor shower. As Jesus told the high priest, He will come with clouds and power (Matthew 26:64). The angels will sound trumpets and gather His elect, His Bride.

Noah and the Rapture

But as the days of Noe were, so shall also the coming of the Son of man be. For as in the days that were before the flood they were eating and drinking, marrying and giving in marriage, until the day that Noe entered into the ark, And knew not until the flood came, and took them all away; so shall also the coming of the Son of man be. Then shall two be in the field; the one shall be <u>taken</u>, and the other left. Two women shall be grinding at the mill; the one shall be <u>taken</u>, and the other left. (Matthew 24:37-41)

Noah's world was acting as if everything was normal when the flood "*took*" the wicked away; that word is *airo*, and means to take or put away. But "*taken*" *is paralambano* meaning "to receive near, associate with oneself (in any familiar or intimate act or relation); receive, take unto, take with." The same Greek word is used by Jesus and translated "*receive*" in the following verse.

And if I go and prepare a place for you, I will come again, and <u>receive</u> you to myself; that where I am, there you may be also. (John 14:3)

It is Christ's Bride who are taken away from the wicked and received by Jesus.

Christ's Bride should be Awake and Watching

Watch therefore: for you know not what hour your Lord does come. But know this, that if the manager of the house had known in what watch the thief would come, he would have watched, and would not have suffered his house to be broken up. Therefore be you also ready: for in such an hour as you think not the Son of man comes. Who then is a faithful and wise servant, whom his lord has made ruler over his household, to give them meat in due season? Blessed is that servant, whom his lord when he comes shall find so doing. Truly I say to you, That he shall make him ruler over all his goods. But and if that evil servant shall say in his heart, My lord delays his coming; And shall begin to smite his fellow servants, and to eat and drink with the drunken; The lord of that servant shall come in a day when he looks not for him, and in an hour that he is not aware of, And shall cut him asunder, and appoint him his portion with the hypocrites: there shall be weeping and gnashing of teeth. (Matthew 24:42-51)

Here the thief is used in the regular sense of someone breaking in to steal, and the believer is represented as <u>the house steward who knew which watch of the night the thief would come</u>. The ancient Jews had three night watches of roughly four hours each, but the Romans instituted four watches of three hours each: dusk to 9 P.M., 9 P.M. to midnight, midnight to 3 A.M., and 3-6 A.M.. But the Son of man would not come like a 'thief' for His Bride from dusk to 9 P.M., as was expected of grooms. Continuing the steward analogy, Jesus encouraged His people to attend the household faithfully, even though the Lord's return seems delayed, and not give up faithful service and be unaware of the timing of the Lord's coming and end up with unbelievers in hell. The parallel passage in Luke 12:35-40 refers to the second and third watches in the night (which contain midnight), and to the Lord's return from the wedding in expectation that <u>His servants will open the door for Him immediately when He knocks</u>. Christ's Bride will be prepared for His coming.

Parable of the Ten Virgins (Preparing and Persevering)

Then shall the kingdom of heaven be likened to ten virgins, which took their lamps, and went forth to meet the bridegroom. And five of them were wise, and five were foolish. They that were foolish took their lamps, and took no oil with them: But the wise took oil in their vessels with their lamps. While the bridegroom tarried, they all slumbered and slept. And at midnight there was a cry made, Behold, the bridegroom comes; go you out to meet him. Then all those virgins arose, and trimmed their lamps. And the foolish said to the wise, Give us of your oil; for our lamps are gone out. But the wise answered, saying, Not so; lest there be not enough for us and you: but go you rather to them that sell, and buy for yourselves. And while they went to buy, the bridegroom came; and they that were ready went in with him to the marriage: and the door was shut. Afterward came also the other virgins, saying, Lord, Lord, open to us. But he answered and said, Truly I say to you, I know you not. Watch therefore, for you know neither the day nor the hour wherein the Son of man comes. (Matthew 25:1-13)

Just as Noah prepared and went through the flood uncomfortably but safely, the Church will go through the Great Tribulation. The "wise virgins" have prepared themselves spiritually to do so, and will be ready for the delay before the Bridegroom comes. Virgins represent the religiously pure, but just as there were many religiously observant Jews who were not saved at Christ's first coming, there will be religiously observant Christians who will not be saved at Christ's second coming. The "foolish virgins" will not be spiritually prepared, and will go back to their religious system to "buy" answers for why they find themselves in the Great Tribulation, and to their dismay will discover they never had a relationship with the Lord Jesus. These are like the seeds who did not take deep root or who were choked out by the cares of this world (Matthew 13:20-22). There is an aspect of the 'wise' (*phronimos*) virgins in that they also provided for themselves for the difficult times ahead much like the unjust steward did in Luke 16:8, and was commended.

Believers in Israel have built bomb shelters and have bought gas masks. Christians should have emergency supplies, including water, on hand to weather coming disasters. More importantly, believers should prepare themselves spiritually to persevere through the trials until Christ's return, and be ready to share the gospel with unbelievers who will be drawn to their peace and faith in the midst of the fire-storms.

Fires

David Wilkerson is the pastor of Times Square Church in New York City. In obedience to God's word to him, he had his church make hundreds of sandwiches on September 10, 2001 for which the rescue crews were very thankful the next day. On March 23, 2009, David Wilkerson distributed his prophecy to prepare Christians for the judgment of God which would come with fire [www.worldchallenge.org/coverletter/an_urgent_message].

Behold, all you that kindle a fire, that compass yourselves about with sparks: walk in the light of your fire, and in the sparks that you have kindled. This shall you have of my hand; you shall lie down in sorrow. (Isaiah 50:11)

The earth also is defiled under the inhabitants thereof; because they have transgressed the laws, changed the ordinance, broken the everlasting covenant. Therefore has the curse devoured the earth, and they that dwell therein are desolate: therefore the inhabitants of the earth are burned, and few men left. (Isaiah 24:5-6)

The first three trumpets of judgment upon the world have to do with fire (Rev. 8:6-9); during the sixth trumpet a third of men are killed by fire and smoke (Rev. 9:13-19). The fourth vial has the sun scorching men with fire and heat (Rev. 16:8-9). The world is finally destroyed by fire (2 Peter 3:7-12). Jesus will Judge the world.

For the Father judges no man, but has committed all judgment to the Son: . . . The hour is coming, and now is, when the dead shall hear the voice of the Son of God: and they that hear shall live. For as the Father has life in himself; so has he given to the Son to have life in himself; And has given him authority to execute judgment also, because he is the Son of man. Marvel not at this: for the hour is coming, in the which all that are in the graves shall hear his voice, And shall come forth; they that have done good, to the resurrection of life; and they that have done evil, to the resurrection of damnation. I can of my own self do nothing: as I hear, I judge: and my judgment is just; because I seek not my own will, but the will of the Father which has sent me. (John 5:22-30 edited)

Parable of the Talents (Judgment, and Rewards in Millennium)

For the kingdom of heaven is as a man traveling into a far country, who called his own servants, and delivered to them his goods. And to one he gave five talents, to another two, and to another one; to every man according to his several ability; and straightway took his journey. Then he that had received the five talents went and traded with the same, and made them other five talents. And likewise he that had received two, he also gained other two. But he that had received one went and dig in the earth, and hid his lord's money. After a long time the lord of those servants comes, and reckons with them. And so he that had received five talents came and brought other five talents, saying, Lord, you delivered to me five talents: behold, I have gained beside them five talents more. <u>His lord said to him, Well done, you good and faithful servant: you have been faithful over a few things, I will make you ruler over many things: enter you into the joy of your lord</u>. He also that had received two talents came and said, Lord, you delivered to me two talents: behold, I have gained two other talents beside them. His lord said to him, Well done, good and faithful servant; you have been faithful over a few things, I will make you ruler over many things: enter you into the joy of your lord. Then he which had received the one talent came and said, Lord, I knew you that you are an hard man, reaping where you have not sown, and gathering where you have not strewed: And I was afraid, and went and hid your talent in the earth: see, there you have that is yours. His lord answered and said to him, You wicked and slothful servant, you knew that I reap where I sowed not, and gather where I have not strewed: You ought therefore to have put my money to the exchangers, and then at my coming I should have received my own with usury. Take therefore the talent from him, and give it to him which has ten talents. For to every one that has shall be given, and he shall have abundance: but from him that has not shall be taken away even that which he has. <u>And cast you the unprofitable servant into outer darkness</u>: there shall be weeping and gnashing of teeth. (Matthew 25:14-30)

 The talent, or treasure, is in some respects your relationship with the Owner. Those who have invested in their relationship with Christ and have shared it with others have increased the kingdom of heaven. But those who are "closet Christians" who never tell anyone about their faith and never develop a personal relationship with the Lord will find they really don't know who He is, and that a "sinner's prayer" won't keep them from hell (John 15:5-6). Whereas others who said a sinner's prayer and continued to follow the Lord's commands afterward, publicly declaring their faith in Jesus through water baptism and partaking of communion, will not be able to keep their joy to themselves (Jn 15:10-17).

 It is this faithfulness to share what God has done in your life with others which the Lord rewards with joy as well as authority during the millennium. In the parallel parable of the ten pounds to the ten servants in Luke 19:12-27, King Jesus gives the faithful cities to rule over in the millennium. It ends with Jesus saying, "*But those my enemies, which would not that I should reign over them, bring here, and slay them before me.*" Those who won't submit to the grace of King Jesus now will have no place in His Kingdom on earth. But those who followed Christ faithfully will be rewarded abundantly.

> *And Jesus said to them, Truly I say to you, That you which have followed me, <u>in the regeneration when the Son of man shall sit in the throne of his glory</u>, you also shall sit on twelve thrones, judging the twelve tribes of Israel. And every one that has forsaken houses, or brothers, or sisters, or father, or mother, or wife, or children, or lands, for my name's sake, shall receive an hundred times, and shall inherit everlasting life. But many that are first shall be last; and the last shall be first. (Matthew 19:28-30)*

"Regeneration" is *paliggenesia* meaning 'genesis anew', a renovation or restoration to the way it was at the beginning. This is the millennial reign of Christ on the new earth. God will restore abundantly those things which believers sacrificed for Jesus' sake. Remember not to be jealous of God's generosity to others.

Parable of Separating Sheep and Goats (Judgment at end of Millennium)

> *<u>When the Son of man shall come in his glory</u>, and all the holy angels with him, then <u>shall he sit on the throne of his glory</u>: And before him shall be gathered all nations: and he shall separate them one from another, as a shepherd divides his sheep from the goats: And he shall set the sheep on his right hand, but the goats on the left. Then shall the King say to them on his right hand, Come, you blessed of my Father, inherit the kingdom prepared for you from the foundation of the world: For I was an hungered, and you gave me meat: I was thirsty, and you gave me drink: I was a stranger, and you took me in: Naked, and you clothed me: I was sick, and you visited me: I was in prison, and you came to me. Then shall the righteous answer him, saying, Lord, when saw we you an hungered, and fed you? or thirsty, and gave you drink? When saw we you a stranger, and took you in? or naked, and clothed you? Or when saw we you sick, or in prison, and came to you? And the King shall answer and say to them, Truly I say to you, Inasmuch as you have done it to one of the least of these my brothers, you have done it to me. Then shall he say also to them on the left hand, Depart from me, you cursed, into everlasting fire, prepared for the devil and his angels: For I was an hungered, and you gave me no meat: I was thirsty, and you gave me no drink: I was a stranger, and you took me not in: naked, and you clothed me not: sick, and in prison, and you visited me not. Then shall they also answer him, saying, Lord, when saw we you an hungered, or thirsty, or a stranger, or naked, or sick, or in prison, and did not minister to you? Then shall he answer them, saying, Truly I say to you, Inasmuch as you did it not to one*

of the least of these, you did it not to me. And these shall go away into everlasting punishment: but the righteous into life eternal. (Matthew 25:31-46)

The period of grace has passed, and King Jesus has been ruling for 1,000 years on earth. The dividing line is how people treated "*the least of these my brothers,*" most likely referring to disadvantaged Israelis or Jews, since at the end of the millennium there will be those who attack His beloved city of Jerusalem (Revelation 20:7-9). Those who mistreat His people during the Millennium go away into everlasting punishment in fire. Those who kindly treat His people enter life eternal.

Summary

The New Testament authors wrote about tribulation, but none of them specified a seven year period of it. John did specify a 3 1/2 year period of Great Tribulation, and God's chosen saints go through it.

Jesus' disciples asked Him two specific questions: when shall these things be? (referring to the Temple's destruction), and what shall be the sign of your coming and the end of the world? Jesus answered both questions in detail. The first was fulfilled within that generation (70 AD).

In answer to the second question, Jesus referred to "*the abomination of desolation, spoken of by Daniel the prophet,*" and told them to pray it did not occur on a Sabbath or during the winter; so it does not start the clock of the Great Tribulation. A "*falling away*" must occur before the "*son of perdition*" is revealed, and there has been great apostasy within Christendom since the lie of evolution in the 1800's. The ousting of our Creator has ushered in lawlessness and violence. The last time the world was filled with corruption and violence (Gen. 6:11), God took away the wicked with a flood, but rescued Noah's family and the animals on the ark.

Jesus described the 'rapture' using an analogy to Noah, but in this case, the believers are taken away from the wicked and received by Jesus. In the Wheat and the Tares He described the angels as the reapers of the harvest. Jesus' parables of the steward and the virgins encourage believers to understand the time and to be awake, prepared, and watching for His return. Jesus described the signs in the sky preceding His return.

The parable of the talents depicts how King Jesus will reward faithfulness with authority over cities during His Millennial reign. The parable of the sheep and the goats depicts how King Jesus at the end of the 1,000 years will separate the wicked from the righteous based upon their treatment of "*the least of these my brothers.*" The wicked are condemned to everlasting punishment while the righteous enjoy everlasting life with Jesus.

Prophecy Outline of Jesus from Matthew
Tribulation in the world from the beginning
Jesus' first coming
Persecution
False Christs
Destruction of Temple and Jerusalem by fire (within "*generation*" 70 AD)
Persecution and "birth pangs" of Israel's rebirth as nation
False Christs (Hitler, others, Antichrist)
    Great Tribulation
      False Christs and false prophets; gospel preached to nations
      "*Abomination of desolation*"; Judeans flee to mountains

      Darkened sun and moon; stars fall, lightning flash
      Trumpet; angels reap (believers taken to Jesus)
    Jesus' second coming
Destruction of earth and the wicked by fire
    Millennial Reign of King Jesus
      Jesus rewards faithful with rule over cities
    Judgment of those at end of Millennial Reign
    Everlasting Punishment or Life Eternal

Judgments and Rewards
(Revelation 2-3)

Do you not know that the saints shall judge the world? . . .
Know you not that we shall judge angels? (1 Cor. 6:2a, 3a)

Before we judge others, we will be judged as believers for our faithfulness and service to Christ. And before Christians were judged, God pronounced judgment upon the Jews.

But the end of all things is at hand: be you therefore sober, and watch to prayer. . . . For the time is come that <u>judgment must begin at the house of God</u>: and if it first begin at us, what shall the end be of them that obey not the gospel of God? And if the righteous scarcely be saved, where shall the ungodly and the sinner appear? Why let them that suffer according to the will of God commit the keeping of their souls to him in well doing, as to a faithful Creator. (1 Peter 4:7, 17-19)

Peter was writing while Nero was emperor of Rome and committing all sorts of atrocities against Christians and Jews. Judgment came upon the Jews first, and then to those who believed in the gospel of God. Peter was crucified three years later in 67 AD, and God's judgment upon the Temple, "*the house of God*", came three years after that.

Jesus Christ is the corner stone and we are living stones built upon Him. The Church has been under the gracious chastening of the Lord for 2,000 years (or two days of the week of earth's history). After Jesus has completed judging the church, then He will judge the world (with Us at His side).

The Angels of the Seven Churches

And in the middle of the seven candlesticks one like to the Son of man, . . . And he had in his right hand seven stars: . . . The mystery of the seven stars which you saw in my right hand, and the seven golden candlesticks. <u>The seven stars are the angels of the seven churches</u>: and the seven candlesticks which you saw are the seven churches. (Revelation 1:13-20 edited)

'Angel', *angelos*, is translated angel or messenger in the New Testament, and is used in reference to demons, humans, and angels. Because pastors bring the message of good news to their churches, it has been supposed these messages were written to them. These churches represent church history, some periods over hundreds of years long, so it could not be referring to human pastors. We are given a special revelation of God's communication with the actual angels He placed in charge over these churches so that each would best know how to protect and persuade its human members.

Overview of Seven Churches

Just as the 7-headed Beast of the Sea represents seven historical periods of moon-worship of Babylon, the 7 churches represent seven historical periods of church history. These church periods were fraught with various troubles and tribulations, but the believers in each period held onto their belief in Jesus through them. "*And you shall be hated of all men for my name's sake: but he that endures to the end shall be saved*" (Matthew 10:22). According to Thayer, 'endures' (*hupomeno*) means to persevere "under misfortunes and trials to hold fast to one's faith in Christ". "*If we suffer, we shall also reign with him: if we deny him, he also will deny us:*" (2 Timothy 2:12). The believers in these seven church periods are corporately the Bride of Christ who have placed their seven seals of acceptance on the wedding contract, the scroll in Revelation 5.

The letters to the seven churches are written in the natural order that a messenger's route would take to deliver them to the physical churches in western Turkey. Revelation 2-3 records Christ's rebukes and praises of the Church throughout history. Christ's critiques of the 7 churches could apply to any church at any time, but are specific to place in history.

30-67   Apostolic Age (Ephesus) *Ephesus* means 'desire'. The believers' love for the Lord was strong until major persecution came. In 66 The Jewish War with Rome began, and in 67 both Paul and Peter were martyred.

67-313   Ten Persecutions (Smyrna) *Smyrna* means 'myrrh', which was a fragrant perfume used in offering sacrifices. The 10 persecutions (ten toes of Rome) occurred during this time; there were many martyrs.

313-622   Constantine to Mohammed (Pergamos) *Pergamos* means 'fortified' or 'mixed marriage'. Constantine forced believers to meet in pagan temples when he declared all in the Roman Empire to now be Christian. Aurelian had previously tried to implement "one god; one empire" under the sun god, but failed. Mohammed united the waring tribes of Medina under the moon god of Islam. Both Constantine and Mohammed created a "mixed marriage" of truth about God with lies.

622-1522 The Dark Ages to Reformation (Thyatira) *Thyatira* means 'continual sacrifice'. Jews and Christians who refused to convert to Islam were subjugated or slaughtered. The Catholic church only read the Bible in Latin, so the hearers remained "in the dark" regarding truth. This period ends with the Reformation when Bibles in the common languages of German and English began to be produced.

1522-1754 Renaissance to Enlightenment (Sardis) *Sardis* means 'remnant' or 'escaping ones'. It was a time many escaped the Inquisitions of Catholicism, and the "conversion" to Islam. Islam controlled Asia (Mughal empire), Persia and India (Safavid empire), and southern Europe and Asia minor (Ottoman empire).

1754-1844 Reason and Revolution (Philadelphia) *Philadelphia* means 'brotherly love'. Benjamin Franklin wrote *The Albany Plan for Union*, *Join or Die*, and *No Taxation without Representation* in 1754 in Philadelphia. Our national capital was there during the Revolution. During the American Revolution, colonists cried, "No king but King Jesus!"

1844-now Evolution and Democracy (Laodicea) *Laodicea* means "people judge"; thus democracy flourishes even through the world wars. *Vestiges of the Natural History of Creation* was published anonymously in 1844 (its author, Robert Chambers, announced after his death), paving the way for people to believe Charles Darwin's theories of evolution and supremacy of the white race. Darwin's theories led to America's Civil War and two world wars. The Scopes Trial was held in Tennessee in 1926 which opened the way for atheism (legally termed "secular humanism") and evolution to take over public education in America; the transformation from a good and godly America to a wicked and ungodly America was completed within two generations (80 years).

Ephesus: exposed false apostles; must renew first love

> *To the angel of the church of Ephesus write; These things said he that holds the seven stars in his right hand, who walks in the middle of the seven golden candlesticks; I know your works, and your labor, and your patience, and how you can not bear them which are evil: and you have tried them which say they are apostles, and are not, and have found them liars: And have borne, and have patience, and for my name's sake have labored, and have not fainted. Nevertheless I have somewhat against you, because you have left your first love. Remember therefore from where you are fallen, and repent, and do the first works; or else I will come to you quickly, and will remove your candlestick out of his place, except you repent. But this you have, that you hate the deeds of the Nicolaitanes, which I also hate. He that has an ear, let him hear what the Spirit said to the churches; To him that overcomes will I give to eat of the tree of life, which is in the middle of the paradise of God. (Revelation 2:1-6)*

Nicolaitanes means 'destruction of the people'. Nicolas was a deacon from Antioch (Acts 6:5), and it's possible he led a sect into false teaching (gnosticism) and practices (celebrating pagan festivals as well as committing fornication). Gnosticism is the belief that salvation can be obtained through special 'knowledge' (*gnosis*) instead faith in Christ.

Jesus praised believers in Ephesus for exposing false apostles and hating their deeds, but He rebuked them for leaving their first love and first works, and threatened to remove their candlestick unless they repented. Overcomers get to eat of the tree of life in paradise.

Smyrna: Martyrs in 10 persecutions until Constantine

> *And to the angel of the church in Smyrna write; These things said the first and the last, which was dead, and is alive; I know your works, and tribulation, and poverty, (but you are rich) and I know the blasphemy of them which say they are Jews, and are not, but are the synagogue of Satan. Fear none of those things which you shall suffer: behold, the devil shall cast some of you into prison, that you may be tried; and you shall have <u>tribulation ten days</u>: be you faithful to death, and I will give you*

a crown of life. He that has an ear, let him hear what the Spirit said to the churches; He that overcomes shall not be hurt of the second death. (Rev. 2:8-11)

The ten days correspond to the "*ten toes*" of Rome in the statue of Daniel 2. There were ten caesars who inflicted seasons of persecution upon believers. Nero and Domitian persecuted Christians while the original apostles still lived. The atrocities they and the others committed are documented in Foxe's *Book of Martyrs:*

"The first of the ten persecutions was stirred up by Nero about 64 A.D. His rage against the Christians was so fierce that Eusebius records, 'a man might see cities full of men's bodies, the old lying together with the young, and the dead bodies of women cast out naked, without reverence of that sex, in the open streets.'"

Nero 64-68	Maximin 235-237
Domitian 95-96	Decius 250-256
Trajan 100-115	Valerian 257-260
Aurelius 168-171	Aurelian 275
Severus 203-210	Diocletian 303-310

"This was the nineteenth year of the reign of Diocletian in Dystrus [March] when the feast of the Saviour's passion was near at hand, and royal edicts were published everywhere, commanding that the churches be razed to the ground, the scriptures destroyed by fire, those who held positions of honor degraded, and the household servants, if they persisted in the Christian profession, be deprived of their liberty. And such was the first decree against us. But issuing [other] decrees not long after, the Emperor commanded that all the rulers of the churches in every place should be first put in prison and afterwards compelled by every device to offer sacrifice." (Medieval Sourcebook: *Diocletian: Edicts Against The Christians*)

Jesus came to them as the resurrected Christ. He had no judgment against the believers of this period, but promised the "*crown of life*" to those who remained faithful unto death. Christian martyrs have no fear of the second death which is everlasting punishment in the lake of fire (Rev. 20:14-15).

Pergamos: fight false teaching

And to the angel of the church in Pergamos write; These things said he which has the sharp sword with two edges; I know your works, and where you dwell, even where Satan's seat is: and you hold fast my name, and have not denied my faith, even in those days wherein Antipas was my faithful martyr, who was slain among you, where Satan dwells. But I have a few things against you, because you have there them that hold the doctrine of Balaam, who taught Balac to cast a stumbling block before the children of Israel, to eat things sacrificed to idols, and to commit fornication. So have you also them that hold the doctrine of the Nicolaitanes, which thing I hate. Repent; or else I will come to you quickly, and will fight against them with the sword of my mouth. He that has an ear, let him hear what the Spirit said to the churches; To him that overcomes will I give to eat of the hidden manna, and will give him a white stone, and in the stone a new name written, which no man knows saving he that receives it. (Revelation 2:12-17)

Though there are fables regarding a bishop of Pergamos named Antipas being martyred during Trajan's persecution, there is nothing conclusive. The Nicolaitanes still persist in the church, and if the true church members don't drive them out, Jesus will Himself. He comes to them with His sharp sword with which He will destroy the wicked (Rev. 19:15, 21)

An altar to Zeus was constructed overlooking the city by Eumenes II (197-159 BC) as a memorial of his victory against the Galatians. The altar was built in the shape of a horseshoe, a seat, with high reliefs depicting the war between the giants and the gods. The Zeus Altar was taken from Pergamon in 1871 and carried to Germany by engineer Carl Humann. It is now exhibited at the Pergamon Museum in Berlin with the Ishtar Gates.

The serpent god, Asklepios, was worshiped in Pergamum. Zeus' symbol was also that of a serpent, and Zeus' altar was "*Satan's seat*". Pergamos was lured into idolatry and fornication like ancient Balaam did to Israel (Numbers 24). Thyatira was lured into fornication and into idolatry like ancient Jezebel did to Israel (1 Kings 18-21). Overcomers will eat the hidden manna and receive a white stone with a special name on it.

Thyatira: charitable, but tolerating Jezebel

And to the angel of the church in Thyatira write; These things said the Son of God, who has his eyes like to a flame of fire, and his feet are like fine brass; I know your works, and charity, and service, and faith, and your patience, and your works; and the last to be more than the first. Notwithstanding I have a few things against you, because you suffer that woman Jezebel, which calls herself a prophetess, to teach and to seduce my servants to commit fornication, and to eat things sacrificed to idols. And I gave her space to repent of her fornication; and she repented not. Behold, I will cast her into a bed, and them that commit adultery with her into great tribulation, except they repent of their deeds. And I will kill her children with death; and all the churches shall know that I am he which searches the reins and hearts: and I will give to every one of you according to your works. But to you I say, and to the rest in Thyatira, as many as have not this doctrine, and which have not known the depths of Satan, as they speak; I will put on you none other burden. But that which you have already hold fast till I come. And he that overcomes, and keeps my works to the end, to him will I give power over the nations: And he shall rule them with a rod of iron; as the vessels of a potter shall they be broken to shivers: even as I received of my Father. And I will give him the morning star. He that has an ear, let him hear what the Spirit said to the churches. (Revelation 2:18-29)

Truly the Dark Ages can be viewed as a time of "*great tribulation*" when truth was shrouded from most people. The Black Death may have killed off half of Europe's population. Was it a fulfillment of killing Jezebel's children? Overcomers will rule with Jesus in the Millennium.

Reformation

In the 1380's, John Wycliff hand-wrote the first complete Bible in the English language. Gutenburg invented the printing press in the 1450's, and the first book printed was a Latin Bible. Erasmus published his Greek/Latin New Testament in 1516. In 1517 Martin Luther nailed his 95 Theses of Contention to the Wittenberg Door. Luther translated Erasmus' New Testament into German and published it in 1522. Luther began to preach the priesthood of all believers and salvation by grace alone through faith (not by works).

William Tyndale translated the Greek New Testament into the plain English of the ploughman, and only a few were printed in 1525 before Tyndale went into hiding from the king's authorities the next eleven years. Myles Coverdale was Tyndale's assistant the last six years of his life. Coverdale finished translating the Old Testament, and the first complete Bible in the English language was published in 1535, and Tyndale was martyred the next year pleading for God to open the king's eyes. In 1539 Myles Coverdale was hired at the bequest of King Henry VIII to publish the Great Bible, a copy of which was chained to every church pulpit. Reformers found refuge in Geneva, Switzerland. Myles Coverdale, John Foxe, John Calvin, and John Knox produced the first English study Bible. The Geneva Bible was published in 1560 and was the first Bible to add verse numberings to the chapters which included extensive marginal notes. The Puritans and Pilgrims brought the Geneva Bible with them to America.

Sardis: repent and watch

And to the angel of the church in Sardis write; These things said he that has the seven Spirits of God, and the seven stars; I know your works, that you have a name that you live, and are dead. Be watchful, and strengthen the things which remain, that are ready to die: for I have not found your works perfect before God. Remember therefore how you have received and heard, and hold fast, and repent. If therefore you shall not watch, I will come on you as a thief, and you shall not know what hour I will come on you. You have a few names even in Sardis which have not defiled their garments; and they shall walk with me in white: for they are worthy. He that overcomes, the same shall be clothed in white raiment; and I will not blot out his name out of the book of life, but I will confess his name before my Father, and before his angels. He that has an ear, let him hear what the Spirit said to the churches. (Revelation 3:1-5)

Some here are close to losing their salvation; having their names blotted out of the book of life. Only a few walk worthy in white. 'Watch' and 'watchful' are *grēgoreuō*, meaning to keep awake and be vigilant. Jesus will appear like a thief at an unknown time to those who refuse to watch for Him. Jesus will confess the names of overcomers before the Father.

Philadelphia: has kept His Word

And to the angel of the church in Philadelphia write; These things said he that is holy, he that is true, he that has the key of David, he that opens, and no man shuts; and shuts, and no man opens; I know your works: behold, I have set before you an open door, and no man can shut it: for you have a little strength, and have kept my word, and have not denied my name. Behold, I will make them of the synagogue of Satan, which say they are Jews, and are not, but do lie; behold, I will make them to come and worship before your feet, and to know that I have loved you. Because you have kept the word of my patience, I also will keep you from the hour of temptation, which shall come on all the world, to try them that dwell on the earth. Behold, I come quickly: hold that fast which you have, that no man take your crown. Him that overcomes will I make a pillar in the temple of my God, and he shall go no more out: and I will write on him the name of my God, and the name of the city of my God, which is new Jerusalem, which comes down out of heaven from my God: and I will write on him my new name. He that has an ear, let him hear what the Spirit said to the churches. (Revelation 3:6-13)

The churches at Smyrna and Philadelphia were the only churches not rebuked by Jesus. 'Keep' is *tereo* from watch; meaning to guard (keep an eye upon; figuratively, to fulfill a command) or to maintain or hold fast. 'Hour' can mean season. 'Temptation' is *pi-ras-mos'* from test; meaning a putting to proof by adversity or trial. The second Great Awakening was from 1790-1840; truly Christianity in America flourished during this time, and it was a safe-haven for Jews. Overcomers were made pillars in God's presence with His name.

Laodicea: self-sufficient; self-deceived

And to the angel of the church of the Laodiceans write; These things said the Amen, the faithful and true witness, the beginning of the creation of God; I know your works, that you are neither cold nor hot: I would you were cold or hot. So then because you are lukewarm, and neither cold nor hot, I will spew you out of my mouth. Because you say, I am rich, and increased with goods, and have need of nothing; and know not that you are wretched, and miserable, and poor, and blind, and naked: I counsel you to buy of me gold tried in the fire, that you may be rich; and white raiment, that you may be clothed, and that the shame of your nakedness do not appear; and anoint your eyes with eye salve, that you may see. As many as I love, I rebuke and chasten: be zealous therefore, and repent. Behold, I stand at the door, and knock: if any man hear my voice, and open the door, I will come in to him, and will sup with him, and he with me. To him that overcomes will I grant to sit with me in my throne, even as I also overcame, and am set down with my Father in his throne. He that has an ear, let him hear what the Spirit said to the churches. (Revelation 3:14-22)

Laos is 'people'; *dike* is 'rights' (as self-evident) or 'justice'. *Laodicea* means 'people judge'; a democracy. The final word of the Scrips' Spelling Bee in 2009 was Laodicean. God has ways of knocking on our door. This city has aqueducts which provided cold water from Colosse and hot water from Hieropolis, but by the time the water arrived at Laodicea, it was luke warm. The Laodiceans judged by outward appearances which deceived many of them into thinking they had a relationship with Jesus Christ when they didn't.

Not every one that said to me, Lord, Lord, shall enter into the kingdom of heaven; but he that does the will of my Father which is in heaven. Many will say to me in that day, Lord, Lord, have we not prophesied in your name? and in your name have cast out devils? and in your name done many wonderful works? And then will I profess to them, I never knew you: depart from me, you that work iniquity. (Matthew 7:21-23)

The Laodiceans physical wealth blinded them to their spiritual needs.

Physical Reality	Spiritual Reality
Luke warm water from aqueducts	Luke-warm people make Jesus vomit
Wealthy in gold and banks	Wretchedly poor
Black wool garments	Naked (white garment)
Curative eye salve	Blind
Christ left outside of church	Christ will dine with individuals

"*And these are they which are sown among thorns; such as hear the word, And the cares of this world, and the <u>deceitfulness of riches, and the lusts of other things entering in, choke the word, and it becomes unfruitful</u>. And these are they which are sown on good ground; such as hear the word, and receive it, and bring forth fruit, some thirty times, some sixty, and some an hundred*" (Mark 4:18-20). Those who maintain a sinful lifestyle are unfruitful. Those who repent and renew spiritual zeal shall sit with Christ on His throne.

He that overcomes shall inherit all things; and I will be his God, and he shall be my son. But the fearful, and unbelieving, and the abominable, and murderers, and fornicators, and sorcerers, and idolaters, and all liars, shall have their part in the lake which burns with fire and brimstone: which is the second death. (Revelation 21:7-8)

Crowns

When Jesus catches away His Bride, we shall rule with Him as His queen (Psalm 45), but the type and number of crowns we have is up to each of us.

Know you not that they which run in a race run all, but one receives the prize? So run, that you may obtain. And every man that strives for the mastery is temperate in all things. Now they do it to obtain a corruptible crown; but we an <u>incorruptible</u>. I therefore so run, not as uncertainly; so fight I, not as one that beats the air: But I keep under my body, and bring it into subjection: lest that by any means, when I have preached to others, I myself should be a castaway. (1 Corinthians 9:24-25)

For what is our hope, or joy, or <u>crown of rejoicing</u>? Are not even you in the presence of our Lord Jesus Christ at his coming? (1 Thessalonians 2:19)

The elders which are among you I exhort, who am also an elder, and a witness of the sufferings of Christ, and also a partaker of the glory that shall be revealed: Feed the flock of God which is among you, taking the oversight thereof, not by constraint, but willingly; not for filthy lucre, but of a ready mind; Neither as being lords over God's heritage, but being ensamples to the flock. And when the chief Shepherd shall appear, you shall receive a <u>crown of glory</u> that fades not away. (1 Peter 5:1-4)

Blessed is the man that endures temptation: for when he is tried, he shall receive the <u>crown of life,</u> which the Lord has promised to them that love him. (James 1:12)

Fear none of those things which you shall suffer: behold, the devil shall cast some of you into prison, that you may be tried; and you shall have tribulation ten days: be you faithful to death, and I will give you a <u>crown of life</u>. (Revelation 2:10)

It is in heaven that we can then honor the Lord by casting our crowns at His feet in worship as the twenty-four elders do (Rev. 4:10), acknowledging that He gave us the abilities for which He then rewarded us.

Faithful Works Remain While Fleshly Works Burn

But without faith it is impossible to please him: for he that comes to God must believe that he is, and that he is a rewarder of them that diligently seek him. (Hebrews 11:6)

Now he that plants and he that waters are one: and every man shall receive his own reward according to his own labor. . . .For other foundation can no man lay than that is laid, which is Jesus Christ. Now if any man build on this foundation gold, silver, precious stones, wood, hay, stubble; Every man's work shall be made manifest: for the day shall declare it, because it shall be revealed by fire; and the fire shall try every man's work of what sort it is. If any man's work abide which he has built thereupon, he shall receive a reward. If any man's work shall be burned, he shall suffer loss: but he himself shall be saved; yet so as by fire. (1 Corinthians 3:8, 11-15)

Our God is just and righteous in all His judgments. Even though our faith in Jesus gives us eternal life with Him, our works will still be judged. Those done while abiding in Him will be rewarded, but those done in our own strength will not.

Rewards

On Earth

Take heed that you do not your alms before men, to be seen of them: otherwise you have no reward of your Father which is in heaven. . . . But when you do alms, let not your left hand know what your right hand does: That your alms may be in secret: and your Father which sees in secret himself shall reward you openly. And when you pray, . . . enter into your closet, and when you have shut your door, pray to your Father which is in secret; and your Father which sees in secret shall reward you openly. . . . But you, when you fast, anoint your head, and wash your face; That you appear not to men to fast, but to your Father which is in secret: and your Father, which sees in secret, shall reward you openly. (Matthew 6:1-18 edited)

Some of our rewards are given to us in this lifetime, and some in the next. Some rewards are given here and have benefits in the hereafter.

And Jesus answered and said, Truly I say to you, There is no man that has left house, or brothers, or sisters, or father, or mother, or wife, or children, or lands, for my sake, and the gospel's, But he shall receive an hundred times now in this time, houses, and brothers, and sisters, and mothers, and children, and lands, with persecutions; and in the world to come eternal life. (Mark 10:29-30)

In Heaven

Blessed are you, when men shall revile you, and persecute you, and shall say all manner of evil against you falsely, for my sake. Rejoice, and be exceeding glad: for great is your reward in heaven: for so persecuted they the prophets which were before you. (Matthew 5:11-12)

He that receives a prophet in the name of a prophet shall receive a prophet's reward; and he that receives a righteous man in the name of a righteous man shall receive a righteous man's reward. And whoever shall give to drink to one of these little ones a cup of cold water only in the name of a disciple, truly I say to you, he shall in no wise lose his reward. (Matthew 10:41-42)

Judgments and Rewards

Living righteously and speaking God's Word, and aiding those who do, is rewarded.

During Millennium

For the Son of man shall come in the glory of his Father with his angels; and then he shall reward every man according to his works. (Matthew 16:27)

And it came to pass, that when he was returned, having received the kingdom, then he commanded these servants to be called to him, to whom he had given the money, that he might know how much every man had gained by trading. Then came the first, saying, Lord, your pound has gained ten pounds. And he said to him, Well, you good servant: because you have been faithful in a very little, have you authority over ten cities. And the second came, saying, Lord, your pound has gained five pounds. And he said likewise to him, Be you also over five cities. (Luke 19:15-19)

At Jesus' second coming, He will reward His saints and then establish His faithful servants as rulers over cities during His millennial reign.

And whatever you do, do it heartily, as to the Lord, and not to men; Knowing that of the Lord <u>you shall receive the reward of the inheritance</u>: for you serve the Lord Christ. But he that does wrong shall receive for the wrong which he has done: and there is no respect of persons. (Colossians 3:23-25)

Rewards and Judgment at Christ's 2nd Coming

And as it is appointed to men once to die, but after this the judgment: So Christ was once offered to bear the sins of many; and to them that look for him shall he appear the second time without sin to salvation. (Hebrews 9:27-28)

And Enoch also, the seventh from Adam, prophesied of these, saying, Behold, the Lord comes with ten thousands of his saints, <u>To execute judgment on all</u>, and to convince all that are ungodly among them of all their ungodly deeds which they have ungodly committed, and of all their hard speeches which ungodly sinners have spoken against him. (Jude 1:14-15)

For <u>the Father judges no man, but has committed all judgment to the Son</u>: That all men should honor the Son, even as they honor the Father. He that honors not the Son honors not the Father which has sent him. Truly, truly, I say to you, He that <u>hears my word, and believes on him that sent me, has everlasting life</u>, and shall not come into condemnation; but is passed from death to life. Truly, truly, I say to you, The hour is coming, and now is, when the dead shall hear the voice of the Son of God: and they that hear shall live. <u>For as the Father has life in himself; so has he given to the Son to have life in himself; And has given him authority to execute</u>

> *judgment also, because he is the Son of man. Marvel not at this: for the hour is coming, in the which **all** that are in the graves shall hear his voice, And shall come forth; they <u>that have done good, to the resurrection of life; and they that have done evil, to the resurrection of damnation</u>. I can of my own self do nothing: as I hear, I judge: and <u>my judgment is just</u>; because I seek not my own will, but the will of the Father which has sent me. (John 5:22-30)*

The dead did hear Jesus' voice and live: Lazarus, Jairus' daughter, and the widow's son. At Jesus' death and resurrection, the First Fruit saints in Jerusalem came out of their graves, but Jesus spoke of a time when "*all*" the dead would hear His voice.

The Father committed all judgment to the Son, yet Jesus judges according to what he hears. It may be from what He hears read from the books regarding each person; whether they are written in the book of life or not. Jesus spoke of two different judgments: first He stated everlasting life is based upon belief in Him (at His coming), but then stated it is based upon having "*done good*" (after His millennial reign).

> *But after your hardness and impenitent heart treasure up to yourself wrath against the day of wrath and revelation of the righteous judgment of God; <u>Who will render to every man according to his deeds</u>: To them who by patient continuance in well doing seek for glory and honor and immortality, eternal life: But to them that are contentious, and do not obey the truth, but obey unrighteousness, indignation and wrath, Tribulation and anguish, on every soul of man that does evil, of the Jew first, and also of the Gentile; But <u>glory, honor, and peace, to every man that works good</u>, to the Jew first, and also to the Gentile: For there is no respect of persons with God. For as many as have sinned without law shall also perish without law: and as many as have sinned in the law shall be judged by the law . . . In the day when God shall judge the secrets of men by Jesus Christ according to my gospel. (Romans 2:5-12, 16)*

At His coming, Jesus will be judging the dead and rewarding the righteous. Newly "*clothed*" (2 Cor. 5:1-8) believers will be busy with Jesus executing wrath upon the wicked.

> *And the nations were angry, and your wrath is come, and the time of the dead, that they should be judged, and that you should give reward to your servants the prophets, and to the saints, and them that fear your name, small and great; and should destroy them which destroy the earth. (Revelation 11:18)*

> *Let the high praises of God be in their mouth, and a two-edged sword in their hand; To execute vengeance on the heathen, and punishments on the people; To bind their kings with chains, and their nobles with fetters of iron; <u>To execute on them the judgment written: this honor have all his saints</u>. Praise you the LORD. (Psalm 149:6-9)*

So while we are still in these earthly suits of skin, we proclaim the precious Spirit of God within us.

Why we labor, that, whether present or absent, we may be accepted of him. For we must all appear before the judgment seat of Christ; that every one may receive the things done in his body, according to that he has done, whether it be good or bad. Knowing therefore the terror of the Lord, we persuade men; but we are made manifest to God; and I trust also are made manifest in your consciences. (2 Corinthians 5:9-11)

Name in Book of Life is Greatest Reward

. . . written in the book of life of the Lamb slain from the foundation of the world. (Revelation 13:8b)

To have one's name in the Book of Life is the greatest reward. It signifies eternal life in relationship with Jesus. Those who obstinately persist in a sinful life prove they have left their love for Jesus. Those who love Jesus walk in His light and confess their occasional sins and are cleansed and assured of their salvation (1 John).

And the LORD said to Moses, Whoever has sinned against me, him will I blot out of my book. (Exodus 32:33)

He that overcomes, the same shall be clothed in white raiment; and I will not blot out his name out of the book of life, but I will confess his name before my Father, and before his angels. (Revelation 3:5)

The Book of Life can have names blotted out of it. It is opened (next two passages) without reference to the need of any seals to be broken. So the Book of Life is not the scroll with the seven seals in Revelation 5.

Judgment at end of Millennial Reign

I beheld <u>till the thrones were cast down, and the Ancient of days did sit</u>, whose garment was white as snow, and the hair of his head like the pure wool: his throne was like the fiery flame, and his wheels as burning fire. A fiery stream issued and came forth from before him: thousand thousands ministered to him, and ten thousand times ten thousand stood before him: the judgment was set, and the books were opened. . . . I saw in the night visions, and, behold, one like the Son of man came with the clouds of heaven, and came to the Ancient of days, and they brought him near before him. And there was given him dominion, and glory, and a kingdom, that all people, nations, and languages, should serve him: his dominion is an everlasting dominion, which shall not pass away, and his kingdom that which shall not be destroyed. (Daniel 7:9-10, 13-14)

And I saw a <u>great white throne, and him that sat on it</u>, from whose face the earth and the heaven fled away; and there was found no place for them. And I saw the dead, small and great, stand before God; and the books were opened: and another book was opened, which is the book of life: and the dead were judged out of those things which were written in the books, according to their works. And the sea gave up the dead which were in it; and death and hell delivered up the dead which were in them: and they were judged every man according to their works. And death and hell were cast into the lake of fire. This is the second death. And whoever was not found written in the book of life was cast into the lake of fire. (Revelation 20:11-14) He that overcomes shall inherit all things; and I will be his God, and he shall be my son. But the fearful, and unbelieving, and the abominable, and murderers, and fornicators, and sorcerers, and idolaters, and all liars, shall have their part in the lake which burns with fire and brimstone: which is the second death. (Rev. 21:7-8)

The Great White Throne judgment is the final reckoning. At Christ's second coming, the overcomers from the church age received specified rewards according to the age they lived through, but to those overcomers from the Millennium are promised the inheritance of all things in addition to continued relationship with Father-God.

Summary

Jesus Christ is the corner stone and we are living stones built upon Him comprising His Church. The Church has been under the gracious chastening of the Lord for 2,000 years. Those who receive the loving chastening of the Lord and repent, develop new spiritual zeal and receive earthly and spiritual rewards. The seven churches in Revelation 2-3 represent seven periods of history of Christianity; they are corporately the Bride of Christ.

30-67   Apostolic Age (Ephesus) *Ephesus* means 'desire'.
67-313   Ten Persecutions (Smyrna) *Smyrna* means 'myrrh'.
313-622   Constantine to Mohammed (Pergamos) *Pergamos* means 'mixed marriage'.
622-1522   The Dark Ages to Reformation (Thyatira) *Thyatira* means 'sacrifice'.
1522-1754 Renaissance to Enlightenment (Sardis) *Sardis* means 'escaping ones'.
1754-1844 Reason and Revolution (Philadelphia) *Philadelphia* means 'brotherly love'.
1844-now Evolution and Democracy (Laodicea) *Laodicea* means 'people judge'.

When Jesus catches away His Bride, we shall rule with Him as His queen (Psalm 45), but the type and number of crowns we have is up to each of us. Those works we've done in the flesh will burn. After Jesus has completed judging His Church, then He will judge the world with Us at His side. Then Jesus will establish His faithful servants as rulers over cities during His millennial reign. At the end of the 1,000 years, Jesus will judge people based upon how they treated "*the least of these my brethren*" (Matthew 25:31-46). Then at the Great White Throne judgment, those who are not written in the Book of Life will be cast into the lake of fire.

Great Tribulation Angels

And I heard the voice of many angels round about the throne and the beasts and the elders: and the number of them was ten thousand times ten thousand, and thousands of thousands; (Revelation 5:11)

This chapter will focus on the angels in Revelation. John begins the book stating God sent an angel to him verifying the visions (Rev. 1:1). John wrote letters to the angels of the seven churches, which was covered in the previous chapter. Angels are involved in the seven seals, trumpets, and vials which we'll study in another chapter.

Angels are God's servants (Psalm 104:4; Hebrews 1:7). Some are mighty to do His bidding (Psalm 103:20-21). Some are guardians over places (Genesis 3:24) or children (Matthew 18:10); they are called cherubim. God created copper-colored serpentine angels called seraphim to worship Him continually.

And before the throne there was a sea of glass like to crystal: and in the middle of the throne, and round about the throne, were four beasts full of eyes before and behind. And the first beast was like a lion, and the second beast like a calf, and the third beast had a face as a man, and the fourth beast was like a flying eagle. And the four beasts had each of them six wings about him; and they were full of eyes within: and they rest not day and night, saying, Holy, holy, holy, LORD God Almighty, which was, and is, and is to come. (Revelation 4:6-8)

Satan, the Rebellious Seraph

Though angels are God's servants, they are not robots void of personality or will. One of the seraphs desired to switch places and be the one worshiped; and when he rebelled, a third of the angels chose to rebel with him. This winged serpent with eyes is also called a dragon; which in Greek is *drakon*, a fabulous kind of serpent which would fascinate those who 'looked' (*derkomai*). But Satan is a seraph without wings, since God removed them in the garden of Eden to make him slither on his belly (Gen 3:14).

*And there appeared another wonder in heaven; and behold a great red dragon, having seven heads and ten horns, and seven crowns on his heads. And his tail drew the third part of the stars of heaven, and did cast them to the earth: . . . And there was war in heaven: **Michael** and his angels fought against the dragon; and the dragon fought and his angels, And prevailed not; neither was their place found any more in heaven. And the great dragon was cast out, that old serpent, called the*

> *Devil, and Satan, which deceives the whole world: he was cast out into the earth, and his angels were cast out with him. (Revelation 12:3-9 edited)*

Demons, the Rebellious Angels

> *I will therefore put you in remembrance, though you once knew this, how that the Lord, having saved the people out of the land of Egypt, afterward destroyed them that believed not. And the <u>angels which kept not their first estate, but left their own habitation, he has reserved in everlasting chains under darkness to the judgment of the great day</u>. . . . Yet **Michael** the archangel, when contending with the devil he disputed about the body of Moses, dared not bring against him a railing accusation, but said, The Lord rebuke you. (Jude 1:5-9 edited)*

According to Job 1 and Psalm 78:49, Satan and his evil angels are still under God's authority, and can not go beyond what He allows them to do. And you'll notice that it is Michael's job to keep them under God's control.

Michael, the archangel

Not only are there different kinds of angels, they also have a hierarchy or 'rank of sacred beings'. In Daniel 10 God revealed a glimpse of the spiritual battles which take place among angels and demons on behalf of people and locations. After battling the demon of Persia for three weeks, Gabriel was able to finally bring a response to Daniel's prayer because Michael intervened. Michael is a key player in the Great Tribulation ("*time of trouble*").

> *And at that time shall Michael stand up, the great prince which stands for the children of your people: and there shall be <u>a time of trouble, such as never was since there was a nation even to that same time</u>: and at that time your people shall be delivered, every one that shall be found written in the book. (Daniel 12:1)*

In a previous chapter we saw from 2 Thessalonians 2:1-5 that "*the son of perdition*", False Prophet and/or False Messiah, would not be revealed until a "*falling away*" occurred first. But there is another being holding back Satan from empowering and revealing the False Prophet. The following verse has often been misinterpreted as the Holy Spirit who is "*what withholds*".

> *And now you know what withholds that <u>he</u> might be revealed in <u>his</u> time. For the mystery of iniquity does already work: only **he** who now lets will let, until **he** be taken out of the way. And then shall <u>that Wicked</u> be revealed, whom the Lord shall consume with the spirit of his mouth, and shall destroy with the brightness of his coming: Even <u>him</u>, whose coming is after the working of Satan with all power and signs and lying wonders, And with all delusion of unrighteousness in them that perish; because they received not the love of the truth, that they might be saved.*

And for this cause God shall send them strong delusion, that they should believe a lie: That they all might be damned who believed not the truth, but had pleasure in unrighteousness. But we are bound to give thanks always to God for you, brothers beloved of the Lord, because God has from the beginning chosen you to salvation through sanctification of the Spirit and belief of the truth. (2 Thessalonians 2:6-13)

'Withholds' and 'lets' are the same word *katecho* in Greek, meaning held back or restrained. In Revelation 12 we are told it is the archangel Michael who restrains Satan and then casts him to earth. So God through His commands to **Michael** is in control of when the the False Prophet is revealed. Michael is most likely the angel who will bind Satan for 1,000 years and then lose him (Rev. 20). Michael is also the archangel who gives the triumphant cry when Jesus shouts that He's returned.

*For if we believe that Jesus died and rose again, even so them also which sleep in Jesus will God bring with him. For this we say to you by the word of the Lord, that we which are alive and remain to the coming of the Lord shall not prevent them which are asleep. For the Lord himself shall descend from heaven with a shout, with the voice of the **archangel**, and with the trump of God: and the dead in Christ shall rise first: Then we which are alive and remain shall be caught up together with them in the clouds, to meet the Lord in the air: and so shall we ever be with the Lord. (1 Thessalonians 4:14-17)*

So far we have Michael and Satan as book-ends of the Great Tribulation with the False Prophet and/or False Messiah making a declaration of deity during it, and Christ destroying him/them at the end of it. In the midst, God is in control of the timing of his angels and their duties. Michael held back Satan, and now four angels will hold back the winds.

Four Angels Withhold Winds

And after these things I saw four angels standing on the four corners of the earth, holding the four winds of the earth, that the wind should not blow on the earth, nor on the sea, nor on any tree. And I saw another angel ascending from the east, having the seal of the living God: and he cried with a loud voice to the four angels, to whom it was given to hurt the earth and the sea, Saying, Hurt not the earth, neither the sea, nor the trees, till we have sealed the servants of our God in their foreheads. And I heard the number of them which were sealed: and there were sealed an hundred and forty and four thousand of all the tribes of the children of Israel. (Revelation 7:1-3)

These four angels are in charge of hurting the earth and the sea, but another angel is sent to delay them until the sealing the 144,000 is completed. So the sealing of the 144,000 occurs prior to the first two trumpets (Rev. 8:6-9) which destroys all of the grass and a third of the trees and the sea.

Holy Spirit Is Present and Active during Great Tribulation

2 Thessalonians 2:6-7 is commonly misinterpreted to say that the Holy Spirit is removed from the earth. The following verses demonstrate that God's Holy Spirit is very active during the Great Tribulation.

> *When I have brought them again from the people, and gathered them out of their enemies' lands, and am sanctified in them in the sight of many nations; Then shall they know that I am the LORD their God, which caused them to be led into captivity among the heathen: but I have gathered them to their own land, and have left none of them any more there. Neither will I hide my face any more from them: for **I have poured out my spirit** on the house of Israel, said the Lord GOD. (Ezekiel 39:27-29)*

After God returned the exiles to Israel and they became a nation again (1948), He poured out His Holy Spirit upon them. In just the last two decades, God has revealed the lost tribes of the house of Israel and has returned many of them to Israel.

> *And it shall come to pass afterward, that **I will pour out my spirit on all flesh**; and your sons and your daughters shall prophesy, your old men shall dream dreams, your young men shall see visions: And also on the servants and on the handmaids in those days **will I pour out my spirit**. And I will show wonders in the heavens and in the earth, blood, and fire, and pillars of smoke. The sun shall be turned into darkness, and the moon into blood, before the great and terrible day of the LORD come. And it shall come to pass, that whoever shall call on the name of the LORD shall be delivered: for in mount Zion and in Jerusalem shall be deliverance, as the LORD has said, and in the remnant whom the LORD shall call. (Joel 2:28-32)*

In the last two decades, Muslims, particularly in closed countries, have been coming to Jesus by the thousands, often by Jesus visiting them in visions and dreams. Muslim conversions to Christianity have never been this dramatic in history. In Israel there are also accounts of Jews being visited by Jesus in their dreams and then they go ask their Messianic brethren how to be saved. Just because Jesus appears to people in dreams does not mean they automatically accept Him as their Lord and Savior.

> *Turn you at my reproof: behold, **I will pour out my spirit to you**, I will make known my words to you. Because I have called, and you refused; I have stretched out my hand, and no man regarded . . . I will mock when your fear comes; When your fear comes as desolation, and your destruction comes as a whirlwind; when distress and anguish comes on you. Then shall they call on me, but I will not answer; they shall seek me early, but they shall not find me: For that they hated knowledge, and did not choose the fear of the LORD: (Proverbs 1:23-29 edited)*

From the fourth vial to the Day of the LORD the phrase "*they repented not*" is repeated regarding those in Babylon. The *day of salvation* (2 Cor. 6:2) is coming to an end.

Seven Thunders and Little Book

And I saw another mighty angel come down from heaven, clothed with a cloud: and a rainbow was on his head, and his face was as it were the sun, and his feet as pillars of fire: And he had in his hand a little book open: and he set his right foot on the sea, and his left foot on the earth, And cried with a loud voice, as when a lion roars: and when he had cried, seven thunders uttered their voices. And when the seven thunders had uttered their voices, I was about to write: and I heard a voice from heaven saying to me, Seal up those things which the seven thunders uttered, and write them not. And the angel which I saw stand on the sea and on the earth lifted up his hand to heaven, And swore by him that lives for ever and ever, who created heaven, and the things that therein are, and the earth, and the things that therein are, and the sea, and the things which are therein, that there should be time no longer: <u>*But in the days of the voice of the seventh angel, when he shall begin to sound, the mystery of God should be finished, as he has declared to his servants the prophets.*</u> *And the voice which I heard from heaven spoke to me again, and said, Go and take the little book which is open in the hand of the angel which stands on the sea and on the earth. And I went to the angel, and said to him, Give me the little book. And he said to me, Take it, and eat it up; and it shall make your belly bitter, but it shall be in your mouth sweet as honey. And I took the little book out of the angel's hand, and ate it up; and it was in my mouth sweet as honey: and as soon as I had eaten it, my belly was bitter. And he said to me, You must prophesy again before many peoples, and nations, and tongues, and kings. (Revelation 10:1-11)*

There is a blessing to all who read Revelation (Rev. 1:3), but it may also be accompanied by bitterness and sorrow as we digest it, for it describes much destruction and death. We need to understand that we have not been told all there is to know about the Great Tribulation. The information contained in the seven thunders remains a mystery to us. But we are told the mystery of God is finished at the sounding of the seventh trumpet.

Angels announce the beginning, the end, and three "woe" time-markers with which a time-line of the Great Tribulation can be produced. After the fourth trumpet is sounded, John wrote, "*And I beheld, and heard an angel flying through the middle of heaven, saying with a loud voice, Woe, woe, woe, to the inhabitants of the earth by reason of the other voices of the trumpet of the three angels, which are yet to sound! (Rev. 8:13)*" These angelic "woes" are the 5th, 6th, and 7th trumpets.

First Woe (5th trumpet for 5 months)

And the fifth angel sounded, and I saw a star fall from heaven to the earth: and to him was given the key of the bottomless pit. And he opened the bottomless pit; and there arose a smoke out of the pit, as the smoke of a great furnace; and the sun and the air were darkened by reason of the smoke of the pit. And there came out of the smoke locusts on the earth: and to them was given power, as the scorpions of the earth have power. And it was commanded them that they should not hurt the grass of the earth, neither any green thing, neither any tree; but only those men which have not the seal of God in their foreheads. And to them it was given that they should not kill them, but that they should be tormented five months: and their torment was as the torment of a scorpion, when he strikes a man. And in those days shall men seek death, and shall not find it; and shall desire to die, and death shall flee from them. And the shapes of the locusts were like to horses prepared to battle; and on their heads were as it were crowns like gold, and their faces were as the faces of men. And they had hair as the hair of women, and their teeth were as the teeth of lions. And they had breastplates, as it were breastplates of iron; and the sound of their wings was as the sound of chariots of many horses running to battle. And they had tails like to scorpions, and there were stings in their tails: and their power was to hurt men five months. (Revelation 9:1-10)

'Locust' is *akris*, meaning to alight on top, from a root *akmen* meaning point or extreme. The "*star*" falling from heaven to earth could be a reference to Satan or an angel, or it could refer to an asteroid strike and the debris in the atmosphere blocking the sun for a time. These could be natural locusts or mutated ones, or demons or man-made vehicles like radio-controlled planes or helicopters using the darkness as cover. Their "*sting*" is like a scorpion's and causes people to seek death. Scorpion stings can cause severe local skin reactions as well as neurologic, respiratory, cardiovascular problems, and death. But these "*locusts*" are commanded not to hurt the 144,000 who were sealed, and only to torment those who are not sealed for five months.

And they had a king over them, which is the angel of the bottomless pit, whose name in the Hebrew tongue is Abaddon, but in the Greek tongue has his name Apollyon. One woe is past; and, behold, there come two woes more hereafter. (Rev. 9:10-12)

Both *Abaddon* and *Apollyon* mean 'destroyer'. It is a destroying demon from the abyss who is the leader of the locusts. According to Thayer, Abaddon is "the minister of death and the author of havoc on the earth," and the root of Apollyon is "to declare that one must be put to death." This "king" is the 'messenger' (angel - *aggelos*) of the bottomless pit. It is the False Prophet who "destroys" (Daniel 8:24); one of the two horns on the young ram which kills those who refuse the mark of the beast on their foreheads (Rev. 13:11-18).

Ahmadinejad, as mayor of Tehran, stated, "Today our nations' great duty and prophetic mission is to prepare for the formation of the the universal rule of the Mahdi." His speech at the "World Without Zionism" conference in 2005 has been greatly amended and retranslated, but the conference itself promoted an end to the Jewish State, and Ahmadinejad also urged Muslims to imagine a world without the United States and to prepare for the day when "our holy hatred expands" and "strikes like a wave". As the president of Iran, Ahmadinejad declared in a speech on October 14, 2006 that he had a divine connection and calling from Allah to produce nuclear power and launch a final round of the Islamic Revolution which would usher in the Twelfth Imam (Mahdi). In April, 2008 the largest cache of Iranian weapons to date were discovered by Iraqi forces. Iran's leading cleric, Mesbah-Yazdi, has sanctioned the use of nuclear weapons and attacks on civilians. [see chapter on "Revolution" of Joel Rosenberg's *Inside the Revolution*, 2009]

While the world has worried about Iran's nuclear weapons program, they've forgotten about their chemical weapons (CW) program. According to the CIA's report in 1997, "Iran already has manufactured and stockpiled CW, including blister, blood and choking agents and the bombs and artillery shells for delivering them," and concluded that Iran was researching various nerve agents as well. A decade later they were no longer sure about the stockpiles, but had verified Iran's research on nerve agents.

On January 14, 2008, the Israeli Military Intelligence research chief Brigadier General Yossi Kuperwasser said that "the possibility certainly exists" for Iran to supply chemical weapons to Hezbollah.

Second Woe and Four Fallen Angels

Armegeddon War: (6th trumpet for 1 year, 1 month, and 1 day)

And the sixth angel sounded, and I heard a voice from the four horns of the golden altar which is before God, Saying to the sixth angel which had the trumpet, Loose the four angels which are bound in the great river Euphrates. And <u>the four angels were loosed, which were prepared for an hour, and a day, and a month, and a year, for to slay the third part of men</u>. And the number of the army of the horsemen were two hundred thousand thousand: and I heard the number of them. And thus I saw the horses in the vision, and them that sat on them, having breastplates of fire, and of jacinth, and brimstone: and the heads of the horses were as the heads of lions; and out of their mouths issued fire and smoke and brimstone. By these three was the third part of men killed, by the fire, and by the smoke, and by the brimstone, which issued out of their mouths. For their power is in their mouth, and in their tails: for their tails were like to serpents, and had heads, and with them they do hurt. And the rest of the men which were not killed by these plagues yet repented not of the works of their hands, that they should not worship devils, and idols of gold, and silver, and brass, and stone, and of wood: which neither can see, nor hear, nor walk: Neither repented they of their murders, nor of their sorceries, nor of their fornication, nor of their thefts. (Rev. 9:13-21 edited)

These four demons have been bound in the Euphrates, likely near Babylon, to slay a third of mankind through a war with a two hundred million man army. Currently no army has a flag or uniform of red, blue, and yellow. Though there is much more text until John explains that the second woe has passed (Rev. 11:14), the beginning of Armageddon is the second woe.

Michael, Protector of Israel at Armegeddon

And I saw an angel standing in the sun; and he cried with a loud voice, saying to all the fowls that fly in the middle of heaven, Come and gather yourselves together to the supper of the great God; That you may eat the flesh of kings, and the flesh of captains, and the flesh of mighty men, and the flesh of horses, and of them that sit on them, and the flesh of all men, both free and bond, both small and great. . . . and all the fowls were filled with their flesh. (Revelation 19:17-21b edited)

As the fowls feast on flesh, the third woe is set to commence; but to understand it, information on some non-angelic beings and their amazing capabilities is needed.

Two Witnesses/Martyrs (Jewish and Gentile Believers)

Many have postulated as to who the "two witnesses" might be: Elijah and Moses, who spoke with Jesus at His first coming, or possibly Enoch and Elijah whom never died. There have been two witnesses to God's glory throughout history, the Hebrews and non-Hebrews, also known as Jews and Gentiles.

Prophesy for 1,260 Days

The "Gentiles" who have had control of the Temple Mount for hundreds of years will continue to control it and tread upon Jerusalem during the Great Tribulation. Some Muslims contest they are not Gentiles because they are circumcised, but all non-Jews are Gentiles. The duration of the Great Tribulation is 42 months, also calculated as 1,260 days, so the months have to be 30 day months using the 360-day year calendar, which gives us 3 1/2 years. The two witnesses prophesy wearing sackcloth. Sackcloth is worn during mourning and grief, and during repentance and humiliation. Just as Jews enter a period of repentance (*teshuvah*) thirty days prior to Rosh Hashanah, so shall Christ's Bride enter a period of repentance during the Great Tribulation prior to her Lord's return.

*And there was given me a reed like to a rod: and the angel stood, saying, Rise, and measure the temple of God, and the altar, and them that worship therein. But the court which is without the temple leave out, and measure it not; for it is given to the Gentiles: and the holy city shall they tread under foot forty and two months. And I will give power to my <u>two witnesses</u>, and they shall prophesy a thousand two hundred and three score days, clothed in sackcloth. These are the <u>two olive trees</u>, and the <u>two candlesticks</u> **standing before the God of the earth**. (Revelation 11:1-4)*

'Witnesses' is *martus*, meaning martyrs. But there were seven candlesticks and no olive trees mentioned in the first few chapters of Revelation, so John is referring to a different prophetic scripture.

And said to me, What see you? And I said, I have looked, and behold a candlestick all of gold, with a bowl on the top of it, and his seven lamps thereon, and seven

> *pipes to the seven lamps, which are on the top thereof: And two olive trees by it, one on the right side of the bowl, and the other on the left side thereof. . . . he shall bring forth the headstone thereof with shoutings, crying, Grace, grace to it. The hands of Zerubbabel have laid the foundation of this house . . . the plummet in the hand of Zerubbabel with those seven; they are the eyes of the LORD, which run to and fro through the whole earth. Then answered I, and said to him, What are these two olive trees on the right side of the candlestick and on the left side thereof? And I answered again, and said to him, What be these <u>two olive branches</u> which through the <u>two golden pipes</u> empty the golden oil out of themselves? . . . Then said he, These are the <u>two anointed ones</u>, that **stand by the LORD of the whole earth**. (Zechariah 4:2-14 edited)*

The "*seven lamps*" are the seven-fold Spirit of God (Rev. 4:5) evident in the seven churches ("*candlesticks*"). The two olive trees in Zechariah 4 were Joshua, the high priest, and Zerubbabel, the governor. The two olive trees are connected with "*those seven*" of the "*house*" of "*grace*" whose "*headstone*" is Jesus. 'Anointed ones' is *ben yitshar*, meaning anointed sons. The sons are described in the next chapter as the Son of God and the "*remnant of her seed*": believing Gentiles and Jews.

> *And she brought forth a man child, who was to rule all nations with a rod of iron: and her child was caught up to God, and to his throne. . . . And they overcame him by the blood of the Lamb, and by the word of their testimony; and they loved not their lives to the death. . . . And the dragon was wroth with the woman, and went to make war with the remnant of her seed, which keep the commandments of God, and have the testimony of Jesus Christ. (Revelation 12:5, 11, 17)*

These are the Hebrew and Gentile believers during the Great Tribulation; the two witnesses that have been made "*one new man*" in Christ (Ephesians 2:11-22). The two witnesses combined constitute the Bride of Christ. The two witnesses are Us. We will be martyred for Our faith and given white robes (5th seal), but We will prophesy of Christ's coming for Us in powerful ways before We die. We will overcome Satan by the blood of Jesus, Our personal testimony, and Our determination to die rather than give up Our faith. We believers hold fast God's commandments and the 'testimony' (*marturia* meaning witness) of Jesus Christ.

Have Miraculous Power Like Elijah

> *And if any man will hurt them, fire proceeds out of their mouth, and devours their enemies: and if any man will hurt them, he must in this manner be killed. These have power to shut heaven, that it rain not in the days of their prophecy: and have power over waters to turn them to blood, and to smite the earth with all plagues, as often as they will. And when they shall have finished their testimony, the beast that*

ascends out of the bottomless pit shall make war against them, and shall overcome them, and kill them. (Revelation 11:5-7)

Real fire may come from Our mouths or at the command from Our mouths (2 Kings 1:10-12), or the Word of God from Our mouths may incense and devour Our enemies from the inside out (Jeremiah 5:14). Elijah was a foreshadow of the Great Tribulation saints, for he prayed it would not rain for 3 1/2 years, and it did not until he prayed that it would (James 5:17-18). Though we may walk in God's great power, many of us will be killed.

For, behold, the day comes, that shall burn as an oven; and all the proud, yes, and all that do wickedly, shall be stubble: and the day that comes shall burn them up, said the LORD of hosts, that it shall leave them neither root nor branch. But to you that fear my name shall the Sun of righteousness arise with healing in his wings; and you shall go forth, and grow up as calves of the stall. And you shall tread down the wicked; for they shall be ashes under the soles of your feet in the day that I shall do this, said the LORD of hosts. Remember you the law of Moses my servant, which I commanded to him in Horeb for all Israel, with the statutes and judgments. Behold, I will send you Elijah the prophet before the coming of the great and dreadful day of the LORD: And he shall turn the heart of the fathers to the children, and the heart of the children to their fathers, lest I come and smite the earth with a curse. (Malachi 4:1-6)

John the Baptist partially fulfilled the last verse regarding returning the hearts of children to their Father through repentance and baptism (Matthew 11:12-14), the rest of the passage won't be fulfilled until Jesus' second coming. Believers should be full of God's Spirit and walking in the same manifestations of Elijah during the Great Tribulation, but that also assumes We are living in righteousness, obedience, and faithful prayer as Elijah did. The Church should be restoring family relationships, especially healing the wounds from abusive or absent fathers. Those who are still seeking a father figure to love and approve of them will be more easily drawn to follow the Antichrist.

Moses and Aaron turned the Nile to blood, and foretold Pharaoh of the plagues about to happen. Will it be the prayers of saints that surround the Arabian Peninsula with seas of blood? Will the saints declare God's judgments like Moses and Aaron did? If so, how? The Beast of Islam will war against Christians and be victorious and kill them.

Third Woe: Seventh Trumpet

<u>The second woe is past; and, behold, the third woe comes quickly</u>. And the seventh angel sounded; and there were great voices in heaven, saying, The kingdoms of this world are become the kingdoms of our Lord, and of his Christ; and he shall reign for ever and ever. And the four and twenty elders, which sat before God on their seats, fell on their faces, and worshipped God, Saying, We give you thanks, O LORD God Almighty, which are, and were, and are to come; because you have

Judgments and Rewards

taken to you your great power, and have reigned. And the nations were angry, and <u>your wrath is come, and the time of the dead, that they should be judged</u>, and that you should give reward to your servants the prophets, and to the saints, and them that fear your name, small and great; and <u>should destroy them which destroy the earth</u>. And the temple of God was opened in heaven, and there was seen in his temple the ark of his testament: and there were lightning, and voices, and thunder, and an earthquake, and great hail. (Revelation 11:14-19)

The third woe comes immediately upon the last day of the Armegeddon War. Then there will be lightning, and voices, and thunder, and great hail, and an earthquake (6th seal), as the seventh seal and seventh vial commence moments before the seventh trumpet. Then We will come with Jesus to destroy the armies of the Antichrist and execute judgment on the wicked with King Jesus in great power and majesty.

Seven Angels

#1-3 Angelic Announcements

And I saw another <u>angel</u> fly in the middle of heaven, having the everlasting gospel to preach to them that dwell on the earth, and to every nation, and kindred, and tongue, and people, Saying with a loud voice, Fear God, and give glory to him; for the hour of his judgment is come: and worship him that made heaven, and earth, and the sea, and the fountains of waters. And there followed another <u>angel</u>, saying, Babylon is fallen, is fallen, that great city, because she made all nations drink of the wine of the wrath of her fornication. And the <u>third angel</u> followed them, saying with a loud voice, If any man worship the beast and his image, and receive his mark in his forehead, or in his hand, The same shall drink of the wine of the wrath of God, which is poured out without mixture into the cup of his indignation; and he shall be tormented with fire and brimstone in the presence of the holy angels, and in the presence of the Lamb: And the smoke of their torment ascends up for ever and ever: and they have no rest day nor night, who worship the beast and his image, and whoever receives the mark of his name. Here is the patience of the saints: here are they that keep the commandments of God, and the faith of Jesus. And I heard a voice from heaven saying to me, Write, Blessed are the dead which die in the Lord from now on: Yes, said the Spirit, that they may rest from their labors; and their works do follow them. (Revelation 14:6-13)

The first angelic announcement is the *"everlasting gospel"* to the world to worship the Creator before He comes to judge His creation. Hour can mean one hour, or season (as I think it is here). This may allude to the SkyAngel satellite and the myriad of Christian broadcasts going throughout the world, or a real angel proclaiming the gospel around the globe with a loud voice. Jesus also spoke of the gospel being preached as a witness to all nations before the end came (Matthew 24:14).

The second angelic announcement is *"Babylon is fallen because she made the nations drink the wine of the wrath of her fornication."*

The third angelic announcement is if anyone worships the beast or takes its mark, he will also experience God's wrath. This announcement may precede or come shortly after the beast requires the mark in order to buy or sell. But the saints are encouraged to keep God's commands even if it means their death.

#2 Babylon is Fallen

And after these things I saw another angel come down from heaven, having great power; and the earth was lightened with his glory. And he cried mightily with a strong voice, saying, Babylon the great is fallen, is fallen, and is become the habitation of devils, and the hold of every foul spirit, and a cage of every unclean and hateful bird. For all nations have drunk of the wine of the wrath of her fornication, and the kings of the earth have committed fornication with her, and the merchants of the earth are waxed rich through the abundance of her delicacies. And I heard another voice from heaven, saying, Come out of her, my people, that you be not partakers of her sins, and that you receive not of her plagues. . . . And a mighty angel took up a stone like a great millstone, and cast it into the sea, saying, Thus with violence shall that great city Babylon be thrown down, and shall be found no more at all. And in her was found the blood of prophets, and of saints, and of all that were slain on the earth. (Revelation 18:1-3, 21, 24)

'Thrown down' is *ballo*, and can mean struck. The "*great city*" of Islam is Mecca. Mohammed expunged hundreds of idols from their holy site, and later placed a meteorite in the Kaaba, the black cube which Muslims are required to visit once in their lifetime. Muslims are required to face Mecca 5 times a day and pray to Allah, the moon-god. Located on the Red Sea 45 miles from Mecca is the commercial capital of Saudi Arabia, Jeddah, which makes the merchants of the earth rich. It is interesting that the city which worships a black stone from the sky may be destroyed by a great stone cast into the sea. 'Violence' is *hormema* (from *horme*, an assault), meaning an attack, a rash act. This word is only used this one time in the Bible.

Osama bin Laden has let it be known that he is ready to attack oil cities in his home nation of Saudi Arabia in order to crush the economy of the rest of the world. Would he nuke Mecca? Could a group of ten (Rev. 17:16) Muslim terrorist leaders plan an attack that would set all the oil fields and refineries of Saudi Arabia on fire? On June 3, 2009, President Obama was in Saudi Arabia seeking the wise counsel of King Abdullah. Could Obama's presence ignite jihadist furor?

During August, 2007, Colorado Representative Tom Tancredo said, "If it is up to me, we are going to explain that an attack on this homeland of that nature would be followed by an attack on the holy sites in Mecca and Medina. Because that's the only thing I can think of that might deter somebody from doing what they otherwise might do." Abdul-Mohsen Al-Sheik, head of Mecca's municipal council, said he was disappointed that the Republican Party did not issue an apology for Representative Tom Tancredo's remarks; and added, "Neither ... Tancredo nor anyone else can strike the Kaaba in Mecca."

As will be shown in the next chapter, the event of Babylon's fall may come exactly one year after the angel announces it. The event is the same as the second trumpet. *"And the second angel sounded, and as it were a great mountain burning with fire was cast into the sea: and the third part of the sea became blood"* (Rev. 8:8). This burning mountain may be an asteroid or a volcano.

#4-6 Angels Reaping Harvest

God sends His angels to reap both the believers and unbelievers from the earth; the unbelievers are burned, and the believers are taken to God's shelter (Matthew 13:39-42).

And I looked, and behold a white cloud, and on the cloud one sat like to the Son of man, having on his head a golden crown, and in his hand a sharp sickle. And another <u>angel</u> came out of the temple, crying with a loud voice to him that sat on the cloud, Thrust in your sickle, and reap: for the time is come for you to reap; for the harvest of the earth is ripe. And he that sat on the cloud thrust in his sickle on the earth; and the earth was reaped. And another <u>angel</u> came out of the temple which is in heaven, he also having a sharp sickle. And another <u>angel</u> came out from the altar, which had power over fire; and cried with a loud cry to him that had the sharp sickle, saying, Thrust in your sharp sickle, and gather the clusters of the vine of the earth; for her grapes are fully ripe. And the angel thrust in his sickle into the earth, and gathered the vine of the earth, and cast it into the great wine press of the wrath of God. And the wine press was trodden without the city, and blood came out of the wine press, even to the horse bridles, by the space of a thousand and six hundred furlongs. (Revelation 14:14-20)

The first angel reaps the righteous with Jesus. The second angel with the "*sharp sickle*" reaps the wicked and gathers them to be crushed in battle by Christ and the righteous, and then the third angel with "*power over fire*" will burn the wicked. This is akin to the process of the angels gathering the wheat into the barn and angels gathering and burning the tares (Matthew 13:24-30, 36-43).

#7 Angel with Gold Censer

And when he had opened the seventh seal, there was silence in heaven about the space of half an hour. . . . And another angel came and stood at the altar, having a golden censer; and there was given to him much incense, that he should offer it with the prayers of all saints on the golden altar which was before the throne. And the

> *smoke of the incense, which came with the prayers of the saints, ascended up before God out of the angel's hand. And the angel took the censer, and filled it with fire of the altar, and cast it into the earth: and there were voices, and thunder, and lightning, and an earthquake. (Revelation 8:1-5 edited)*

This will occur at the opening of the seventh seal with all the shaking in heaven and earth preceding our Lord's second coming and the fire of the destruction of the wicked. This is in answer to the prayers of the saints who have cried out for deliverance from the wicked and have prayed for Christ's kingdom to come and His will to be done on earth. The 7th seal is connected to the 7th angel.

Believers and Angels "taking vengeance" on Unbelievers

Vengeance on the wicked is the Lord's affair (Romans 12:19). God will make sure to trouble those who have troubled us. His vengeance is just and righteous. They will "*suffer the vengeance of eternal fire*" (Jude 1:7).

> *For the day of the LORD is near on all the heathen: as you have done, it shall be done to you: your reward shall return on your own head. (Obadiah 1:15)*

> *Seeing it is a righteous thing with God to recompense tribulation to them that trouble you; And to you who are troubled rest with us, <u>when the Lord Jesus shall be revealed from heaven with his mighty angels, In flaming fire taking vengeance on them that know not God, and that obey not the gospel of our Lord Jesus Christ:</u> Who shall be punished with everlasting destruction from the presence of the Lord, and from the glory of his power; When he shall come to be glorified in his saints, and to be admired in all them that believe (because our testimony among you was believed) <u>in that day</u>. (2 Thessalonians 1:6-10)*

But on "*that day*" believers will join their Lord in His vengeance to execute on the wicked "*the judgment written*". God will "*avenge the blood of his servants, and will render vengeance to his adversaries*".

> *Let the saints be joyful in glory: let them sing aloud on their beds. Let the high praises of God be in their mouth, and a two-edged sword in their hand; To execute <u>vengeance on the heathen</u>, and punishments on the people; To bind their kings with chains, and their nobles with fetters of iron; <u>To execute on them the judgment written: this honor have all his saints</u>. Praise you the LORD. (Psalm 145:5-9)*

The judgment was written in Deuteronomy 32 by Moses, and the victorious Bride will sing that song in God's presence.

> *See now that I, even I, am he, and there is no god with me: I kill, and I make alive; I wound, and I heal: neither is there any that can deliver out of my hand. For I lift up my hand to heaven, and say, I live for ever. If I whet my glittering sword, and my*

*hand take hold on judgment; I will render vengeance to my enemies, and will reward them that hate me. I will make my arrows drunk with blood, and my sword shall devour flesh; and that with the blood of the slain and of the captives, from the beginning of revenges on the enemy. Rejoice, O you nations, with his people: for he will avenge the blood of his servants, and will render vengeance to his adversaries, and will be merciful to his land, and to his people. And **Moses** came and spoke all the words of this **song** in the ears of the people. (Deuteronomy 32:39-44a)*

*And I saw as it were a sea of glass mingled with fire: and them that had gotten the victory over the beast, and over his image, and over his mark, and over the number of his name, stand on the sea of glass, having the harps of God. And they sing the **song of Moses** the servant of God, and the song of the Lamb, saying, Great and marvelous are your works, Lord God Almighty; just and true are your ways, you King of saints. Who shall not fear you, O Lord, and glorify your name? for you only are holy: for all nations shall come and worship before you; for your judgments are made manifest. (Revelation 15:2-4)*

God will destroy those who hate Him and His people. Those people and nations remaining will love the "*King of saints*" and worship Jesus. "*That at the name of Jesus every knee should bow, of things in heaven, and things in earth, and things under the earth; And that every tongue should confess that Jesus Christ is Lord, to the glory of God the Father*" (Phil. 2:10-11).

Parallels

God's Team	Satan's Team
Christ	Antichrist (Mahdi)
7 Churches	7-headed Beast of Sea
Two Witnesses	2-horned Beast of Earth
Bride of Christ	Whore
Michael	**Destroying Angel from Abyss**
other angels	**other demons**

Summary

Angels are God's servants who do His bidding, and they are key players in the book of Revelation. Michael is the archangel in charge of protecting Israel and withholding Satan. Michael begins the Great Tribulation by casting Satan to earth at God's command; and Michael ends the Great Tribulation by binding Satan for 1,000 years.

There are three angelic "woes" and other interactions which are time markers during the Great Tribulation. There are four angels in charge of sealing the 144,000 at the beginning of the Great Tribulation. The first woe is a five month period in which the destroying demon from the abyss leads "locusts" to sting and afflict people. The second woe is at the beginning of the Armegeddon War. There are four demons bound in the Euphrates who will help a two hundred million man army slay a third of mankind through the Armegeddon war for one year, one month, and one day. The third woe is the 7th trumpet, the day of the Lord's return when the heavens and earth will shake, and He will call His people to Him on September 16, 2012.

Using the 360-day calendar, "*a day, and a month, and a year*" equals 391 days. The year 2012 on our calendar is a leap year having one extra day. Counting backwards 391 days from the calculated date of Christ's return, the war of Armegeddon should commence on August 23, 2011. Counting backward 150 days (5 thirty-day months) from that, the first woe should commence on March 26, 2011.

There are seven special angels: three make proclamations near the beginning of the Great Tribulation, three help reap the harvest, and one casts to earth his golden censer of the prayers of the saints and fire from the altar right before Christ's coming. The first angelic announcement is the "everlasting gospel" to the world to worship the Creator before He comes to judge His creation. The second angelic announcement is "*Babylon is fallen because she made the nations drink the wine of the wrath of her fornication.*" The third angelic announcement is if anyone worships the beast or takes its mark, he will also experience God's wrath.

The two witnesses are the Hebrew and Gentile believers during the Great Tribulation who have been made "*one new man*" in Christ. Believers will be 'destroyed' and 'martyred' by the 2-horned young ram (False Prophet) and given white robes (5th seal).

Believers will prophesy of Christ's coming for Us in powerful ways like Elijah before We die. After We are resurrected or raptured, We will take vengeance upon the wicked unbelievers with Jesus and His angels. God will burn the wicked and the earth with fire and recreate a new heaven and earth. The saints will worship King Jesus as He rules and reigns 1,000 years.

The Beasts and Whore of Babylon

There appeared another wonder in heaven;
and behold a great red dragon,
having seven heads and ten horns,
and seven crowns on his heads.
(Revelation 12:3)

The beast that gives authority and power to all the other nasties in Revelation is Satan, the red dragon. Satan had seven empires (heads with crowns) which worshiped him as the moon-god with ten notable leaders (horns). Satan established a religion in his image ("*beast of the sea*") which worships him as the moon-god.

Satan, the Deceiver

And the great dragon was cast out, that old serpent, called the Devil, and Satan, which deceives the whole world: he was cast out into the earth, and his angels were cast out with him. . . . Therefore rejoice, you heavens, and you that dwell in them. Woe to the inhabitants of the earth and of the sea! for the devil is come down to you, having great wrath, because he knows that he has but a short time. And when the dragon saw that he was cast to the earth, he persecuted the woman which brought forth the man child. (Revelation 12:9, 12-13)

Satan and his angels, now demons, deceive the whole world during the Great Tribulation of 3 1/2 short years. Satan wants to deceive and destroy all humans, but especially the Jews and Christians. The people of the earth and sea need to be aware of Satan's wrath. This chapter will focus on Satan's team in the Great Tribulation. Just because there are parallels does not mean there is equality of power.

God's Team	Satan's Team
Jerusalem	"*Mystery Babylon*"
Jesus Christ	Antichrist (Mahdi)
7 Churches	7-headed Beast of Sea (Sunni)
Two Witnesses	2-horned Beast of Earth (Shia)
Bride of Christ	Whore (Wahhabi)
Michael	Destroying Angel from Abyss
other angels	other demons

The Beast of the Earth is referred to as as the economical/religious system and "*the false prophet*" (or "voice"). The Beast of the Sea (which appears in Daniel 7 as the 4th beast) is sometimes referred to as the political/religious system, and sometimes referred to as the Antichrist leader ("*little horn*" or "*mouth*") who comes from it, and also correlates to the Muslims' Mahdi. The Antichrist and False Prophet will relate to each other much as Moses and Aaron did (Exodus 7:1, 10, 19; 8:5-6, 16-17), with Aaron performing the miraculous signs at Moses' command; the Mahdi giving the orders, and the False Prophet carrying them out.

Beasts are empires in prophetic scriptures. The two main religious empires of Islam are Sunni (7-headed Beast of the Sea) and Shia (2-horned Beast of theEarth). The most powerful sect of Sunnism is Wahhabism, which is the Whore of Mystery Babylon.

Mystery Babylon (Middle-east Islam)

The satanic system of "*Mystery Babylon*" in the last days is middle-eastern Islam. It is divided between the Sunnis (Beast of the Sea), the Shia (Beast of the Earth), and the Wahhabis (the Whore that rides the Beast of the Sea).

When Mohammed died in 632 AD, there was an unclear succession. His cousin/son-in-law gathered a following known as Shia, while Mohammed's companion and general, Abu Bakr, became the first caliph and his followers were called Sunni. Mohammed's companions wrote down Mohammed's sayings now known as *hadiths*, and the Sunnis follow these as closely as they do the Quran. Shia reject the hadiths.

The Sunni sect is the largest with dozens of national adherents. The Sunnis believe Mohammed's generals and their descendants have power over the people. They also believe Allah does not resemble his creation in any way, and to imagine him in a form is idolatry. Yet they pray to saints to aid their prayers, which the Wahhabis consider idolatry.

In 1740, the house of Saud invited Ibn Abd al-Wahhab to settle near them because they were intrigued with his ideas to return to a stricter adherence of the Quran and the hadiths. The Wahhabis believe Allah has a physical body and sits on a throne, and is a unique unity. They insist on hatred and violence toward Muslims and non-Muslims who disagree with them. The House of Saud, which rules Saudi Arabia, funds the indoctrination of other Muslims into this sect. They would like to remain wealthy and in power, and do not ascribe to the eschatology of the Shia (whom they consider apostates). The bordering countries of Kuwait and United Arab Emirates are also Wahhabi, while Yemen is Shia. The Sunni countries on the Arabian Peninsula are Qatar, Oman, and tiny Bahrain.

The Shia, predominant in Iran with large populations in Iraq and Afghanistan, believe the descendants of Mohammed (religious leaders called Imams) have special political and religious power over the people. Shia believe they must create world-wide chaos before their savior, the Mahdi (12th Imam) will return to rule the world. The Shia and the Sunnis despise the house of Saud and Wahhabism for their decadence and opulence in Westernizing themselves.

Beast of the Sea (Sunni Confederation)

And I stood on the sand of the sea, and saw a beast rise up out of the sea, having seven heads and ten horns, and on his horns ten crowns, and on his heads the name of blasphemy. (Revelation 13:1)

Normal animals are usually called "beasts of the field". The phrase "*sand of the sea*" is used throughout the Bible to describe an innumerable multitude. This beast is comprised of people. It is very similar to the dragon Satan, with a difference in the number of crowns. With the dragon, the crowns were worn by each empire. With the Beast of the Sea, the crowns equal the number of leaders (horns), and are worn by individuals.

And the beast which I saw was like to a leopard, and his feet were as the feet of a bear, and his mouth as the mouth of a lion: and the dragon gave him his power, and his seat, and great authority.(Revelation 13:2)

This particular beast is a Frankenstein of empires first introduced in Daniel 7. These empires persecuted the Jews prior to the rebirth of the nation of Israel: lion of England, bear of Russia, and the leopard (panther) of Germany. But now the main body of this beast is based upon Nazi Germany (leopard) with the 'feet'/'arm'ament (armament) and transportation of Russia (bear), and the communication broadcasting system of the BBC (lion). Each of these countries are aiding the Muslim Beast, and each has a large population of Muslims.

*And four great beasts came up from the sea . . . The first was like a lion, . . . a second, like to a bear, . . . another, like a leopard, . . . and behold a fourth beast, dreadful and terrible, and strong exceedingly; and it had great iron teeth: <u>it devoured and broke in pieces</u>, and <u>stamped the residue with the feet</u> of it: and it was diverse from all the beasts that were before it; and it had ten horns. I considered the horns, and, behold, there came up among them another little horn, before whom there were three of the first horns plucked up by the roots: and, behold, in this horn were eyes like the eyes of man, and a **mouth** speaking great things. . . . Thus he said, The fourth beast shall be the fourth kingdom on earth, which shall be diverse from all kingdoms, and <u>shall devour the whole earth</u>, and <u>shall tread it down, and break it in pieces</u>. (Daniel 7:3-23 edited)*

The Sunnis have been devouring the whole earth; they've expanded into most of the 10° X 40° window. Those who don't convert are either killed or subjugated. They break up whatever government was in power and tread down the society to its basest level.

*And I saw one of his heads as it were wounded to death; and his deadly wound was healed: and all the world wondered after the beast. And they **worshipped** the dragon which gave power to the beast: and they **worshipped** the beast, saying, Who is like to the beast? who is able to make war with him? And there was given to him*

> *a **mouth** speaking great things and blasphemies; and power was given to him to continue forty and two months. And **he** opened his mouth in blasphemy against God, to blaspheme his name, and his tabernacle, and them that dwell in heaven. And it was given to **him** to make war with the saints, and to overcome them: and power was given him over all kindreds, and tongues, and nations. And all that dwell on the earth shall **worship** him, whose names are not written in the book of life of the Lamb slain from the foundation of the world. (Revelation 13:3-8)*

Satan and the Beast of Islam will be worshiped, and its spread seemingly unstoppable. According to Thayer, "worship (*proskuneō*) among the Persians means to fall upon the knees and touch the ground with the forehead as an expression of profound reverence; a probable derivative of dog (*kuon*), meaning to kiss, like a dog licking his master's hand." Islam is an enslaving religion which makes "converts" with the sword. Those who refuse to convert must be enslaved or killed.

Although this beast already has the "*mouth of a lion*", another "***mouth***" is given to it. This Sunni 'mouth' is Al-Jazeera which has close ties to Al-Qaeda, the Muslim Brotherhood, and other terrorist Sunni groups. Al-Jazeera was started by the emir of Qatar. In February 2008 Egypt and Saudi Arabia convened a meeting of the Arab League to impose restrictions on all satellite channels in the Arab world. Qatar and Lebanon refused to endorse it, so Al Jazeera continues to be a threat to Arab regimes.

The "Little Horn" chapter documented the seven middle-eastern empires which worshiped Satan as the moon-god: Sumerian, Assyrian, Babylonian, Media-Persian, Grecian, Roman, and Ottoman. The Ottoman Empire was dealt a death blow after WWI, but has since revived. All Muslim countries have a large Sunni population except for Iran and Iraq (Shia). The "Little horn" with the blasphemous mouth (Antichrist/Mahdi), arises from the large sea of Muslims.

Muqtada Al-Sadr from Iraq descended from Mohammed and leads the Mahdi Army of black flags while keeping connections with his father's social services network throughout Iraq; a combination of combat and compassion which has done well for Hezbollah and Hamas. He is currently a Shia cleric studying in Iran to become an ayatollah. Osama ben Laden was/is a Sunni from Saudi Arabia who located his base, *Al Qaeda*, in Afghanistan. If he is still alive, he might be considered a candidate for Antichrist/Mahdi, even though he's Shia, because he has great wealth and has had many victorious battles against infidels.

> *If any man have an ear, let him hear. He that leads into captivity shall go into captivity: he that kills with the sword must be killed with the sword. Here is the patience and the faith of the saints. (Revelation 13:9-10)*

The Antichrist/Mahdi will be given power over the whole world to make war with the saints and overcome them. Just as Muslims have captured and killed millions of Christians in Sudan, Muslims will continue to be victorious throughout the world. Christians need to

Beast of the Earth (Shia Confederation)

And I beheld another beast coming up out of the earth; and he had two horns like a lamb, and he spoke as a dragon. (Revelation 13:11)

'Lamb' is *arnion* meaning lambkin or young lamb or **ram**.

And he exercises all the power of the first beast before him, and causes the earth and them which dwell therein to worship the first beast, whose deadly wound was healed. And he does <u>great wonders</u>, so that he makes fire come down from heaven on the earth in the sight of men, And deceives them that dwell on the earth by the means of those <u>miracles</u> which he had power to do in the sight of the beast; saying to them that dwell on the earth, <u>that they should make an image to the beast, which had the wound by a sword, and did live</u>.(Revelation 13:12-14)

The seventh head of the beast of the sea was the Ottoman empire which was dissected at the end of WWI, yet it survived and revived. This lamb-like beast with two horns comes afterward saying they should redo the ancient Ottoman empire and have one caliph again. These Shia Muslims will deceive with miracles and wonders and their "*fire*"-power (nukes). They will initiate a new holocaust and call for a new world-wide Muslim empire or caliphate ("*image to the beast*"), a likeness to the Ottoman Empire. The ayatollah Khomeini openly opposed the shah of Iran in 1978, and the next year was welcomed as the revered leader of the country. His brand of radicalized Shia eschatology rebirthed the beast of the Medes and Persians.

Revived Ram: Medes and Persians (Afghanistan and Iran)

*The **ram** which you saw having two horns are the kings of Media and Persia. (Daniel 8:20)*

Japheth's son, Madai (hence Medes), occupied the lands now known as Afghanistan. In the third and second centuries BC, the Parthians, a nomadic Iranian people, arrived in ancient Afghanistan. The Parthians established control in most of what is Iran as early as the middle of the 3rd century BC; about 100 years later another Indo-European group from the north entered the region that is now Afghanistan and established an empire lasting almost four centuries. There remains a strong Shia dominance in central Afghanistan, urban centers and the Herat province. The horn in Afghanistan was/is Osama ben Laden, though he is Sunni; it's possible a Shia could take his place. The horn in Iran is Achmajinedab.

Iran has the largest Shia population. Central Afghanistan and eastern Iraq also have large Shia populations. Oman has a large Ibaldi (derived from Shia) population, and it controls the land opposite the Straits of Hormuz from Iran; together they could blockade oil tankers. The United Arab Emirates, Yemen, and Lebanon have small Shia populations.

Image of the Beast of the Sea

The "*beast of the earth*" will have power to give life (*pneuma*, spirit or soul) to the image of the "*beast of the sea*". Achmajinedab has voiced its purpose is to create chaos for Mahdi's return. The Beast of the Sea represents Islam globally, and Sunnism specifically. The 'image' is *eikon;* from it we get icon. The icon of Islam is the crescent moon; it's on top of almost every mosque and most flags of Muslim countries. Will Achmajinedab make a statue of a crescent moon talk, or make the gold dinar the monetary standard?

> *And he had power to give life to the image of the beast, that the image of the beast should both speak, and cause that as many as would not worship the image of the beast should be killed. And he causes all, both small and great, rich and poor, free and bond, to receive a mark in their right hand, or in their foreheads: And that no man might buy or sell, save he that had the mark, or the name of the beast, or the number of his name. Here is wisdom. Let him that has understanding count the number of the beast: for it is the number of a man; and his number is Six hundred three score and six. (Revelation 13:15-18)*

Like the Hindus place a dot on their foreheads, will Muslims be required to place a crescent moon? To require a crescent moon tattoo to buy or sell would not be difficult for Muslims under Sharia law to accept, but it will mean death for Jews and Christians. My best stab at calculating the number of the Beast is that Muslims will represent 2/3 of the world population (2/3 is .666 repeating) at some point before Christ's return.

Muslim Gold Dinar to Replace US Dollar as International Standard

In addition to its dedication to create nuclear bombs, Iran is cooperating with Malaysia to reestablish the gold dinar to replace paper currency; thus dropping an economic bomb on the world. From Islam's early beginnings, the gold dinar remained the official Islamic currency until the collapse of the Ottoman Empire in 1924. After George Soros raided Asian currencies in 1997, Malaysia has sought a more stable unit. On Nov. 7, 2001 the Islamic Dinar was officially re-launched by the Islamic Mint in West Malaysia. On the obverse it has a picture of a mosque with a crescent moon on top. The main pillar of Osama bin Laden's strategy to bring down the United States has been to ruin it economically, just as he did the former USSR; hence the destruction of the Trade Towers on Sept. 11, 2001, and the costly wars in Afghanistan and Iraq.

Most Middle Eastern gold is primarily held in London, in violation of the Quran. Thus the Muslims either need to make Britain a Muslim country or move their gold to a Muslim country. Iran might become the center of the Middle East's gold holding because it will be protected militarily by Putin's Russia. Iran could promote the gold dinar as a superior currency to the US dollar under nuclear threat or threat of closing Strait of Hormuz.

The Whore (Wahhabi Confederation)

Countries with large Wahhabi populations are Saudi Arabia, Kuwait, and United Arab Emirates. The heart of Wahhabism is the Kaaba in Mecca; the black cube that devout Muslim pilgrims march around at least once in their lifetime. Islam is a religion for men, promising them virgins for their pleasure in paradise. But there are many more sexual connotations.

Ishtar ruled the moon, and the morning and evening stars. Ishtar is in the Bible as Ashtoreth, Anath, Asherah, and the 'Queen of Heaven'. Ishtar is the virgin warrior, the benevolent mother, and the wise old woman. She is also called the Great Whore and the Mother of Harlots, the Goddess Har, and the compassionate prostitute. Men communed with her through sexual rites with her priestesses at the Har-em (temple of women). The black stone surrounded by silver (in the shape of a vulva) is located on the southeastern corner of the *Haram*, another name for the cube in Mecca. When male priests took over the care of the Haram, they were called "sons of Shayban" or "sons of the wise old woman".

*And he said to me, What see you? And I answered, I see a flying roll; the length thereof is twenty cubits, and the breadth thereof ten cubits. Then said he to me, This is the curse that goes forth over the face of the whole earth: for **every one that steals** shall be cut off as on this side according to it; and **every one that swears** shall be cut off as on that side according to it. . . .And I said, What is it? And he said, This is an ephah that goes forth. He said moreover, **This is their resemblance through all the earth.** And, behold, there was lifted up a talent of lead: and this is **a woman** that sits in the middle of the ephah. And he said, **This is wickedness.** And he cast **it** into the middle of the ephah; and he cast the weight of lead on the mouth thereof. Then lifted I up my eyes, and looked, and, behold, there came out two women, and the wind was in their wings; for they had wings like the wings of a stork: and they lifted up the ephah between the earth and the heaven. Then said I to the angel that talked with me, Where do these bear the ephah? And he said to me, <u>To build **it** an house in the land of Shinar: and **it** shall be established, and set there on **her** own base.</u> (Zechariah 5:2-3, 6b-11)*

The land of Shinar is what we call Mesopotamia, where Nimrod ("*a mighty hunter AGAINST the Lord*") began constructing the tower of Babel; and so it represents the center of opposition to God - Babylon. Muslims are commanded to steal and to lie if it will further Islam. Thus the wicked base of Islam is associated with Babylon and the physical base is almost a cube like the "*bases*" in 1 Kings 7:27. John places the whore in the wilderness (*eremos*) which is often translated 'desert'. Saudi Arabia is 98% desert.

*And there came one of the seven angels which had the seven vials, and talked with me, saying to me, Come here; I will show to you the judgment of <u>the great whore that sits on many waters</u>: With whom the kings of the earth have committed fornication, and the inhabitants of the earth have been made drunk with the **wine** of*

> *her fornication. So he carried me away in the spirit into the wilderness: and I saw a woman sit on a scarlet colored beast, full of names of blasphemy, having seven heads and ten horns. And the woman was arrayed in purple and scarlet color, and decked with gold and precious stones and pearls, having a golden cup in her hand full of abominations and filthiness of her fornication: . . . And he said to me, The <u>waters which you saw, where the whore sits, are peoples, and multitudes, and nations, and tongues</u>. (Revelation 17:1-4, 15)*

The whore is seated upon the waters (has a vast population) and is seated upon the Beast of the Sea (Rev. 13:1; Sunni Islam). Wahhabis came from the Sunnis and consider themselves superior to them. The judgment of the seven vials is associated with the whore for seducing others with "*the wine of her fornication*". The "wine" of the Wahabbis which lures nations into addiction to it is oil, but it also causes them to submit to her fornication with the moon-god. President George W. Bush continued to blaspheme Almighty God by equating the Muslim god to Him. President Jimmy Carter fully supports the Palestinians against Israel. The U.S. is Saudi Arabia's largest trading partner, and Saudi Arabia is the largest U.S. export market in the Middle East. God has used Babylon as a golden cup to make the nations drunk, but now she thinks she possesses the cup as a queen.

Wine of Wrath

> *Flee out of the middle of Babylon, and deliver every man his soul: <u>be not cut off in her iniquity</u>; for this is the time of the LORD's vengeance; he will render to her a recompense.* **Babylon has been a golden cup in the LORD's hand, that made all the earth drunken: the nations have drunken of her wine; therefore the nations are mad.** *Babylon is suddenly fallen and destroyed: howl for her. (Jer. 51:6-8a)*

Quite often in scripture there is a past example of a future fulfillment to come; a precursor which points to a similar prophecy. In both cases God commands His people to flee from Babylon before He pours out His wrath upon her sins.

> *For all nations have drunk of the* **wine of the wrath of her fornication**, *and the kings of the earth have committed fornication with her, and the merchants of the earth are waxed rich through the abundance of her delicacies. And I heard another voice from heaven, saying, Come out of her, my people, that you be not partakers of her sins, and that you receive not of her plagues. For her sins have reached to heaven, and <u>God has remembered her iniquities</u>. (Revelation 18:3-5)*

> *And <u>great Babylon came in remembrance before God, to give to her</u> the* **cup of the wine of the fierceness of his wrath**. *(Revelation 16:19b)*

When God pours out His wrath upon the whore for leading people away from Him, the angels encourage Him to "*Reward her even as she rewarded you, and double to her double according to her works: in the cup which she has filled fill to her double*" (Rev. 18:6).

The Mother of Idolatry

God has not forgotten the source of idolatry is Satan. Ever since Satan deceived Eve to turn from obedience to God in order to become "*like God*", he has been deceiving the whole world to do the same. For hundreds of years Satan's seat of opposition to God was in Babylon, so the whore is given the name "*mystery, Babylon the great*". Satan used his various religious systems to kill those who believed in the promised Messiah ("*the saints*") along with those who believed in Messiah Jesus after He came ("*martyrs of Jesus*").

And on her forehead was a name written, MYSTERY, BABYLON THE GREAT, THE MOTHER OF HARLOTS AND ABOMINATIONS OF THE EARTH. And I saw the woman drunken with the blood of <u>the saints</u>, and with the blood of <u>the martyrs of Jesus</u>: and when I saw her, I wondered with great admiration. And the angel said to me, Why did you marvel? I will tell you the mystery of the woman, and of the beast that carries her, which has the seven heads and ten horns. . . .And here is the mind which has wisdom. The seven heads are seven mountains, on which the woman sits. . . . And the woman which you saw is that great city, which reigns over the kings of the earth. (Revelation 17:5-7, 9, 18)

The whore does not do the killing herself, but promotes others to do it for her. She uses her charms and wealth to train and support her murderous beast of Islam all around the world (even in the US). According to Simon Altaf, Mecca is surrounded by seven mountains (*Jabal* in Arabic): Jabal Quba, Jabal Al-Qinaa, Jabal Li Aali, Jabal Jifan, Jabal Jiyad, Jabal Abi Qubais, and Jabal Hindi. Mecca sits in the 'well' of these mountains. This religious whore is a great city which reigns over the kings of the earth because it holds the cards of wealth, oil, and the holiest city. The whore is Mecca.

The Trade of Mecca and Jeddeh

This list is similar to the list of merchandise that went in and out of Tyre in Ezekiel 27.

And the merchants of the earth shall weep and mourn over her; for no man buys their merchandise any more: The merchandise of gold, and silver, and precious stones, and of pearls, and fine linen, and purple, and silk, and scarlet, and all thyine wood, and all manner vessels of ivory, and all manner vessels of most precious wood, and of brass, and iron, and marble, And cinnamon, and odors, and ointments, and frankincense, and wine, and oil, and fine flour, and wheat, and beasts, and sheep, and horses, and chariots, and slaves, and souls of men. (Revelation 18:11-13)

According to Saudia-online.com, Saudi Arabia imports and exports the following: base metals; pearls; precious and semi-precious stones; jewelry; wood and cork, basket ware; textiles; articles of human hair; paper making material; footwear, headgear; artificial flowers; artificial resins; prepared foodstuffs; beverages; spirits and vinegar; live animals; leather, fur skin, tobacco; machinery; electrical equipment; transport equipment;

instruments; works of art; and arms and ammunition. Crude and refined oil account for 75% of Saudi Arabia's exports. Jeddeh held the first Islamic Trade Fair with over forty countries in June, 2001.

'Thyine' means to sacrifice. It is a Mediterranean citron wood that the Romans used in their sacrifices because of its sweet scent. It was very valuable and used to make expensive furniture. Its bark yields a resin used in varnishes. The Bedouin call the thyine tree the "cursed lemon" because it grows in the salt lands that surround the Dead Sea where Sodom and Gomorrah once were.

Many Saudis are very rich. They hire foreigners for house servants who then find it very difficult to leave the country. Saudi clerics say that Islam advocates slavery. They also don't mind kidnapping foreign women (infidels) for their harems. "Many religious leaders feel that it is a woman's place to provide pleasure to the male and bear children without receiving pleasure themselves, especially if they are infidel women," according to Egyptian Doctor Muzaffar who performs female circumcision on many concubines in Saudi Arabia.

The City of "Babylon" is Fallen

*And the ten horns which you saw on the beast, these shall hate the whore, and shall make her desolate and naked, and shall eat her flesh, and **burn her with fire**. For God has put in their hearts to fulfill his will, and to agree, and give their kingdom to the beast, until the words of God shall be fulfilled. (Revelation 17:16-17)*

And there followed another angel, saying, Babylon is fallen, is fallen, that great city, because she made all nations drink of the wine of the wrath of her fornication. (Revelation 14:8)

And after these things I saw another angel come down from heaven, having great power; and the earth was lightened with his glory. And he cried mightily with a strong voice, saying, Babylon the great is fallen, is fallen, and is become the habitation of devils, and the hold of every foul spirit, and a cage of every unclean and hateful bird. (Revelation 18:1-2)

Ten Horns Will Torch the Whore of Islam

John wrote of the ten horns (kings) having power at the same time with the Antichrist for one hour (Rev. 17:12). The ten Sunni leaders and the Antichrist will burn Mecca with fire. Sunni Wahhabis have attacked Mecca before in 1979. A band of native Saudis under the leadership of Juhayman Al Uteybi captured the Grand Mosque of Mecca with hundreds of pilgrims inside by chaining the 51 gates shut and setting up their sharp-shooters on the seven minarets. Juhayman thought the Saudis were too Westernized for the Mahdi's imminent return (within two weeks on the first day of the new Muslim century), and this rash act gave him a platform to purge and purify them. The Saudis called in a French special force to help them retake the area, which was accomplished with heavy casualties after two weeks.

According to the US State Department, "In May 2003, a terrorist organization directly affiliated with al-Qaida launched a violent campaign of terror in Saudi Arabia. On May 12, suicide bombers killed 35 people, including nine Americans, in attacks at three housing compounds for Westerners in Riyadh. On November 8, 2003 terrorists attacked another compound housing foreign workers from mainly Arab countries. At least 18 people, including 5 children died in this attack, and more than 100 were injured. On May 1, 2004 terrorists killed two Americans in the Yanbu oil facility in the western part of the country. On May 29, 2004 terrorists killed one American and wounded several others in attacks on an official building and housing compound in al-Khobar in the Eastern Province. On June 6, terrorists shot and killed a BBC journalist. On June 9 and June 12, 2004 terrorists killed Americans Robert Jacobs and Kenneth Scroggs. On June 18, 2004 terrorists kidnapped and beheaded American Paul Johnson. On December 6, 2004 terrorists attacked the U.S. Consulate in Jeddah, killing five consulate employees. Terrorists also targeted and killed other foreign nationalities during this time. . . . In May 2006, terrorists attempted to attack the major ARAMCO oil-processing facility at Abqaiq."

Most of Saudi Arabia's oil fields are on the east coast, but there is an east-west crude oil pipeline and refineries in the port city of Jeddeh. Jeddeh is 45 miles west of Mecca and it has an offshore oil terminal for tankers as well. And in "*one hour*" the whore (Mecca/Jeddeh) will be destroyed and made desolate.

*How much she has glorified herself, and lived deliciously, so much torment and sorrow give her: for she said in her heart, I sit a queen, and am no widow, and shall see no sorrow. Therefore shall <u>her plagues come in one day</u>, death, and mourning, and famine; and she shall be **utterly burned with fire**: for strong is the Lord God who judges her. And the kings of the earth, who have committed fornication and lived deliciously with her, shall mourn her, and lament for her, when they shall see **the smoke of her burning**, Standing afar off for the fear of her torment, saying, Alas, alas that great city Babylon, that mighty city! for <u>in one hour is your judgment come</u>. . . . And the fruits that your soul lusted after are departed from you, and all things which were dainty and goodly are departed from you, and you shall find them no more at all. The merchants of these things, which were made rich by her, shall stand afar off for the fear of her torment, weeping and wailing, And saying, Alas, alas that great city, that was clothed in fine linen, and purple, and scarlet, and decked with gold, and precious stones, and pearls! For <u>in one hour so great riches is come to nothing</u>. And every shipmaster, and all the company in ships, and sailors, and as many as trade by sea, stood afar off, And cried when they saw **the smoke of** *her burning, saying, What city is like to this great city! And they cast dust on their heads, and cried, weeping and wailing, saying, Alas, alas that great city, wherein were made rich all that had ships in the sea by reason of her costliness! for <u>in one hour is she made desolate</u>. (Revelation 18:7-19 edited)*

Because of the wrath of the LORD it shall not be inhabited, but it shall be wholly desolate: every one that goes by Babylon shall be astonished, and hiss at all her plagues. (Jeremiah 50:13)

Recall pictures of the oil fields of Iraq set on fire and belching black smoke across the sky; the same may happen to Mecca and Jeddeh, and possibly the oil fields on the east coast as well. Both Sunni and Shia leaders have threatened to burn oil fields in order to bring down America. And there may be a different scenario.

God Will Send an Asteroid or Volcano

*Rejoice over her, you heaven, and you holy apostles and prophets; for God has avenged you on her. And a mighty angel took up a stone like **a great millstone**, and <u>cast it into the sea</u>, saying, Thus with violence shall that great city Babylon be thrown down, and shall be found no more at all. And the voice of harpers, and musicians, and of pipers, and trumpeters, shall be heard no more at all in you; and no craftsman, of whatever craft he be, shall be found any more in you; and the sound of a millstone shall be heard no more at all in you; And the light of a candle shall shine no more at all in you; and the voice of the bridegroom and of the bride shall be heard no more at all in you: for your merchants were the great men of the earth; for by your sorceries were all nations deceived. And in her was found the blood of prophets, and of saints, and of all that were slain on the earth. (Revelation 18:20-24)*

'Violence' here means a rash attack. Will someone nuke Mecca on impulse? Or will it be a calculated purging of evil like Juhayman did? Jesus wrote about tying a "*millstone*" to a person who led little ones astray and drowning him in the sea (Matthew 18:6). Will Mecca's destruction be an act of God using an asteroid to bring judgment on the Wahhabis for leading so many little ones and nations astray?

"*And the second angel sounded, and as it were **a great mountain burning with fire** was <u>cast into the sea</u>: and the third part of the sea became blood*" (Rev. 8:8).

Mecca and Jeddeh are in western Saudi Arabia. Western Saudi Arabia has several volcanic fields. One volcano there erupted as recently as one hundred years ago.

God's Judgment of Babylon is Celebrated

And after these things I heard a great voice of much people in heaven, saying, Alleluia; Salvation, and glory, and honor, and power, to the Lord our God: For *true and righteous are his judgments: for he has judged the great whore, which did corrupt the earth with her fornication, and has <u>avenged the blood of his servants at her hand</u>. And again they said, Alleluia And her smoke rose up for ever and ever. And the four and twenty elders and the four beasts fell down and worshipped God that sat on the throne, saying, Amen; Alleluia. And a voice came out of the throne, saying, Praise our God, all you his servants, and you that fear him, both small and great. (Revelation 19:1-5)*

The "*much people*" in heaven include the Great Tribulation witnesses who were killed by Islamic terrorists, and they state God has "*avenged the blood of his servants at her hand*". When God destroys the great whore of Islam, believers should praise Him. The great whore is only kept in power by the Sunnis until their Mahdi/Antichrist arises and gives power to ten kings who will make her desolate.

Seven Heads of the Beast of the Sea

I saw a woman sit on a scarlet colored beast, full of names of blasphemy, having seven heads and ten horns. . . . And on her forehead was a name written, MYSTERY, BABYLON THE GREAT, THE MOTHER OF HARLOTS AND ABOMINATIONS OF THE EARTH. And I saw the woman drunken with the blood of the saints, and with the blood of the martyrs of Jesus: . . . I will tell you the mystery of the woman, and of the beast that carries her, which has the seven heads and ten horns. The beast that you saw was, and is not; and shall ascend out of the bottomless pit, and go into perdition: and they that dwell on the earth shall wonder, whose names were not written in the book of life from the foundation of the world, when they behold the beast that was, and is not, and yet is. And here is the mind which has wisdom. The seven heads are seven mountains, on which the woman sits. And there are seven kings: five are fallen, and one is, and the other is not yet come; and when he comes, he must continue a short space. And the beast that was, and is not, even he is the eighth, and is of the seven, and goes into perdition. (Revelation 17:3b-11)

The seven dynasties which controlled Babylon with their notable king are as follows:
1. Sumerian - (Nimrod, then Marduk, then) Nebu
2. Assyrian - Shalmaneser
3. Babylonian - Nebucchadnezzar (to Nabonidas)
4. Mede & Persian - (Darius &) Cyrus
5. Macedonian (Greek) - Alexander
6. Roman - Caesar
7. Ottoman - <u>Mohammed</u>
8. Revived Muslim - Mahdi

John wrote Revelation between 95-96 AD; he died in 99. During his lifetime Rome ruled the world, which was the "*one is*". The five dynasties which were fallen were the Sumerian, Assyrian, Babylonian, Mede/Persian, and Macedonian. The dynasty which had not yet come was the Ottoman.

Ten Horns of the Beast of the Sea

And the ten horns which you saw are ten kings, which have received no kingdom as yet; but receive power as kings one hour with the beast. These have one mind, and shall give their power and strength to the beast. These shall make war with the Lamb, and the Lamb shall overcome them: for he is Lord of lords, and King of kings: and they that are with him are called, and chosen, and faithful. And he said to me, The waters which you saw, where the whore sits, are peoples, and multitudes, and nations, and tongues. And the ten horns which you saw on the beast, these shall hate the whore, and shall make her desolate and naked, and shall eat her flesh, and burn her with fire. For God has put in their hearts to fulfill his will, and to agree, and give their kingdom to the beast, until the words of God shall be fulfilled. And the woman which you saw is that great city, which reigns over the kings of the earth. (Rev. 17:12-18)

The ten horns with crowns signifying ten kings. They may be kings in exile since they have "*no kingdom as yet*", or they may not be kings at all until the beast gives them power to rule one hour with him; the same "*one hour*" it takes to destroy the whore of Babylon. The ten horns who hate the whore may include the two on the beast of the earth (Achmajinedab and Osama ben Laden, or his replacement). Four more horns may be the leaders of United Arab Emirates, Yemen, Lebanon, and tiny Bahrain which have small Shia populations. The other four kings may be from countries nearby.

*Behold, I will stir up the Medes against them, which shall not regard silver; and as for gold, they shall not delight in it. Their bows also shall dash the young men to pieces; and they shall have no pity on the fruit of the womb; their eyes shall not spare children. And Babylon, the glory of kingdoms, the beauty of the Chaldees' excellency, shall be as when God overthrew Sodom and Gomorrah. It shall never be inhabited, neither shall it be dwelled in from generation to generation: neither shall the **Arabian** pitch tent there; neither shall the shepherds make their fold there. (Isaiah 13:17-20)*

When the Medes and Persians conquered Babylon, they did not destroy the city, and people continued to dwell there; though Cyrus did give a speech which intimated the Medes weren't in it for the money. We are given several clues that this event is still future. The Taliban in Afghanistan, ancient land of the Medes, could not be persuaded with riches when President George W. Bush sought to make a deal with them to construct a 1,000 mile natural gas pipeline to the Caspian Sea. The Taliban are known for their ruthless acts of

The Beasts and Whore of Babylon

violence toward young and old. This glorious Babylon will be burned with fire and never inhabited again like Sodom and Gomorrah. The "*Arabian*" won't dwell there.

The Arab League

The Arab League was founded in Cairo in 1945 by Egypt, Iraq, Lebanon, Saudi Arabia, Syria, Jordan, and Yemen (who joined within months of founding). So it began with seven countries.

All members of Arab League are also members of the Organization of the Islamic Conference. The Arab League initiated the creation of the Palestine Liberation Organization (PLO). Of the Arab League nations, Jordan, Saudi Arabia, Morocco, and Bahrain are kingdoms and they call their leader by the title 'king'; but except for Jordan, they are seen as dictators by the world as are the leaders of most of the other countries.

A list of the ten 'kings' of the Arab League excluding Saudi Arabia would be Bahrain, Jordan, Morocco, Kuwait, Qatar, UAE, Oman, Sudan, Libya, and Egypt. Though these Arab League nations are likely candidates for the ten horns/kings, there are other possible combinations of Muslim nations which should be considered.

Ten Horns but Three Old Ones Get Uprooted

After this I saw in the night visions, and behold a fourth beast, dreadful and terrible, and strong exceedingly; and it had great iron teeth: it devoured and broke in pieces, and stamped the residue with the feet of it: and it was diverse from all the beasts that were before it; and it had ten horns. I considered the horns, and, behold, there came up among them another <u>little horn, before whom there were three of the first horns plucked up by the roots</u>: and, behold, in this horn were eyes like the eyes of man, and a mouth speaking great things. . . . Thus he said, The fourth beast shall be the fourth kingdom on earth, which shall be diverse from all kingdoms, and shall devour the whole earth, and shall tread it down, and break it in pieces. And the ten horns out of this kingdom are ten kings that shall arise: and <u>another shall rise after them; and he shall be diverse from the first, and he shall subdue three kings</u>. And he shall speak great words against the most High, and shall wear out the saints of the most High, and think to change times and laws: and they shall be given into his hand until a time and times and the dividing of time. But the judgment shall sit, and they shall take away his dominion, to consume and to destroy it to the end. (Daniel 7:7-8, 23-26)

Islam uses a strict lunar calendar, and they also impose Sharia law. The phrase "*time and times and the dividing of time*" (see Revelation 12:14) signals the Little Horn will be active during the Great Tribulation. These ten horns/kings are already in place prior to the arrival of the Antichrist/Mahdi. But in John's description, it seems the ten kings only rise to power for the "one hour" to destroy the whore of Islam. Using Daniel's description and the

Awake, Bride

leaders of the Arab League: Bahrain, Jordan, Morocco, Kuwait, Qatar, UAE, Oman, Sudan, Libya, and Egypt; which three kings might the little horn uproot?

Kuwait and UAE are both Wahhabi. Qatar is also wealthy and has allowed US soldiers to launch attacks from its soil. All three are located on the Arabian Peninsula, and may be taken out when the whore of Saudi Arabia is burned and made desolate.

Summary

Satan established moon-worship in the middle east. The current form of that religion is Islam. Islam has two main branches: Shia and Sunni, which has a sect called Wahhabi. In Revelation, Satan is the dragon, the Sunnis are the Beast of the Sea, the Shia are the Beast of the Earth, and the Wahhabis are the Whore that rides the Beast of the Sea. The Shia and the Sunnis despise the Wahhabis for their decadence in Westernizing themselves, and the Wahhabis consider everyone else to be apostate.

The Beast of the Sea is a conglomeration of Nazi Germany (leopard) determination to exterminate the Jews with the 'armament and transportation of Russia (bear), and the communication broadcasting system of the BBC (lion). Each of these countries is aiding the Muslim Beast, and each has a growing population of Muslims. This beast also has seven heads which were past empires. It has ten horns with ten crowns which are ten kings. This beast is given a blasphemous mouth to "*make war with the saints and overcome them*". Daniel's "*little horn*" is the Antichrist to Christians; but to Muslims, he is their savior, the Mahdi, who will create a new Muslim empire (caliphate) during the Great Tribulation.

This caliphate will be supported by the Beast of the Earth, which is a Shia confederation led by two horns/leaders from Afghanistan and Iran. The horn in Afghanistan was/is Osama ben Laden, though he is Sunni. The horn in Iran is Achmajinedab. These Muslims will deceive with miracles and wonders and their "fire"-power (nukes). The icon of Islam is the crescent moon. People say, "money talks", so it may be that the Islamic Dinar picturing a mosque with a crescent moon on top will be the icon of their economy. No one can buy or sell without the mark.

The Whore which rides the Beast of the Sea is Wahhabism, primarily in Saudi Arabia. The heart of Wahhabism is the Kaaba in Mecca. This is a shrine to the compassionate prostitute, the goddess Har, who communed with men through her sexual rites with her priestesses at the Har-em (temple of women). The judgment of the seven vials is associated with the Whore for seducing others with "*the wine of her fornication*". For hundreds of years Satan's seat of opposition to God was in Babylon, so the Whore is given the name "*mystery, Babylon the great*". This religious whore is a great city which reigns over the kings of the earth because it holds the wealth, oil, and the holiest city. The whore is Mecca.

The port city 45 miles west of Mecca is Jeddeh. It held the Islamic Trade Fair. The religious center of Mecca combined with the economic trade center of Jeddeh make the "great city" of Babylon which will be destroyed in "one hour". The ten horns/kings of the Beast of the Sea will carry out God's will in burning this great city. Additionally, God will wipe it out with a "natural" disaster.

7 Seals, 7 Trumpets and 7 Vials

Blessed is he that reads, and they that hear the words of this prophecy, and keep those things which are written therein: for the time is at hand.(Revelation 1:3)

"Call to me, and I will answer you, and show you great and mighty things, which you know not" (Jeremiah 33:3). Jesus is the Word of God, and the testimony of Jesus is the spirit of prophecy (Rev. 19:10c, 13b); so we come to worship God as we study His Word, and call to Him for revelation.

Book of Revelation

Apocalypse means 'lifting of the veil' or 'revealing'; hence 'revelation'. The revelation is of Jesus Christ and His Bride; it is a positive word which has only been associated with the tribulations which surround it. The book of the time of the end which Daniel, the beloved prophet, was told to seal (Daniel 12:4) was revealed to John, the beloved apostle, on the isle of Patmos. John used much of Daniel's imagery.

John was describing things in an orderly fashion, but some things are coupled to others, and some things overlap or coincide with others. If John had hyper-linked text, he could have written a linear time-line of what was to take place. John used the writing style of the Bible in which an outline or overview is given, followed by details, which eventually come back around to the time-line. With this Hebrew cyclical writing style in mind, the prophecies can be grouped according to their timings and commonalities. The seals, trumpets and vials are found in the following chapters of Revelation:

<u>Revelation Chapters</u>
- 5   Lamb to break seals
- 6   Six seals
- 8   7th seal & 4 trumpets
- 9   5th & 6th trumpets
- 11   7th trumpet
- 14-16 7 vials of wrath

The 7 seals are global in their impact, with the first four seals before the Great Tribulation and the three remaining seals at the end. The 7 vials are poured out on Babylon (Islam) and those who worship the beast, while the 7 trumpets are experienced by the rest of the world; God making a distinction like He did between the Egyptians and the Hebrews. The trumpets and vials are done in tandem. [*Encyclopedia of Biblical Prophecy* by J. Barton Payne, p.598] The 7th seal, vial, and trumpet are simultaneous, culminating in King Jesus' return to reign and lead His army to victory (Rev. 19).

Awake, Bride

The Scroll with the Seven Seals: The Marriage Contract

I am indebted to Edward Chumney who wrote of the Hebrew marriage traditions and their Biblical fulfillments in "*The Seven Festivals of the Messiah*" which was published by Treasure House in 1994.

Hebrew Marriage Traditions	Fulfillment in Scripture
The father chose the bride for his son.	God chose us. (Eph. 1:4; 2 Thess. 2:13)
Wedding covenant was a witnessed and sealed contract called a *ketubah*.	New covenant is "*Love one another*" sealed in blood. (Jer. 31:31; Heb. 12:24)
If the woman drank the wine offered, that sealed the covenant; they were 'betrothed'.	The disciples (Bride) drank the "new testament" in Christ's blood. (Luke 22:20)
The groom would pay "bride price" to the father of the bride.	Jesus paid Father God with His life-blood, so ketubah is also a will.
Bride accepts a gift from groom; *kiddushin*, which means sanctification.	Jesus gave us His Holy Spirit, sanctifying and sealing us to Himself (Eph. 1:13; 4:30)
Bride had a ritual immersion [baptism] transferring her obedience to her husband.	Baptism and obedience Romans 6-8
Groom returned to his father's house to build an addition, the bridal chamber.	New Jerusalem John 14:2-3 and Rev. 21:9-27
After father deemed bridal chamber finished, he allowed son to leave at sunset to get bride.	"*Only the Father knows*" Mark 13:32-37
Groom to bride's house with shofars, shouting,"*Behold, the bridegroom comes*".	Trumpets are *shofars* (1 Thess. 4:16-17). Matthew 25:6
Wedding ceremony took place under a *chupah*, a white canopy.	Bride meets Groom in clouds. Acts 1:9-11; 1 Thess. 4:14-18
The cantor greeted groom like a king, "Blessed is he who comes".	When Jews chant same, Jesus will come. Matthew 23:39
Vows consummated that night; celebrate the wedding feast for seven days.	Tishri 2-9, 2012 in New Jerusalem cube

7 Seals, 7 Trumpets and 7 Vials

The scroll in Revelation 5 is the ketubah, or marriage covenant, which has been agreed to and sealed by seven churches (Rev. 2-3) over time, of which we are the last (Laodicea, Rev. 3:14-22). That is why the scroll has seven seals on it. It was also a Roman custom during Christ's life to have a will witnessed and sealed by seven people. Since Christ's bride price was His own life, the ketubah scroll is also His will. The opportunity to be included in the new covenant of receiving God's grace through faith in the blood of Jesus Christ becomes successively more difficult with the breaking of each seal, and comes to an end when Jesus breaks the seventh seal. Then those bridal virgins who were prepared will go into the wedding, and those who went back into the world "to buy oil" because they didn't have a personal relationship with Jesus will be shut out (Matthew 25:1-13).

Jesus Purchased the Right to Open the Seven Seals

*In the dispensation of the fulness of times, <u>to re-establish all things in Christ, that are in heaven **and on earth**</u>, in him. In whom we also are called by lot, being predestinated according to the purpose of him who worketh all things according to the counsel of his will. That we may be unto the praise of his glory: we who before hoped in Christ: In whom you also, after you had heard the word of truth (the gospel of your salvation), in whom also believing, you were signed with the holy Spirit of promise. Who is the pledge of our inheritance, <u>unto the redemption of acquisition</u>, unto the praise of his glory. . . .according to the operation of the might of his power, Which he wrought in Christ, raising him up from the dead and setting him on his right hand in the heavenly places. Above all principality and power and virtue and dominion and every name that is named, <u>not only in this world, but also **in that which is to come**</u>. (Ephesians 1:3-14 edited)*

For we know that the whole creation groans and travails in pain together until now. And not only they, but ourselves also, which have the first fruits of the Spirit, even we ourselves groan within ourselves, waiting for the adoption, to wit, the redemption of our body. (Romans 8:22-23)

'Redemption' in both passages is *apolutrosis*, meaning liberation procured by the payment of a ransom. 'Acquisition' is *peripoiesis*, meaning possession of one's own property. Jesus gave His life to redeem His own property He created. Jesus prevailed over sin and death. He was the victor in His life, death and resurrection. He was slain to redeem mankind (those written in the Book of Life) and the earth. Jesus will remove the curse and all its effects from the earth, and God will make a new heaven and earth (2 Peter 3:13). Believers will receive immortal bodies, and then we shall reign with Christ on the new earth He creates.

And I saw in the right hand of him that sat on the throne a book written within and on the backside, sealed with seven seals. . . . And I wept much, because no man was found worthy to open and to read the book, neither to look thereon. And one of the *elders said to me, Weep not: behold, the Lion of the tribe of Juda, the Root of David, has prevailed to open the book, and to loose the seven seals thereof. . . . And he came and took the book out of the right hand of him that sat on the throne. And when he had taken the book, the four beasts and four and twenty elders fell down before the Lamb, having every one of them harps, and <u>golden vials full of odors, which are the prayers of saints</u>. And they sung a new song, saying, You are worthy to take the book, and to open the seals thereof: for you were slain, and have redeemed us to God by your blood out of every kindred, and tongue, and people, and nation; And have made us to our God kings and priests:* **and we shall reign on the earth**. *And I beheld, and I heard the voice of many angels round about the throne and the beasts and the elders: and the number of them was ten thousand times ten thousand, and thousands of thousands; Saying with a loud voice, Worthy is the Lamb that was slain to receive power, and riches, and wisdom, and strength, and honor, and glory, and blessing. (Revelation 5:1-12 edited)*

'Redeemed' is *agorazo*, meaning purchased. After all the seals have been opened, Jesus will receive His purchased possession, His Bride; and He will receive all power and authority as King over the whole earth, and His saints will serve Him and bless Him and give King Jesus the riches and honor He deserves.

When God delivered the Hebrews from Egypt and plagued the Egyptians and destroyed the Egyptian army, it was in answer to prayers (Exodus 3:7-10). Similarly, Christians have been crying out to God for deliverance from Muslim oppression. The cries of millions of faithful martyrs have been heard and stored as fragrant aromas in 24 golden vials. In Revelation 15:7, "*one of the four beasts gave to the seven angels seven golden vials full of the wrath of God.*" Whether these seven are from the twenty-four is not stated; nor does it say golden vials full of prayers have now become vials full of God's wrath. But these prayers may have been imprecations seeking God's destruction of their enemies like in Psalm 83, or seeking temporary hardship of their enemy to bring repentance (Acts 13:8-12). Or there may be plenty of gold vials/bowls in heaven for these various uses.

The 7th angel will cast his golden censer to the earth when the 7th seal is broken (Rev. 8:1-5). There is a special golden censer used in the Holy of Holies (Hebrews 9:3-4) which is patterned on the one used in heaven. It too is associated with God's wrath and the prayers of the saints after the trumpets are handed to the seven angels.

Though there are seven each of the seals, trumpets and vials; the first group of four of each object is a distinct grouping. The first four trumpets and vials parallel each other as they make a distinction between those who worship the Beast of Islam, and those who do not. Prior to them and the beginning of the Great Tribulation are the first four seals which are also known as the four horsemen of the apocalypse. Scripture gives no indication these four horsemen appear before the Great Tribulation begins, but our recent history does.

Four Horsemen (Seals #1-4)

Though there have always been conquerors bent on taking over the world, and wars, and economic problems and death in various places of the globe; the four horsemen are felt by the whole world at the same time. They are a prelude to the 3 ½ year Great Tribulation to awaken the world out of its slumber, yet they will continue into the Great Tribulation. **September 11**th is the day Jesus was born in 3 BC; it was Rosh Hashanah, Jewish New Year. Using September 11th and dates near Rosh Hashanah was a way to awaken Christ's Bride as to His soon return. This assumes Christ's Bride knows His birthday.

Seal #1

And I saw when the Lamb opened one of the seals, and I heard, as it were the noise of thunder, one of the four beasts saying, Come and see. And I saw, and behold a white horse: and he that sat on him had a bow; and a crown was given to him: and he went forth conquering, and to conquer. (Revelation 6:1-2)

Though Islamic terrorists had bombed many embassies worldwide, it was the attack on **September 11**, 2001 (Rosh Hashanah was a week later) which awakened the world to the "peaceful" **white horse** of Islam attempting to conquer the world without "*arrows*" (nukes). To view Islam's violent toll of conquest, visit www.thereligionofpeace.com which keeps track of each Muslim attack worldwide.

New York City

And I will give power to my two witnesses, and they shall prophesy a thousand two hundred and three score days, clothed in sackcloth. These are the <u>two olive trees</u>, and the <u>two candlesticks</u> standing before the God of the earth. . . .And their dead bodies shall lie in the street of the great city, which spiritually is called Sodom and Egypt, where also our Lord was crucified. And they of the people and kindreds and tongues and nations shall see their dead bodies three days and an half, and shall not suffer their dead bodies to be put in graves. And they that dwell on the earth shall rejoice over them, and make merry, and shall send gifts one to another; because these two prophets tormented them that dwelled on the earth. And after three days and an half the spirit of life from God entered into them, and they stood on their feet; and great fear fell on them which saw them. And they heard a great voice from heaven saying to them, Come up here. And they ascended up to heaven in a cloud; and their enemies beheld them. (Revelation 11:8-12)

During the Revolutionary War New York City was greatly damaged twice by fires, laid siege to, and many battles were fought there with patriots crying, "No king but King Jesus!" From 1788 to 1790, New York City was the capital of the United States of America. (Jerusalem is Israel's capital in which Jesus was crucified as King of the Jews, and later laid siege to and burned.) New York City is currently the most populous city ("*great city*") of the United States with over eight million people, and it is the city with the largest Jewish population outside of Israel (like Egypt housed the Hebrews for hundreds of years). It also has a large homosexual community ("*Sodom*"). The two olive trees and two candlesticks represent God's two anointed 'sons' (Zechariah 4:14), Jews and Gentiles. 'Witness' is another word for 'martyr'. Those who died in the 9/11 attacks were martyred for living in a Christian country which protected the Jews.

On September 11, 2001 Islamic terrorists flew planes into the Twin Towers, and almost 3,000 people from 90 different countries died. The Muslims in Palestine were shown dancing in the streets and celebrating by passing out candy. This was the "*white horse*" of the first seal. Muslims have been slaughtering Christians around the world and leaving their corpses to rot. The "*three and a half days*" refers to the 3½ years of the Great Tribulation in which there will be more martyrs. The slaughter of believers will continue and increase until Rosh Hashanah, September 16, 2012 when the heavens and earth will shake at the Lord's coming, and He will call His people to Him.

The mastermind of the 9/11 attack, and many other Al Qaeda attacks, was Khalid Sheikh Mohammed who was born in Pakistan but received his mechanical engineering degree in the US. According to notes of his interrogation on the internet titled "Substitution for the Testimony of Khalid Sheikh Mohammed," "Sheikh Mohammed said that the purpose of the attack on the Twin Towers was to 'wake the American people up'."

I will also gather all nations, and will bring them down into the valley of Jehoshaphat, and will plead with them there for my people and for my heritage Israel, whom they have scattered among the nations, and parted my land. *Proclaim you this among the Gentiles; Prepare war,* **wake up** *the mighty men, let all the men of war draw near; let them come up: Let the heathen be wakened, and come up to the valley of Jehoshaphat: for there will I sit to judge all the heathen round about. (Joel 3:2, 9, 12)*

The purpose of the first four seals is to get people to "*wake up*" and recognize God's judgment is coming soon. That judgment includes how we have treated the Jews and the land which God gave them.

"On **September 11**, 2008 US Consul General Jacob Walles admitted during an interview with a Palestinian newspaper that there were secret negotiations taking place to divide Jerusalem. The US State Department and Israeli officials were quick to deny such negotiation. Consul General Walles is second in command under the US ambassador to Israel and knows what is going on. I feel he let "the cat out of the bag." Walles' statement was in perfect agreement with Secretary Rice's actions. This admission by the Consul General was on Thursday, **September 11**. At the very time of this admission, Hurricane Ike was rushing toward Texas. This was a massive hurricane 600 miles wide! It struck late Friday and the eye went directly up Galveston Bay. Entire towns were destroyed and Houston was crippled. The rippling effect is not known at this time. The damaged is estimated now at $20 billion and counting. This was bad enough but then Lehman Brothers, one of the largest Wall Street banks, collapsed right on the heels of the hurricane. Then the domino effect hit the stock market." [John McTernan from http://johnmcternansinsights.blogspot.com, emphasis added]

Seal #2

And when he had opened the second seal, I heard the second beast say, Come and see. And there went out another horse that was red: and power was given to him that sat thereon to take peace from the earth, and that they should kill one another: and there was given to him a great sword. (Revelation 6:3-4)

The **red horse** of Islamic terrorism has "*taken peace from the earth*". Not content to just kill infidels, the Muslims also kill other Muslims ("*they should kill one another*"). According to Gunnar Heinsohn and Daniel Pipes, "some 11,000,000 Muslims have been violently killed since 1948, . . . over 90 percent of the 11 million who perished were killed by fellow Muslims" [Front Page Magazine, October 8, 2007]. For example, on **September 11**, 2006 a 12-year-old boy was among six people murdered by a suicide bomber at a funeral for a previous victim of a suicide bombing in Afghanistan; thirty-six were wounded.

Seal #3

And when he had opened the third seal, I heard the third beast say, Come and see. And I beheld, and see a black horse; and he that sat on him had a pair of balances in his hand. And I heard a voice in the middle of the four beasts say, A measure of wheat for a penny, and three measures of barley for a penny; and see you hurt not the oil and the wine. (Revelation 6:5-6)

Again it was during the "days of awe" between Rosh Hashanah and Yom Kippur (Sept. 29 and Oct. 9, 2008) that the **black horse** of economic ruin traveled the globe. (Was it just Democrats causing runs on banks to create economic uncertainty to shift the focus off of the war in Iraq so that their candidate would be elected? Or were rich terrorists making large computer transactions ½ hour before closing for twelve days?) One day's worth of food for one day's wage is mere subsistence. There may yet come a blight on wheat and barley until it gets to the point where "daily bread" will cost a day's wages (Rev. 6:6).

Seal #4

And when he had opened the fourth seal, I heard the voice of the fourth beast say, Come and see. And I looked, and behold a pale horse: and his name that sat on him was Death, and Hell followed with him. And power was given to them over the fourth part of the earth, to kill with sword, and with hunger, and with death, and with the beasts of the earth. (Revelation 6:7-8)

Then comes the **pale horse** of Death. Currently Islam has a majority in one fourth of the world. Russia still has a large Muslim population even after all the "-istan" secessions. Current Muslim world population is estimated between 21% and 27%. [Only 2% of US population is Muslim.] And in those parts of the world in which Islam has power, it is killing through war and famine. There is another form of world-wide death to consider.

The 1918 flu pandemic was mild in the spring but then mutated and returned in the fall with a vengeance. It is estimated that 2% - 5% of the world population died. Twenty years prior in Russia, a virulent flu followed the same pattern: mild in spring and devastatingly deadly in the late summer and fall. The 1918 flu was an H1N1 type. Take wise precautions in Fall 2009.

What Event Started the 3 1/2 Year Clock?

God started the Great Tribulation clock. God told Michael to release Satan (2 Thess. 2:3), and Satan *"knows that his time is short"*. Prior to the first trumpet, God will tell the four angels to start sealing the 144,000.

> *But the court which is without the temple leave out, and measure it not; for it is given to the Gentiles: and the holy city shall they tread under foot forty and two months. And I will give power to my two witnesses, and they shall prophesy a thousand two hundred and three score days, clothed in sackcloth.(Rev. 11:2-3)*

Two groups who will be involved throughout the Great Tribulation. The Muslims ("*Gentiles*") continue to occupy the Temple Mount, continuing to do so for another 42 months will not seem unusual. The Two Witnesses (Jewish and Gentile believers) are already present and proclaiming the gospel, though not to the point of withholding rain or praying plagues upon our enemies to demonstrate God's power yet. Counting backwards 1,260 days from September 16, 2012, the Great Tribulation clock began on **April 6, 2009**.

All Great Tribulation days and times are according to Hebrew days and Jerusalem time. I don't know what occurred at dusk in Jerusalem on (Nisan 12) April 6, 2009, but I bet the cabinet members were discussing how to eliminate Iran's nuclear threat.

Power and Influence of USA Is Removed

> *And now you know <u>what withholds that he might be revealed in his time</u>. For the mystery of iniquity does already work: only he who now lets will let, until he be taken out of the way. And then shall that Wicked be revealed." (2 Thess. 2:3-8a)*

Barnes' Bible Commentary on this verse states: "The most natural interpretation is that which refers it to civil power, meaning that there was something in the form of the existing administration which would prevent this development until that restraint should be removed." What civil restraining power has been present in the Middle East?

In order for God to accomplish what He intends to do in the Middle East, He needed to remove the United States of America. The black horse of economic ruin has already removed the US dollar as the standard of world currency, and continued reckless government spending will keep it suppressed. The first war the United States of America encountered after becoming a nation was with the Muslims in 1801 who had declared war on all Christian nations. They were known as the Barbary Pirates of the Mediterranean. General Eaton of the US Navy said prior to his marines success at Tripoli, "It is a maxim of the Barbary States, that 'The Christians who would be on good terms with them must fight well or pay well.'" America's commander-in-chief has declared to the Muslims that we are not a Christian nation and are not at war with Islam. So the US will "pay" for peace.

On **April 6, 2009**, President Obama declared to the Turkey parliament, "Let me say this as clearly as I can: The United States is not, and will never be, at war with Islam." He further clarified, "Our partnership with the Muslim world is critical in rolling back a fringe ideology that people of all faiths reject." The purpose of Islam is to subject the world to Islam through peaceful or forceful conversion. As a child, Obama attended both a Muslim school and a Catholic school for two years each. He knows the basic tenets of each religion. Obama is wearing out the saints through a barrage of law changes (Daniel 7:25) toward an immoral, socialist dictatorship while he strengthens his relationships with the dictators of the world. On the first day of the Great Tribulation, Obama announced to the Muslims that America will no longer be a restraining force (to their plans to annihilate Israel). He later set a date for the withdrawal of troops from Iraq in 2010. Obama told Netanyahu that by the end of 2009, he might consider stronger sanctions against Iran. Yet Obama will soon present Netanyahu with a "peace plan" with a binding timetable for negotiations with the Palestinians for a final resolution to their conflict. The Aryan (*Iranian*) "final solution" to the presence of Jews is the same as Nazi Germany which is the same as the PLO has written in Article 15 of their own charter; the elimination of all Jews.

There are three woes which are time markers. The first woe (March 6, 2011) begins five months of locusts. The second woe begins the Armegeddon War (August 23, 2011) which lasts for one year, one month, one day, and one hour. The third woe is the 7th trumpet which begins the Day of the Lord. There are also three angelic announcements at the beginning of the Great Tribulation. The <u>first angelic announcement</u> is the everlasting gospel to the world (Rev. 14:6-7).

Babylon is Fallen

The <u>second angelic announcement</u> is the fall of the great city Babylon (Mecca), taken out by a meteor or a bomb. According to "The Samson Option" written by reporter Seymour Hersh, Israel may have 200 to 400 atomic warheads, ready to use as a last resort to preserve the existence of the country. Osama bin Laden has denounced the house of Saud and let it be known that he is ready to attack oil cities in his home nation of Saudi Arabia in order to crush the economy of the rest of the world. Osama is a Sunni, but most of Saudi Arabia is Wahhabi (apostates according to Sunnis). Al-Qaeda might bomb Mecca and its port city Jeddah. *Osama* means 'lion' in Arabic.

> *The burden of the desert of the sea. As whirlwinds in the south pass through; so it comes from the desert, from a terrible land. A grievous vision is declared to me; the treacherous dealer deals treacherously, and the spoiler spoils. Go up, O Elam: besiege, O Media; all the sighing thereof have I made to cease. Therefore are my loins filled with pain: pangs have taken hold on me, as the pangs of a woman that travails: I was bowed down at the hearing of it; I was dismayed at the seeing of it. . . . And he cried, A **lion**: My lord, I stand continually on the watchtower in the daytime, and I am set in my ward whole nights: And, behold, here comes a chariot of men, with a couple of horsemen. And he answered and said, <u>Babylon is fallen</u>, is fallen; and all the graven images of her gods he has broken to the ground. . . . The burden of Dumah. . . . The burden on Arabia. In the forest in Arabia shall you lodge, O you traveling companies of Dedanim. . . .The inhabitants of the land of Tema brought water to him that was thirsty, they prevented with their bread him that fled. For they fled from the swords, from the drawn sword, and from the bent bow, and from the grievousness of war. For thus has the LORD said to me, <u>Within a year, according to the years of an hireling, and all the glory of Kedar shall fail</u>: And the residue of the number of archers, the mighty men of the children of Kedar, shall be diminished: for the LORD God of Israel has spoken it. (Isaiah 21:1-17 edited)*

The Elamites lived in what is now the province of Khuzestan, Iran which borders the Persian Gulf. The name "Persia" was not used until after Babylonian captivity. And Media is the Medes (now Afghanistan). Though Persia has borders with seas, its desert is inland. The Medes and Persians did besiege and conquer Babylon more than a hundred years after this prophecy.

This burden or oracle also has a future fulfillment regarding Arabia. Dumah is now called Dumat el Janda, located near Medina. Dumah and Kedar were sons of Ishmael. Mohammed was of the lineage of Kedar. Mohammed first promoted his new religion in Mecca, who cast him out. He fled north to Medina. [Continuing on the road north of Medina are Hafirat al Ayda (where Dedan settled) and Tayma (Tema).] Medina accepted his religion and authority, and Mohammed returned to Mecca with armed men from Medina. Mohammed threw out all the idols from Mecca, except the Kaaba to the moon god which he then proclaimed to be "The Deity" (Al-Ilah, which was shortened to Allah). The Hebrew words for 'fail' and 'diminished' could also be translated to bring Kedar to an 'end' and to 'bring to nothing'. Arabian desert of the sea is prophetically connected to Babylon and the Medes and Persians destruction of it, and it may also fall within a 360-day year of the announcement of its destruction.

With the Wahhabis and Saudi oil out of the way, the Beast of the Earth (the Shia of Iraq, Afghanistan and Iran), will then require all people to wear a mark of allegiance to

7 Seals, 7 Trumpets and 7 Vials

Islam on their arm or forehead in order to buy or sell. Peaople will eventually to be killed if they refuse the mark. The <u>third angelic announcement</u> is if anyone worships the Beast or takes its mark, he will also experience God's wrath poured out on the Beast (through the seven vials).

First Four Trumpets and Vials

The first angel sounded, and there followed hail and fire mingled with blood, and they were cast on the earth: and the third part of trees was burnt up, and all green grass was burnt up. And the second angel sounded, and as it were <u>a great mountain burning</u> with fire was cast into the sea: and the third part of the sea became blood; And the third part of the creatures which were in the sea, and had life, died; and the third part of the ships were destroyed. And the third angel sounded, and there fell <u>a great star from heaven, burning</u> as it were a lamp, and it fell on the third part of the rivers, and on the fountains of waters; And the name of the star is called Wormwood: and the third part of the waters became wormwood; and many men died of the waters, because they were made bitter. And the fourth angel sounded, and the third part of the sun was smitten, and the third part of the moon, and the third part of the stars; so as the third part of them was darkened, and the day shone not for a third part of it, and the night likewise. (Revelation 8:7-12)

At the first trumpet "hail and fire mingled with blood" (Rev. 8:7) were cast on the earth. It may be literal blood, or it may be a clue that biological weapons will be used. Blood is weaponized throughout the first four trumpets and vials. The second trumpet has something like a great burning mountain which is thrown into the sea, whereas the third trumpet states a great burning star fell from heaven; one sounds man-made while the other sounds God-made. The fourth trumpet takes away one third of daylight and night light, but it does not make a black sun and a red moon as the 6th seal does.

<u>First Four Trumpets</u> (upon **world**)
1st   All grass burnt; 1/3 trees
2nd 1/3 sea, sea-life & ships
3rd   1/3 rivers; & bitter waters
4th   1/3 of sun, moon & stars

<u>First Four Vials</u> (upon "**Babylon**")
1st   Sores upon worshipers of Beast
2nd Sea to blood; all sea-life dies
3rd   All rivers and fountains to blood
4th   Use sun to scorch men with fire

It is unclear when in the first two years of the Great Tribulation these sets of four will occur, or how much time is allotted to each or between each. Though between the second angelic announcement and the actual fall of Babylon at the 2nd trumpet and vial may be a period of one year. The Sea of Babylon is most likely the Arabian Sea surrounding the Arabian Peninsula with its arms of the Red Sea, Gulf of Oman, and the Persian Gulf. Thus, the Whore of Babylon-Islam and its great cities of Mecca and Jeddeh will be destroyed.

Awake, Bride

> *And the first went, and poured out his vial on the earth; and there fell a noisome and grievous sore on the men which had the mark of the beast, and on them which worshipped his image. And the second angel poured out his vial on the sea; and it became as the blood of a dead man: and every living soul died in the sea. And the third angel poured out his vial on the rivers and fountains of waters; and they became blood. And I heard the angel of the waters say, You are righteous, O Lord, which are, and were, and shall be, because you have judged thus. For they have shed the blood of saints and prophets, and you have given them blood to drink; for they are worthy. And I heard another out of the altar say, Even so, Lord God Almighty, true and righteous are your judgments. And the fourth angel poured out his vial on the sun; and power was given to him to scorch men with fire. And men were scorched with great heat, and blasphemed the name of God, which has power over these plagues: and they repented not to give him glory. (Revelation 16:2-9)*

There is no statement that the people of "Babylon" repent from this time forward. Their murderous acts have made them "worthy" of the judgment of a righteous God. Even though one third of the sunlight no longer reaches earth, the sun still has the ability to scorch with great heat. The sun's last cycle (23) of sun spots went unusually long and demonstrated large solar flares; the scorching may be the result of solar flares.

5th Trumpet and Vial (First Woe)

> *And there came out of the smoke locusts on the earth: and to them was given power, as the scorpions of the earth have power. And it was commanded them that they should not hurt the grass of the earth, neither any green thing, neither any tree; but only those men which have not the seal of God in their foreheads. And to them it was given that they should not kill them, but that <u>they should be tormented five months: and their torment was as the torment of a scorpion</u>, when he strikes a man. And in those days shall men seek death, and shall not find it; and shall desire to die, and death shall flee from them. And the shapes of the locusts were like to horses prepared to battle; and on their heads were as it were crowns like gold, and their faces were as the faces of men. And they had hair as the hair of women, and their teeth were as the teeth of lions. And they had breastplates, as it were breastplates of iron; and the sound of their wings was as the sound of chariots of many horses running to battle. <u>And they had tails like to scorpions, and there were stings in their tails: and their power was to hurt men five months</u>. (Revelation 9:3-10)*

John, the apostle, is trying to describe something he's never seen before by relating it to things he knows. Locusts with breastplates of iron with the roar of their wings like many chariots, yet with men's faces best describes helicopters. The women's hair may be rope ladders. The sting could be biological or chemical weapons spewed from their *"tails"*, or traditional weapons. Counting backwards from the date of Christ's return as September 16, 2012, the fifth trumpet and fifth vial should commence on March 26, 2011.

And the fifth angel poured out his vial on <u>the seat of the beast</u>; and his kingdom was full of darkness; and they gnawed their tongues for pain, And blasphemed the God of heaven because of their pains and their sores, and repented not of their deeds. (Revelation 16:10-11)

The "*seat of the beast*" given by Satan (Rev. 13:2) is not the same as the "*great city*" of the Whore. The Beast's seat of power will most likely be Baghdad or a rebuilt Babylon. 'Darkness' is *skotoo*, meaning to obscure or blind. This word is only used once in the New Testament; usually *skotos* or *skotinos* are used for outer or inner darkness respectively. It may be that the chemical warfare produces very painful sores and cloudy vision. The pattern after the fourth and fifth vials is that the Beast worshipers cursed the God of heaven and did not repent.

5th Seal (Great Tribulation Martyrs)

*And when he had opened the fifth seal, I saw under the altar the souls of them that were <u>slain for the word of God, and for the testimony which they held</u>: And they cried with a loud voice, saying, How long, O Lord, holy and true, do you not judge and avenge our blood on them that dwell on the earth? And **white robes** were given to every one of them; and it was said to them, that they should rest yet for a little season, until their fellow servants also and their brothers, that should be killed as they were, should be fulfilled. (Revelation 6:9-11)*

*After this I beheld, and, see, a great multitude, which no man could number, of all nations, and kindreds, and people, and tongues, stood before the throne, and before the Lamb, clothed with white robes, and palms in their hands; And cried with a loud voice, saying, Salvation to our God which sits on the throne, and to the Lamb. . . . And one of the elders answered, saying to me, What are these which are arrayed in **white robes**? and from where came they? And I said to him, Sir, you know. And he said to me, These are they which <u>came out of great tribulation</u>, and have washed their robes, and made them white in the blood of the Lamb. Therefore are they before the throne of God, and serve him day and night in his temple: and he that sits on the throne shall dwell among them. They shall hunger no more, neither thirst any more; neither shall the sun light on them, nor any heat. For the Lamb which is in the middle of the throne shall feed them, and shall lead them to living fountains of waters: and God shall wipe away all tears from their eyes. (Rev. 7:9-17 edited)*

These courageous saints will be persecuted for their faith. They will hunger and thirst, possibly because they refuse the mark of the Beast and can not buy or sell. They will be killed for following Jesus, but then their King will feed and comfort them. Since they only wait a "*little season*", this seal occurs during the Armegeddon War before Jesus' return.

6th Vial and Trumpet (Armageddon War: Second Woe)

With the 6th trumpet and vial the prior distinction between them (vials upon Babylon and trumpets upon the rest of the world) is diminished as the "*kings of the earth*" are brought together to Mount Megiddo in Israel. The word for mountain is *Har*, and so we get (H)ar Megiddo(n), or Armegeddon. The 6th vial dries up the Euphrates so the kings of the east can more easily transport their armies to Israel. Whether this is accomplished using a man-made dam, weather conditions, or a miracle is unclear. Three demons are sent to entice the kings of the earth to make war at Armegeddon.

Countries immediately east of the Euphrates river are Shiite south-eastern Iraq, and Shiite Iran and Afghanistan which constitute the Shia Beast of the Earth. These countries are what used to be the Persian empire. The Persian empire once sought to exterminate the Jews, when Queen Esther foiled their plans (Purim); but they are planning to do so again, and this time with nuclear weapons.

*And the sixth angel poured out his vial on the great river **Euphrates**; and the water thereof was dried up, that the way of the kings of the east might be prepared. And I saw three unclean spirits like frogs come out of the mouth of the dragon, and out of the mouth of the beast, and out of the mouth of the false prophet. For they are the spirits of devils, working miracles, which go forth to the kings of the earth and of the whole world, to gather them to the battle of that great day of God Almighty. Behold, I come as a thief. Blessed is he that watches, and keeps his garments, lest he walk naked, and they see his shame. And he gathered them together into a place called in the Hebrew tongue Armageddon. (Revelation 16:12-16)*

*And the sixth angel sounded, and I heard a voice from the four horns of the golden altar which is before God, Saying to the sixth angel which had the trumpet, Loose the four angels which are bound in the great river **Euphrates**. And the four angels were loosed, which were prepared for an hour, and a day, and a month, and a year, for to slay the third part of men. And the number of the army of the horsemen were two hundred thousand thousand: and I heard the number of them. And thus I saw the horses in the vision, and them that sat on them, having breastplates of fire, and of jacinth, and brimstone: and the heads of the horses were as the heads of lions; and out of their mouths issued fire and smoke and brimstone. By these three was the third part of men killed, by the fire, and by the smoke, and by the brimstone, which issued out of their mouths. For their power is in their mouth, and in their tails: for their tails were like to serpents, and had heads, and with them they do hurt. And the rest of the men which were not killed by these plagues yet repented not of the works of their hands, that they should not worship devils, and idols of gold, and silver, and* *brass, and stone, and of wood: which neither can see, nor hear, nor walk: Neither repented they of their murders, nor of their sorceries, nor of their fornication, nor of their thefts. (Revelation 8:13-21)*

This time John seems to be describing fire-throwing tanks with small caliber weapons in their rear, along with a two hundred million man army. Jihadists have shown they can transport their men to the theater of battle in great numbers. The people are killed by the fire, smoke, and brimstone which are then called plagues; so this is chemical warfare. This time it is recorded under the trumpet that the survivors of the world who worshiped other gods did not repent.

The breastplates are fire, jacinth, and brimstone. Fire is red or red-orange. Jacinth is a semi-precious stone and flower that is also known as hyacinth. The flower is blue. The stone jacinth is a lustrous orange-yellow, orange-red, yellow, or yellow-brown; but when it's cut and polished it is blue-white. Brimstone is equated with sulfur. In its natural state, sulfur is yellow; when it's melted, it turns blood red. Sulphur produces a blue flame when it's burned. Red, orange, brown, blue, and yellow may be the colors of a new U.N. army or the new Muslim Caliphate army, even though the preferred color representing Islam is green. More likely, John is describing fire protective gear.

Using the 360-day calendar, "*a day, and a month, and a year*" equals 391 days. The year 2012 on our calendar is a leap year having one extra day. Counting backwards 391 days from the calculated date of Christ's return on September 16, 2012, the war of Armegeddon should commence on August 23, 2011.

Mount (*Har*) Meggido overlooks the Valley of Esdraelon. Mount Gilboa to its east overlooks the Valley of Jezreel. The armies will be gathered to these valleys, scripturally known as the "*valley of Jehoshaphat* (God's judgment)," where God plans to destroy them.

6th Seal: Jerusalem Will Be Divided Into Three Parts

And the great city was divided into three parts, and the cities of the nations fell: and great Babylon came in remembrance before God, to give to her the cup of the wine of the fierceness of his wrath. <u>And every island fled away, and the mountains were not found.</u> (Revelation 16:19-20)

"*Great city*" refers to Jerusalem here. One of the divisions will be the Mount of Olives (Zechariah 14:4) to make a way of escape for Jews out of the city. The description of islands and mountains vanishing may be the result of soil liquefaction in which soil suddenly goes from a solid state to a liquefied state, like quicksand. This occurred in the 1964 earthquakes in Japan and Alaska.

And I beheld when he had opened the sixth seal, and, see, there was a <u>great earthquake</u>; and the sun became black as sackcloth of hair, and the moon became as blood; And the stars of heaven fell to the earth, even as a fig tree casts her untimely figs, when she is shaken of a mighty wind. And the heaven departed as a *scroll when it is rolled together; <u>and every mountain and island were moved out of their places</u>. And the kings of the earth, and the great men, and the rich men, and the chief captains, and the mighty men, and every slave, and every free man, hid themselves in the dens and in the rocks of the mountains; And said to the mountains and rocks, Fall on us, and hide us from the face of him that sits on the throne, and from the wrath of the Lamb: For the great day of his wrath is come; and who shall be able to stand? (Revelation 6:12-17)*

*Enter into the rock, and hide you in the dust, for fear of the LORD, and for the glory of his majesty. The lofty looks of man shall be humbled, and the haughtiness of men shall be bowed down, and the LORD alone shall be exalted in **that day**. For the **day of the LORD** of hosts shall be on every one that is proud and lofty, and on every one that is lifted up; and he shall be brought low: . . . And the loftiness of man shall be bowed down, and the haughtiness of men shall be made low: and the LORD alone shall be exalted in **that day**. And the idols he shall utterly abolish. And they shall go into the holes of the rocks, and into the caves of the earth, for fear of the LORD, and for the glory of his majesty, when <u>he rises to shake terribly the earth</u>. In that day a man shall cast his idols of silver, and his idols of gold, which they made each one for himself to worship, to the moles and to the bats; To go into the clefts of the rocks, and into the tops of the ragged rocks, for fear of the LORD, and for the glory of his majesty, when <u>he rises to shake terribly the earth</u>. (Is. 2:10-21 edited)*

Just like Adam and Eve, sinners will seek in vain to hide from the LORD. The severity of the global "earth shake" just prior to Christ's return is unimaginable. No one will be able to stand physically but will all be brought to their hands and knees or faces, and they will have to acknowledge the Creator of Heaven and Earth and humble themselves before the majesty of His appearing.

Dark Sun and Moon

The heavens and earth are falling apart, and people cry out for a quick death and to be hidden from the coming Judge and His judgment. God will humble the wicked. The light from the sun, moon, and stars have been at two-thirds strength reaching the earth, and now they're getting dimmer. The sun and moon will appear dark to everyone on earth.

Behold, the day of the LORD comes, cruel both with wrath and fierce anger, to lay the land desolate: and he shall destroy the sinners thereof out of it. <u>For the stars of heaven and the constellations thereof shall not give their light: the sun shall be darkened in his going forth, and the moon shall not cause her light to shine</u>. And I will punish the world for their evil, and the wicked for their iniquity; and I will cause the arrogance of the proud to cease, and will lay low the haughtiness of the terrible. (Isaiah 13:9-11 to Babylon)

> *The earth shall quake before them; the heavens shall tremble: the sun and the moon shall be dark, and the stars shall withdraw their shining: And the LORD shall utter his voice before his army: for his camp is very great: for he is strong that executes his word: for the **day of the LORD** is great and very terrible; and who can abide it? Therefore also now, said the LORD, turn you even to me with all your heart, and with fasting, and with weeping, and with mourning: And rend your heart, and not your garments, and turn to the LORD your God: for he is gracious and merciful, slow to anger, and of great kindness, and repents him of the evil. . . . And I will show wonders in the heavens and in the earth, blood, and fire, and pillars of smoke. The sun shall be turned into darkness, and the moon into blood, before the great and terrible **day of the LORD** come. (Joel 2:10-13, 31 to Zion)*

Some lunar eclipses are called "blood moons". The longest central total eclipse for the next thousand years occurred on July, 16, 2000; it was dark red, but it was observed from the Pacific Ocean. Prophecies regarding the sun and moon to Israel must be observable from Israel. The last total eclipse of the moon observable from Israel was on February 21, 2008, and it had a slight red tinge; the next will be on December 21, 2010. The total solar eclipse of March 29, 2006 will be the only one visible from Jerusalem, Israel until 2021. Thus these prophecies are not likely to be the result of common eclipses. The darkening of the sun may be due to continued erratic sun spot activity and the ash of volcanic eruptions. Ash in the atmosphere would also block out starlight and color the moon.

Signs Immediately Before Christ's Second Coming:
(Voices, Lightning, Thunder, Hail, and a Great Earthquake)

> *And out of the throne proceeded lightning and thunder and voices: and there were seven lamps of fire burning before the throne, which are the seven Spirits of God. (Revelation 4:5)*

> *I have looked, and behold a candlestick all of gold, with a bowl on the top of it, and his seven lamps thereon, and seven pipes to the seven lamps, which are on the top thereof: . . . This is the word of the LORD to Zerubbabel, saying, Not by might, nor by power, but by my spirit, said the LORD of hosts. Who are you, O **great mountain**? before Zerubbabel you shall become a plain: and he shall bring forth the headstone thereof with shoutings, crying, Grace, grace to it. Moreover the word of the LORD came to me, saying, The hands of Zerubbabel have laid the foundation of this house; his hands shall also finish it; and you shall know that the LORD of hosts has sent me to you. For who has despised the day of small things? for they shall rejoice, and shall see the plummet in the hand of Zerubbabel with those seven; they are the eyes of the LORD, which run to and fro through the whole earth. (Zechariah 4:2-10)*

From the throne of God proceed lightning and thunder and voices. On the Day of the LORD everyone will experience a glimpse of God's majesty from His throne in heaven as His kingdom comes to be established upon the earth. The "*great mountain*" is the empire of Babylon, which is called the "*destroying mountain*" in Jeremiah 51:24-25. Christ's kingdom had "*small beginnings*" upon the earth, but Islam and the earth shall be leveled before Him, and He shall build His temple and kingdom on earth with Himself as the "*cornerstone*". Those of the seven churches of God throughout history will rejoice. The following events are in very quick succession.

7th Vial

And I saw another sign in heaven, great and marvelous, seven angels having the seven last plagues; for in them is filled up the wrath of God. . . . And the temple was filled with smoke from the glory of God, and from his power; and no man was able to enter into the temple, till the seven plagues of the seven angels were fulfilled. (Revelation 15:1, 8)

The seven 'last' is *eschatos* in Greek, meaning end of or final; from which we get the word eschatology. These seven vials of plagues upon Babylon must be fulfilled and concluded prior to the 7th trumpet. So the 7th vial precedes the 7th seal and trumpet.

And the seventh angel poured out his vial into the air; and there came a great voice out of the temple of heaven, from the throne, saying, It is done. And there were <u>voices, and thunders, and lightning; and there was a great earthquake,</u> such as was not since men were on the earth, so mighty an earthquake, and so great. And the great city was divided into three parts, and the cities of the nations fell: and great Babylon came in remembrance before God, to give to her the cup of the wine of the fierceness of his wrath. And every island fled away, and the mountains were not found. And there fell on men a <u>great hail</u> out of heaven, every stone about the weight of a talent: and men blasphemed God because of the plague of the hail; for the plague thereof was exceeding great. (Revelation 16:17-21)

7th Seal

And when he had opened the seventh seal, there was silence in heaven about the space of half an hour. . . .And another angel came and stood at the altar, having a golden censer; and there was given to him much incense, that he should offer it with the prayers of all saints on the golden altar which was before the throne. And the smoke of the incense, which came with the prayers of the saints, ascended up before God out of the angel's hand. And the angel took the censer, and filled it with fire of the altar, and cast it into the earth: and there were <u>voices, and thunder, and lightning, and an earthquake.</u> (Revelation 8:1-5 edited)

7th Trumpet: Third Woe

*There **should be time no longer**: But in the days of the voice of the seventh angel, when he shall begin to <u>sound</u>, the mystery of God should be **finished**, as he has declared to his servants the prophets. (Revelation 10:6d-7)*

"*Time no longer*" means no further delay. It is the same word (*teleo*) translated "*finished*" here and when Jesus cried from the cross (John 19:30). God's master plan comes to completion in King Jesus ruling and reigning the nations through the consummation of His wrath and judgment. The 7th trumpet, the last trumpet, that heralds the Day of the Lord as "*declared to his servants the prophets*":

And the LORD shall be seen over them, and his arrow shall go forth as the lightning: and the LORD God shall blow the <u>trumpet</u>. (Zechariah 9:14)

That day is a day of wrath, a day of trouble and distress, a day of devastation . . . A day of the <u>trumpet</u> and alarm . . . (Zephaniah 1:15-16 edited)

*The second woe is past; and, behold, the third woe comes quickly. And the seventh angel **sounded**; and there were great voices in heaven, saying, The kingdoms of this world are become the kingdoms of our Lord, and of his Christ; and he shall reign for ever and ever. And the four and twenty elders, which sat before God on their seats, fell on their faces, and worshipped God, Saying, We give you thanks, O LORD God Almighty, which are, and were, and are to come; because you have taken to you your great power, and have reigned. And the nations were angry, and your wrath is come, and the time of the dead, that they should be judged, and that you should give reward to your servants the prophets, and to the saints, and them that fear your name, small and great; and should destroy them which destroy the earth. And the temple of God was opened in heaven, and there was seen in his temple the ark of his testament: and there were <u>lightning, and voices, and thunder, and an earthquake, and great hail</u>. (Revelation 11:14-19)*

King Jesus Returns and Fights, and Reigns

The following passage is directed to Jerusalem, "*the city where David dwelled*" but prophetically called "*Ariel*" which means 'lion of God'. Thus it is a prophecy regarding when Jerusalem shall become the city of the "*Lion of the tribe of Judah*" who was called "*the son of David*". King Jesus will defeat all the nations who come against Israel.

Moreover the multitude of your strangers shall be like small dust, and the multitude of the terrible ones shall be as chaff that passes away: yes, it shall be at an instant suddenly. You shall be visited of the LORD of hosts <u>with thunder, and with earthquake, and great noise, with storm and tempest, and the flame of devouring</u>

> *fire. And the multitude of all the nations that fight against Ariel, even all that fight against her and her fortification, and that distress her, shall be as a dream of a night vision. . . . For the LORD has poured out on you the spirit of deep sleep, and has closed your eyes: <u>the prophets and your rulers, the seers has he covered. And the vision of all is become to you as the words of a book that is sealed</u>, . . . Woe to them that seek deep to hide their counsel from the LORD, and their works are in the dark, and they say, Who sees us? and who knows us? <u>Surely your turning of things upside down shall be esteemed as the potter's clay:</u> for shall the work say of him that made it, He made me not? or shall the thing framed say of him that framed it, He had no understanding? Is it not yet a very little while, and **Lebanon** shall be turned into a fruitful field, and the fruitful field shall be esteemed as a forest? And in that day shall the deaf hear the words of the book, and the eyes of the blind shall see out of obscurity, and out of darkness. The meek also shall increase their joy in the LORD, and the poor among men shall rejoice in the Holy One of Israel. <u>For the terrible one is brought to nothing, and the scorner is consumed, and all that watch for iniquity are cut off:</u> That make a man an offender for a word, and lay a snare for him that reproves in the gate, and turn aside the just for a thing of nothing. Therefore thus said the LORD, who redeemed Abraham, concerning the house of Jacob, Jacob shall not now be ashamed, neither shall his face now wax pale. But when he sees his children, the work of my hands, in the middle of him, they shall sanctify my name, and sanctify the Holy One of Jacob, and shall fear the God of Israel. They also that erred in spirit shall come to understanding, and they that murmured shall learn doctrine. (Isaiah 29:5-24 edited)*

Sadly, the Jewish rulers and prophets will not understand the prophecies regarding the end-times in which they live. They will focus more on the oral traditions of the elders (Matthew 15:1-20), the *Mishnah*, which caused them to be blinded to Christ's first coming. But God, the Potter (Isaiah 64:8), will use His vessels according to His own plans (Romans 9:20-28; Rev. 2:25-27). The restoration of Jewish Israel was also a restoration of Christian Lebanon (until the Shia Muslims took over). Christians began to understand end-times better only after Israel became a nation again, and began to look for the "*terrible one*" whom God will destroy. A person that "*reproves in the gate*" is a leader of the city. And the Jews shall also come to understand their place in prophecy. Israel's prime minister Netanyahu is going to have people come after him over trivial matters, and those within his government will try to overturn his plans.

> *Behold, the day of the LORD comes, and your spoil shall be divided in the middle of you. For I will gather all nations against Jerusalem to battle; and the city shall be taken, and the houses rifled, and the women ravished; and half of the city shall go forth into captivity, and the residue of the people shall not be cut off from the city. Then shall the LORD go forth, and fight against those nations, as when he fought in the day of battle. And his feet shall stand in that day on the mount of Olives, which*

*is before Jerusalem on the east, and the mount of Olives shall split in the middle thereof toward the east and toward the west, and there shall be a very great valley; and half of the mountain shall remove toward the north, and half of it toward the south. And you shall flee to the valley of the mountains; for the valley of the mountains shall reach to Azal: yes, you shall flee, like as you fled from before the earthquake in the days of Uzziah king of Judah: <u>and the LORD my God shall come, and all the saints with you</u>. And it shall come to pass in that day, that the light shall not be clear, nor dark: But it shall be one day which shall be known to the LORD, not day, nor night: but it shall come to pass, that at evening time it shall be light. . . . And the LORD shall be king over all the earth: in that day shall there be one LORD, and his name one. . . . And this shall be the **plague** with which the LORD will smite all the people that have fought against Jerusalem; **Their flesh shall consume away while they stand on their feet, and their eyes shall consume away in their holes, and their tongue shall consume away in their mouth.** And it shall come to pass in that day, that a great tumult from the LORD shall be among them; and they shall lay hold every one on the hand of his neighbor, and his hand shall rise up against the hand of his neighbor. And Judah also shall fight at Jerusalem; and the wealth of all the heathen round about shall be gathered together, gold, and silver, and apparel, in great abundance. And so shall be the **plague** of the horse, of the mule, of the camel, and of the ass, and of all the beasts that shall be in these tents, as this plague. (Zechariah 14:1-15 edited)*

The saints shall be resurrected and raptured and shall come with Jesus to Jerusalem to fight on behalf of Israel. Jesus will stand on the Mount of Olives, and an earthquake will split it so that Jews can escape the city safely. This "*plague*" is similar to the results of an atomic bomb, but God could use a different method, because the jihadists might not ever complete there "*mischievous device*".

Your hand shall find out all your enemies: your right hand shall find out those that hate you. You shall make them as a fiery oven in the time of your anger: the LORD shall swallow them up in his wrath, and the fire shall devour them. Their fruit shall you destroy from the earth, and their seed from among the children of men. For they intended evil against you: they imagined a <u>mischievous device</u>, which they are not able to perform. Therefore shall you make them turn their back, when you shall make ready your arrows on your strings against the face of them. (Psalms 21:8-12)

Order and Timing of Seals, Trumpets and Vials

John described these things in an orderly fashion. The first group of four of each object is a distinct grouping. With understanding their groupings and timings, the following order can be made.

Seal #1 (Conquering white horse - 9/11/01 to 09/16/2012)
Seal #2 (Red war horse of Islam; from 9/11/01 to 09/16/2012)
Seal #3 (Black horse of economic ruin; from Sept. 2008 to 09/16/2012)
Seal #4 (Pale horse of death; from 9/11/01 to 09/16/2012)
   Great Tribulation began 4/6/09 (counting backwards 1,260 days
   from calculated date of Christ's return on September 16, 2012)
Trumpets #1-4 (1/3 of world's trees, seas, and rivers are spoiled)
Vials #1-4 (all of Arabia's rivers and sea to blood; Muslims afflicted by sores and heat)
Vial #5 (Darkness/Pain) and Trumpet #5 ('Locusts' for 5 months; March 26, 2011)
Trumpet and Vial #6 (Armegeddon War 1 1/2 years; beginning August 23, 2011)
Seal #5 (Great Tribulation Martyrs during Armegeddon War)
Seal #6 (? 09/15/2012)
Vial #7 (09/16/2012)
Seals #7 (09/16/2012)
Trumpet #7 (09/16/2012)

Summary

Though there are seven each of the seals, trumpets and vials; the first group of four of each object is a distinct grouping. The 7 seals are global in their impact, with the first four seals before the Great Tribulation and the three remaining seals at the end. The 7 vials are poured out on Babylon (Islam) and those who worship the beast, while the 7 trumpets are experienced by the rest of the world. The first four trumpets and vials parallel each other as they make a distinction between those who worship the Beast of Islam, and those who do not, just as God made a distinction between the Egyptians and the Hebrews during the ten plagues. The trumpets and vials are not done in succession, but in tandem. The 7th seal, the 7th vial, and the 7th trumpet are almost simultaneous, culminating in King Jesus' return to reign and lead His army to victory.

The seven seals are opened by the "*Lamb who was slain*" who purchased the right to do so in preparation to retrieve His Bride. Israel became a nation again, and we have divided its land. The Lamb of God has determined it is time to redeem and judge the earth, and the first four seals wake up people to prepare for judgment (Joel 2 and Rev. 5). Al Qaeda demonstrated to the the world what damage it could do without nukes on 9/11/01 (white horse). By that act Muslim terrorists have "*removed peace from the earth*" and have continued killing (red horse). Exactly seven years later the US entered secret negotiations to divide Jerusalem, and a devastating hurricane and economic ruin (black horse) followed a few days later. Currently Islam constitutes one fourth of the world population, and has a majority in one fourth of the world's countries, where it exercises its power to kill through war and famine (pale horse).

God started the Great Tribulation clock with commands to angels and with the removal of the USA from world influence and interference in the middle-east. The destruction of the great city Babylon (Mecca with its port, Jeddeh) will likely occur within a year of its angelic announcement. With the Saudis out of the way, Iran (threatening blockade of the Straits of Hormuz or nuclear war) will then require all people to wear a mark of allegiance to Islam on their arm or forehead in order to buy or sell (international monetary standard of the 'gold dinar'). Muslims will behead those who refuse the mark. The "*mark of the beast*" may be a simple crescent moon tattoo or a computer chip placed beneath the skin. It may be the name of the Muslim Mahdi or possibly the number of his name somehow equaling 666. But whatever it is, don't take it! Those who do will experience God's wrath.

The trumpets and vials are concurrent with each other. The 1st trumpet burns all grass and a third of the trees; which could occur anytime before March 2011 along with the next three trumpets: 2nd, 1/3 of seas to blood and 1/3 of ships destroyed; 3rd, 1/3 of rivers and fountains made bitter and undrinkable; and 4th, 1/3 of sunlight and star/moonlight doesn't reach earth. Except for all our grass burnt, America might be in the fortunate 2/3 which isn't effected until the 4th trumpet. The 4th trumpet will likely be close to March 2011, because the planet won't last long on 2/3 light. [see graphic in Appendix]

First Four Trumpets (upon world)	First Four Vials (upon Babylon)
1st All grass burnt; 1/3 trees	1st Sores upon worshipers of Beast
2nd 1/3 sea, sea-life & ships	2nd Sea to blood; all sea-life dies
3rd 1/3 rivers; & bitter waters	3rd All rivers and fountains to blood
4th 1/3 of sun, moon & stars	4th Use sun to scorch men with fire

3/26/2011-8/23/2011 (prelude to Armegeddon)

TRUMPETS	VIALS
5th Chemical war with helicopters	5th Painful sores & darkness

8/23/2011-9/16/2012 (Armegeddon War)

6th Chemical/Fire tanks	[5th seal during Armegeddon War]
	6th Dry Euphrates for Shia armies

6th seal
9/16/2012 (Day of the LORD) 7th Seal and Vial and Trumpet

The 6th seal is most likely broken within a few hours of the day of the Lord. The 7th vial will be poured out over Babylon (Islam) completing God's wrath upon them. Then the 7th seal is broken and the 7th trumpet sounds over the world as voices, lightning, thunder, hail, and a great earthquake are experienced around the globe. The sun will be dark and the moon look like blood, but the brightness of Christ's coming will illuminate the world. Jesus will bring the resurrected saints with Him and collect His living saints en route to Jerusalem where we will fight for Israel and be victorious over the Antichrist and all nations gathered against Israel.

Awake, Bride

Day of the LORD

*The sun shall be turned into darkness,
and the moon into blood,
before the great and terrible
day of the LORD come. (Joel 2:31)*

From calculations in Daniel, Messiah Yeshua will most likely return in 2012. According to the feasts yet to be fulfilled, Hebrew wedding traditions, and Jesus' teaching on His coming in Matthew 24 and 25, He will return at midnight on Rosh Hashanah for His Bride. Rosh Hashanah, Tishri 1, will be Sunday, September 16th in 2012. Traditionally, the feast of trumpets is celebrated for two days which are considered one long day, so the "Day of the LORD" will continue until dusk on September 18, 2012.

The Day of the LORD is referred to by many other names: "The Day of Vengeance of our God", "The Day of God's Wrath", "The Day of God's Judgment", "The Great and Dreadful Day", and more. The Day of the LORD is referred to so often, it is also abbreviated to just "That Day" or "The Day". It is the climax of human history and God's prophecies. It is the day when King Jesus returns to earth with His resurrected saints, snatches His Bride still alive, and conquers those who have attacked Israel, judging and destroying the wicked.

Possible Day of the LORD Time-Line

Dusk — Silence in heaven for half an hour
Jesus is coronated with "many crowns" in heaven.
Voices, Lightnings, Thunders, and Great Hail and an Earthquake on earth

Midnight — *"The Brightness of His Coming"* as *"Lightning from the east to the west"*
Resurrection and Rapture of Saints *"in the twinkling of an eye"*
Jesus, "*the Breaker*", destroys those attacking "*Bozrah*" (Petra)

Dawn — Jesus stands on the Mount of Olives, splitting it in two so Jews can escape.
Jesus and His saints destroy the wicked in Jerusalem.

Noon — Saints ride with Jesus to battle the wicked at Armegeddon (Rev. 19:17) and the Antichrist and his armies are defeated and the fowls feast on their flesh.

Dusk — The dead are judged (Rev. 11:18)

Awake, Bride

Midnight   "*At evening time it shall be light.*" (Zech. 14:7)

Dawn   Antichrist and False Prophet are cast into the Lake of Fire.
Satan is bound for 1,000 years.

Noon   Jesus takes His Beloved to the Bridal chamber He made, the New Jerusalem, while the earth is destroyed by fire.

Dusk   The Wedding ceremony

These are estimations. So much more is accomplished during the Day of the LORD that entire books could be written, but this chapter will focus on the highlights in Revelation 19. [Revelation 20 opens with Satan being bound.]

Jesus' Coronation

The Feast of Trumpets is a memorial of the day Joseph ascended to rule Egypt (the world power of that time). The Hebrews calculated a king's reign from this feast on Tishri 1. Jesus was born on this day in 3 BC with shofars heralding the King of the Jews, and in 2012 He will return to fulfill His destiny as King of kings and Lord of lords.

There will be awe and silence in heaven for thirty minutes, as all of heaven contemplates the coming events. The litany of "*holy, holy, holy*" from the seraphim will cease; the harps be stilled. Father God will officially bestow upon His Son the crowns of all the kingdoms of the earth, accompanied by many voices. These are the voices and thunder heard on earth as the temple in heaven is opened. "*And the temple of God was opened in heaven, and there was seen in his temple the ark of his testament: and there were lightning, and voices, and thunder, and an earthquake, and great hail*" (Revelation 11:19).

> *And I heard as it were the voice of a great multitude, and as the voice of many waters, and as the voice of mighty thunder, saying, Alleluia: for the Lord God omnipotent reigns. Let us be glad and rejoice, and give honor to him: for the marriage of the Lamb is come . . . His eyes were as a flame of fire, and on his head were many crowns; and he had a name written, that no man knew, but he himself.* (Revelation 19:6-7, 12)

This is the day King Jesus makes Himself known to the whole earth as King of kings and LORD of Lords. He is ready to judge the nations. As the few remaining faithful Jews on earth blow their shofars on Rosh Hashanah, 2012 in hope the King of the Jews will appear to save them . . . He will!

Because the sun and moon will no longer be producing sufficient light at that time, Jesus will be the light with the "*brightness of His coming*". The New Jerusalem will also be a source of light in the sky.

And it shall come to pass in that day, that the light shall not be clear, nor dark: But it shall be one day which shall be known to the LORD, not day, nor night: but it shall come to pass, that <u>at evening time it shall be light</u>. (Zechariah 14:6-7)

But the state of the sky prior to Christ's coming is void of light in the midst of noises.

Dark, Gloomy, and Full of Despair

*The great day of the LORD is near, it is near, and hastens greatly, even the <u>voice</u> of the day of the LORD: <u>the mighty man shall cry there bitterly. That day is a day of wrath, a day of trouble and distress, a day of devastation and desolation, a day of darkness and gloominess, a day of clouds and thick darkness</u>, A day of the **trumpet** and alarm against the fenced cities, and against the high towers. And I will bring distress on men, that they shall walk like blind men, because they have sinned against the LORD: and their blood shall be poured out as dust, and their flesh as the dung. Neither their silver nor their gold shall be able to deliver them in the day of the LORD's wrath; but the whole land shall be devoured by the **fire** of his jealousy: for he shall make even a speedy riddance of all them that dwell in the land. (Zephaniah 1:14-18)*

The burden of Babylon, which Isaiah the son of Amoz did see. Lift you up a banner on the high mountain, exalt the voice to them, shake the hand, that they may go into the gates of the nobles. I have commanded my sanctified ones, I have also called my mighty ones for my anger, even them that rejoice in my highness. <u>The noise of a multitude in the mountains, like as of a great people; a tumultuous noise of the kingdoms of nations gathered together: the LORD of hosts musters the host of the battle. They come from a far country, from the end of heaven, even the LORD, and the weapons of his indignation, to destroy the whole land. Howl you; for the day of the LORD is at hand; it shall come as a destruction from the Almighty</u>. Therefore shall all hands be faint, and every man's heart shall melt: And they shall be afraid: pangs and sorrows shall take hold of them; they shall be in pain as a woman that travails: they shall be amazed one at another; their faces shall be as flames. Behold, the day of the LORD comes, cruel both with wrath and fierce anger, to lay the land desolate: and <u>he shall destroy the sinners thereof out of it. For the stars of heaven and the constellations thereof shall not give their light: the sun shall be darkened in his going forth, and the moon shall not cause her light to shine</u>. And I will punish the world for their evil, and the wicked for their iniquity; and I will cause the arrogance of the proud to cease, and will lay low the haughtiness of the terrible. I will make a man more precious than fine gold; even a man than the golden wedge of Ophir. Therefore <u>I will shake the heavens</u>, and the earth shall remove out of her place, in the wrath of the LORD of hosts, and in the day of his fierce anger. (Isaiah 13:1-13)

Awake, Bride

There is ample reason for the great despair because King Jesus has come to destroy the wicked. It is the end of the world, and God will have His vengeance upon those who refused to submit to Him. They loved the darkness and abhorred the light, and they will be cast into "*outer darkness*".

Black Sun, Red Moon, and Fallen Stars

*And there shall <u>be signs in the sun, and in the moon, and in the stars</u>; and on the earth **distress of nations, with perplexity**; the sea and the waves roaring; **Men's hearts failing them for fear, and for looking after those things which are coming on the earth:** for <u>the powers of heaven shall be shaken</u>. And then shall they see the Son of man coming in a cloud with power and great glory. And when these things begin to come to pass, then look up, and lift up your heads; for your redemption draws near. . . . And take heed to yourselves, lest at any time your hearts be overcharged with surfeiting, and drunkenness, and cares of this life, and so that day come on you unawares. For as a snare shall it come on all them that dwell on the face of the whole earth. (Luke 21:25-35 edited)*

*And I beheld when he had opened the sixth seal, and, see, there was a great earthquake; and <u>the sun became black as sackcloth of hair, and the moon became as blood; And the stars of heaven fell to the earth</u>, even as a fig tree casts her untimely figs, when she is shaken of a mighty wind. And the heaven departed as a scroll when it is rolled together; and every mountain and island were moved out of their places. And the kings of the earth, and the great men, and the rich men, and the chief captains, and the mighty men, and every slave, and every free man, **hid themselves in the dens and in the rocks of the mountains**; And said to the <u>mountains and rocks, Fall on us, and hide us from the face of him that sits on the throne, and from the wrath of the Lamb: For the great day of his wrath is come;</u> and who shall be able to stand? (Revelation 6:12-17)*

Isaiah described the dark sun upon its *"going forth"* (Is. 13:10), so it is not an eclipse. Scientists watched a car-sized asteroid explode in earth's atmosphere on March 26, 2009, and then they tracked and recovered pieces of it in Sudan. Such events will become more commonplace during the Great Tribulation, as will an increase in "natural disasters". Like Adam and Eve did after they sinned, people will attempt to hide themselves from God.

Sinners Hide in the Rocks from Jesus' Wrath

<u>Enter into the rock, and hide you in the dust, for fear of the LORD, and for the glory of his majesty.</u> The lofty looks of man shall be humbled, and the haughtiness of men shall be bowed down, and the LORD alone shall be exalted in that day. For the day of the LORD of hosts shall be on every one that is proud and lofty, and on every one that is lifted up; and he shall be brought low: And on all the cedars of Lebanon,

that are high and lifted up, and on all the oaks of Bashan, And on all the high mountains, and on all the hills that are lifted up, And on every high tower, and on every fenced wall, And on all the ships of Tarshish, and on all pleasant pictures. And the loftiness of man shall be bowed down, and the haughtiness of men shall be made low: and the LORD alone shall be exalted in that day. And the idols he shall utterly abolish. <u>And they shall go into the holes of the rocks, and into the caves of the earth, for fear of the LORD, and for the glory of his majesty, when he rises to shake terribly the earth.</u> In that day a man shall cast his idols of silver, and his idols of gold, which they made each one for himself to worship, to the moles and to the bats; <u>To go into the clefts of the rocks, and into the tops of the ragged rocks, for fear of the LORD, and for the glory of his majesty, when he rises to shake terribly the earth.</u> Cease you from man, whose breath is in his nostrils: for wherein is he to be accounted of? (Isaiah 2:10-22)

During earthquakes most people don't run into caves. It is a vain effort to try to escape the judgment of the LORD. Even pleading for the rocks to end life quickly won't keep anyone from appearing before God's judgment.

Great Earthquakes at Earth's Displacement

Therefore <u>I will shake the heavens, and the earth shall remove out of her place</u>, in the wrath of the LORD of hosts, and in the day of his fierce anger. (Isaiah 13:13)

Whether God sovereignly moves the earth out of its orbit or uses an asteroid flyby or collision to do it, the heavens and earth will be ripped apart; people crying out for a quick death from the falling rocks will seek to be hidden from the coming Judge and judgment.

*<u>The earth shall quake before them</u>; the heavens shall tremble: the **sun** and the **moon** shall be dark, and the stars shall withdraw their shining. (Joel 2:10)*

*And I beheld when he had opened the sixth seal, and, see, there was a <u>great earthquake</u>; and the **sun** became black as sackcloth of hair, and the **moon** became as blood; And the stars of heaven fell to the earth, even as a fig tree casts her untimely figs, when she is shaken of a mighty wind. <u>And the heaven departed as a scroll when it is rolled together; and every mountain and island were moved out of their places.</u> (Revelation 6:12-14)*

The 6th seal, and the 7th vial and trumpet all speak of a great earthquake preceding Christ's return.

The Resurrection and Rapture . . .

The resurrection and rapture are concurrent with a great earthquake, a great voice, a shout, lightning, clouds, a trumpet, and great hail. There has never been, nor will ever be again, a day like it. "*Remember Lot's wife*," and don't longing look back at your old life.

...Are Concurrent with a Great Earthquake

*And they heard a **great voice** from heaven saying to them, <u>Come up here. And they ascended up to heaven in a **cloud**</u>; and their enemies beheld them. <u>And the same hour was there a great **earthquake**</u>, and the tenth part of the city fell, and in the earthquake were slain of men seven thousand: and the remnant were affrighted, and gave glory to the God of heaven. The second woe is past; and, behold, the third woe comes quickly. <u>And **the seventh angel sounded**</u>; and there were great voices in heaven, saying, <u>The kingdoms of this world are become the kingdoms of our Lord, and of his Christ; and he shall reign for ever and ever.</u> And the four and twenty elders, which sat before God on their seats, fell on their faces, and worshipped God, Saying, We give you thanks, O LORD God Almighty, which are, and were, and are to come; because you have taken to you your great power, and have reigned. <u>And the nations were angry, and your wrath is come, and the time of the dead, that they should be judged, and that you should give reward to your servants the prophets, and to the saints, and them that fear your name</u>, small and great; and should destroy them which destroy the earth. And the temple of God was opened in heaven, and there was seen in his temple the ark of his testament: and there were <u>lightning, and voices, and thunder, and an earthquake, and great hail</u>. (Revelation 11:12-19)*

The two witnesses are the Jewish and Gentile believers in Messiah Jesus. As noted in the chapter on "Resurrections and Rapture", believers will be "*caught up*" to Jesus in the "*clouds*". In that same moment ("*hour*" can also mean instant) as the earthquake is the 7th trumpet blown and the kingdoms come under the control of King Jesus and His wrath.

...Are Concurrent with a Shout

*God is gone up with a **shout**, the LORD with the sound of a **trumpet**. Sing praises to God, sing praises: sing praises to our King, sing praises. (Psalm 47:5-6)*

*Therefore prophesy you against them all these words, and say to them, <u>The LORD shall **roar** from on high, and utter his **voice** from his holy habitation; he shall mightily **roar** on his habitation; he shall give a **shout**, as they that tread the grapes, against all the inhabitants of the earth. A noise shall come even to the ends of the earth; for the LORD has a controversy with the nations, he will plead with all flesh; he will give them that are wicked to the sword, said the LORD.</u> Thus said the LORD of hosts, Behold, evil shall go forth from nation to nation, and a great whirlwind shall be raised up from the coasts of the earth. And the slain of the LORD shall be at that day from one end of the earth even to the other end of the earth: they shall not be lamented, neither gathered, nor buried; they shall be dung on the ground. (Jeremiah 25:30-33)*

This is a warrior's shout of battle, a victorious shout of triumph. If the Hebrews could not endure to hear God's voice when He was lovingly proclaiming His commandments to them (Hebrews 12:18-29), how much more will the shout of Christ at His return cause His enemies to fear. Note the consistent theme of God's judgment and destruction of evil.

. . . Are Concurrent with Lightning

*And the LORD shall be seen over them, and his arrow shall go forth as the **lightning**: and the LORD God shall blow the **trumpet**, and shall go with whirlwinds of the south. (Zechariah 9:14)*

In Clarke's commentary on the LORD "*over them*", he wrote, God was "*refreshing them, as the cloud did the camp in the wilderness.*" This is similar to "*times of refreshing shall come from the presence of the Lord*" (Acts 3:19b). Lightning and a trumpet blown are clear signs in the 6th seal and 7th vial and trumpet.

*For as the **lightning**, that lightens out of the one part under heaven, shines to the other part under heaven; so shall also the Son of man be in his day. . . . In that day, he which shall be on the housetop, and his stuff in the house, let him not come down to take it away: and he that is in the field, let him likewise not return back. Remember Lot's wife. Whoever shall seek to save his life shall lose it; and whoever shall lose his life shall preserve it. I tell you, in that night there shall be two men in one bed; the one shall be taken, and the other shall be left. Two women shall be grinding together; the one shall be taken, and the other left. (Luke 17:24-35 edited)*

. . . Are Concurrent with Clouds and a Trumpet

*And when he had spoken these things, while they beheld, he was taken up; and a **cloud** received him out of their sight. And while they looked steadfastly toward heaven as he went up, behold, two men stood by them in white apparel; Which also said, You men of Galilee, why stand you gazing up into heaven? this same Jesus, which is taken up from you into heaven, shall so come in like manner as you have seen him go into heaven. (Acts 1:9-11)*

*Immediately after the tribulation of those days shall the sun be darkened, and the moon shall not give her light, and the stars shall fall from heaven, and the powers of the heavens shall be shaken: And then shall appear the sign of the Son of man in heaven: and then shall all the tribes of the earth mourn, and they shall see the Son of man coming in the **clouds** of heaven with power and great glory. And he shall send his angels with a great sound of a **trumpet**, and they shall gather together his elect from the four winds, from one end of heaven to the other. (Matthew 24:29-31)*

*Behold, I show you a mystery; We shall not all sleep, but we shall all be changed, In a moment, in the twinkling of an eye, at the last trump: for the **trumpet** shall sound, <u>and the dead shall be raised incorruptible, and we shall be changed</u>. For this corruptible must put on incorruption, and this mortal must put on immortality. (I Corinthians 15:51-53)*

*For if we believe that Jesus died and rose again, even so them also which sleep in Jesus will God bring with him. For this we say to you by the word of the Lord, that we which are alive and remain to the coming of the Lord shall not prevent them which are asleep. For the Lord himself shall descend from heaven with a shout, with the voice of the archangel, and with the **trump** of God: <u>and the dead in Christ shall rise first: Then we which are alive and remain shall be caught up together with them in the **clouds**, to meet the Lord in the air: and so shall we ever be with the Lord</u>. Why comfort one another with these words. (1 Thessalonians 4:14-18)*

This is the 7th trumpet being blown after the 7th vial poured and the 7th seal opened.

. . . Are Concurrent with Great Hail

*<u>Behold, I come as a thief</u>. Blessed is he that watches, and keeps his garments, lest he walk naked, and they see his shame. And he gathered them together into a place called in the Hebrew tongue Armageddon. And the seventh angel poured out his vial into the air; and there came a great voice out of the temple of heaven, from the throne, saying, <u>It is done</u>. And there were <u>voices, and thunders, and lightning; and there was a great earthquake</u>, such as was not since men were on the earth, so mighty an **earthquake**, and so great. And the great city was divided into three parts, and the cities of the nations fell: and great Babylon came in remembrance before God, to give to her the cup of the wine of the fierceness of his wrath. And every island fled away, and the mountains were not found. And there fell on men a **great hail** out of heaven, every stone about the weight of a talent: and men blasphemed God because of the **plague of the hail**; for the plague thereof was exceeding great. (Revelation 16:15-21)*

Notice how all these things are happening simultaneously. There are voices and thunders and lightning. The earth quakes so violently that cities are leveled and broken apart, and islands and mountains vanish. The last plague (hail) falls upon the lands of Babylon (Islam). Jesus returns to earth for His Bride "*as a thief*" and defeats those gathered at Armageddon.

"*It is done*" is *ginomai* in Greek, meaning to do with 'generations', but which is also translated "*married*" in Romans 7:3-4. (When Jesus says, "*It is finished*" in John 19:30 and Rev. 10:7, it is *teleo*, which means 'completed'.) After the 7th vial and trumpet, Father God pronounces us "Man and Wife" and sends His Son to fetch His Bride.

Let us be glad and rejoice, and give honor to him: <u>for the marriage of the Lamb is come, and his wife has made herself ready</u>. And to her was granted that she should be arrayed in fine linen, clean and white: for the fine linen is the righteousness of saints. And he said to me, Write, Blessed are they which are called to the marriage supper of the Lamb. And he said to me, These are the true sayings of God. (Revelation 19:7-9)

Christ's Bride has "*made herself ready*" by being "*sincere and without offense till the day of Christ. Being filled with the fruits of righteousness*" (Philippians 1:10b-11a). She is prepared for His coming. God will dress us all in the white righteousness Christ has imparted to us.

. . . As a Thief, so Watch

Watch *therefore: for you know not what hour your Lord does come. But know this, that if the manager of the house had known in what watch the **thief** would come, he would have watched, and would not have suffered his house to be broken up. Therefore be you also ready: for in such an hour as you think not the Son of man comes. (Matthew 42-44)*

*But of the times and the seasons, brothers, you have no need that I write to you. For yourselves know perfectly that the day of the Lord so comes as a **thief** in the night. For when they shall say, Peace and safety; then <u>sudden destruction</u> comes on them, as travail on a woman with child; and <u>they shall not escape</u>. But you, brothers, are not in darkness, that that day should overtake you as a **thief**. You are all the children of light, and the children of the day: we are not of the night, nor of darkness. Therefore let us not sleep, as do others; but let us **watch** and be sober. (1 Thessalonians 5:1-4)*

*But the day of the Lord will come as a **thief** in the night; in the which <u>the heavens shall pass away with a great noise</u>, and the elements shall melt with fervent heat, the earth also and the works that are therein shall be burned up. Seeing then that all these things shall be dissolved, what manner of persons ought you to be in all holy conversation and godliness, **Looking for** and hastening to the coming of the day of God, wherein the heavens being on fire shall be dissolved, and the elements shall melt with fervent heat? (2 Peter 3:10-12)*

Notice the "*Thief*" coming for His Bride is accompanied with a great noise and the the heavens dissolving with heat, and the destruction of the wicked. King Jesus makes us His Warrior Queen, and immediately begins to take care of business. The resurrection and rapture are important, but so is the deliverance of the Hebrew people and Jerusalem on the Day of the LORD.

The Breaker at "Bozrah"

Who is this that comes from Edom, with <u>dyed garments</u> from Bozrah? this that is glorious in his apparel, traveling in the greatness of his strength? I that speak in righteousness, mighty to save. Why are you <u>red in your apparel</u>, and your garments like him that treads in the winefat? I have trodden the wine press alone; and of the people there was none with me: for I will tread them in my anger, and trample them in my fury; and <u>their blood shall be sprinkled on my garments, and I will stain all my raiment</u>. **For the day of vengeance is in my heart, and the year of my redeemed is come.** *And I looked, and there was none to help; and I wondered that there was none to uphold: therefore my own arm brought salvation to me; and my fury, it upheld me. And I will tread down the people in my anger, and make them drunk in my fury, and I will bring down their strength to the earth. I will mention the loving kindnesses of the LORD, and the praises of the LORD, according to all that the LORD has bestowed on us, and the great goodness toward the house of Israel, which he has bestowed on them according to his mercies, and according to the multitude of his loving kindnesses. For he said, Surely they are my people, children that will not lie: so he was their Savior. In all their affliction he was afflicted, and the angel of his presence saved them: in his love and in his pity he redeemed them; and he bore them, and carried them all the days of old. (Isaiah 63:1-9)*

Edom is now located in the land of Jordan. "*Bozrah*" means 'sheepfold', and it is likely the place of safety a Jewish remnant occupies during the Great Tribulation. It may be that others also sought refuge with the Jews (Rev. 6:15-17). The enemies of the Jews have found their hiding place and begin their attack when Jesus shows up and slaughters them.

I will surely assemble, O Jacob, all of you; I will surely gather the remnant of Israel; I will put them together as the sheep of Bozrah, as the flock in the middle of their fold: they shall make great noise by reason of the multitude of men. <u>The breaker</u> is come up before them: they have broken up, and have passed through the gate, and are gone out by it: and their king shall pass before them, and the LORD on the head of them. (Micah 2:12-13)

"*Bozrah*" is most likely Petra. From Jerusalem to Petra is about 37 miles. Petra is like a sheepfold in that it has a narrow (10-20 ft wide and a mile long) approach with high cliffs (seen in "Indiana Jones and the Last Crusade") and is easily defended. Its engineers included rock-hewn gutters which caught rainwater and deposited it into cisterns. This, plus its springs, give Petra enough fresh water to accommodate 100,000 people.

*Come near, you nations, to hear; and listen, you people: let the earth hear, and all that is therein; the world, and all things that come forth of it. For the **indignation** of the LORD is on <u>all nations, and his fury on all their armies: he has utterly destroyed them, he has delivered them to the slaughter.</u> Their slain also shall be* *cast out, and their stink shall come up out of their carcasses, and the mountains shall be melted with their blood. And all <u>the host of heaven shall be dissolved, and the heavens shall be rolled together as a scroll</u>: and all their host shall fall down, as the leaf falls off from the vine, and as a falling fig from the fig tree. For my sword shall be bathed in heaven: behold, it shall come down on Idumea, and on the people of my curse, to judgment. <u>The sword of the LORD is filled with blood</u>, it is made fat with fatness, and with the blood of lambs and goats, with the fat of the kidneys of rams: for the LORD has a sacrifice in Bozrah, and a great slaughter in the land of Idumea. And the unicorns shall come down with them, and the bullocks with the bulls; and their land shall be soaked with blood, and their dust made fat with fatness. For it is the day of the LORD's **vengeance**, and the **year of recompenses for the controversy of Zion.** And the streams thereof shall be turned into pitch, and the dust thereof into brimstone, and the land thereof shall become burning pitch. It shall not be quenched night nor day; the smoke thereof shall go up for ever: from generation to generation it shall lie waste; none shall pass through it for ever and ever. (Isaiah 34:1-10)*

Surrounding the Dead Sea are pits of pitch. Edom's burning pitch will be a reminder upon the new Earth. Notice Christ's slaughter in Bozrah is accompanied by the skies being dissolved. This one battle Jesus does alone; it's personal. Messiah Jesus is their Deliverer. In the upcoming battle, Christ's Bride joins Him; the immortal saints, will not be wounded.

Bride and Bridegroom in Battle

*Blow you the **trumpet** in Zion, and sound an alarm in my holy mountain: let all the inhabitants of the land <u>tremble: for the day of the LORD comes</u>, for it is near at hand; <u>A day of darkness and of gloominess, a day of clouds and of thick darkness</u>, as the morning spread on the mountains: a great people ['am] and a strong; there has not been ever the like, neither shall be any more after it, even to the years of many generations. A **fire** devours before them; and behind them a flame burns: the land is as the garden of Eden before them, and behind them a desolate wilderness; yes, and <u>nothing shall escape</u> them. The appearance of them is as the appearance of horses; and as horsemen, so shall they run. Like the noise of chariots on the tops of mountains shall they leap, like the noise of a flame of fire that devours the stubble, as **a strong people set in battle array**. Before their face <u>the people shall be much pained: all faces shall gather blackness</u>. They shall run like mighty men; they shall climb the wall like men of war; and they shall march every one on his ways, and they shall not break their ranks: Neither shall one thrust another; they shall walk every one in his path: and **when they fall on the sword, they shall not be wounded.** They shall run to and fro in the city; they shall run on the wall, they shall climb up on the houses; they shall enter in at the windows like a thief. <u>The earth shall quake before them; the heavens shall tremble: the sun and the moon shall be dark, and the</u>*

> *stars shall withdraw their shining: And the LORD shall utter his voice before **his army**: for his camp is very great: **for he is strong that executes his word**: for the day of the LORD is great and very terrible; and who can abide it? . . . Blow the trumpet in Zion, sanctify a fast, call a solemn assembly: Gather the people, sanctify the congregation, assemble the elders, gather the children, and those that suck the breasts: let the bridegroom go forth of his chamber, and the **bride** out of her closet. (Joel 2:1-16 edited with addition)*

Though *'am* is translate 'people' over a thousand times, it is once made reference to the conies (rabbits) as 'folk', and so commentators wrote that this passage was about locusts. It does have similarities to John's description of locusts which plague men five months.

> *For, behold, the day comes, that shall burn as an oven; and all the proud, yes, and all that do wickedly, shall be stubble: and the day that comes shall **burn** them up, said the LORD of hosts, that it shall leave them neither root nor branch. But to you that fear my name shall the Sun of righteousness arise with healing in his wings; and you shall go forth, and grow up as calves of the stall. And **you shall tread down the wicked**; for they shall be ashes under the soles of your feet in the day that I shall do this, said the LORD of hosts. (Malachi 3:1-3)*

Those preparing for marriage are called to sanctification, fasting, and the battle. The immortal believers, Christ's Bride, will have strength and exuberance that defies gravity. There is a combination of battle and burning which will take place upon the wicked.

Jesus Stands on Mount of Olives

> *Behold, the day of the LORD comes, and your spoil shall be divided in the middle of you. For I will gather all nations against Jerusalem to battle; and the city shall be taken, and the houses rifled, and the women ravished; and half of the city shall go forth into captivity, and the residue of the people shall not be cut off from the city. Then shall the LORD go forth, and fight against those nations, as when he fought in the day of battle. And his feet shall stand in that day on the mount of Olives, which is before Jerusalem on the east, and the mount of Olives shall split in the middle thereof toward the east and toward the west, and there shall be a very great valley; and half of the mountain shall remove toward the north, and half of it toward the south. And you shall flee to the valley of the mountains; for the valley of the mountains shall reach to Azal: yes, you shall flee, like as you fled from before the **earthquake** in the days of **Uzziah** king of Judah: and the LORD my God shall come, and all the saints with you. And it shall come to pass in that day, that the light shall not be clear, nor dark: But it shall be one day which shall be known to the LORD, not day, nor night: but it shall come to pass, that at evening time it shall be light. (Zechariah 14:1-7)*

*The words of Amos, who was among the herdsmen of Tekoa, which he saw concerning Israel in the days of **Uzziah** king of Judah, and in the days of Jeroboam the son of Joash king of Israel, two years before the **earthquake**. (Amos 1:1-2)*

Amos wrote about this earthquake in 783 BC, so the earthquake was in 781 BC. Isaiah also wrote about the earthquake during king Uzziah's reign (Isaiah 5:25). There are adjoining east-west streets running from the Mount of Olives to Azal, Rub'a el-Adawiya and Al Shaykh. The distance to Azal from the mount of Olives is just a couple miles, but it will link people to an escape route out of Jerusalem. The saints may join Jesus in Jerusalem to battle the enemy forces there.

Jews Acknowledge Their Messiah

The burden of the word of the LORD for Israel, said the LORD, which stretches forth the heavens, and lays the foundation of the earth, and forms the spirit of man within him. Behold, I will make Jerusalem a cup of trembling to all the people round about, when they shall be in the siege both against Judah and against Jerusalem. <u>And in that day will I make Jerusalem a burdensome stone for all people: all that burden themselves with it shall be cut in pieces, though all the people of the earth be gathered together against it.</u> In that day, said the LORD, I will smite every horse with astonishment, and his rider with madness: and I will open my eyes on the house of Judah, and will smite every horse of the people with blindness. And the governors of Judah shall say in their heart, The inhabitants of Jerusalem shall be my strength in the LORD of hosts their God. In that day will I make the governors of Judah like an hearth of fire among the wood, and like a torch of fire in a sheaf; and they shall devour all the people round about, on the right hand and on the left: and Jerusalem shall be inhabited again in her own place, even in Jerusalem. <u>The LORD also shall save the tents of Judah first</u>, that the glory of the house of David and the glory of the inhabitants of Jerusalem do not magnify themselves against Judah. <u>In that day shall the LORD defend the inhabitants of Jerusalem; and he that is feeble among them at that day shall be as David;</u> and the house of David shall be as God, as the angel of the LORD before them. And it shall come to pass <u>in that day, that I will seek to destroy all the nations that come against Jerusalem. And I will pour on the house of David, and on the inhabitants of Jerusalem, the spirit of grace and of supplications</u>: and **they shall look on me whom they have pierced, and they shall mourn for him, as one mourns for his only son**, *and shall be in bitterness for him, as one that is in bitterness for his firstborn. In that day shall there be a great mourning in Jerusalem, as the mourning of Hadadrimmon in the valley of Megiddon. (Zechariah 12:1-11)*

The original mourning was for King Josiah who was killed trying to keep Neco, pharaoh of Egypt, from going through his land to attack a city in Syria (2 Chron. 35:20-27).

Syria and Egypt were constantly cutting through this trade route of Israel to war with each other. King Josiah died trying to stop it, as many before him had.

> "For five millennia, the city of Megiddo stood at one of the most important junctions in the ancient Near East, the Nahal Iron Pass. This pass was the only means of traversing the Carmel-Gilboa mountain range on the road from Damascus to Egypt. By controlling this route, Megiddo commanded the course of trade and the march of armies in the Holy Land. Excavations suggest the city was repeatedly devastated by some large force." (Ellen Licking, *Stanford Report Online*, 11/12/97)

> *But <u>Israel shall be saved in the LORD with an everlasting salvation</u>: you shall not be ashamed nor confounded world without end. For thus said the LORD that created the heavens; God himself that formed the earth and made it; he has established it, he created it not in vain, he formed it to be inhabited: I am the LORD; and there is none else. I have not spoken in secret, in a dark place of the earth: I said not to the seed of Jacob, Seek you me in vain: I the LORD speak righteousness, I declare things that are right. Assemble yourselves and come; draw near together, <u>you that are escaped of the nations</u>: they have no knowledge that set up the wood of their graven image, and pray to a god that cannot save. Tell you, and bring them near; yes, let them take counsel together: who has declared this from ancient time? who has told it from that time? have not I the LORD? and there is no God else beside me; a just God and a Savior; there is none beside me. <u>Look to me, and be you saved, all the ends of the earth: for I am God, and there is none else</u>. I have sworn by myself, the word is gone out of my mouth in righteousness, and shall not return, <u>That to me every knee shall bow, every tongue shall swear</u>. Surely, shall one say, in the LORD have I righteousness and strength: even to him shall men come; and all that are incensed against him shall be ashamed. In the LORD shall all the seed of Israel be justified, and shall glory. (Isaiah 45:17-25 edited)*

"*All Israel shall be saved*" (Jeremiah 23:5-6 and Romans 11:25-26) is a recurring theme in Scripture, and it will be fulfilled "*in that day*". Also, every person will acknowledge Jesus is God from every tribe and nation (ethnicity).

> *Why God also has highly exalted him, and given him a name which is above every name: That at the name of Jesus every knee should bow, of things in heaven, and things in earth, and things under the earth; And that every tongue should confess that Jesus Christ is Lord, to the glory of God the Father. (Philippians 2:9-11)*

From Jerusalem to Armegeddon

After the 6th vial the armies of the "*whole world*" (Rev. 16:14) are gathered to the spot where God plans to destroy them. This is not the past battle of Gog and Magog (Ezekiel

38-39), nor is it the future battle of Gog and Magog which occurs at the end of the millennium (Rev. 20:7-15). It is the Antichrist and all nations gathered at Armegeddon to destroy Israel during the Great Tribulation.

Valley of Jehoshaphat/Decision

I will also gather all nations, and will bring them down into the valley of Jehoshaphat, and will plead with them there for my people and for my heritage Israel, whom they have scattered among the nations, and parted my land. (Joel 3:2)

There is no actual "*Valley of Jehoshaphat*" in Israel. *Jehoshaphat* means 'Jehovah judges'. He will judge the nations for scattering the Jews and dividing the land of Israel which He gave them and He calls "*My land*". The word 'plead' is *shaphat*, meaning to judge, pronounce sentence, or punish.

Assemble yourselves, and come, all you heathen, and gather yourselves together round about: thither cause your mighty ones to come down, O LORD. <u>Let the heathen be wakened, and come up to the valley of Jehoshaphat: for there will I sit to judge all the heathen round about</u>. Put you in the sickle, for <u>the harvest is ripe</u>: come, get you down; for the press is full, the fats overflow; for their wickedness is great. Multitudes, multitudes in the valley of decision: for the day of the LORD is near in the valley of decision. <u>The sun and the moon shall be darkened, and the stars shall withdraw their shining</u>. <u>The LORD also shall roar out of Zion, and utter his voice from Jerusalem; and the heavens and the earth shall shake</u>: but the LORD will be the hope of his people, and the strength of the children of Israel. So shall you know that I am the LORD your God dwelling in Zion, my holy mountain: then shall Jerusalem be holy, and there shall no strangers pass through her any more. (Joel 3:11-17)

God's voice caused the earth to shake when He wed Israel at Mount Sinai (Hebrew 12:18-29). Now God's Son causes the earth to shake as the Lion of Judah roars from Jerusalem with His Bride mounted on white horses.

The kingdom of heaven is like to a certain king, which made a marriage for his son, And sent forth his servants to call them that were bidden to the wedding: and they would not come. . . . And the remnant took his servants, and entreated them spitefully, and slew them. But when the king heard thereof, he was wroth: and he sent forth his armies, and destroyed those murderers, and burned up their city. (Matthew 22:2-7 edited)

King Jesus and Saints War Against the Wicked

And I saw heaven opened, and <u>behold a white horse; and he that sat on him was called Faithful and True, and in righteousness he does judge and make war</u>. His

> *eyes were as a flame of fire, and on his head were many crowns; and he had a name written, that no man knew, but he himself. And he was clothed with a clothing dipped in blood: and his name is called The Word of God. <u>And the armies which were in heaven followed him on white horses, clothed in fine linen, white and clean</u>. And out of his mouth goes a sharp sword, that with it he should smite the nations: and he shall rule them with a rod of iron: and he treads the wine press of the fierceness and wrath of Almighty God. And he has on his clothing and on his thigh a name written, KING OF KINGS, AND LORD OF LORDS. (Revelation 19:11-16)*

Jesus is the Word of God, which is the "*sword of the Spirit*", and He is also able to wield it in judgment (Hebrews 4:12-13). Jesus and His army of resurrected saints deal with the wicked swiftly. Then an angel calls upon the birds to feast.

> *And I saw an angel standing in the sun; and he cried with a loud voice, saying to all the fowls that fly in the middle of heaven, Come and gather yourselves together to the supper of the great God; That you may eat the flesh of kings, and the flesh of captains, and the flesh of mighty men, and the flesh of horses, and of them that sit on them, and the flesh of all men, both free and bond, both small and great. And I saw the beast, and the kings of the earth, and their armies, gathered together to make war against <u>him that sat on the horse, and against his army</u>. . . . And the remnant were slain with the sword of him that sat on the horse, which sword proceeded out of his mouth: and all the fowls were filled with their flesh. (Revelation 19:17-19, 21)*

At this time angels are reaping the wicked into the "winepress" to be judged by Jesus.

> *When the Lord Jesus shall be revealed from heaven with his mighty angels, In **flaming fire** taking **vengeance** on them that know not God, and that obey not the gospel of our Lord Jesus Christ: <u>Who shall be punished with everlasting destruction from the presence of the Lord</u>, and from the glory of his power; When he shall come to be glorified in his saints, and to be admired in all them that believe (because our testimony among you was believed) in that day. (2 Thessalonians 1:7b-10)*

> *And another angel came out from the altar, which had power over **fire**; and cried with a loud cry to him that had the sharp sickle, saying, Thrust in your sharp sickle, and gather the clusters of the vine of the earth; for her grapes are fully ripe. And the angel thrust in his sickle into the earth, and gathered the vine of the earth, and cast it into <u>the great wine press of the wrath of God</u>. And the wine press was trodden without the city, and blood came out of the <u>wine press</u>, even to the horse bridles, by the space of a thousand and six hundred furlongs. (Revelation 14:18-20)*

Vengeance and destroying the wicked with fire seem to go together. God will destroy the wicked and the earth with fire (2 Peter 3:7-13). And then Jesus will also judge the dead to damnation.

For the Father judges no man, but has committed all judgment to the Son: That all men should honor the Son, even as they honor the Father. He that honors not the Son honors not the Father which has sent him. Truly, truly, I say to you, He that hears my word, and believes on him that sent me, has everlasting life, and shall not come into condemnation; but is passed from death to life. Truly, truly, I say to you, The hour is coming, and now is, when <u>the dead shall hear the voice of the Son of God</u>: and they that hear shall live. For as the Father has life in himself; so has he given to the Son to have life in himself; And has <u>given him authority to execute judgment also, because he is the Son of man</u>. Marvel not at this: for the hour is coming, in the which <u>all that are in the graves shall hear his voice, And shall come forth; they that have done good, to the resurrection of life; and they that have done evil, to the resurrection of damnation</u>. I can of my own self do nothing: as I hear, I judge: and <u>my judgment is just</u>; because I seek not my own will, but the will of the Father which has sent me. (John 5:22-30)

Beasts of the Sea and The Earth Cast into Lake of Fire

And the beast was taken, and with him the false prophet that worked miracles before him, with which he deceived them that had received the mark of the beast, and them that worshipped his image. These both were cast alive into a lake of fire burning with brimstone. (Revelation 19:20)

This is talking about two individuals, the Antichrist and the False Prophet, who are cast alive into the lake of fire. "*That Wicked*" and wonder-working liar is the False Prophet.

And then shall that Wicked be revealed, whom the Lord shall consume with the spirit of his mouth, and shall destroy with the brightness of his coming: Even him, whose coming is after the working of Satan with all power and signs and lying wonders. (2 Thessalonians 2:8-9)

Summary

According to calculations from Matthew and Daniel, the "Day of the LORD" will be from dusk on Sunday, September 16, 2012 to dusk on September 18, 2012. It is the day when King Jesus returns to earth with His resurrected saints, snatches His Bride still alive, and conquers those who have attacked Israel, judging and destroying the wicked.

Possible Day of the LORD Time-Line

The 6th seal is opened hours before the Day of the LORD, with its darkened sun and moon and fallen stars and earthquake, and great fear and despair among the people. From dusk to midnight on Sunday, September 16, 2012, Jesus will be coronated in heaven while the 7th vial is poured out upon Babylon. Then the angel of the 7th seal casts its golden censer to earth and the 7th angel sounds the trumpet. These all contain a similar list of signs: voices and lightning, and thunder, and an earthquake, and great hail.

Dusk	Silence in heaven for half an hour Jesus is coronated with "many crowns" in heaven. Voices, Lightnings, Thunders, and Great Hail and an Earthquake on earth
Midnight	"*The Brightness of His Coming*" as "*Lightning from the east to the west*" Resurrection and Rapture of Saints "in the twinkling of an eye" Jesus, "*the Breaker*", destroys those attacking "*Bozrah*" (Petra)
Dawn	Jesus stands on the Mount of Olives, splitting it in two so Jews can escape. Jesus and His saints destroy the wicked in Jerusalem.
Noon	Saints ride with Jesus to battle the wicked at Armegeddon (Rev. 19:17) and the Antichrist and his armies are defeated and the fowls feast on their flesh.
Dusk	The dead are judged (Rev. 11:18)
Midnight	"*At evening time it shall be light.*" (Zech. 14:7)
Dawn	Antichrist and False Prophet are cast into the Lake of Fire. Satan is bound for 1,000 years.
Noon	Jesus takes His Beloved to the Bridal chamber He made, the New Jerusalem, while He destroys the earth with fire.
Dusk	The Wedding ceremony

This is the day King Jesus makes Himself known to the whole earth as King of kings and LORD of lords and Judge of the nations. It is also the day His Bride has been preparing to welcome Him as King. First alone at "*Bozrah*", and then with His Bride at Jerusalem and Armegeddon, Jesus will take vengeance upon the wicked.

The Jews will acknowledge Jesus as their Messiah, and "*all Israel will be saved*". And every knee will bow and tongue confess that Jesus Christ is Lord God (Phil. 2:9-11). The angels will reap the living wicked into the "*winepress*" to be judged by Jesus, and Jesus will also judge the dead to damnation. The Antichrist and the False Prophet will be cast alive into the lake of fire.

Millennium

They lived and reigned with Christ a thousand years.
(Revelation 20:4e)

A Thousand Years As One Day

Return, you children of men. For a thousand years in your sight are but as yesterday when it is past, and as a watch in the night. (Psalm 90:3b-4)

But, beloved, be not ignorant of this one thing, that one day is with the Lord as a thousand years, and a thousand years as one day. The Lord is not slack concerning his promise, as some men count slackness; but is long-suffering to us-ward, not willing that any should perish, but that all should come to repentance. (2 Pet. 3:8-9)

Throughout human history, God has patiently waited for people to repent and return to Him. According to Bishop Ussher, human history began in 4004 BC. John Eddy, a leading solar astronomer, told a symposium on time that "we could live with Bishop Ussher's value for the age of the earth and sun." [reported by Raphael Kazmann in the *Geotimes* on September 18, 1978] Now, 6,000 years later, Jesus is about to begin His millennial reign and we shall "*enter His rest*". When God created the heavens and earth He did it in six days and then rested on the seventh as a pattern for us. The seven days of the week roughly correlate to 7,000 years of earth history which was divided midway by Christ's first coming.

4004 BC	Adam and Eve and their seed are redeemed by "*the Seed*", the "*Lamb slain from the foundation of the world*".
3017 BC	God 'raptured' righteous Enoch.
2348 BC	God rescued eight righteous people in an ark with animals.
1491 BC	God ransomed the Hebrew people from Egypt at the cost of lambs and first born sons.
3 BC - 33 AD	King Jesus is born to die as the "*Lamb of God which takes away the sin of the world*", and to resurrect as the "*first fruits of them that slept*".
1099-1291 AD	Men fight eight crusades trying to restore Christianity to Jerusalem, but God continued to redeem lives through His gospel in Jesus.
2012 AD	King Jesus returns to rule on earth for 1,000 years.
3013 AD	Great White Throne Judgment, and the righteous spend eternity with God.

So from an overview of God's plan of redemption over time, we now return to Christ's redemption of His Bride and the heavens and earth during the "Day of the LORD".

Awake, Bride

First Few Days of Millennium

September 18, 2012 (Last portion of the "Day of the LORD")
Dawn   Satan is bound for 1,000 years.
Noon   Believers' unloving works are burned.
          Jesus takes His Beloved to the Bridal chamber He made, the New Jerusalem, while He destroys the earth with fire.
Dusk   The Wedding ceremony

Dusk September 18 to dusk on September 25
    The seven day Wedding Feast, "*Marriage Supper of the Lamb*" convenes.
    God restores the Heavens and terra-forms the Earth again in six days.
Dusk September 25th to dusk on September 26th (Yom Kippur)
    Fasting in holy awe of the Creator of a new heaven and new earth;
    a perfect "wedding gift".
Dusk September 26th to dusk on September 30th
    Bride returns to earth with Jesus, and begins building booths.
    New boundaries for the tribes of Israel established.
Dusk September 30th to dusk on October 8th (Succoth/Feast of Booths)
    Curses are removed. Longevity of human life is restored.
    Beasts are now vegetarian and no longer fear nor harm man.
    Jesus places the earthly New Jerusalem and Temple which He's constructed.

Satan Bound for 1,000 Years

And I saw an angel come down from heaven, having the key of the bottomless pit and a great chain in his hand. And he laid hold on the dragon, that old serpent, which is the Devil, and <u>Satan, and bound him a thousand years</u>, And cast him into the bottomless pit, and shut him up, and set a seal on him, that he should deceive the nations no more, till the thousand years should be fulfilled: and after that he must be loosed a little season. (Revelation 20:1-3)

Since Michael has been responsible for restraining Satan, he is likely the angel here. God still has a purpose for Satan. People will be born during the Millennium who will not choose to worship Jesus. Strangely enough they will congregate in the ancient lands of Gog and Magog.

Believers' Unloving Works are Burned

According to the grace of God which is given to me, as a wise master builder, I have laid the foundation, and another builds thereon. But let every man take heed how he builds thereupon. For other foundation can no man lay than that is laid, which is Jesus Christ. Now if any man build on this foundation gold, silver, *precious stones, wood, hay, stubble; <u>Every man's work shall be made manifest: for</u> <u>**the day** shall declare it, because it shall be revealed by fire</u>; and the fire shall try every man's work of what sort it is. If any man's work abide which he has built thereupon, he shall receive a reward. <u>If any man's work shall be burned, he shall</u> <u>suffer loss: but he himself shall be saved; yet so as by fire</u>. (1 Corinthians 3:10-15)*

We all need to be more in love with Jesus than what we do for Him. Works motivated by our love for Him will be rewarded later, but during "*the day of the LORD*" any works not built upon the foundation of our love for Jesus will be burned up.

Don't Love This World and This Life

He that loves his life shall lose it; and he that hates his life in this world shall keep it to life eternal. If any man serve me, let him follow me; and where I am, there shall also my servant be: if any man serve me, him will my Father honor. (Jn. 12:25-26)

Love not the world, neither the things that are in the world. If any man love the world, the love of the Father is not in him. For all that is in the world, the lust of the flesh, and the lust of the eyes, and the pride of life, is not of the Father, but is of the world. <u>And the world passes away, and the lust thereof: but he that does the will of</u> <u>God stays for ever.</u> (1 John 2:15-17)

Paul lamented, "*For Demas has forsaken me, having loved this present world, and is departed to Thessalonica*" (2 Timothy 4:10a). We have a better world to look forward to with King Jesus. We are "*citizens with the saints*" and are merely "*pilgrims on this earth*". We are thankful for the blessings God has given us in this life, but we are ready to leave it all behind to follow Jesus and be with Him.

Heavenly New Jerusalem: Bridal Chamber

Jesus will take all the members of His Bride to safety in the space cube, New Jerusalem. She will prepare Herself for a proper wedding ceremony. Afterwards, the Bride and Jesus will enjoy a 7-day honeymoon. Jesus' prayer for all believers to be one with Him (John 17:20-26) is finally answered.

*And there came to me one of the seven angels which had the seven vials full of the seven last plagues, and talked with me, saying, Come here, I will show you <u>the</u> <u>bride, the Lamb's wife</u>. And he carried me away in the spirit to a great and high mountain, and showed me <u>that great city, the holy Jerusalem, descending out of</u> <u>heaven from God, Having the glory of God: and her light was like to a stone most</u> <u>precious</u>, even like a jasper stone, clear as crystal; . . . And he that talked with me had a golden reed to measure the city, and the gates thereof, and the wall thereof. And the city lies foursquare, and the length is as large as the breadth: and he measured the city with the reed, twelve thousand **furlongs**. The length and the*

> *breadth and the height of it are equal. And he measured the wall thereof, an hundred and forty and four cubits, according to the measure of a man, that is, of the angel. And the building of the wall of it was of jasper: and the city was pure gold, like to clear glass. . . . And **I saw no temple therein**: for the Lord God Almighty and the Lamb are the temple of it. And the city had no need of the sun, neither of the moon, to shine in it: for the glory of God did lighten it, and the Lamb is the light thereof. And the nations of them which are saved shall walk in the light of it: (Revelation 21:9-24a edited)*

Like any Jewish man of his time, Jesus went away to *"prepare a place"* for His Bride - a bridal chamber which is called the New Jerusalem. It is a huge space cube. A third of the day and night are gone at the time of His appearing, so it may act as an additional luminary in the sky, since it is about one half the size of the moon. It does not reflect light, but God emanates light from within it.

The base of the New Jerusalem would have been equal to 144 million square stadia. A furlong or stadia is about 600 feet, thus the area of the base (and each face of the cube) is roughly 1500 miles by 1500 miles, or a volume of 3.375 billion cubic miles. If resting upon the Earth, its ceiling would be inside our current exosphere (the last layer before space), and its base would cut a trench in the earth up to 70 feet deep near its center. John says it comes down out of heaven, but he doesn't say it lands or rests upon the earth. Since its base would take up half or more of any continent and would greatly depress the earth's crust, and the nations walk by its light, it sounds much more like a small moon. Its presence at Christ's 2nd coming allows Rosh Hashanah to have light at all hours.

There would be plenty of space for every believer in Yahweh since creation in it. God chose to dwell in a cubical called the Holy of Holies on earth (1 Kings 6:20), so His Bride will now dwell in holiness with Him in a space cube.

Pearl Gates and Precious Stone Foundations

> *And had a wall great and high, and had <u>twelve gates</u>, and at the gates twelve angels, and names written thereon, which are <u>the names of the twelve tribes of the children of Israel</u>: On the east three gates; on the north three gates; on the south three gates; and on the west three gates. And the wall of the city had <u>twelve foundations, and in them the names of the twelve apostles of the Lamb</u>. . . . And the twelve gates were twelve pearls: every several gate was of one pearl: and the street of the city was pure gold, as it were transparent glass. . . . And the foundations of the wall of the city were garnished with all manner of precious stones. The first foundation was jasper; the second, sapphire; the third, a chalcedony; the fourth, an emerald; The fifth, sardonyx; the sixth, sardius; the seventh, chrysolyte; the eighth, beryl; the ninth, a topaz; the tenth, a chrysoprasus; the eleventh, a jacinth; the twelfth, an amethyst. (Revelation 21:12-20 edited)*

The twelve gates have the names of the twelve tribes of Israel. The twelve foundations have the names of the twelve apostles. These correlated to the twenty-four elders around the throne. Pure gold is soft and malleable, but God has tempered it in such a way that it is clear and strong enough to walk upon.

Heaven and Earth Destroyed by Fire

After the Great Tribulation, the heavens and earth will need a complete overhaul, so they will be torched by God to make way for a New Heaven and Earth. The Father and Holy Spirit will be busy destroying and then re-creating the heavens and the earth.

And, You, Lord, in the beginning have laid the foundation of the earth; and the heavens are the works of your hands: They shall perish; but you remain; and <u>they all shall wax old as does a garment; And as a clothing shall you fold them up, and they shall be changed</u>: but you are the same, and your years shall not fail. (Hebrews 1:10-12)

Knowing this first, that there shall come in the last days scoffers, walking after their own lusts, And saying, Where is the promise of his coming? for since the fathers fell asleep, all things continue as they were from the beginning of the creation. For this they willingly are ignorant of, that by the word of God the heavens were of old, and the earth standing out of the water and in the water: Whereby the world that then was, being overflowed with water, perished: But the <u>heavens and the earth</u>, which are now, by the same word are kept in store, <u>reserved to fire against the day of judgment and perdition of ungodly men</u>. . . .But the day of the Lord will come as a thief in the night; in the which <u>the heavens shall pass away with a great noise, and the elements shall melt with fervent heat, the earth also and the works that are therein shall be burned up</u>. Seeing then that <u>all these things shall be dissolved</u>, what manner of persons ought you to be in all holy conversation and godliness, Looking for and hastening to the coming of the day of God, wherein <u>the heavens being on fire shall be dissolved, and the elements shall melt with fervent heat</u>? Nevertheless we, according to his promise, look for new heavens and a new earth, wherein dwells righteousness. Why, beloved, seeing that you look for such things, be diligent that you may be found of him in peace, without spot, and blameless. . . .You therefore, beloved, seeing you know these things before, beware lest you also, being led away with the error of the wicked, fall from your own steadfastness. But grow in grace, and in the knowledge of our Lord and Savior Jesus Christ. To him be glory both now and for ever. Amen. (2 Peter 3:3-18 edited)

God could miraculously scorch the earth, or He could choose to send gamma rays or solar flares; or send one or more large asteroids to hit the earth, thus sending debris into the upper atmosphere which would then rain down again as meteors or burning hail. There are several mentions in Revelation of falling stars and burning mountains thrown into the sea.

Awake, Bride

We are aware of the power unleashed by single asteroids like the ones which devastated the areas of Yucatan, Mexico and Tunguska, Russia. Russians spoke of a "deafening bang" and seismic instruments recorded effects 600 miles away. Having several asteroids hit simultaneously would certainly dissolve the elements with "*fervent heat*" and "*great noise*".

A team of scientists reported in the 1999 issue of *Geo-Marine Letters* that in earth's distant past, undersea methane gas ruptures from the Yucatan asteroid (Chicxulub) impact caused a firestorm on earth's surface and up into the atmosphere. According to Naval Research Laboratory scientist Barton Hurdle, "The theoretical fire would have burned near the ground and high into the atmosphere. The fire would have incinerated land creatures. There was a lot of soot, and that soot has been found." After impact millions of tons of rock were sent into the atmosphere, and re-entered the Earth's at high speed as "shooting stars" igniting the trees and the methane gas. [Report by Robert Roy Britt on space.com] This impact may have occurred just prior to Noah's flood, causing the earth's crust to crack (oceanic trenches) and releasing the "*fountains of the deep*" and the "*waters above*" to quench the fire.

Bride Gets a Pure Language

Therefore wait you on me, said the LORD, until the day that I rise up to the prey: for my determination is to gather the nations, that I may assemble the kingdoms, to pour on them my indignation, even all my fierce anger: for all the earth shall be devoured with the fire of my jealousy. For then will I turn to the people a pure language, that they may all call on the name of the LORD, to serve him with one consent. (Zephaniah 3:8-9)

The earth is destroyed by fire while the Bride is safe in New Jerusalem with Jesus. And God will restore a pure language to us so that we can all communicate and worship Him with a unified voice. It may be the language Adam and Eve spoke.

Marriage Supper of the Lamb

*Let us be glad and rejoice, and give honor to him: for the marriage of the Lamb is come, and his wife has made herself ready. And to her was granted that she should be arrayed in fine linen, clean and white: for the fine linen is the righteousness of saints. And he said to me, Write, Blessed are they which are **called** to the marriage supper of the Lamb. And he said to me, These are the true sayings of God. (Revelation 19:7-9)*

'Called' is *kaleo* which is often used of our "*calling*" into Christ (Eph. 4:4). Jesus ended His parable of the "*king who made a marriage for his son*" with "*For many are called [kletos], but few are chosen [eklektos]*" (Matthew 22:14). *Kletos* means to be invited to a banquet or appointed. *Eklektos* means to be chosen or selected; the 'elect'. As Jesus' Father, Father God chose Us to be His Son's Bride, and to live righteously.

*Blessed be the God and Father of our Lord Jesus Christ, who has blessed us with all spiritual blessings in heavenly places in Christ: According as <u>he has **chosen** us in him before the foundation of the world</u>, that we should be holy and without blame before him in love: (Ephesians 1:3-4)*

God chose Christ's Bride, the Church composed of Jews and Gentiles, before creation.

Father, I will that they also, whom you have given me, be with me where I am; that they may behold my glory, which you have given me: for <u>you loved me before the foundation of the world</u>. (John 17:24)

Father God chose to give Us to His beloved Son, and established the 'Bride price'.

*But with the **precious blood of Christ**, as of a lamb without blemish and without spot: Who truly was foreordained <u>before the foundation of the world</u>, but was manifest in these last times for you, (1 Peter 1:19-20)*

And he shall set the sheep on his right hand, but the goats on the left. Then shall the King say to them on his right hand, Come, you blessed of my Father, <u>inherit the kingdom prepared for you from the foundation of the world</u>: (Matthew 25:33-34)

Prior to creating the heavens and earth, God knew He would have to recreate them to present as a wedding gift to His Son and His Bride.

New Heavens and New Earth and Earthly New Jerusalem

Two days of Rosh Hashanah, and 7 days while the new heaven and earth are being recreated has us celebrating Yom Kippur, the day of atonement on a new earth that has been completely redeemed from the curse and no longer groans, but rejoices. We may keep the fast in awe of all that God has done.

*And I saw <u>a new heaven and a new earth</u>: for the first heaven and the first earth were passed away; and there was no more sea. And I John saw <u>the holy city, new Jerusalem, coming down from God out of heaven, prepared as a bride adorned for her husband</u>. And I heard a great voice out of heaven saying, Behold, the **tabernacle of God is with men, and he will dwell with them**, and they shall be his people, and God himself shall be with them, and be their God. And God shall wipe away all tears from their eyes; and <u>there shall be no more death</u>, neither sorrow, nor crying, neither shall there be any more pain: <u>for the former things are passed away.</u> And he that sat on the throne said, Behold, I make all things new. (Revelation 21:1-5a)*

This new holy city does have a tabernacle among men and God dwells with them, so it is the earthly New Jerusalem. There is no more death for saints whether they remain in heavenly New Jerusalem or return to the new earth.

> *And you shall number seven sabbaths of years to you, seven times seven years; and the space of the seven sabbaths of years shall be to you forty and nine years. <u>Then shall you cause the trumpet of the jubilee to sound on the tenth day of the seventh month, in the day of atonement shall you make the trumpet sound throughout all your land.</u> . . . A jubilee shall that fiftieth year be to you: you shall not sow, neither reap that which grows of itself in it, nor gather the grapes in it of your vine undressed. (Leviticus 25:8-9)*

It may be that the year our Lord returns is also a jubilee year to be celebrated on Yom Kippur. If so, we will not sow that year, but eat the fruit of the trees. On Yom Kippur the curse is removed from the earth and the Adamic sin nature from the human race. Truly the slaves have all been set free, and the land has returned to its rightful Owner and Creator.

> *For, behold,<u> I create new heavens and a new earth: and the former shall not be remembered, nor come into mind</u>. But be you glad and rejoice for ever in that which I create: for, behold, I create Jerusalem a rejoicing, and her people a joy. And I will rejoice in Jerusalem, and joy in my people: and the voice of weeping shall be no more heard in her, nor the voice of crying. <u>There shall be no more there an **infant** of days, nor an old man that has not filled his days: for the child shall **die** an hundred years old; but the sinner being an hundred years old shall be accursed.</u> And they shall build houses, and inhabit them; and they shall plant vineyards, and eat the fruit of them. They shall not build, and another inhabit; they shall not plant, and another eat: for <u>as the days of a tree are the days of my people</u>, and my elect shall long enjoy the work of their hands. They shall not labor in vain, nor bring forth for trouble; for they are the seed of the blessed of the LORD, and their offspring with them. And it shall come to pass, that before they call, I will answer; and while they are yet speaking, I will hear. The wolf and the lamb shall feed together, and <u>the lion shall eat straw like the bullock</u>: and dust shall be the serpent's meat. They shall not hurt nor destroy in all my holy mountain, said the LORD. (Isaiah 65:17-25)*

God may adjust our memories, or just allow the past to fade away much like the ark of the covenant did (Jeremiah 31:16). Our future labor in planting and reaping will no longer be "*in vain*" struggling against thorns (Genesis 3:17-19). Also God's curse on limited human years of life is removed (Genesis 6:3), and our telomeres will no longer unravel. People born will have the ability to live for hundreds of years like the people before Noah's flood before we die. The fear of man will no longer be upon the animals (Genesis 9:2-3; Isaiah 11:6-9), and we and the animals will return to a more vegetarian diet.

Infants are mentioned. Those raptured believers (who did not die) will return to the new earth. Those who were married will remain married (it's legally binding until death; 1 Cor. 7:39). They will have sex and produce children, and their children will be able to die during the millennium. Although those born on the new earth no longer have the Adamic sin nature, they still have free will and can choose to sin. But God promised His Spirit and Word would be in His people and their "*seed's seed for ever*" (Isaiah 59:21).

Resurrected immortals will also be on the earth, specifically those who were martyred during the Great Tribulation will reign with Christ (Rev. 20:4-6). They shall be like the angels and neither marry nor have sex.

Familiar but New Terrain

And it shall be in that day, that living waters shall go out from Jerusalem; half of them toward the former sea, and half of them toward the hinder sea: in summer and in winter shall it be. And the LORD shall be king over all the earth: in that day shall there be one LORD, and his name one. All the land shall be turned as a plain from Geba to Rimmon south of Jerusalem: and it shall be lifted up, and inhabited in her place, from Benjamin's gate to the place of the first gate, to the corner gate, and from the tower of Hananeel to the king's winepresses. And men shall dwell in it, and there shall be no more utter destruction; but Jerusalem shall be safely inhabited. (Zechariah 14:8-11)

Currently al-Geba is six miles north of Jerusalem, and Rimmon is thirty-five miles south of Jerusalem (5 miles north of Beer-sheba). New Jerusalem will be "*lifted up*" on a high plateau forty miles long. The basic continents will be there with many of the rivers, seas, and oceans still familiar, but topography will be drastically different, and possibly returned to pre-flood status. Particularly, two new rivers will flow from New Jerusalem; one eastward to the former Dead Sea, and one westward to the Mediterranean.

The River of Life with Trees of Healing

*Now when I had returned, behold, at the bank of the river were very many **trees** on the one side and on the other. Then said he to me, These waters issue out toward the east country, and go down into the desert, and go into the sea: which being brought forth into the sea, the <u>waters shall be healed</u>. And it shall come to pass, that every thing that lives, which moves, wherever the rivers shall come, shall live: and there shall be a very great multitude of fish, because these waters shall come thither: for they shall be healed; and every thing shall live where the river comes. . . . And by the river on the bank thereof, on this side and on that side, shall grow all trees for meat, whose **leaf** shall not fade, neither shall the fruit thereof be consumed: it shall bring forth new fruit according to his months, because their waters they issued out of the sanctuary: and the fruit thereof shall be for meat, and the **leaf** thereof for **medicine**. (Ezekiel 47:7-9, 12)*

And he that sat on the throne said, Behold, I make all things new. And he said to me, Write: for these words are true and faithful. And he said to me, It is done. I am Alpha and Omega, the beginning and the end. I will give to him that is thirsty of the fountain of the water of life freely. He that overcomes shall inherit all things; and I will be his God, and he shall be my son. But the fearful, and unbelieving, and the abominable, and murderers, and fornicators, and sorcerers, and idolaters, and all liars, shall have their part in the lake which burns with fire and brimstone: which is the second death. (Revelation 21:5-8)

*And he showed me <u>a pure river of water of life</u>, clear as crystal, proceeding out of the throne of God and of the Lamb. In the middle of the street of it, and on either side of the river, was there the **tree of life**, which bore twelve manner of fruits, and yielded her fruit every month: and the **leaves** of the tree were for the **healing** of the nations. . . . Blessed are they that do his commandments, that they may have right to the tree of life, and may enter in through the gates into the city. For without are dogs, and sorcerers, and fornicators, and murderers, and idolaters, and whoever loves and makes a lie. . . . And the Spirit and the bride say, Come. And let him that hears say, Come. And let him that is thirsty come. And whoever will, let him take the <u>water of life</u> freely. (Revelation 22:1-2,14-15,17)*

Those who sin in the millennial kingdom of Christ can be cleansed by drinking from the river of the water of life which issues as a fountain from the throne of God. Jesus will be physically present with the scars in His wrists and side; His crucifixion an uncontested fact. Instead of a dead wooden cross, there will be a tree of life which produces fruit of life and leaves for healing, but only those who obey Christ's command may eat of it. Sadly, there will be those who refuse to submit to King Jesus and drink of the water of life which flows from His throne in earthly New Jerusalem, and so they will not be allowed to enter the city.

Feast of Booths/Tabernacles

Back to our first week on the new earth: from Yom Kippur we will have a few days to make latrines and simple shelters for ourselves in which to celebrate the Feast of Booths.

*You shall bring down the noise of strangers, as the heat in a dry place; even the heat with the shadow of a cloud: the branch of the terrible ones shall be brought low. <u>And in this mountain shall the LORD of hosts make to all people a feast of fat things, a feast of wines on the lees, of fat things full of marrow, of wines on the lees well refined.</u> And he will destroy in this mountain the face of the covering cast over all people, and the veil that is spread over all nations. He will swallow up death in victory; and the Lord GOD will wipe away tears from off all faces; and the rebuke of his people shall he take away from off all the earth: for the LORD has spoken it. And it shall be said **in that day**, See, this is our God; we have waited for him, and he will save us: this is the LORD; we have waited for him, we will be glad and rejoice in his salvation. (Isaiah 25:5-9)*

Mountains refer to empires, and here it refers to Christ's kingdom on earth. This feast follows the Day of the LORD in which He destroyed the *"terrible ones"* and brought forth salvation and resurrection. There are three feasts which will be celebrated during the millennium: the feast of unleavened bread, the feast of the early harvest of Pentecost, and the feast of the latter harvest of Tabernacles (Exodus 23:14-17; Deuteronomy 16:16; 2 Chronicles 8:13). It will still be required to go to Jerusalem, or at least send a representative from your country, during these feasts.

And it shall come to pass, that every one that is left of all the nations which came against Jerusalem shall even go up from year to year to worship the King, the LORD of hosts, and to keep the feast of tabernacles. And it shall be, that whoever will not come up of all the families of the earth to Jerusalem to worship the King, the LORD of hosts, even on them shall be no rain. <u>*And if the family of Egypt go not up, and come not, that have no rain; there shall be the plague, with which the LORD will smite the heathen that come not up to keep the feast of tabernacles.*</u> *This shall be the punishment of Egypt, and the punishment of all nations that come not up to keep the feast of tabernacles. In that day shall there be on the bells of the horses, HOLINESS UNTO THE LORD; and the pots in the LORD's house shall be like the bowls before the altar. Yes, every pot in Jerusalem and in Judah shall be holiness to the LORD of hosts: and all they that sacrifice shall come and take of them, and seethe therein: and in that day there shall be no more the Canaanite in the house of the LORD of hosts. (Zechariah 14:16-21)*

Healing Waters on the 8th Day of *Sukkot*/Booths

On the eighth day of the feast, the high priest would draw water from the pool of Siloam in a golden vase. *Siloam* means 'gently flowing waters'. Flowing waters are also called living waters because you can safely drink from them. The source of the pool of Siloam is the spring under the Temple Mount. A flute player, called "the pierced one", would lead the procession back to the Temple. The high priest would declare "*Behold, God is my salvation; I will trust, and not be afraid: for the LORD JEHOVAH is my strength and my song; he also is become my salvation;*" (Isaiah 12:2), and the people would respond with the following verse, "*Therefore with joy shall you draw water out of the wells of salvation.*" Then they prayed for winter rains. After the other priests had sacrificed the required animals for the day. The high priest would pour the water onto the altar, and another priest would pour the silver vase of wine. Just as Christ's pierced heart gushed water and blood together to atone for our sins. Jesus is a covering or *sukkah* to those who believe.

The fulfillment of the 8th day in the Millennium will be when Jesus brings down His new city of Jerusalem with its Temple and places it upon the earth, and the Temple Mount spring gushes forth living water which brings healing (Ezekiel 47).

Original/New Boundaries for Israel

Israel's tribal boundaries during the millennium are based upon God's covenant with Abraham in Genesis15:18 *"In the same day the LORD made a covenant with Abram, saying, To your seed have I given this land, from the river of Egypt to the great river, the river Euphrates;"* and Ezekiel's prophecies. [See map in Appendix by Clarence Larkin.] Ezekiel 45:1-8 contains the boundaries of the holy portion and the prince's portion. Joshua 13 and Numbers 34 can also be taken into account. The description of borders for the twelve tribes begins in Ezekiel 47:13 and ends in 48:35. There were 144,000 Jews sealed prior to Christ's return, and a Jewish remnant of at least 100,000 more saved in Petra. So there is a good Jewish population with which to start the new country of Israel.

*Therefore will I save my flock, and they shall no more be a prey; and I will judge between cattle and cattle. And I will set up one shepherd over them, and he shall feed them, even my servant David; he shall feed them, and he shall be their shepherd. And I the LORD will be their God, and my servant David a prince among them; I the LORD have spoken it. And I will make with them a <u>covenant of peace</u>, and will cause the evil beasts to cease out of the land: and they shall dwell safely in the wilderness, and sleep in the woods. And I will make them and the places round about my hill a blessing; and I will cause the shower to come down in his season; there shall be showers of blessing. And the tree of the field shall yield her fruit, and the earth shall yield her increase, and they shall be safe in their land, and shall know that I am the LORD, when I have broken the bands of their yoke, and delivered them out of the hand of those that served themselves of them. And they shall no more be a prey to the heathen, neither shall the beast of the land devour them; but they shall dwell safely, and none shall make them afraid. And I will raise up for them a **plant of renown**, and they shall be no more consumed with hunger in the land, neither bear the shame of the heathen any more. Thus shall they know that I the LORD their God am with them, and that they, even the house of Israel, are my people, said the Lord GOD. And you my flock, the flock of my pasture, are men, and I am your God, said the Lord GOD. (Ezekiel 34:22-31)*

The "*plant of renown*" is the tree of life. All Israelis will finally be safe and blessed with their Messiah reigning the whole earth from Jerusalem (Jeremiah 23:5-6). The millennium sinners won't harm them and neither will the beasts.

New Jerusalem on Earth

*And it shall come to pass **in the last days**, that the mountain of the <u>LORD's house shall be established in the top of the mountains, and shall be exalted above the hills</u>; and all nations shall flow to it. And many people shall go and say, Come you, and let us go up to the mountain of the LORD, to the house of the God of Jacob; and he will teach us of his ways, and we will walk in his paths: for out of Zion shall* *go forth the law, and the word of the LORD from Jerusalem. And he shall judge among the nations, and shall rebuke many people: and they shall beat their swords into plowshares, and their spears into pruning hooks: nation shall not lift up sword against nation, <u>neither shall they learn war any more</u>. O house of Jacob, come you, and let us walk in the light of the LORD. (Isaiah 2:2-5)*

Again, the New Jerusalem will be elevated above the hills. The new tabernacle/temple will be the LORD's dwelling and throne and classroom, and will radiate with His glory. They will no longer "*learn war*" (Zechariah 9:10).

In that day *shall the branch of the LORD be beautiful and glorious, and the fruit of the earth shall be excellent and comely for them that are escaped of Israel. And it shall come to pass, that he that is left in Zion, and he that remains in Jerusalem, shall be called holy, even every one that is written among the living in Jerusalem: When the Lord shall have washed away the filth of the daughters of Zion, and shall have purged the blood of Jerusalem from the middle thereof by the spirit of judgment, and by the spirit of burning. And the LORD will create on every dwelling place of mount Zion, and on her assemblies, a cloud and smoke by day, and the <u>shining of a flaming fire by night: for on all the **glory** shall be a defense. And there shall be a **tabernacle** for a shadow in the day time from the heat, and for a place of refuge, and for a covert from storm and from rain</u>. (Isaiah 4:2-6)*

"*When the Lord shall have washed away the filth of the daughters of Zion*" was Jesus' first coming. During His second coming He will have "*purged the blood of Jerusalem from the middle thereof by the spirit of judgment, and by the spirit of burning*". Then King Jesus will establish His glorious kingdom and His tabernacle/temple.

New Temple

Only the righteous written in the book of life have access to the heavenly New Jerusalem. Because it is illuminated by the glory of the LORD, it is always bright and never night.

Just as the heavenly New Jerusalem (Hebrew 12:22) was constructed by Jesus and comes down from heaven, so does the earthly New Jerusalem, as a fully built city. Regarding the heavenly New Jerusalem, John stated: "*And I saw no temple therein: for the Lord God Almighty and the Lamb are the temple of it.*" (Revelation 21:22) But there is definitely a temple/tabernacle in the earthly New Jerusalem, which Jesus has built (Zechariah 6:12-13) and it is described in Ezekiel 40-47.

To the overcomers from the church of Philadelphia, Jesus promised, "*Him that overcomes will I make a pillar in the **temple** of my God, and he shall go no more out: and I will write on him the name of my God, and the name of the city of my God, which is <u>new Jerusalem</u>, which comes down out of heaven from my God: and I will write on him my new name.*" (Revelation 3:12)

*And I will make them one nation in the land on the mountains of Israel; and one king shall be king to them all: and they shall be no more two nations, neither shall they be divided into two kingdoms any more at all. Neither shall they defile themselves any more with their idols, nor with their detestable things, nor with any of their transgressions: but I will save them out of all their dwelling places, wherein they have sinned, and will cleanse them: so shall they be my people, and I will be their God. And David my servant shall be king over them; and they all shall have one shepherd: they shall also walk in my judgments, and observe my statutes, and do them. And they shall dwell in the land that I have given to Jacob my servant, wherein your fathers have dwelled; and they shall dwell therein, even they, and their children, and their children's children for ever: and my servant David shall be their prince for ever. Moreover I will make a <u>covenant of peace</u> with them; it shall be an everlasting covenant with them: and I will place them, and multiply them, and <u>will set my sanctuary in the middle of them for ever more. My **tabernacle** also shall be with them: yes, I will be their God, and they shall be my people. And the heathen shall know that I the LORD do sanctify Israel, when my sanctuary shall be in the middle of them for ever more.</u> (Ezekiel 37:22-28)*

Sin and Sinners Have No Access

*And I heard a great voice out of heaven saying, Behold, the **tabernacle** of God is with men, and he will dwell with them, and they shall be his people, and God himself shall be with them, and be their God. . . . and the kings of the earth do bring their glory and honor into it. And the gates of it shall not be shut at all by day: for there shall be no night there. And they shall bring the glory and honor of the nations into it. And there shall in no wise enter into it any thing that defiles, neither whatever works abomination, or makes a lie: but they which are written in the Lamb's book of life. (Revelation 21:3, 24b-27 edited)*

King Jesus will have saved His people and fulfilled His promises to them regarding the land of Israel. The Gentiles will acknowledge that fact as King Jesus rules from Jerusalem.

King Jesus Rules the Earth

For to us a child is born, to us a son is given: and the government shall be on his shoulder: and his name shall be called Wonderful, Counselor, The mighty God, The everlasting Father, The Prince of Peace. <u>Of the increase of his government and peace there shall be no end, on the throne of David, and on his kingdom, to order it, and to establish it with judgment and with justice from now on even for ever.</u> The zeal of the LORD of hosts will perform this. (Isaiah 9:6-7)

O clap your hands, all you people; shout to God with the voice of triumph. For the LORD most high is terrible; he is a great King over all the earth. He shall subdue the people under us, and the nations under our feet. He shall choose our inheritance for us, the excellency of Jacob whom he loved. Selah. God is gone up with a shout, the LORD with the sound of a trumpet. Sing praises to God, sing praises: sing praises to our King, sing praises. For God is the King of all the earth: sing you praises with understanding. God reigns over the heathen: God sits on the throne of his holiness. The princes of the people are gathered together, even the people of the God of Abraham: for the shields of the earth belong to God: he is greatly exalted. (Psalms 47:1-7)

Yet have I set my king on my holy hill of Zion. I will declare the decree: the LORD has said to me, You are my Son; this day have I begotten you. Ask of me, and I shall give you the heathen for your inheritance, and the uttermost parts of the earth for your possession. You shall break them with a rod of iron; you shall dash them in pieces like a potter's vessel. Be wise now therefore, O you kings: be instructed, you judges of the earth. Serve the LORD with fear, and rejoice with trembling. Kiss the Son, lest he be angry, and you perish from the way, when his wrath is kindled but a little. Blessed are all they that put their trust in him. (Psalms 2:6-12)

That you keep this commandment without spot, unrebukable, until the appearing of our Lord Jesus Christ: Which in his times he shall show, who is the blessed and only Potentate, the King of kings, and Lord of lords; (1 Timothy 6:14-15)

But the LORD shall endure for ever: he has prepared his throne for judgment. And he shall judge the world in righteousness, he shall minister judgment to the people in uprightness. (Psalms 9:7-8)

There are many scriptures which refer to Christ reigning and pronouncing judgment over all the earth. The fulfillment of His Kingdom on earth is what the last 6,000 years have been building toward, and it will soon become a reality.

Those Who Suffered (Martyrdom) Reign With Christ

It is a faithful saying: For if we be dead with him, we shall also live with him: If we suffer, we shall also reign with him: if we deny him, he also will deny us: (2 Timothy 2:11-12)

And he that overcomes, and keeps my works to the end, to him will I give power over the nations: And he shall rule them with a rod of iron; as the vessels of a potter shall they be broken to shivers: even as I received of my Father. (Revelation 2:26-27)

God's promise to His suffering saints is that they will reign with Him.

And I saw thrones, and they sat on them, and judgment was given to them: and I saw the souls of them that were beheaded for the witness of Jesus, and for the word of God, and which had <u>not worshipped the beast, neither his image, neither had received his mark on their foreheads, or in their hands; and they lived and reigned with Christ a thousand years</u>. But the rest of the dead lived not again until the thousand years were finished. This is the first resurrection. Blessed and holy is he that has part in the first resurrection: on such the second death has no power, but they shall be priests of God and of Christ, and shall reign with him a thousand years. (Revelation 20:4-6)

And there shall be no more curse: but the throne of God and of the Lamb shall be in it; and his servants shall serve him: And they shall see his face; <u>and his name shall be in their foreheads.</u> And there shall be no night there; and they need no candle, neither light of the sun; for the Lord God gives them light: and they shall reign for ever and ever. (Revelation 22:3-5)

Only the righteous dead are resurrected at Christ's second coming, which is called the "*first resurrection*" here. There is a distinction of suffering, enduring faith, and martyrdom in order to reign with Christ. Those who specifically suffered for refusing to worship the beast or receive his mark will have the name of the Lamb in their foreheads. We are all kings (Rev. 1:5-6) and priests (1 Peter 2:9) by His Spirit in this life, but not necessarily in the next.

The Faithful are Restored and Rule Cities

And Jesus said to them, Truly I say to you, That you which have followed me, in the regeneration when the Son of man shall sit in the throne of his glory, you also shall sit on twelve thrones, judging the twelve tribes of Israel. And every one that has forsaken houses, or brothers, or sisters, or father, or mother, or wife, or children, or lands, for my name's sake, shall receive an hundred times, and shall inherit everlasting life. But many that are first shall be last; and the last shall be first. (Matthew 19:28-30)

'Regeneration' is *paliggenesia* meaning 'genesis anew', a renovation or restoration to the way it was at the beginning. This is the millennial reign of Christ on the new earth. God will restore abundantly those things which believers sacrificed for Jesus' sake. Remember not to be jealous of God's generosity to others.

He said therefore, A certain nobleman went into a far country to receive for himself a kingdom, and to return. And he called his ten servants, and delivered them ten pounds, and said to them, Occupy till I come. But his citizens hated him, and sent a message after him, saying, We will not have this man to reign over us. And it came *to pass, that when he was returned, having received the kingdom, then he commanded these servants to be called to him, to whom he had given the money, that he might know how much every man had gained by trading. Then came the first, saying, Lord, your pound has gained ten pounds. And he said to him, <u>Well, you good servant: because you have been faithful in a very little, have you authority over ten cities.</u> And the second came, saying, Lord, your pound has gained five pounds. And he said likewise to him, <u>Be you also over five cities.</u> . . . But those my enemies, which would not that I should reign over them, bring here, and slay them before me. (Luke 19:12-19, 27)*

The American Colonies began with many people who truly sought to live in a manner which pleased Jesus in accordance with the Bible. After two hundred years, many still upheld those values, but after 400 years less than half could truly be called Christians, and the government and its institutions became anti-Christian. So during 1,000 years, even though Satan is bound, there will be those who no longer enjoy being ruled by King Jesus. And at the end of the 1,000 years, Satan will be released and lead many to rebel.

Satan is loosed -- Gog and Magog Attack Israel

And he laid hold on the dragon, that old serpent, which is the Devil, and Satan, and bound him a thousand years, And cast him into the bottomless pit, and shut him up, and set a seal on him, that he should deceive the nations no more, till the thousand years should be fulfilled: and after that he must be loosed a little season. . . . <u>And when the thousand years are expired, Satan shall be loosed out of his prison, And shall go out to deceive the nations which are in the four quarters of the earth, Gog, and Magog, to gather them together to battle</u>: the number of whom is as the sand of the sea. And they went up on the breadth of the earth, and compassed the camp of the saints about, and the beloved city: and fire came down from God out of heaven, and devoured them. And the devil that deceived them was cast into the lake of fire and brimstone, where the beast and the false prophet are, and shall be tormented day and night for ever and ever. (Revelation 20:2-10 edited)

The world population will be close to the population before Noah's flood, since human longevity has been restored. The sinners have congregated around the ancient lands of Gog and Magog which are currently located between the northern ends of the Black and Caspian Seas in southern Russia. All the kings of the earth are not coming to this battle as at Armegeddon, but like those armies, they will all be burned up. Satan will be cast into the lake of fire where the beasts of the sea and earth have been tormented the last 1,000 years.

Second Death in Lake of Fire

Parable of Separating Sheep and Goats

When the Son of man shall come in his glory, and all the holy angels with him, then shall he sit on the throne of his glory: And before him shall be gathered all nations: and he shall separate them one from another, as a shepherd divides his sheep from the goats: And he shall set the sheep on his right hand, but the goats on the left. Then shall the King say to them on his right hand, Come, you blessed of my Father, inherit the kingdom prepared for you from the foundation of the world: . . . Truly I say to you, Inasmuch as you have done it to one of the least of these my brothers, you have done it to me. Then shall he say also to them on the left hand, <u>Depart from me, you cursed, into everlasting fire, prepared for the devil and his angels:</u> For I was an hungered, and you gave me no meat: I was thirsty, and you gave me no drink: I was a stranger, and you took me not in: naked, and you clothed me not: sick, and in prison, and you visited me not. Then shall they also answer him, saying, Lord, when saw we you an hungered, or thirsty, or a stranger, or naked, or sick, or in prison, and did not minister to you? Then shall he answer them, saying, Truly I say to you, Inasmuch as you did it not to one of the least of these, you did it not to me. And these shall go away into everlasting punishment: but the righteous into life eternal. (Matthew 25:31-46 edited)

King Jesus has been ruling for 1,000 years on earth. The dividing line is how people treated *"the least of these my brothers,"* most likely referring to disadvantaged Israelis or Jews, since at the end of the millennium there will be those who attack His beloved city of Jerusalem (Revelation 20:7-9). Those who mistreat His people during the Millennium go away into everlasting punishment in fire which was prepared for the devil and his angels (2 Peter 2:4). Those who kindly treat His people enter life eternal.

Great White Throne Judgment

And I saw a great white throne, and him that sat on it, from whose face the earth and the heaven fled away; and there was found no place for them. And I saw the dead, small and great, stand before God; and the books were opened: and another book was opened, which is the book of life: and the dead were judged out of those things which were written in the books, according to their works. And the sea gave up the dead which were in it; and death and hell delivered up the dead which were in them: <u>and they were judged every man according to their works. And death and hell were cast into the lake of fire. This is the second death. And whoever was not found written in the book of life was cast into the lake of fire.</u> (Revelation 20:11-15)

The unbelievers who died before Christ's second coming are judged by their works because they refused to accept the finished work of Jesus on their behalf. Those who died during the millennium who are not written in the book of life are also judged according to their works because they did not treat His brethren kindly. But believing overcomers shall not be hurt by the "*second death*" (Rev. 2:11b).

He that overcomes shall inherit all things; and I will be his God, and he shall be my son. But the fearful, and unbelieving, and the abominable, and murderers, and fornicators, and sorcerers, and idolaters, and all liars, shall have their part in the <u>lake which burns with fire and brimstone: which is the second death</u>. (Revelation 21:7-8)

Eternity

After all have been judged and judgment has been carried out, then those who love Jesus and His righteousness will live in eternity with Him without wickedness ever intruding again. Eternal life is knowing and being with Jesus.

The righteous perishes, and no man lays it to heart: and merciful men are taken away, none considering that the righteous is taken away from the evil to come. He shall enter into peace: they shall rest in their beds, each one walking in his uprightness. . . . For thus said <u>the high and lofty One that inhabits eternity, whose name is Holy; I dwell in the high and holy place, with him also that is of a contrite and humble spirit, to revive the spirit of the humble, and to revive the heart of the contrite ones</u>. For I will not contend for ever, neither will I be always wroth: for the spirit should fail before me, and the souls which I have made. (Isaiah 57:1-2, 15-16)

And this is life eternal, that they might know you the only true God, and Jesus Christ, whom you have sent. (John 17:3)

Final Warnings About the Book of Revelation

Behold, I come quickly: <u>blessed is he that keeps the sayings of the prophecy of this book</u>. And I John saw these things, and heard them. And when I had heard and seen, I fell down to worship before the feet of the angel which showed me these things. Then said he to me, See you do it not: for I am your fellow servant, and of your brothers the prophets, and of them which <u>keep the sayings of this book</u>: worship God. And he said to me, <u>Seal not the sayings of the prophecy of this book: for the time is at hand</u>. He that is unjust, let him be unjust still: and he which is filthy, let him be filthy still: and he that is righteous, let him be righteous still: and he that is holy, let him be holy still. . . . For I testify to every man that hears the words of the prophecy of this book, <u>If any man shall add to these things, God shall add to him the plagues that are written in this book: And if any man shall take away from the words of the book of this prophecy, God shall take away his part out of the</u>

Awake, Bride

book of life, and out of the holy city, and from the things which are written in this book. He which testifies these things said, Surely I come quickly. Amen. Even so, come, Lord Jesus. The grace of our Lord Jesus Christ be with you all. Amen. (Revelation 22:7-21 edited)

The book of Revelation is also precious to the angels who "*keep its sayings*". It is something to treasure and hold closely, and not to be flippant or haphazard about. Saints for almost 2,000 years have hoped in the imminent return of our Lord Jesus Christ. Truly, He will now come quickly.

Summary

Tishri 2, 2012 (Rosh Hashanah, Last portion of the "Day of the LORD")
    Satan is bound for 1,000 years.
    Believers' unloving works are "burned".
    Jesus takes His Beloved to the Bridal chamber He made, the New Jerusalem, while He destroys the earth with fire.
    The Wedding ceremony

Tishri 3-9
    The seven day Wedding Feast, "*Marriage Supper of the Lamb*" convenes.
    God restores the Heavens and terra-forms the Earth again in six days.

Tishri 10 (Yom Kippur, Day of Atonement)
    Fasting in holy awe of the Creator of a new heaven and new earth.

Tishri 11-14
    Bride returns to earth with Jesus, and begins building "booths".
    New boundaries for the tribes of Israel established.

Tishri 15-23 (Succoth, Feast of Booths)
    Curses are removed. Longevity of human life is restored.
    Beasts are now vegetarian and no longer fear nor harm man.
    Jesus places the earthly New Jerusalem and Temple which He's constructed.

Over the years cities are built and the faithful rule over them. Jesus and other saints reign over the earth; Jesus judges in righteousness and truth with a "*rod of iron*", but there will be sinners who need to be imprisoned. Many sinners will gather in the ancient lands of Gog and Magog. After 1,000 years, Satan will be released and will compel these people to attack Israel. God will consume them with fire and throw Satan into the lake of fire where others, who were not written in the book of life, will join him. Then the righteous will enjoy eternity with Jesus.

Conclusions

The Lord God of the holy prophets sent his angel to show to his servants the things which must shortly be done. Behold, I come quickly: blessed is he that keeps the sayings of the prophecy of this book. And I John saw these things, and heard them. (Revelation 22:6b-8a)

As we read the prophecies of Revelation and keep watch over them, we are truly blessed as we await our Lord's arrival. God desires to show "*His servants*" (plural) those things which "*must shortly be done*" (*tachos*). And Jesus says He comes "*quickly*" (*tachu*) or 'suddenly'. When we begin to see and hear the things which the apostle John did, we know Jesus will return soon. Our Lord God wants to reveal Jesus Christ and His future plans to us, so we will be ready for His coming. God is not being secretive. Understanding God's future plans is not relegated to a few prophets, but is available to all who serve the Lord Jesus.

Surely the Lord GOD will do nothing, but he reveals his secret to his servants the prophets. The lion has roared, who will not fear? the Lord GOD has spoken, who can but prophesy? (Amos 3:7)

Follow after charity, and desire spiritual gifts, but rather that you may prophesy. . . . But he that prophesies speaks to men to edification, and exhortation, and comfort. He that speaks in an unknown tongue edifies himself; but he that prophesies edifies the church. (1 Corinthians 14:1, 3-4)

But the prophet, which shall presume to speak a word in my name, which I have not commanded him to speak, or that shall speak in the name of other gods, even that prophet shall die. And if you say in your heart, How shall we know the word which the LORD has not spoken? When a prophet speaks in the name of the LORD, if the thing follow not, nor come to pass, that is the thing which the LORD has not spoken, but the prophet has spoken it presumptuously: you shall not be afraid of him. (Deuteronomy 18:20-22)

The prophet Jonah was given a word from the LORD for Nineveh's destruction, "*Yet forty days, and Nineveh shall be overthrown*" (Jonah 3:3b). This was not a conditional statement; yet because of their repentance, God relented (Jonah 3:10). According to Moses' command, Jonah should have been killed because his prophecy did not come to pass, but Jonah sought death out of anger at God (Jonah 4:3). God taught him compassion instead.

There have been many prophets predicting Christ's return in the last 100 years: some "*presumptuously*" (pridefully), and others humbly; some for gain, while others spent all they had to proclaim it. Since God reveals what He's about to do to His prophets, eventually some will get it right for the right reasons. Prior to Christ's first coming, regular people were anticipating His arrival: unbelieving Jews (John 10:24), seeking Samaritan woman, (John 4:25), and believing Martha (John 11:27). Several false messiahs led people astray during and soon after Christ's life (Acts 5:36-37). The same is true today.

People around the world are clamoring for a messiah to put an end to corruption (sin) and to establish peace throughout the world. Currently, a vast majority are expecting Barack Hussein Obama to be that messiah. Newsweek's Evans Thomas said on MSNBC, "In a way Obama's standing above the country – above the world, he's sort of God" [June 5, 2009]. Obama is neither Father God nor Jesus, but a false messiah. The true Messiah Jesus will return to earth from heaven at the end of the Great Tribulation, after the sun goes dark and the moon turns red, with the resurrected saints and voices and lightning and thunder and hail and a world-wide earthquake. Jesus warned His "*elect*", 'chosen' ones, not to be deceived by false Christs and false prophets (Matthew 24:24)

The "Church" contains all His chosen ones from Hebrew and non-Hebrew ancestry, as His Chosen Bride for Jesus. The word "*church*" was used by Jesus in Matthew 18:17 to refer to a 'gathering' of Jews. It was a common non-religious term used for civil affairs (1 Kings 12:3), for war (1 Samuel 17:46-47), and for God's gathering of the Hebrews at Mt. Sinai (Acts 7:38). Gentile believers have been grafted into the marvelous Hebrew stock through the blood of Jesus Christ. The knowledge of Hebrew culture helps the Bride of Christ understand the last days we are living in.

Hebrew Marriage Traditions	Fulfillment in Scripture
Groom returned to his father's house to build an addition, the bridal chamber.	Heavenly New Jerusalem John 14:2-3 and Rev. 21:9-27
After father deemed bridal chamber finished, he allowed son to leave at sunset to get bride.	"*Only the Father knows*" Mark 13:32-37
Groom to bride's house with shofars, shouting, "*Behold, the bridegroom comes.*"	Trumpets are *shofars* (1 Thess. 4:16-17). Matthew 25:6
Wedding ceremony took place under a *chupah*, a white canopy.	Bride meets Groom in clouds. Acts 1:9-11; 1 Thess. 4:14-18

Father God' Marriage Arrangement for His Son

When Father God arranged the marriage of the Hebrew nation (the Church) and His Son, He established the 'bride price' of His "*firstborn*" Son as the "*passover*" lamb (Exodus 11:5-11). In the light of the full moon they left Egypt, and a week later God parted the Red Sea while they crossed to Arabia safely, and then He closed the sea upon their enemies, giving the Hebrews the gift of freedom from bondage. Six weeks later, Father God as a fire spoke the bride's contract, the Ten Commandments, and the people responded with a fearful 'I do' (Exodus 19:1, 19). The pattern is the bride price is given on Passover, freedom from bondage is given on First Fruits, and the wedding contract is spoken with fire on Feast of Weeks (Pentecost).

When Jesus proclaimed the bride price of the "*new covenant*" to His Bride (the Church), many were offended at the thought of eating His body and drinking His blood (John 6), except for His disciples (Mark 14:22-24). After eating the Passover meal that night, Jesus became the Passover Lamb that day, then three days later arose victorious over sin and death and appeared to hundreds of witnesses for forty days. The disciples prayed for a week and then were baptized with the Holy Spirit on Pentecost. Jesus died on Passover, rose on First Fruits, and sent His Comforter with tongues of fire on Pentecost.

The old covenant was sealed by 70 elders on Mount Sinai. The new covenant, the scroll with seven seals, was sealed by the seven churches (Rev. 2-3). The opportunity to be included in Christ's Bride becomes successively more difficult with the breaking of each seal, and comes to an end when Jesus breaks the seventh seal. Then those bridal virgins who were prepared will go into the wedding, and those who went back into the world "to buy oil" because they didn't have a personal relationship with Jesus will be shut out (Matthew 25:1-13).

Jesus told this parable to His disciples to answer their question, "*What shall be the sign of your coming, and of the end of the world?*" (Matthew 24:3) In the parable, the groom arrives at midnight, which was considered late. A groom usually arrived at his bride's house soon after dusk so that the wedding ceremony could be held before midnight.

If you were to ask any betrothed Jewish man of Jesus' time, "When is the date of your wedding?" He would respond, "No one knows the day or the hour, except my father." The groom could not fetch his bride until his father declared the groom had finished the bridal chamber. After the betrothal it could take a year or two before all the preparations had been completed for the bridal chamber and the wedding ceremony. If word had been brought to the bride by a traveling family member that the bridal chamber was completed, then she would know it was a matter of days. The bride would prepare a lamp each night so she could light it and go to meet her groom as soon as she was awakened by the trumpets announcing his arrival. Her family would join her in a grand procession to his father's house for the wedding. But if the groom was delayed several hours after dusk, the family might think it was a "*thief in the night*" stealing their daughter away.

Awake, Bride

Day of the LORD was Known Exactly

We are to be on "*watch*" (Matthew 24:42-44) for Jesus in a way that we are not caught 'off guard' or 'overtaken' at His coming (Rev. 3:3). Jesus has not kept us 'in the dark' regarding His return.

*But of the times and the seasons, brothers, you have no need that I write to you. <u>For yourselves **know perfectly** that the day of the Lord so comes as a thief in the night.</u> For when they shall say, Peace and safety; then sudden destruction comes on them, as travail on a woman with child; and they shall not escape. <u>But you, brothers, are not in darkness, that that day should overtake you as a thief.</u> You are all the children of light, and the children of the day: we are not of the night, nor of darkness. Therefore let us not sleep, as do others; but let us watch and be sober. For they that sleep sleep in the night; and they that be drunken are drunken in the night. But let us, who are of the day, be sober, putting on the breastplate of faith and love; and for an helmet, the hope of salvation. <u>For God has not appointed us to wrath, but to obtain salvation by our Lord Jesus Christ, Who died for us, that, whether we wake or sleep, we should live together with him.</u> Why comfort yourselves together, and edify one another, even as also you do. . . . <u>Prove all things; hold fast that which is good.</u> Abstain from all appearance of evil. And the very God of peace sanctify you wholly; and I pray God your whole spirit and soul and body <u>be preserved blameless to the coming of our Lord Jesus Christ.</u> Faithful is he that calls you, who also will do it. (1 Thessalonians 5:1-24 edited)*

The wicked are appointed unto wrath, and "*they shall not escape*" destruction, but we are to "*abstain from all appearance of evil*" and "*obtain salvation*". The Day of the LORD will also be the end of the current heaven and earth. "*Heaven and earth shall pass away, but my words shall not pass away. But of that day and hour knows no man, no, not the angels of heaven, but my Father only*" (Matthew 24:35-36).

Rosh Hashanah, Jewish New Year, is the only feast day which occurs on the first of the month with a new moon; it is also the only feast without a name given to it in the Bible. Since those in Israel had to wait for Sanhedrin verification and the signal fires to begin the celebration, they "did not know the day or hour"; so it was determined to celebrate for two days which were considered one long day. To "not know the day or hour" was a code to Hebrews who celebrate Rosh Hashanah. Jesus then tells them the time plainly in the next few verses of the wedding parable. "*While the bridegroom tarried, they all slumbered and slept. And at **midnight** there was a cry made, Behold, the bridegroom comes; go you out to meet him*" (Matthew 25:5-6). So they were to expect Jesus to return at midnight on Rosh Hashanah. Why didn't Jesus just say clearly, "I'm returning at midnight on Rosh Hashanah"? Likely for the same reason He never corrected anyone who thought He was born in Nazareth. But Jesus did attempt to correct their notion that His Kingdom would come soon.

Conclusions

And as they heard these things, he added and spoke a parable, because he was near to Jerusalem, and <u>because they thought that the kingdom of God should immediately appear</u>. He said therefore, A certain nobleman went into a far country to receive for himself a kingdom, and to return. And he called his ten servants, and delivered them ten pounds, and said to them, Occupy till I come. (Luke 19:11-13)

There are several other corrections needed to understand Christ's return for His Bride. Daniel 11 and Ezekiel 38-39 were fulfilled in the centuries before Jesus was born. The ten toes of Nebuchadnezzar's statue and the 70th week of Daniel were fulfilled in the first centuries after Christ.

Daniel 11 and Ezekiel 38-39 Have Been Fulfilled

Gog and his Hebrew descendants originally occupied lands to the west and east of the Sea of Galilee before the Assyrians led them into captivity north between the Black and Caspian Seas (1 Chronicles 5:3-20, 734 BC), and later (Shalmaneser V, 724 BC) west into the land of the Medes (2 Kings 17:6). Gog's people intermarried with Assyrians and became Assyrian/Syrian. Antiochus III and IV both went to war against Egypt through Israel and Judah (Daniel 11:10-33). Antiochus IV is "*Gog*" of Ezekiel 38 and 39 who used mercenary troops from the countries listed therein to attack Israel. During the first seven years of the Macabbean Wars (167-161 BC), one quarter million of Gog's troops were killed. They provided enough wooden weaponry to stoke the fires for those seven years (Ezekiel 39:6-10). One of the attacks was near the "*former sea*" (Ezekiel 39:11) Lake Hula in the valley of Hazor which leads to a narrow passage along the Jordan which is the "*valley of the passengers*" and the "*valley of Hamongog*". Thus the people of Gog were buried back home in their own region in Israel. Only Ezekiel 38:19-23 is yet to be fulfilled "*in that day*" of the great earthquake at Christ's coming.

Nebuchadnezzar's Statue Prophecy Was Fulfilled

There won't be a revived Roman empire of ten nations. Ten different Caesars beginning with Nero led persecutions against the Christians. The ten toes were ten kings/caesars.

*And as <u>the toes</u> of the feet were part of iron, and part of clay, so the kingdom shall be partly strong, and partly broken. And whereas you saw iron mixed with miry clay, they shall mingle themselves with the seed of men: but they shall not join one to another, even as iron is not mixed with clay. And in the days of <u>these kings</u> shall the God of heaven set up **a kingdom, which shall never be destroyed**: and the kingdom shall not be left to other people, **but it shall break in pieces and consume all these kingdoms, and it shall stand for ever.** For as much as you saw that the stone was cut out of the mountain without hands, and that it broke in pieces the iron, the brass, the clay, the silver, and the gold; the great God has made known to* *the king what shall come to pass hereafter: and the dream is certain, and the interpretation thereof sure." (Daniel 2:42-45)*

The kingdoms of the statue (including Rome) were consumed by the kingdom of Christianity after Constantine declared it the state religion. The kingdom of Christ "*shall stand for ever*". But do look for ten kings to give their power to the "*little horn*" (Daniel 7:7-27) for "*one hour*" (Rev. 17:12).

70th Week of Daniel 9 Was Fulfilled by 70 AD

God gave Daniel a prophecy of a period of seventy weeks for His people and Jerusalem to complete all punishment and be forgiven all sin. God's command to start the 490 year period corresponds with king Artaxerxes decree in his 20th year (454 BC) to Nehemiah to rebuild Jerusalem. After 483 years Jesus is baptized and declared to be God's anointed Son, the Messiah and Prince; and the Lamb of God of the new covenant. Jesus ministered during the first half of the 70th week, and then was "*cut off*" with His blood as the bride price of the new covenant. The last half of the 70th week occurred within that "*generation*" (in accordance with Jesus' prophecy in Matthew 24:2, 33-34), beginning with Vespasian troops attacking Israel's northern coast and Galilee in the spring of 67 AD, and ending with the siege and destruction of Jerusalem and its Temple in the summer of 70 AD. The entire 70 weeks prophecy has been fulfilled. Christ's Bride should not be anticipating any seven year treaty with Israel nor a seven year period of tribulation.

Church Has Been In Tribulation and Will Go Through Great Tribulation

Jesus and Paul and the other NT writers spoke of current tribulation and persecution. The Church has been in the Tribulation since Christ was born (John 16:33). John, who wrote the book of Revelation after the Temple's destruction, clarified in "*times*", months, and days that the Great Tribulation would be exactly 3 1/2 years, 42 months, and 1,260 days. Periods of seven are typical for punishment and forgiveness (Leviticus 26:16-19; Dan. 9:2, 24), but Jesus stated the period would be shortened for the sake of the elect (Mat. 24:21-22). The Church will go through the Great Tribulation, but they will be spared from the plagues of the seven vials of God's wrath (1 Thess. 5:9) much like the Hebrews were spared from the plagues poured out on the Egyptians; with God making a distinction between those who have "*the mark of the beast, and on them which worshipped his image*" and "*shed the blood of saints and prophets*" (Rev. 16:2, 6), and those who do not. Then after the 7th vial, Christ will come for His Church to join Him (resurrection and rapture) and the saints from heaven (1 Thess. 4:14-18) in destroying the armies of the wicked at Armageddon (Rev. 16:14-21).

Resurrection and Rapture at Christ's Second Coming

Jesus described Tribulation and the Great Tribulation prior to His return and rapture of saints as recorded by Matthew 24 and Luke 17 & 21. The early church fathers recorded the same progression in Didache 16. Jesus will remain in heaven until His "*appearing*" (Acts 3:20-21). The 2nd Coming of Christ, His "*glorious appearing*" (Titus 2:13; 2 Tim. 4:1-8), will be at the end of the Great Tribulation; that appearing is also known as "*the day of the Lord*" (Zechariah 14:1-21).

The separation of Christ's one appearing into two episodes was done by Catholics around 500 AD to keep Protestants from calling the pope the antichrist. They deduced if a rapture of the church occurs before the antichrist declares himself diety in the temple, they could no longer accuse the pope of being "*that Wicked*" one. The author of the often used Catholic quote was Psuedo Ephrem (the original Ephrem lived 306-373 AD). These two appearings of Christ were later popularized among Protestants by John Darby in the early 1800s. Pre-tribulation rapture is a false doctrine. Saints miraculously living through God's judgment of the wicked is Biblical: Jesus gave Noah and Lot (Luke 17:24-37) as examples.

The resurrection of the dead occurs prior to the rapture of those still alive at Christ's coming. "*In a moment, in the twinkling of an eye, at the last **trump**: for the trumpet shall sound, and the dead shall be raised incorruptible, and we shall be changed.*" (1 Corinthians 15:52). "*And with the **trump** of God: and <u>the dead in Christ shall rise first: Then we which are alive and remain shall be caught up together with them in the **clouds**, to meet the Lord in the air</u>: and so shall we ever be with the Lord*" (1 Thessalonians 4:14-17). In a blink of an eye the dead saints are raised first and then the living saints are caught up (raptured) with them and Jesus in the clouds.

Abominations

> *Seventy weeks are determined on your people and on your holy city . . . And after threescore and two weeks shall <u>Messiah</u> be cut off, but not for himself: and the people of the prince that shall come shall destroy the city and the sanctuary; and the end thereof shall be with a flood, **and unto the end of the war desolations are determined**. And <u>he</u> shall confirm the covenant with many for one week: and in the midst of the week <u>he</u> shall cause the sacrifice and the oblation to cease, and **for the overspreading of abominations <u>he</u> shall make it desolate**, even until the consumption, and that determined shall be poured upon the desolate. (Daniel 9:24-27 edited)* Jesus fulfilled His part by His sacrifice on April 3, 33 AD which rent the veil in the Temple, and the Syrian troops of Titus fulfilled their part by destroying the Temple and Jerusalem within a generation in 70 AD.

Three times Daniel mentions the abomination of desolation. Jesus made the Temple "*desolate*" because of the overspreading of Israel's "*abominations*" (Daniel 9:27), and the "*seventy weeks*" prophecy was completely fulfilled by 70 AD, and provided a clue regarding the "*the people of the prince that shall come*" would be Syrian, referring to Antiochus IV and his army's abomination of desolation. Antiochus Epiphanes IV with his Syrian army fulfilled Daniel 8:8-14 and 11:31, leaving the last one of Daniel's "*abomination*" prophecies to be fulfilled (Daniel 12:11-12).

*And **arms** shall stand on his part, and **they** shall pollute the sanctuary of strength, and shall take away the daily sacrifice, and **they** shall place the abomination that makes desolate. (Daniel 11:31)* Antiochus Epiphanes IV and his Syrian army fulfilled this in 167 BC. Thus, "*the people*" - Syrians, "*of the prince that shall come*" - Antiochus IV, destroyed the Temple and Jerusalem in 70 AD.

And from the time that the daily sacrifice shall be taken away, and the abomination that makes desolate set up, *there shall be a thousand two hundred and ninety days. Blessed is he that waits, and comes to the thousand three hundred and five and thirty days. (Daniel 12:11-12 edited)* This is the passage referred to by Jesus as to be fulfilled prior to the Great Tribulation. These numbers (1, 290 and 1,335) coupled with the numbers from Daniel 8:7 and 14 (2,300 and date of 333 when goat conquered ram), lead to the year 2012 for Christ's second coming.

333 BC the goat conquered the ram; Alexander conquered Darius III Codomannus.
   From Daniel 8, we have 2300 - 333 = 1967.
677 The date for the completion of the Al-Aqsa Mosque is between 674 and 679.
   I chose 677 because it yields the 1967 year. 677 + 1,290 = 1967.
1967 Jews regain control of Jerusalem after 6-day war. Though the Jews recaptured Jerusalem, the abomination of Muslim structures on the Temple Mount remained. 677 + 1,335 = 2012.
2012 Those waiting and "*looking for that blessed hope*" will see "*the glorious appearing of our Savior Jesus Christ*" (Titus 2:13) on His birthday, Tishri 1, Rosh Hashanah; which is September 16, 2012.

In answering the disciples' question of "*what shall be the sign of your coming, and of the end of the world?*" (Mat. 24:3b), Jesus replied in verse 15, "*When you therefore shall see the abomination of desolation, spoken of by Daniel the prophet, stand in the holy place, (whoever reads, let him understand:)*". 'Understand' is *noieo*, which means to 'exercise the mind'. "*It is the glory of God to conceal a thing: but the honor of kings is to search out a matter*" (Proverbs 25:2). The treasure of the truth of the year of Christ's second coming has been waiting in Scripture for those willing to search for it.

Antichrist: The Little Horn with the Blasphemous Mouth

Regarding the "*little horn*" of the end times, Daniel wrote, "*And in the latter time of their kingdom, when the transgressors are come to the full, a king of fierce countenance, and understanding dark sentences, shall stand up. And his power shall be mighty, but not by his own power: and he shall destroy wonderfully, and shall prosper, and practice, and shall destroy the mighty and the holy people. And through his policy also he shall cause craft to prosper in his hand; and he shall magnify himself in his heart, and by peace shall destroy many: he shall also stand up against the Prince of princes; but he shall be broken without hand.*" (Daniel 8:23-25) And "*a **mouth speaking great things**.*" (Daniel 7:8e)

*And there was given to him a **mouth speaking great things** <u>and blasphemies</u>; and power was given to him to continue forty and two months. And he opened his mouth in <u>blasphemy against God, to blaspheme his name, and his tabernacle, and them that dwell in heaven</u>. And it was given to him to make war with the saints, and to overcome them: (Revelation 13:5-7a)*

Now we beseech you, brothers, by the coming of our Lord Jesus Christ, and by our gathering together to him, . . . Let no man deceive you by any means: for that day shall not come, except there come a falling away first, and that man of sin be revealed, the son of perdition; <u>Who opposes and exalts himself above all that is called God, or that is worshipped; so that he as God sits in the temple of God, showing himself that he is God</u>. (2 Thessalonians 2:1, 3-4)

Though the Antichrist will blaspheme against God and His Name and tabernacle, the False Prophet and/or False Messiah exalts himself above God and sits in the place of His Temple. Our gathering to Jesus at His coming will not occur until after the False Prophet/False Messiah declares himself deity. Because this announcement will have immediate devastating consequences for Israel, Jesus told them to pray it might not happen on a sabbath or in winter (Matthew 24:20).

In Islamic eschatology, the distorted Jesus (Isa) of the Quran will return bodily to defeat the bad al-Dajjal (False Messiah), who leads Muslims astray. The Muslim savior, al-Mahdi, will be a direct descendant of Mohammed. He will unite Muslims as one caliphate again and lead the army of black flags to conquer the Jews and establish a base at Jerusalem, but have his headquarters in Iraq. Iran's Ahmadinejad believes causing world chaos will hasten the arrival of the Muslim Mahdi, and that he will come before the end of his presidency (election is June 12, 2009) [*Ahmadinejad: The Secret History of Iran's Radical Leader* by Kasra Naji in 2008, p92]. Ahmadinejad is already acting as the False Prophet, preparing to welcome and support the Mahdi. The Mahdi will likely be a Sunni Muslim from the ancient lands of Assyria.

Babylonian Empire Has Revived

The revived Babylonian empire includes the people and the lands of the Medes & Persians, Greeks, and Romans who once conquered it. Islam is Daniel's 4th beast (Daniel 7:19-25) and the "*beast of the sea*" (Rev.13:1-8; 17:3-18). Islam is both a religion and a governing state. The US poured billions of dollars into restoring Iraq's infrastructure, who then demanded their constitution be based upon Sharia law as in Afghanistan. God used America to empower the ancient seat of Babylon. As soon as the US pulls its troops out of Iraq, Iraq will become a Muslim epicenter of power; its current population is dominated by Shiites. Iran's Ahmadinejad plans to cause world chaos so that the Muslim Mahdi will arise from a well/"*pit*" to take control of the world. The Mahdi is the "*Little horn*" (Daniel 8) with the blasphemous mouth, the Antichrist.

Awake, Bride

God's Team	Satan's Team
Jerusalem	Babylon
Jesus Christ	Antichrist (Muslim Mahdi)
7 Churches	7-headed Beast of Sea (Sunni)
Two Witnesses	2-horned Beast of Earth (Shia)
Bride of Christ	Whore (Wahhabi)
Michael	Destroying Angel from Abyss
other angels	other demons

The Beast of the Earth is referred to as economic/religious system and "*the false prophet*"; and the Beast of the Sea is sometimes referred to as the political/religious system, and sometimes as the Antichrist leader ("little horn") who comes from it. The False Prophet will perform miraculous signs of bringing fire down from heaven (nukes?) and beheading those who do not worship the Beast of the Sea (Rev. 20:4).

Beasts are empires in prophetic scriptures. The two main religious empires of Islam are Sunni (7-headed Beast of Sea) and Shia (2-horned Beast of Earth). The most powerful sect of Sunnism is Wahhabism, which is the Whore that rides the 7-headed beast. The 7 heads represent the seven moon-worshiping empires over time based from Babylon, just as the 7 churches represent Christianity in history.

The Sunni sect is the largest with dozens of national adherents. The Shia are predominant in Iran with large populations in Iraq and Afghanistan. The Wahhabis control Saudi Arabia and most of the Arabian Peninsula. Shia and Sunnis despise the house of Saud and Wahhabism for their decadence and opulence in Westernizing themselves.

Four Horsemen

Three and a half prophetic years is 1,260 days. Rosh Hashanah begins at sundown on Sept. 16, 2012 with the rest of the 'day' following on the 17th. Counting backwards from Sunday, Sept. 16th we arrive at Monday, April 6, 2009 for the beginning of the Great Tribulation. Prior to this, the four horses of the first four seals came first to wake us up. September 11, 2001 was the day the world woke up to the four horsemen, and the description of the terrorist attack on the Twin Towers in New York City was included in Revelation 11:8-12 to verify the timing. The 'wake up' period is roughly seven and a half years (2,665 days); could they have included the "*seven thunders*" (Rev. 10:3-4)?

Though Islamic terrorists had bombed many embassies worldwide, it was the attack on September 11, 2001 which awakened the world to the "peaceful" **white horse** of Islam attempting to conquer the world without "arrows" (nukes). This leads us to the **red horse** of terrorism which has "*taken peace from the earth.*" Not content to just kill infidels, the Muslims also kill other Muslims ("*they should kill one another*"). On September 11, 2008 the US was involved in secret negotiations to divide Jerusalem as Hurricane Ike headed toward Texas. The **black horse** of economic ruin was acknowledged a few weeks later on

Conclusions

September 29th, 2008. The **pale horse** of Death controls a quarter of the world. Currently Islam has a majority in one fourth of the world and comprises one fourth of the population.

Great Tribulation

April 6, 2009 was the first day of the Great Tribulation. On that day a unique sign in the heavens was reported by Fox News: "In a new image from NASA's Chandra X-ray Observatory, high-energy X-rays emanating from the nebula around PSR B1509-58 have been colored blue to reveal a structure resembling a hand reaching for some eternal red cosmic light."

Your hand shall find out all your enemies: <u>your right hand shall find out those that hate you. You shall make them as a fiery oven in the time of your anger</u>: the LORD shall swallow them up in his wrath, and the fire shall devour them. Their fruit shall you destroy from the earth, and their seed from among the children of men. **For they intended evil against you: they imagined a mischievous device, which they are not able to perform.** *Therefore shall you make them turn their back, when you shall make ready your arrows on your strings against the face of them. (Psalms 21:8-12)*

<u>Though I walk in the middle of trouble, you will revive me: you shall stretch forth your hand against the wrath of my enemies, and your right hand shall save me</u>. The LORD will perfect that which concerns me: your mercy, O LORD, endures for ever: forsake not the works of your own hands. (Psalms 138:7-8)

God has begun the process of destroying those who hate Him and delivering those who love Him. I pray that the terrorists are unable to secure or produce a nuclear weapon ("*mischievous device*") before Christ returns. God may use Israel to stop them.

Power and Influence of USA Was Removed

And now you know <u>what withholds that he might be revealed in his time</u>. For the mystery of iniquity does already work: only he who now lets will let, until he be taken out of the way. And then shall that Wicked be revealed." (2 Thess. 2:3-8a)

This verse primarily refers to the archangel Michael withholding Satan until the Great Tribulation, but it has a clear secondary meaning as well. Barnes' Bible Commentary on this verse states: "The most natural interpretation is that which refers it to civil power, meaning that there was something in the form of the existing administration which would prevent this development until that restraint should be removed."

In order for God to accomplish what He intends to do in the Middle East, He needed to remove the United States of America. The black horse of economic ruin has already removed the US dollar as the standard of world currency, and continued reckless government spending will keep it suppressed. On April 6, 2009 America's commander-in-chief declared to the Muslims in Turkey that we are not a Christian nation and are not and will never be at war with Islam. President Obama announced the withdrawal of troops from Iraq by the end of August, 2010. Each demonstration of American weakness and withdrawal emboldens the jihadists. After troops have left Iraq, I expect the Mahdi and his army to arise. The best candidate is Muqtada Sadr who stood down his Mahdi army in Iraq in August 2008, but could revive it easily.

Great Tribulation Time-line

The first angelic announcement is the everlasting gospel with a loud voice to the world (Rev. 14:6-7). The second angelic announcement is the fall of the great city Babylon (Mecca), taken out by a meteor and/or fires. With the Wahhabis and Saudi oil out of the way, the Beast of the Earth (the Shiites) will then require all people to wear a mark of allegiance to Islam on their arm or forehead in order to buy or sell (possible international monetary standard of the 'gold dinar') or be beheaded if they refuse the mark. The third angelic announcement is if anyone worships the Beast or takes its mark, he will also experience God's wrath poured out on the Beast.

I suspect the trumpets and vials to begin sometime after all American combat troops are pulled out of Iraq. It is unclear how much time is allotted to each trumpet or vial or between each. All the Great Tribulation days and times are according to Hebrew days and Jerusalem time, but I use traditional calendar dates here. The trumpets and vials are concurrent with each other.

First Four Trumpets (upon world)	First Four Vials (upon Babylon)
1st All grass burnt; 1/3 trees	1st Sores upon worshipers of Beast
2nd 1/3 sea, sea-life & ships	2nd Sea to blood; all sea-life dies
3rd 1/3 rivers; & bitter waters	3rd All rivers and fountains to blood
4th 1/3 of sun, moon & stars	4th Use sun to scorch men with fire

3/26/2011-8/23/2011 (prelude to Armegeddon)

    5th Chemical war with helicopters   5th Painful sores & darkness

8/23/2011-9/16/2012 (Armegeddon War)   [5th seal during Armegeddon War]

    6th Chemical/Fire tanks   6th Dry Euphrates for Shia armies
6th seal
9/16/2012 (Day of the LORD) 7th Seal and Vial and Trumpet

The 6th seal is broken within a few hours of the day of the Lord. The 7th vial will be poured out over Babylon (Islam) completing God's wrath upon them, and the 7th seal and the 7th trumpet over the world as voices, lightning, thunder, hail, and a great earthquake are experienced around the globe. The sun will be dark and the moon look like blood, but the brightness of Christ's coming will illuminate the world. Jesus will bring the resurrected saints with Him and collect His living saints en route to Jerusalem where the Bride fights for Israel and is victorious over the Antichrist and all nations gathered against Israel. ["*All kings*" are enticed to the battle of Armegeddon, not just those listed in Ezekiel 38.]

Day of the LORD

Jesus, the Lamb of God was born on Rosh Hashanah, September 11, 3 BC, and He will return on His birthday at the end of the Great Tribulation as the Lion of the tribe of Judah to rescue the righteous and to destroy the wicked. His Bride needs to wake up and live righteously, and lovingly proclaim the good news of grace in Jesus while there is still time. Jesus, the King of kings, will return to establish His kingdom on earth at midnight on Rosh Hashanah, Tishri 1; Sunday, September 16, 2012. Traditionally, the feast of trumpets is celebrated for two days which are considered one long day, so the "Day of the Lord" will continue until dusk on September 18, 2012.

The Day of the LORD is referred to by many other names: "The Day of Vengeance of our God", "The Day of God's Wrath", "The Day of God's Judgment", "The Great and Dreadful Day", and more. The Day of the LORD is referred to so often, it is also abbreviated to just "That Day" or "The Day". It is the climax of human history and God's prophecies. It is the day when King Jesus returns to earth with His resurrected saints, snatches His Bride still alive, and conquers those who have attacked Israel, judging and destroying the wicked.

Day of the LORD Time-Line

These are estimations. Much more is accomplished during the Day of the LORD.
Tishri 1-2: Sunday, September 16, 2012 at dusk until dusk on September 18, 2012.

Dusk	Silence in heaven for half an hour Jesus is coronated with "*many crowns*" in heaven. Voices, Lightnings, Thunders, and Great Hail and an Earthquake on earth
Midnight	"*The Brightness of His Coming*" as "*Lightning from the east to the west*" Resurrection and Rapture of Saints "*in the twinkling of an eye*" Jesus, "*the Breaker*", destroys those attacking "*Bozrah*" (Petra)
Dawn	Jesus stands on the Mount of Olives, splitting it in two so Jews can escape. Jesus and His saints destroy the wicked in Jerusalem.
Noon	Saints ride with Jesus to battle the wicked at Armegeddon (Rev. 19:17) and the Antichrist and his armies are defeated and the fowls feast on their flesh.
Dusk	The dead are judged (Rev. 11:18)

Awake, Bride

Midnight	*"At evening time it shall be light."* (Zech. 14:7)
Dawn	Beasts of Sea and Earth are cast into the Lake of Fire. Satan is bound for 1,000 years. Believers' unloving works are burned.
Noon	Jesus takes His Beloved to the Bridal chamber He made, the New Jerusalem, while He destroys the earth with fire.
Dusk	The Wedding ceremony: we are made one in answer to Jesus' prayer in John 17:20-26.

Earth Destroyed by Fire while Bride is in Heavenly New Jerusalem

Jesus went away to *"prepare a place"* for us - a bridal chamber which is called the New Jerusalem. According to its description in Revelation 20, the area of each face of the cube is roughly 1500 miles by 1500 miles for a volume of 3.375 billion cubic miles; half the size of the moon. Since its base would take up half or more of any continent and would greatly depress the earth's crust, and *"the nations walk by its light"*. A third of the day and night are gone, so it may act as an additional luminary in the sky. It does not reflect light, but emanates light from within. It is a huge, glowing, space cube. Its presence at Christ's 2nd coming allows Rosh Hashanah to have light at all hours.

Since the battle of the armies at Armageddon may be nuclear (Zechariah 14:11-15; Ezekiel 38:17-23) and the earth is a mess after the Great Tribulation (seas and rivers of blood, no grass, etc.), God will purge the world by fire.

> *Seeing then that all these things shall be dissolved, what manner of persons ought you to be in all holy conversation and godliness, <u>Looking for and hastening to the coming of the day of God, wherein the heavens being on fire shall be dissolved, and the elements shall melt with fervent heat?</u> Nevertheless we, according to his promise, look for new heavens and a new earth, wherein dwells righteousness. Why, beloved, seeing that you look for such things, be diligent that you may be found of him in peace, without spot, and blameless. (2 Peter 3:11-14)*

Those who will *"ever be with the Lord"* will be housed in the New Jerusalem, our Bridal chamber, until a New Heaven and Earth is prepared for us (terra-formed again in 6 days during our honeymoon with Jesus). Resurrected immortals will live in the heavenly New Jerusalem or the new earth without marriage or sex like the angels (Mat. 22:30). Raptured immortals who were married will continue their marriage on the new earth and be able to procreate. Their children will not be immortal or have a sin-nature, but they can still chose to sin; there are infants, sin, and death during the millennium (Isaiah 65:17-20).

Conclusions

First Few Days of Millennial Reign

Dusk September 18 to dusk on September 25
> The seven day Wedding Feast, "*Marriage Supper of the Lamb*" convenes.
> God restores the Heavens and terra-forms the Earth again in six days.

Dusk September 25th to dusk on September 26th (Yom Kippur)
> Fasting in holy awe of the Creator of a new heaven and new earth.

Dusk September 26th to dusk on September 30th
> Bride returns to earth with Jesus, and begins building booths.
> New boundaries for the tribes of Israel established.

Dusk September 30th to dusk on October 8th (Succoth/Feast of Booths)
> Curses are removed. Longevity of human life is restored.
> Beasts are now vegetarian and no longer fear nor harm man.
> Jesus places the earthly New Jerusalem and Temple which He's constructed.

Earthly New Jerusalem and Temple

And <u>David my servant shall be king over them</u>; and they all shall have one shepherd: they shall also walk in my judgments, and observe my statutes, and do them. And they shall dwell in the land that I have given to Jacob my servant, wherein your fathers have dwelled; and they shall dwell therein, even they, and their children, and their children's children for ever: and <u>my servant David shall be their prince for ever</u>. Moreover I will make a covenant of peace with them; it shall be an everlasting covenant with them: and I will place them, and multiply them, and <u>will set my sanctuary in the middle of them for ever more. My tabernacle also shall be with them: yes, I will be their God, and they shall be my people. And the heathen shall know that I the LORD do sanctify Israel, when my sanctuary shall be in the middle of them for ever more.</u> (Ezekiel 37:24-28)

Jesus, the descendant of king David, shall be King of the Hebrews in the land He promised them. There is no temple in the heavenly space cube New Jerusalem, but there is a temple in the earthly city of New Jerusalem. It is the temple described to Ezekiel in chapters 40-47 and built by Jesus (Zechariah 6:12-13).

Healing Waters on the Last Day of *Sukkot*/Booths

On the eighth day of the feast, the high priest would declare "*Behold, God is my salvation; I will trust, and not be afraid: for the LORD JEHOVAH is my strength and my song; he also is become my salvation;*" (Isaiah 12:2), and the people would respond with the following verse, "*Therefore with joy shall you draw water out of the wells of salvation.*"

Awake, Bride

The fulfillment of this "*great day*" in the Millennium will be when Jesus brings down His new city of Jerusalem with its Temple and places it upon the earth, and the Temple Mount spring gushes forth living water from the throne in the Holy of Holies which brings healing (Ezekiel 47).

The River of Life with Trees of Healing

Those who sin in the millennial kingdom of Christ can be cleansed by drinking from the river of the water of life which issues as a fountain from the throne of God. Jesus will be physically present with the scars in His wrists and side from His crucifixion. Instead of a dead wooden cross which represented the tree of the knowledge of good and evil (the Law in Col. 2:14), there will be a tree of life which produces fruit of life and leaves for healing, but only those who obey Christ's command may eat of it. Sadly, there will be those who refuse to submit to King Jesus and drink of the water of life which flows from His throne in earthly New Jerusalem, and so they will not be allowed to enter the city.

And he that sat on the throne said, Behold, I make all things new. And he said to me, Write: for these words are true and faithful. And he said to me, It is done. I am Alpha and Omega, the beginning and the end. <u>*I will give to him that is thirsty of the fountain of the water of life freely.*</u> *He that overcomes shall inherit all things; and I will be his God, and he shall be my son. But the fearful, and unbelieving, and the abominable, and murderers, and fornicators, and sorcerers, and idolaters, and all liars, shall have their part in the lake which burns with fire and brimstone: which is the second death. (Revelation 21:5-8)*

And he showed me <u>*a pure river of water of life*</u>*, clear as crystal,* <u>*proceeding out of the throne of God and of the Lamb*</u>*. In the middle of the street of it, and on either side of the river, was there the* **tree of life**, *which bore twelve manner of fruits, and yielded her fruit every month: and the* **leaves** *of the tree were for the* **healing** *of the nations. . . . Blessed are they that do his commandments, that they may have right to the tree of life, and may enter in through the gates into the city. For without are dogs, and sorcerers, and fornicators, and murderers, and idolaters, and whoever loves and makes a lie. . . . And the Spirit and the bride say, Come. And let him that hears say, Come. And let him that is thirsty come. And whoever will, let him take the water of life freely. (Revelation 22:1-2,14-15,17)*

Now when I had returned, behold, <u>*at the bank of the river were very many* **trees** *on the one side and on the other*</u>*. Then said he to me, These waters issue out toward the east country, and go down into the desert, and go into the sea: which being brought forth into the sea, the waters shall be healed. And it shall come to pass, that every thing that lives, which moves,* <u>*wherever the rivers shall come, shall live*</u>*: and there shall be a very great multitude of fish, because these waters shall come thither: for they shall be healed; and* <u>*every thing shall live where the river comes*</u>*. And it shall come to pass, that the fishers shall stand on it from Engedi even to Eneglaim; they shall be a place to spread forth nets; their fish shall be according to their kinds, as the fish of the great sea, exceeding many. But the miry places thereof and the marshes thereof shall not be healed; they shall be given to salt. And by the river on the bank thereof, on this side and on that side, shall grow all trees for* *meat, whose **leaf** shall not fade, neither shall the fruit thereof be consumed: it shall bring forth new fruit according to his months, <u>because their waters they issued out of the sanctuary</u>: and the fruit thereof shall be for meat, and the **leaf** thereof for **medicine**. (Ezekiel 47:7-12)*

"*Healed*" water means drinkable, fresh water as opposed to salt. En Gedi is on the southwest shore of the Dead Sea, and Eneglaim is on the northern shore. In addition to fruit and grains, we will also eat fish.

Over the years cities are built and the faithful rule over them. Jesus and other saints reign over the earth; Jesus judges in righteousness and truth with a "*rod of iron*", but there will be sinners who gather in the ancient lands of Gog and Magog. After 1,000 years, Satan will be released and will compel these people to attack Israel. God will consume them with fire and throw Satan into the lake of fire where others, who were not written in the book of life (Great White Throne Judgment), will join him. Then the righteous will enjoy eternity with Jesus (John 17:3).

For thus said the high and lofty One that inhabits eternity, whose name is Holy; I dwell in the high and holy place, with him also that is of a contrite and humble spirit, to revive the spirit of the humble, and to revive the heart of the contrite ones. (Isaiah 57:15)

Bride Fasts while the Bridegroom is Away

Jesus is the Bridegroom (John 3:27-29), and believers in Him are His Bride.

*And Jesus said to them, Can the children of the bridal chamber **mourn**, as long as the bridegroom is with them? but the days will come, when the bridegroom shall be taken from them, and then shall they **fast**. No man puts a piece of new cloth to an old garment, for that which is put in to fill it up takes from the garment, and the rent is made worse. Neither do men put new wine into old bottles: else the bottles break, and the wine runs out, and the bottles perish: but they put new wine into new bottles, and both are preserved. (Matthew 9:15-17)*

Mark and Luke also record the analogies of the cloth and wineskins following Christ's declaration that the children awaiting the bridegroom will fast when he's gone. The *ketubah*, the Spirit of the Groom's covenant had to fulfill and supersede the *erusin*, the Law of the Bride's covenant. The Bride was to acknowledge her failure (sin) to keep the Law in order to receive the bride price of forgiveness in Christ through faith. "*The law was our schoolmaster to bring us to Christ, that we might be justified by faith. But after that faith is come, we are no longer under a schoolmaster*" (Galatians 3:23-24).

There is therefore now no condemnation to them which are in Christ Jesus, who walk not after the flesh, but after the Spirit. For the law of the Spirit of life in Christ Jesus has made me free from the law of sin and death. (Romans 8:1-2)

Awake, Bride

Yet in this freedom, the Bride is to fast while the Bridegroom is away. The Hebrews fast thirty days during the month of Elul prior to Rosh Hashanah, and another ten days until after Yom Kippur for a total of forty days. They are days of repentance, *teshuvah*, when the trumpet is blown in repetition. Moses and Christ physically fasted forty days, and there may be those who chose to follow their example. Elul 1 will occur on August 21, 2009; August 11, 2010; August 31, 2011; and August 19, 2012.

*Cry aloud . . . <u>lift up your voice like a trumpet</u>, and show my people their transgression . . . you shall not fast as you do this day . . . Is not this the **fast** that I have chosen? to loose the bands of wickedness, to undo the heavy burdens, and to let the oppressed go free, and that you break every yoke? Is it not to deal your bread to the hungry, and that you bring the poor that are cast out to your house? when you see the naked, that you cover him; and that you hide not yourself from your own flesh? Then shall your light break forth as the morning, and your health shall spring forth speedily: and your righteousness shall go before you . . . <u>Then shall you call, and the LORD shall answer; you shall cry, and he shall say, Here I am</u>. If you take away from the middle of you the yoke, the putting forth of the finger, and speaking vanity; And if you draw out your soul to the hungry, and satisfy the afflicted soul; then shall your light rise in obscurity, and your darkness be as the noon day: And the LORD shall guide you continually . . . and <u>you shall be like a watered garden, and like a spring of water, whose waters fail not</u>. . . . But your iniquities have separated between you and your God, and your sins have hid his face from you, that he will not hear. . . . We roar all like bears, and <u>mourn sore like doves</u>: we look for judgment, but there is none . . . For our transgressions are multiplied before you . . . and the LORD saw . . . that there was no man, and wondered that there was no <u>intercessor</u>: therefore his arm brought salvation to him; and his righteousness, it sustained him. For he put on righteousness as a breastplate, and an helmet of salvation on his head; and he put on the garments of vengeance for clothing, and was clad with zeal as a cloak. . . . And the Redeemer shall come to Zion, and to them that turn from transgression in Jacob . . . this is my covenant with them, said the LORD; My spirit that is on you, and my words which I have put in your mouth, shall not depart out of your mouth . . . Arise, shine; for your light is come, and the glory of the LORD is risen on you. . . . the darkness shall cover the earth . . . but the LORD shall arise on you . . . And the Gentiles shall come to your light . . . For the nation and kingdom that will not serve you shall perish . . . and you shall know that I the LORD am your Savior and your Redeemer . . . The sun shall be no more your light by day; neither for brightness shall the moon give light to you: but the LORD shall be to you an everlasting light . . . <u>and the days of your **mourning** shall be ended</u>. Your people also shall be all righteous: they shall inherit the land for ever . . . that I may be glorified. . . . (Isaiah 58-60 edited)*

Our fasting and mourning will end when our King arrives. In the Song of Solomon, the Bridegroom is called the 'Beloved', and His Bride is called a 'garden' and a 'dove' among lilies. Psalm 45 foretells of King Jesus' wife, the queen, praising Him and raising children to be princes.

Upon Shoshannim [white trumpets like lilies]. . . a song of the Beloved. . . . You are fairer than the children of men: grace is poured into your lips: therefore God has blessed you for ever. Gird your sword on your thigh, O most mighty, with your glory and your majesty. And in your majesty ride prosperously because of truth and meekness and righteousness . . . Your arrows are sharp in the heart of the king's enemies; whereby the people fall under you. Your throne, O God, is for ever and ever: the scepter of your kingdom is a right scepter. You love righteousness, and hate wickedness: therefore God, your God, has anointed you with the oil of gladness . . . your garments smell of myrrh, and aloes, and cassia, out of the ivory palaces, whereby they have made you glad. . . . on your right hand did stand the <u>queen</u> in gold of Ophir . . . her clothing is of worked gold. She shall be brought to the king in raiment of needlework: the virgins her companions that follow her shall be brought to you. With gladness and rejoicing shall they be brought: they shall enter into the king's palace. Instead of your fathers shall be your children, whom you may make princes in all the earth. <u>I will make your name to be remembered in all generations: therefore shall the people praise you for ever and ever</u>. (Psalm 45:1-17 edited with addition)

Awake, Bride

And there shall be signs in the sun, and in the moon, and in the stars; and on the earth distress of nations, with perplexity; the sea and the waves roaring; Men's hearts failing them for fear, and for looking after those things which are coming on the earth: for the powers of heaven shall be shaken. And then shall they see the Son of man coming in a cloud with power and great glory. <u>And when these things begin to come to pass, then look up, and lift up your heads; for your redemption draws near</u>. (Luke 21:25-28)

'Look up' is *anakupto*, meaning to unbend as in a reversal. Don't be hunched over in grief, but rise up and stand tall. 'Lift up' is *epairo*, meaning to be lifted up with pride or to exalt one's self. Be proud of your relationship with Christ and invite those around you to join the sweet fellowship you have in His Spirit by submitting to Jesus as Lord and Savior. 'Redemption' is *apolutrosis*, meaning to ransom in full. Jesus, our Groom, has paid the bride price, and He is coming to claim His purchased possession -- Us.

Don't Be Fearful; Be Faithful and Loving

Awake, Bride

> *Beloved, believe not every spirit, . . . Every spirit that confesses that Jesus Christ is come in the flesh is of God: And every spirit that confesses not that Jesus Christ is come in the flesh is not of God: and this is that spirit of antichrist, . . . <u>You are of God, little children, and have overcome them: because greater is he that is in you, than he that is in the world</u>. They are of the world: therefore speak they of the world, and the world hears them. We are of God: he that knows God hears us; he that is not of God hears not us. Beloved, let us love one another: for love is of God; and every one that loves is born of God, and knows God. . . . <u>God sent his only begotten Son into the world, that we might live through him.</u> Herein is love, not that we loved God, but that he loved us, and sent his Son to be the propitiation for our sins. . . . Hereby know we that we dwell in him, and he in us, because he has given us of his Spirit. And we have seen and do testify that the Father sent the Son to be the Savior of the world. <u>Whoever shall confess that Jesus is the Son of God, God dwells in him, and he in God</u>. And we have known and believed the love that God has to us. God is love; and he that dwells in love dwells in God, and God in him. <u>Herein is our love made perfect, that we may have boldness</u> **in the day of judgment**: <u>because as he is, so are we in this world</u>. **There is no fear in love; but perfect love casts out fear: because fear has torment**. He that fears is not made perfect in love. (1 John 4:1-18 edited)*

Muslims don't believe Jesus is the Son of God. Do not be drawn into their worship of the Antichrist. Muslims worship a false god and especially seek to destroy those who worship the true God. Muslims seek to convert or destroy Christians who believe in Messiah Jesus, and Jews who await Messiah 'Salvation' (*Yeshua*). When Messiah Jesus comes to judge the world, we have nothing to fear because we have received His love and grace. Hold onto your faith in Jesus, the Son of God; your faith will overcome the world even if it means being martyred in the process. Our bodies may be tortured and killed, but we will have eternal life with Jesus in immortal bodies.

> *<u>For whatever is born of God overcomes the world</u>: and **this is the victory that overcomes the world, even our faith**. Who is he that overcomes the world, but he that believes that Jesus is the Son of God? . . . And this is the record, that God has given to us eternal life, and this life is in his Son. He that has the Son has life; and he that has not the Son of God has not life. <u>These things have I written to you that believe on the name of the Son of God; that you may know that you have eternal life</u>, and that you may believe on the name of the Son of God. And this is the confidence that we have in him, that, if we ask any thing according to his will, he hears us: And if we know that he hear us, whatever we ask, we know that we have the petitions that we desired of him. . . . And we know that the Son of God is come, and has given us an understanding, <u>that we may know him that is true, and we are in him that is true, even in his Son Jesus Christ. This is the true God, and eternal life</u>. (1 John 5:4-20 edited)*

Sources and Resources

Truth only comes from Jesus and His Holy Word. I have gleaned information and facts from the following, but that does not mean I agree with or endorse their ideas.

Books

Archaeological Study Bible - NIV, Zondervan, 2005.
Berry, George R., *Interlinear Greek-English New Testament*, Baker Book House, 1981.
Bullinger, E.W., *The Witness of the Stars,* 1893. [http://philologos.org/__eb-tws/]
Chumney, Edward, *The Seven Festivals of the Messiah,* Treasure House, 1994.
Cooper, Bill, *After the Flood,* New Wine Press, 1995
        [http://ldolphin.org/cooper/index.html]
Dougherty, Haskew, Jestice, and Rice, *Battles of the Bible*, Metro Books, 2008.
Elad, Amikam, *Medieval Jerusalem and Islamic Worship*, Brill, 1994.
Ferguson, Clyde, *The Stars and the Bible,* Exposition Press, 1978.
Finegan, Jack, *Handbook of Biblical Chronology*, Hendrickson Publishers, 1964.
Fleming, Kenneth C., *God's Voice in the Stars*, Loizeaux Brothers, 1981.
Foxe, John, *Foxe's Christian Martyrs of the World*, Barbour Books, 1989.
Hoerth, Alfred J., *Archaeology & the Old Testament*, Baker Books, 1998.
Jamieson, Fausset, & Brown's *Commentary on the Whole Bible*, Zondervan, 1999.
Lubenow, Marvin L., Bones of Contention, Baker Books, 1992. Solar neutrinos and
        John Eddy's statement, page 205.
Payne, J. Barton, *Encyclopedia of Biblical Prophecy*, Baker Books, 1973.
        (trumpets and vials in tandem)
Perry, Richard H., *Of The Last Days*, Guardian Books, 2003.
Perry, Richard H., *The Complete Idiot's Guide to the Last Days*, Alpha Books, 2006.
Richardson, Joel, *Antichrist: Islam's Awaited Messiah*, Pleasant Word of
        WinePress Pub., 2006.
Rosenberg, Joel C., *Epicenter*, Tyndale House Publishers, 2006.
Rosenberg, Joel C., *Inside the Revolution*, Tyndale House Publishers, 2009.
Scarlatta, Robin and Pierce, Linda, *A Family Guide to the Biblical Holidays*,
        Heart of Wisdom Publishing, 1999.
Shoebat, Walid, *Why I Left Jihad*, Top Executive Media, 2005.
Thiele, Edwin, *The Mysterious Numbers of the Hebrew Kings*,
        Kregel Publications, 1983.
Ussher, James, *The Annals of World History*, Master Books, 2003.
Ussher, James, *The Wall Chart of World History*, Third Millennium Trust, 1997.
Wierwille, Victor Paul, *Jesus Christ, Our Promised Seed,*
        American Christian Press, 1982.
Zubair Ali, Mohammed Ali, *Signs of Qiyamah,* Islamic Book Service, 2000.

Websites

www.wikipedia.org
www.360calendar.com on Hebrew calendar
www.hebcal.com Hebrew/Gregorian calendar converter
IDEA www.webexhibits.org on Sumerians
http://bsimmons.wordpress.com/2006/11/14/netanyahu-its-1938-and-iran-is-germany-ahmadinejad-is-preparing-another-holocaust/
http://www.globalpolitician.com/23370-russia Report on weaponry be Natalya Hmelik
http://www.earlychristianwritings.com/text/didache-hoole.html
http://www.yeshua.co.uk on archaeological moon-worship artifacts
www.wyattmuseum.com Exodus to Mount Sinai
www.christianmedianetwork.com/lastdays.html
    Lion=England, Bear=Russia, and Leopard=Germany
http://philologos.org/__eb-tws/ E.W. Bullinger's *The Witness of the Stars*
http://www.prophecyinthenews.com/articledetail.asp?Article_ID=238 on Obama
http://newsgroups.derkeiler.com/Archive/Soc/soc.culture.israel/2006/04/msg00915.html report by Chuck Morse, April 14, 2006, on modern Israel's beginnings
www.jewishvoice.org Information of the lost tribes of Israel
http://johnmcternansinsights.blogspot.com
http://www.earlyjewishwritings.com/1maccabees.html
http://www.earlyjewishwritings.com/2maccabees.html
http://news.stanford.edu/news/1997/november12/nurearthquake.html
    Ellen Licking report

Movies and Television

Against All Odds on DVD regarding God's miracles in modern Israel
Zola Levitt Presents TV show; also www.levitt.com on prophecy fulfillment in Israel
The Jewish Jesus TV show with Hebrew insights into the Bible
The 700 Club TV show; also www.cbn.com current news regarding Israel

Software

Open Office, a free program at www.openoffice.org
e-sword by Rick Meyers, a free program at www.e-sword.net.com;
    contains Strong's Concordance among others.
The Sword Project, a free program at www.crosswire.org; contains the
American King James Bible, and Barnes and Clarke's Bible Commentaries among others.

Biblical Hebrew Year = 360 days

Number 32:14 "And the LORD's anger was kindled against Israel, and he made them wander in the wilderness <u>forty years</u>, until all the <u>generation</u>, that had done evil in the sight of the LORD, was consumed."

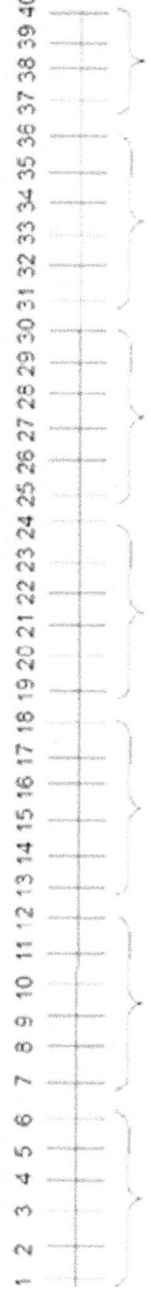

2,190 days 2,190 days 2,190 days 2,190 days 2,190 days 2,190 days 1,470 days

$(5 \times 12 \times 30) + (1 \times 13 \times 30) = 2{,}190$ $(3 \times 12 \times 30) + (1 \times 13 \times 30) = 1{,}470$

Total number of days is 14,610 days which = **365.25 days × 40 years**

2,190 = 6 years of 5(360) + 1(390)
2,190 = 6 years
2,190 = 6 years
2,190 = 6 years
2,190 = 6 years
2,190 = 6 years
+1,470 = 4 years of 3(360) + 1(390)
14,610 = 40 years

So multiples of 40 years in Biblical prophecy will align with our 365.25 day calendars.

Graphic: Eve Clarity © 11/13/2008   Concept: www.360calendar.com

Appendix

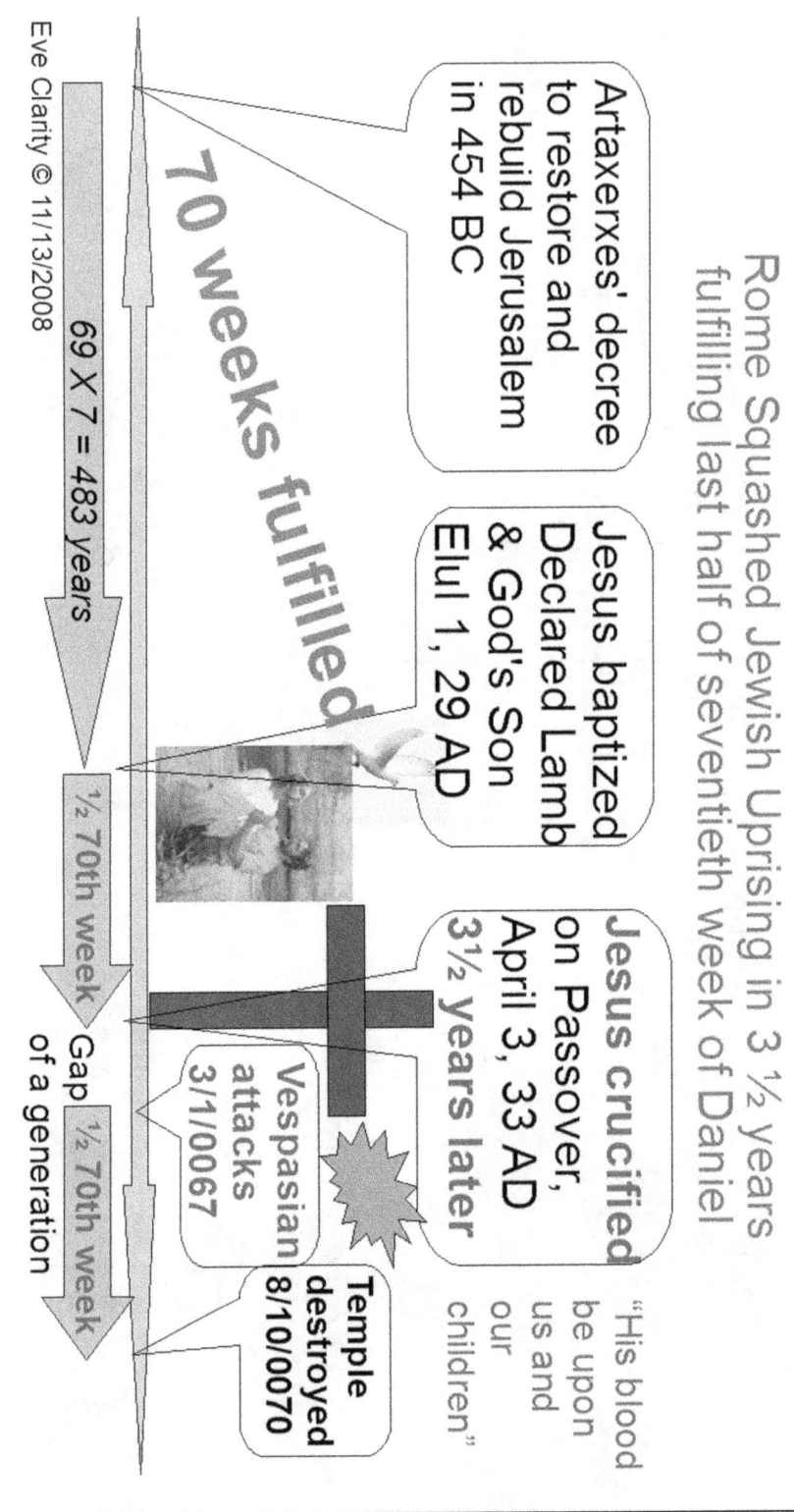

346

Appendix

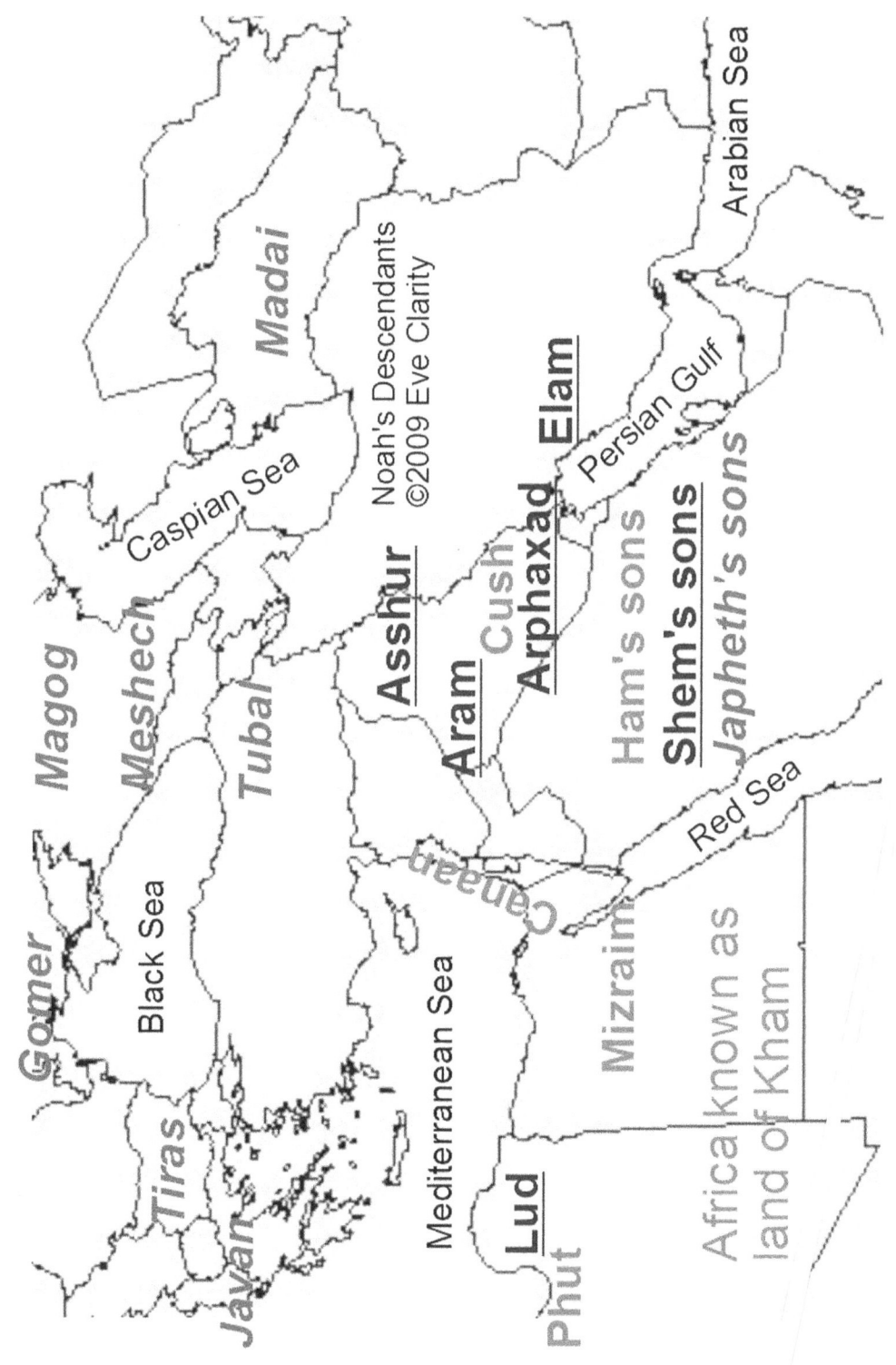

Appendix

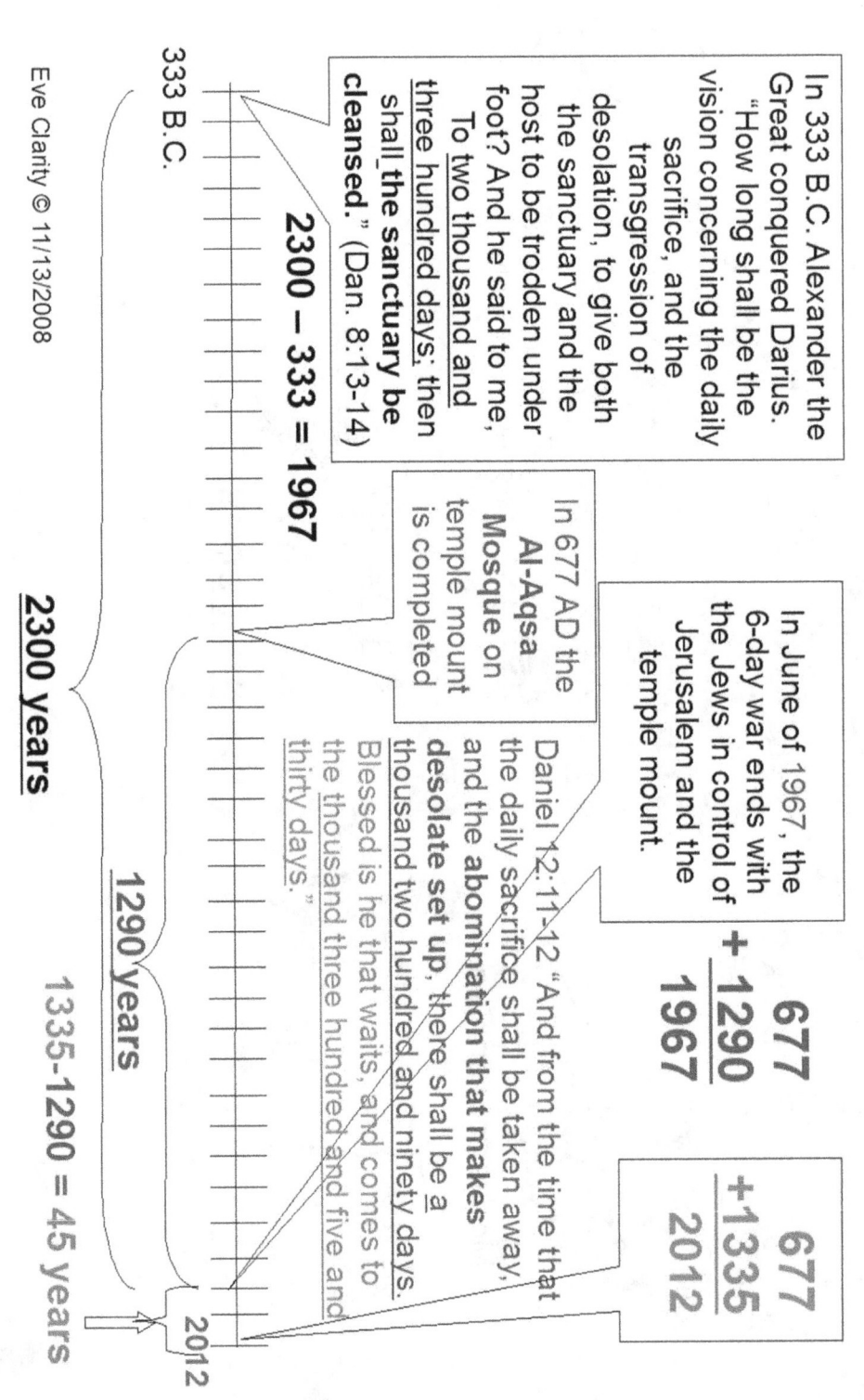

348

Appendix

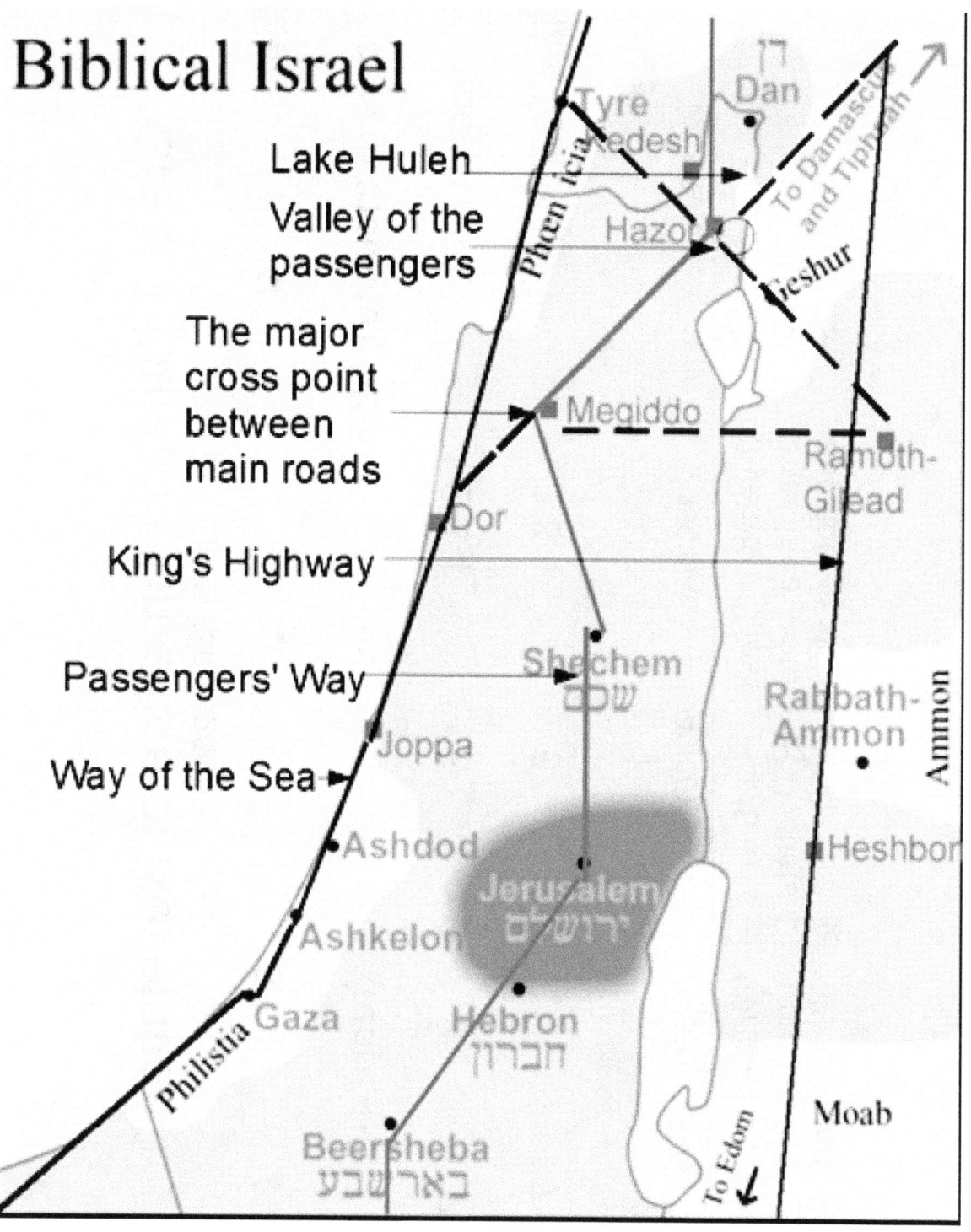

Great Tribulation Time-line of Revelation
Eve Clarity © 04/02/2009

Seals	1	2	3	4	5	6	7
Angels (announce)	1	2	3			(reap) 4-6	7
Trumpets (world)	1	2	3	4	5	6	7
Vials (Babylon)	1	2	3	4	5	6	7
Woes				1		2	3

Wake up	<<<	=	5 m locusts	=	1 yr 1 m 1 d Armegeddon Kills 1/3 world	>>>
9/11/01	4/06/09	1,260 days	3/26/11	42(30)	8/23/11 3.5(360)	9/16/12
		2 years, 1/3 less trees, sea, water, and light in sky				

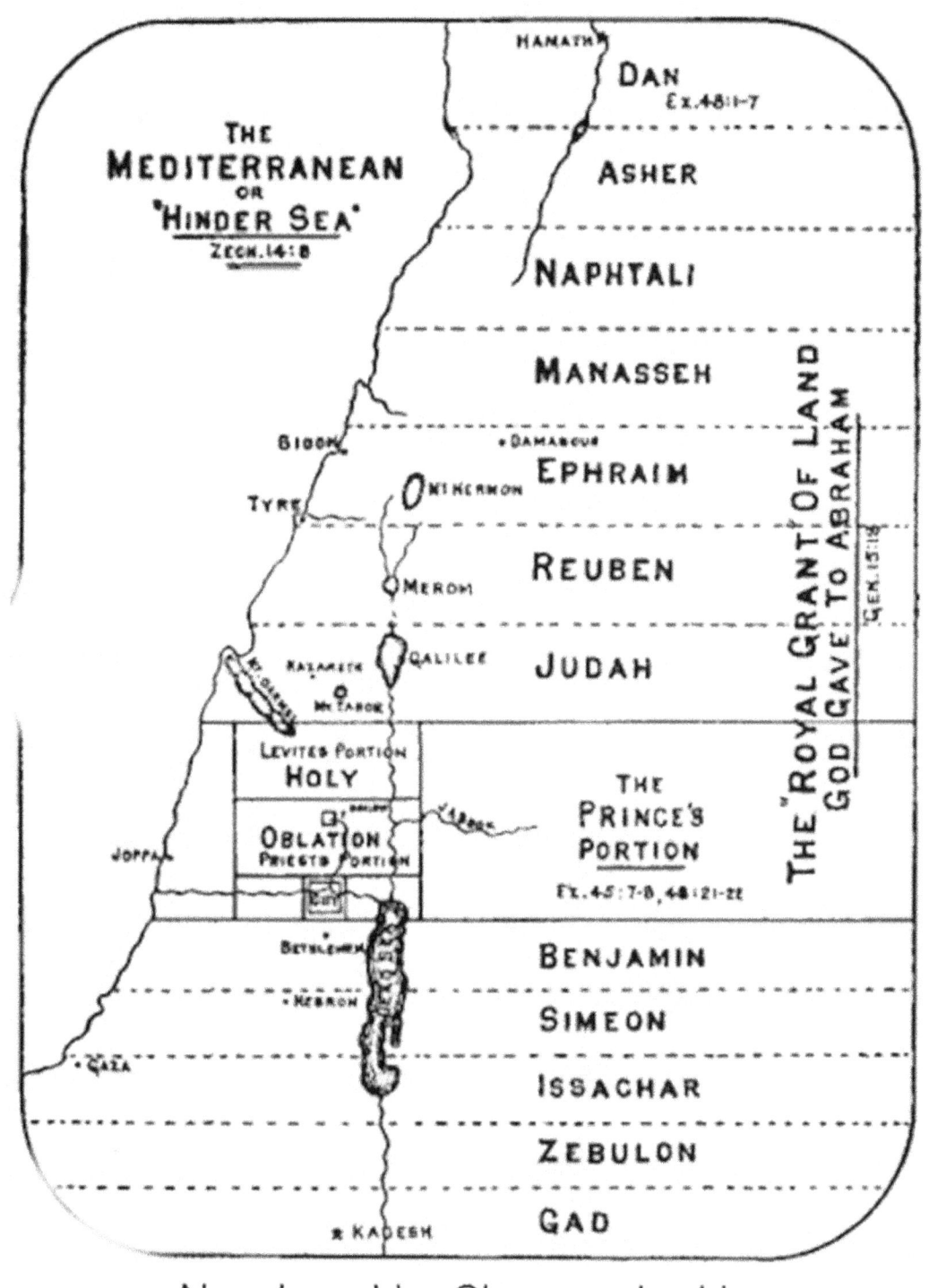

New Israel by Clarence Larkin

www.ingramcontent.com/pod-product-compliance
Lightning Source LLC
Chambersburg PA
CBHW080331170426
43194CB00014B/2519